W9-CCH-681

A long time ago in a galaxy far, far away....

LETTERERS:
JIM NOVAK, TOM ORZECHOWSKI, CAROL LAY & MIKE ROYER

EDITORS:
ROY THOMAS & ARCHIE GOODWIN

COVER ART:
ADI GRANOV

BACK COVER ART:
HOWARD CHAYKIN & EDGAR DELGADO

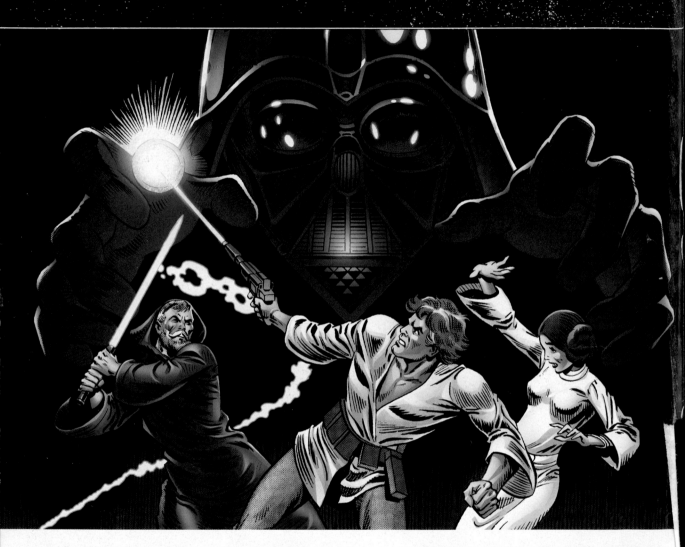

COLLECTION EDITOR: **MARK D. BEAZLEY**
ASSISTANT MANAGING EDITOR: **JOE HOCHSTEIN**
ASSOCIATE MANAGING EDITOR: **ALEX STARBUCK**
EDITOR, SPECIAL PROJECTS: **JENNIFER GRÜNWALD**
SENIOR EDITOR, SPECIAL PROJECTS: **JEFF YOUNGQUIST**
PRODUCTION: **COLORTEK & M. HANDS**
BOOK DESIGN: **RODOLFO MURAGUCHI**

SVP PRINT, SALES & MARKETING: **DAVID GABRIEL**
EDITOR IN CHIEF: **AXEL ALONSO**
CHIEF CREATIVE OFFICER: **JOE QUESADA**
PUBLISHER: **DAN BUCKLEY**
EXECUTIVE PRODUCER: **ALAN FINE**

Special Thanks to JENNIFER HEDDLE & LUCASFILM, DAVID MANDEL, TOM PALMER, MIKE FICHERA, GARY HENDERSON and MILE HIGH COMICS' CHUCK ROZANSKI & CHRIS BOYD

STAR WARS: EPISODE IV — A NEW HOPE. Contains material originally published in magazine form as STAR WARS #1-6. First printing 2015. ISBN# 978-0-7851-9348-7. Published by MARVEL WORLDWIDE, INC., a subsidiary of MARVEL ENTERTAINMENT, LLC. OFFICE OF PUBLICATION: 135 West 50th Street, New York, NY 10020. STAR WARS and related text and illustrations are trademarks and/or copyrights, in the United States and other countries, of Lucasfilm Ltd. and/or its affiliates. © & TM Lucasfilm Ltd. No similarity between any of the names, characters, persons, and/or institutions in this magazine with those of any living or dead person or institution is intended, and any such similarity which may exist is purely coincidental. Marvel and its logos are TM Marvel Characters, Inc. **Printed in the U.S.A.** ALAN FINE, EVP - Office of the President, Marvel Worldwide, Inc. and EVP & CMO Marvel Characters B.V.; DAN BUCKLEY, Publisher & President - Print, Animation & Digital Divisions; JOE QUESADA, Chief Creative Officer; TOM BREVOORT, SVP of Publishing; DAVID BOGART, SVP of Operations & Procurement, Publishing; C.B. CEBULSKI, SVP of Creator & Content Development; DAVID GABRIEL, SVP Print, Sales & Marketing; JIM O'KEEFE, VP of Operations & Logistics; DAN CARR, Executive Director of Publishing Technology; SUSAN CRESPI, Editorial Operations Manager; ALEX MORALES, Publishing Operations Manager; STAN LEE, Chairman Emeritus. For information regarding advertising in Marvel Comics or on Marvel.com, please contact Niza Disla, Director of Marvel Partnerships, at ndisla@marvel.com. For Marvel subscription inquiries, please call 800-217-9158. **Manufactured between 2/27/2015 and 4/13/2015 by WORZALLA PUBLISHING CO., STEVENS POINT, WI, USA.**

10987654321

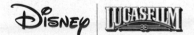

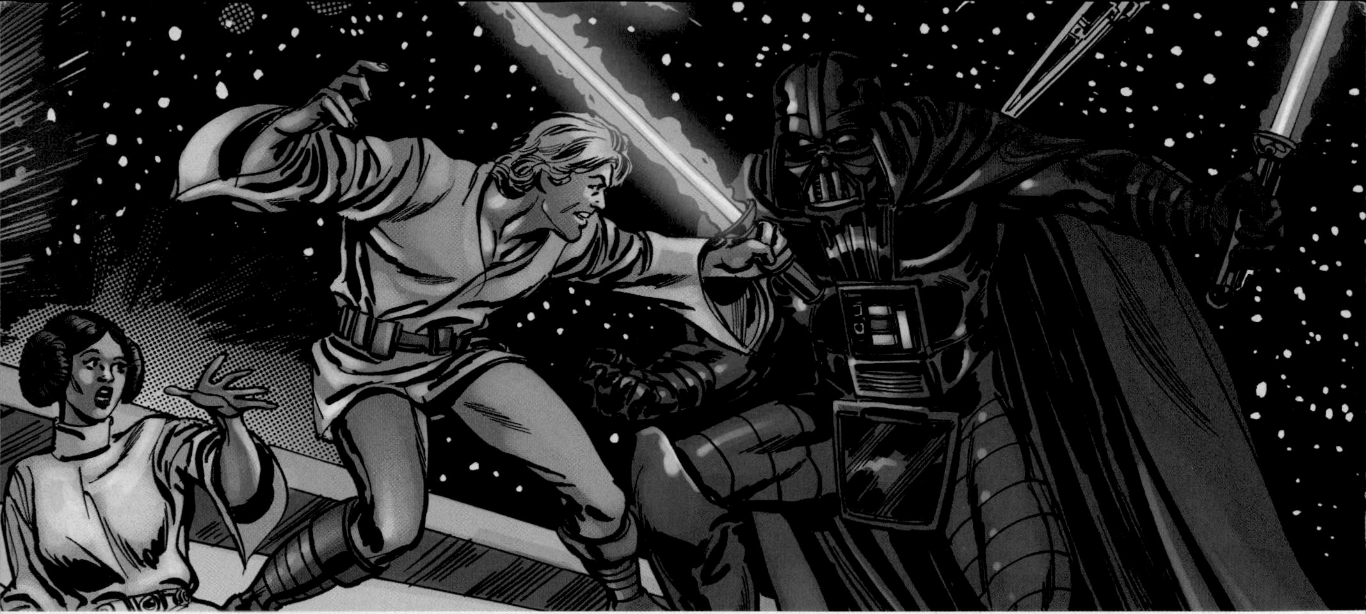

STAR WARS®

EPISODE IV

A NEW HOPE

WRITER:
ROY THOMAS

PENCILER:
HOWARD CHAYKIN

INKERS:
HOWARD CHAYKIN, STEVE LEIALOHA,
RICK HOBERG & BILL WRAY

COLORIST:
SOTOCOLOR

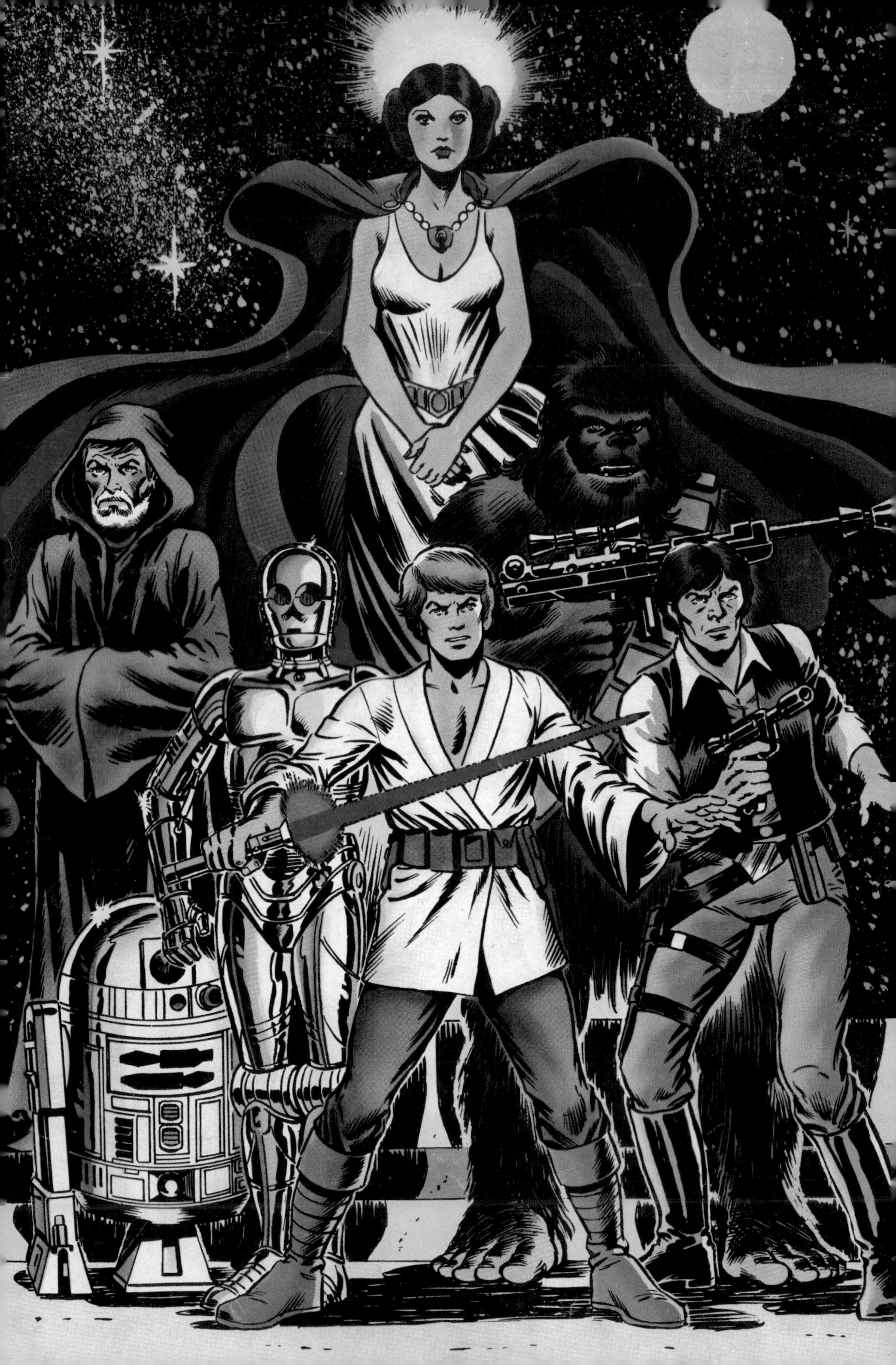

INTRODUCTION
BY PETER MAYHEW

Over the last 40 years I've had the privilege to be able to watch, from the co-pilot seat of the *Millennium Falcon*, the *Star Wars* Universe change the face of science fiction. *Star Wars* has inspired generations of dreamers. For me personally, it has allowed me to be able to travel the world, I met my wife at a comic convention, and I've been a part of the best family of fans of any genre.

As a child growing up in the 1950s in Britain I always enjoyed reading illustrated stories of the American Old West. Although they differed in style from the comic books of today, it was still a wonderful way to escape into another world — a world where the good guys wore white hats and the bad guys were fast with their weapons. These books gave us a glimpse into a world of courage, bravery and the triumph of good over evil. They helped fuel a love of reading. Our imaginations can take us anywhere as we learn and explore our world.

I still remember the feeling of excitement I experienced when I saw the original issues of Marvel's *Star Wars*. All those wonderful memories of quiet lazy afternoons losing myself in the books of my youth and this time I WAS IN THE COMIC! It was wonderful to be able to see Chewbacca and the rest of the characters given new life by Marvel and their incredible artists.

The freedom of a comic book is very different from film. Comics can be read at your own pace, interpreted in your own way, and everything that happens between the panels can be filled in with your own imagination. I often find myself going back to the comics when I am puttering in the Chewie Museum and am always surprised to find time disappear as I relive those adventures time and again. Needless to say, my original 1977 issues are a bit threadbare! And for all of you collectors that are cringing right now hearing that, I sincerely apologize.

Comic books are magical. It's magic to see the way the writers and illustrators are able to convey so much emotion and detail into a two-dimensional format. I love that Chewbacca, a character that speaks no Basic language, still emotes through sounds and motions and comes across just as powerfully in the panels of the comic. Through amazing artistry Marvel is able to convey so much of the original look and feel of my big furry friend and all the rest of the cast as well.

Star Wars is unique in that it began as a film and was later released as books and comics rather than the other way around. This made for people having strong opinions on what each character meant to them before they read their stories. In the comics, Chewbacca often comes off as a barrel-chested bruiser rather than the gentle giant he was in the films. Seeing another artist's interpretation of the characters, whether it be in comics or book form, is always fun for me.

When I was informed that Marvel was going to reissue the original saga in an all new edition with new coloring I felt that same sense of excitement I felt originally, as that meant a way for a new generation of readers to discover the magic that is *Star Wars*. With the expansion of the *Star Wars* Universe to include new movies, new shows and new books, I am glad that the coloring of the original trilogy comic is being updated as well. Howard Chaykin's work is amazing, so putting a fresh face on his art and this timeless story will really help to engage readers of every age and creed. My hope is that it'll allow you to lose yourself the same way I did my first time reading the comics so many years ago. So from the depth of my heart and with a heartfelt RAWHOOL ROWR YRROONN, prepare yourself to be transported back to a galaxy far, far away....

Cheers,
PETER MAYHEW

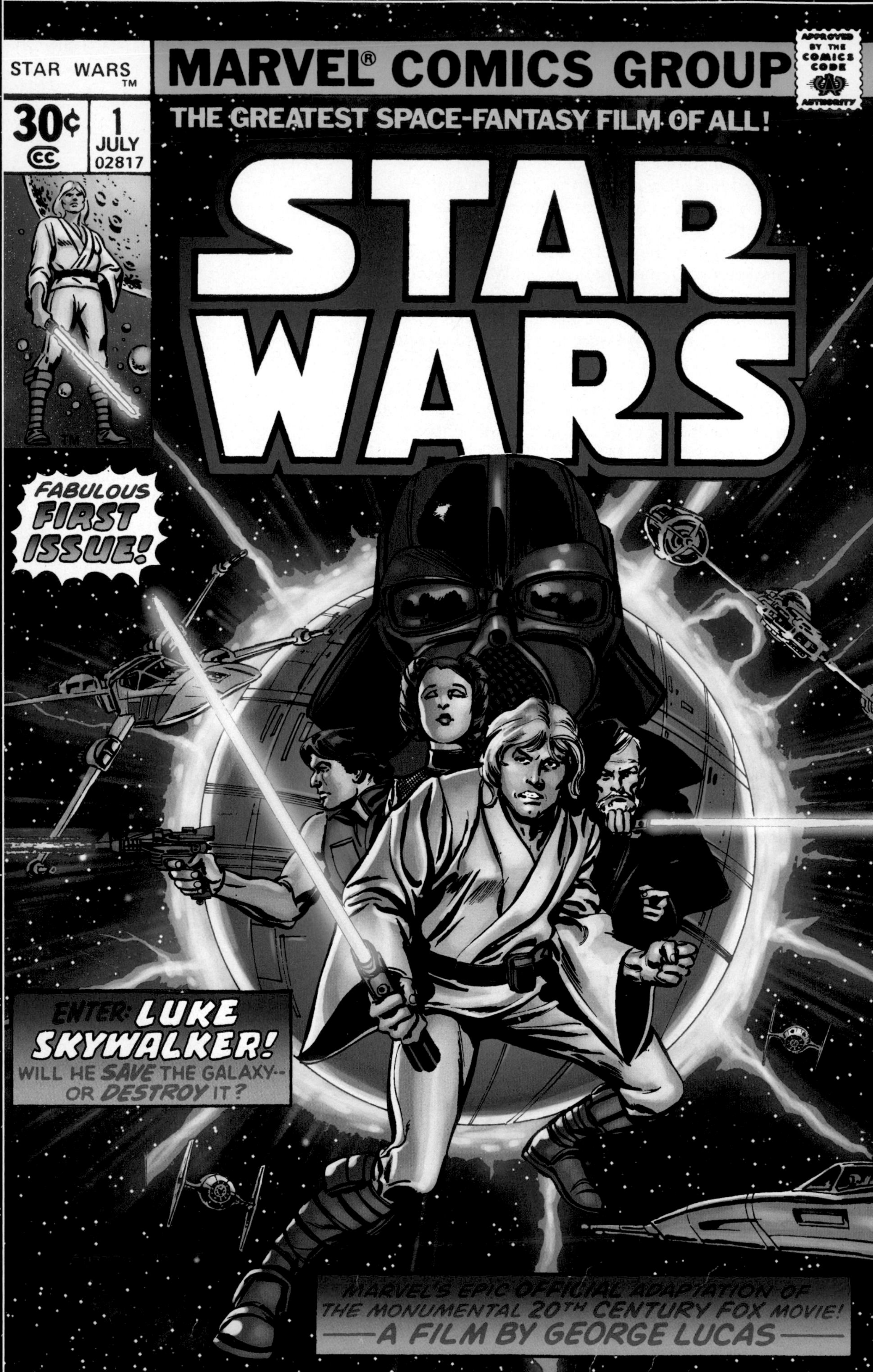

STAR WARS TM
MARVEL® COMICS GROUP
APPROVED BY THE COMICS CODE AUTHORITY
30¢
1
JULY
02817
THE GREATEST SPACE-FANTASY FILM OF ALL!
STAR WARS
FABULOUS FIRST ISSUE!
ENTER: LUKE SKYWALKER!
WILL HE SAVE THE GALAXY--OR DESTROY IT?
MARVEL'S EPIC OFFICIAL ADAPTATION OF THE MONUMENTAL 20TH CENTURY FOX MOVIE!
—A FILM BY GEORGE LUCAS—

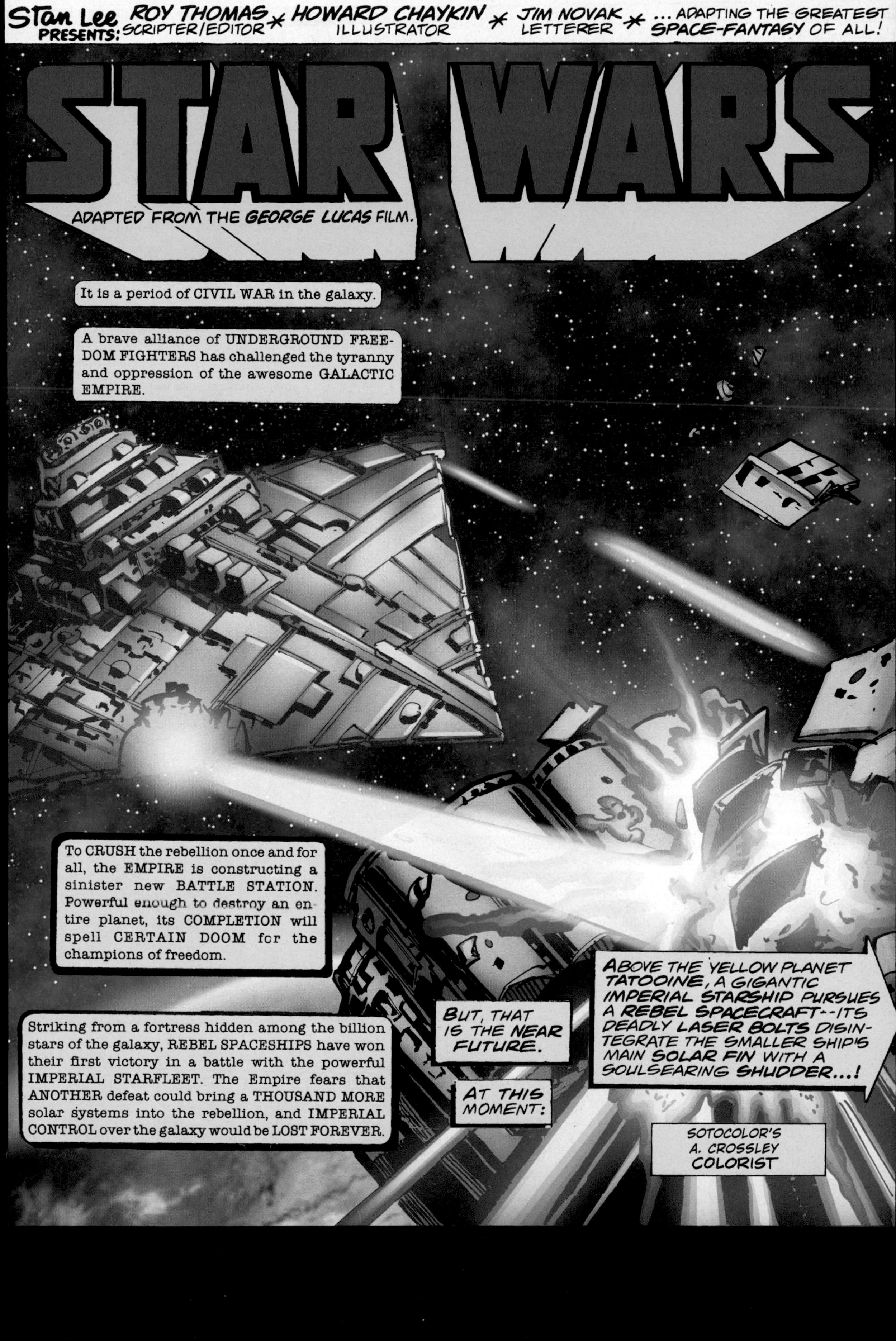
Stan Lee PRESENTS: ROY THOMAS SCRIPTER/EDITOR * HOWARD CHAYKIN ILLUSTRATOR * JIM NOVAK LETTERER * ... ADAPTING THE GREATEST SPACE-FANTASY OF ALL!
STAR WARS
ADAPTED FROM THE GEORGE LUCAS FILM.
It is a period of CIVIL WAR in the galaxy.
A brave alliance of UNDERGROUND FREEDOM FIGHTERS has challenged the tyranny and oppression of the awesome GALACTIC EMPIRE.
To CRUSH the rebellion once and for all, the EMPIRE is constructing a sinister new BATTLE STATION. Powerful enough to destroy an entire planet, its COMPLETION will spell CERTAIN DOOM for the champions of freedom.
Striking from a fortress hidden among the billion stars of the galaxy, REBEL SPACESHIPS have won their first victory in a battle with the powerful IMPERIAL STARFLEET. The Empire fears that ANOTHER defeat could bring a THOUSAND MORE solar systems into the rebellion, and IMPERIAL CONTROL over the galaxy would be LOST FOREVER.
BUT, THAT IS THE NEAR FUTURE.
AT THIS MOMENT:
ABOVE THE YELLOW PLANET TATOOINE, A GIGANTIC IMPERIAL STARSHIP PURSUES A REBEL SPACECRAFT--ITS DEADLY LASER BOLTS DISINTEGRATE THE SMALLER SHIP'S MAIN SOLAR FIN WITH A SOULSEARING SHUDDER...!
SOTOCOLOR'S A. CROSSLEY COLORIST

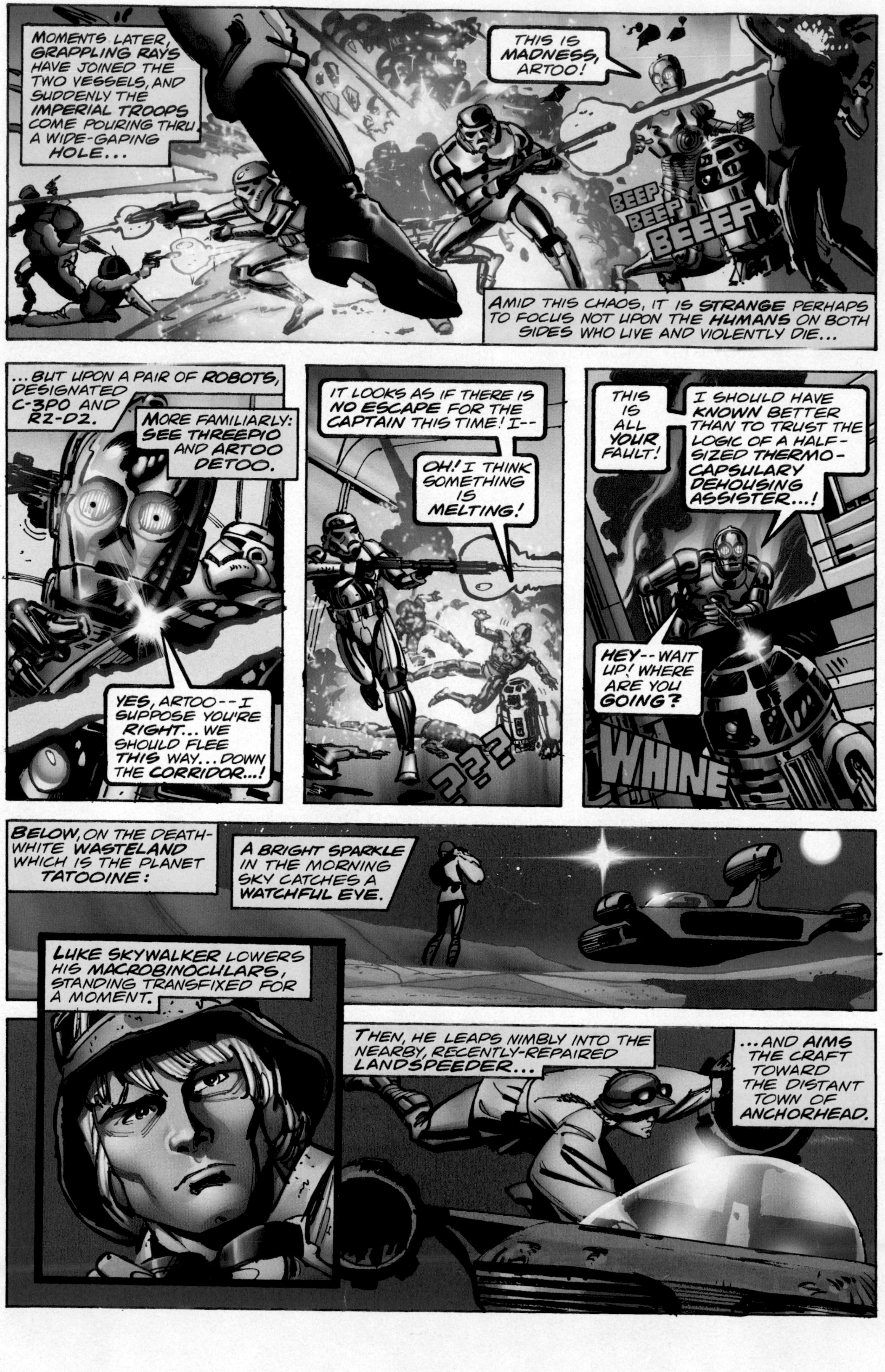
MOMENTS LATER, GRAPPLING RAYS HAVE JOINED THE TWO VESSELS, AND SUDDENLY THE IMPERIAL TROOPS COME POURING THRU A WIDE-GAPING HOLE...
THIS IS MADNESS, ARTOO!
BEEP BEEP BEEEP
AMID THIS CHAOS, IT IS STRANGE PERHAPS TO FOCUS NOT UPON THE HUMANS ON BOTH SIDES WHO LIVE AND VIOLENTLY DIE...
...BUT UPON A PAIR OF ROBOTS, DESIGNATED C-3PO AND R2-D2.
MORE FAMILIARLY: SEE THREEPIO AND ARTOO DETOO.
YES, ARTOO--I SUPPOSE YOU'RE RIGHT... WE SHOULD FLEE THIS WAY... DOWN THE CORRIDOR...!
IT LOOKS AS IF THERE IS NO ESCAPE FOR THE CAPTAIN THIS TIME! I--
OH! I THINK SOMETHING IS MELTING!
???
THIS IS ALL YOUR FAULT!
I SHOULD HAVE KNOWN BETTER THAN TO TRUST THE LOGIC OF A HALF-SIZED THERMO-CAPSULARY DEHOUSING ASSISTER...!
HEY--WAIT UP! WHERE ARE YOU GOING?
WHINE
BELOW, ON THE DEATH-WHITE WASTELAND WHICH IS THE PLANET TATOOINE:
A BRIGHT SPARKLE IN THE MORNING SKY CATCHES A WATCHFUL EYE.
LUKE SKYWALKER LOWERS HIS MACROBINOCULARS, STANDING TRANSFIXED FOR A MOMENT.
THEN, HE LEAPS NIMBLY INTO THE NEARBY, RECENTLY-REPAIRED LANDSPEEDER...
...AND AIMS THE CRAFT TOWARD THE DISTANT TOWN OF ANCHORHEAD.

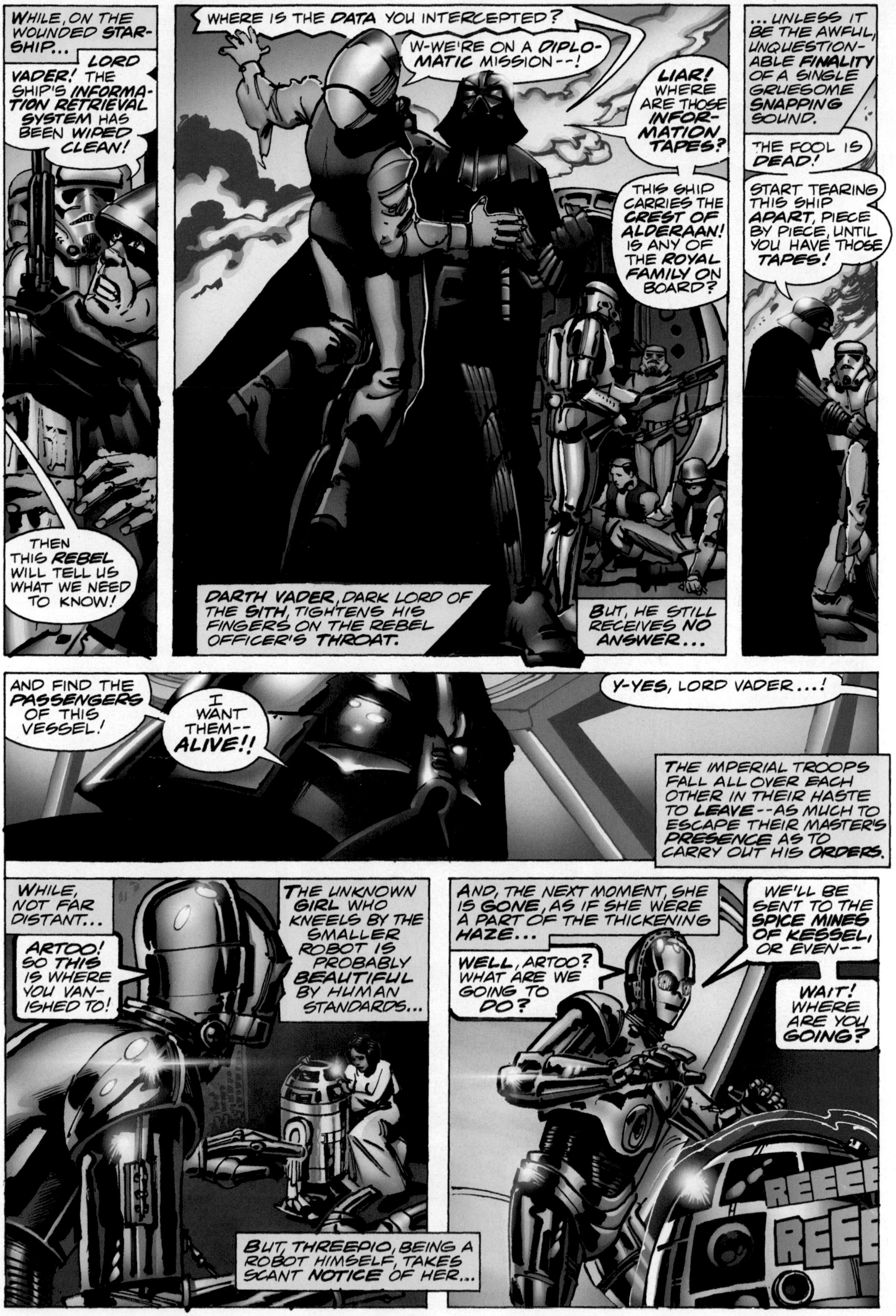
WHILE, ON THE WOUNDED STARSHIP...
LORD VADER! THE SHIP'S INFORMATION RETRIEVAL SYSTEM HAS BEEN WIPED CLEAN!
THEN THIS REBEL WILL TELL US WHAT WE NEED TO KNOW!
WHERE IS THE DATA YOU INTERCEPTED?
W-WE'RE ON A DIPLOMATIC MISSION--!
LIAR! WHERE ARE THOSE INFORMATION TAPES?
THIS SHIP CARRIES THE CREST OF ALDERAAN! IS ANY OF THE ROYAL FAMILY ON BOARD?
DARTH VADER, DARK LORD OF THE SITH, TIGHTENS HIS FINGERS ON THE REBEL OFFICER'S THROAT.
BUT, HE STILL RECEIVES NO ANSWER...
...UNLESS IT BE THE AWFUL, UNQUESTIONABLE FINALITY OF A SINGLE GRUESOME SNAPPING SOUND.
THE FOOL IS DEAD!
START TEARING THIS SHIP APART, PIECE BY PIECE, UNTIL YOU HAVE THOSE TAPES!
AND FIND THE PASSENGERS OF THIS VESSEL!
I WANT THEM--ALIVE!!
Y-YES, LORD VADER...!
THE IMPERIAL TROOPS FALL ALL OVER EACH OTHER IN THEIR HASTE TO LEAVE--AS MUCH TO ESCAPE THEIR MASTER'S PRESENCE AS TO CARRY OUT HIS ORDERS.
WHILE, NOT FAR DISTANT...
ARTOO! SO THIS IS WHERE YOU VANISHED TO!
THE UNKNOWN GIRL WHO KNEELS BY THE SMALLER ROBOT IS PROBABLY BEAUTIFUL BY HUMAN STANDARDS...
BUT, THREEPIO, BEING A ROBOT HIMSELF, TAKES SCANT NOTICE OF HER...
AND, THE NEXT MOMENT, SHE IS GONE, AS IF SHE WERE A PART OF THE THICKENING HAZE...
WELL, ARTOO? WHAT ARE WE GOING TO DO?
WE'LL BE SENT TO THE SPICE MINES OF KESSEL, OR EVEN--
WAIT! WHERE ARE YOU GOING?
REEEE
REEE

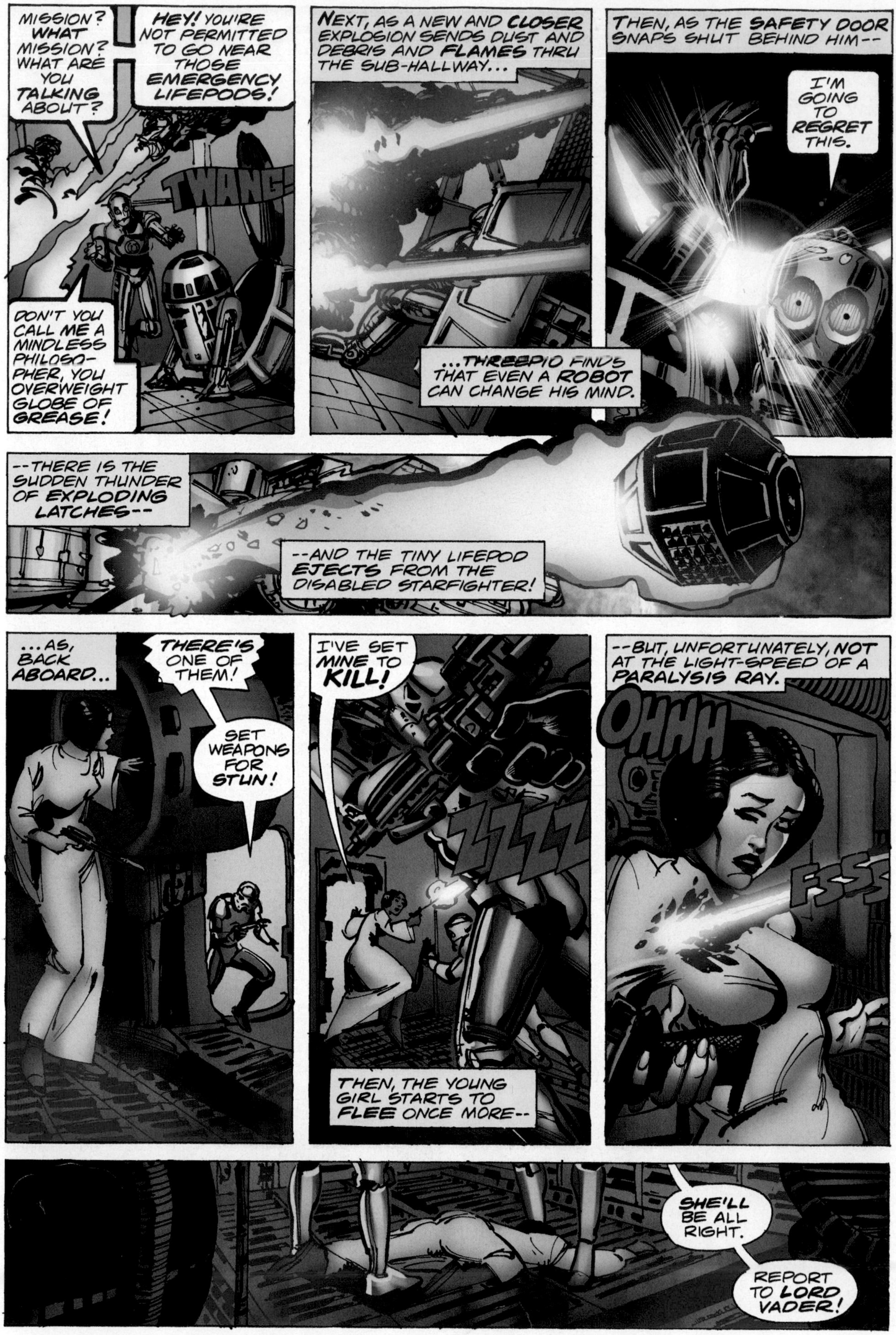
MISSION? WHAT MISSION? WHAT ARE YOU TALKING ABOUT?
HEY! YOU'RE NOT PERMITTED TO GO NEAR THOSE EMERGENCY LIFEPODS!
TWANG
DON'T YOU CALL ME A MINDLESS PHILOSOPHER, YOU OVERWEIGHT GLOBE OF GREASE!
NEXT, AS A NEW AND CLOSER EXPLOSION SENDS DUST AND DEBRIS AND FLAMES THRU THE SUB-HALLWAY...
...THREEPIO FINDS THAT EVEN A ROBOT CAN CHANGE HIS MIND.
THEN, AS THE SAFETY DOOR SNAPS SHUT BEHIND HIM--
I'M GOING TO REGRET THIS.
--THERE IS THE SUDDEN THUNDER OF EXPLODING LATCHES--
--AND THE TINY LIFEPOD EJECTS FROM THE DISABLED STARFIGHTER!
...AS, BACK ABOARD...
THERE'S ONE OF THEM!
SET WEAPONS FOR STUN!
I'VE SET MINE TO KILL!
ZZZZ
THEN, THE YOUNG GIRL STARTS TO FLEE ONCE MORE--
--BUT, UNFORTUNATELY, NOT AT THE LIGHT-SPEED OF A PARALYSIS RAY.
OHHH
FSSS
SHE'LL BE ALL RIGHT.
REPORT TO LORD VADER!

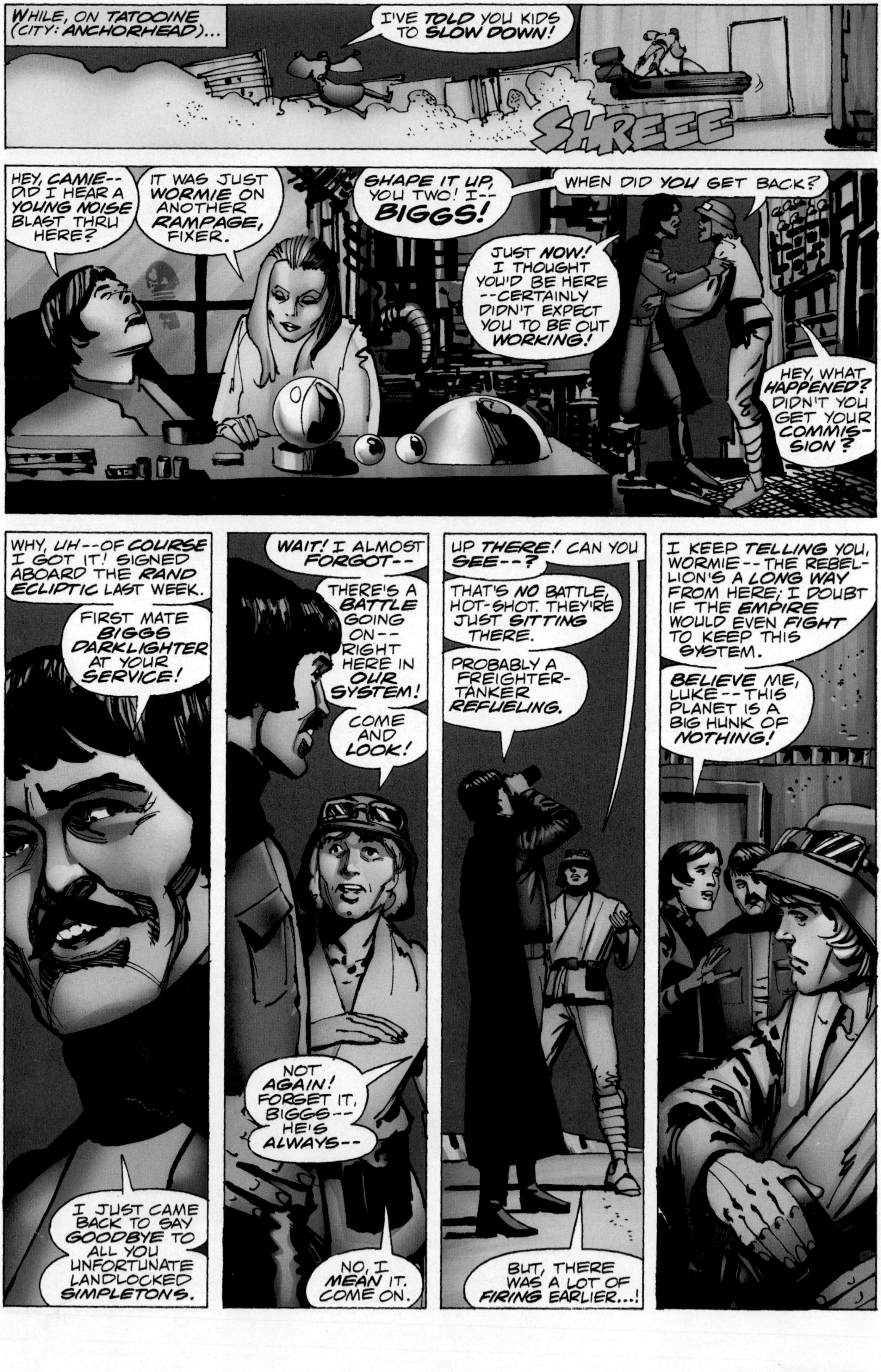
WHILE, ON TATOOINE (CITY: ANCHORHEAD)...
I'VE TOLD YOU KIDS TO SLOW DOWN!
SHREEE
HEY, CAMIE-- DID I HEAR A YOUNG NOISE BLAST THRU HERE?
IT WAS JUST WORMIE ON ANOTHER RAMPAGE, FIXER.
SHAPE IT UP, YOU TWO! I-- BIGGS!
WHEN DID YOU GET BACK?
JUST NOW! I THOUGHT YOU'D BE HERE --CERTAINLY DIDN'T EXPECT YOU TO BE OUT WORKING!
HEY, WHAT HAPPENED? DIDN'T YOU GET YOUR COMMISSION?
WHY, UH--OF COURSE I GOT IT! SIGNED ABOARD THE RAND ECLIPTIC LAST WEEK.
FIRST MATE BIGGS DARKLIGHTER AT YOUR SERVICE!
I JUST CAME BACK TO SAY GOODBYE TO ALL YOU UNFORTUNATE LANDLOCKED SIMPLETONS.
WAIT! I ALMOST FORGOT--
THERE'S A BATTLE GOING ON-- RIGHT HERE IN OUR SYSTEM!
COME AND LOOK!
NOT AGAIN! FORGET IT, BIGGS-- HE'S ALWAYS--
NO, I MEAN IT. COME ON.
UP THERE! CAN YOU SEE--?
THAT'S NO BATTLE, HOT-SHOT. THEY'RE JUST SITTING THERE.
PROBABLY A FREIGHTER-TANKER REFUELING.
BUT, THERE WAS A LOT OF FIRING EARLIER...!
I KEEP TELLING YOU, WORMIE--THE REBELLION'S A LONG WAY FROM HERE; I DOUBT IF THE EMPIRE WOULD EVEN FIGHT TO KEEP THIS SYSTEM.
BELIEVE ME, LUKE--THIS PLANET IS A BIG HUNK OF NOTHING!

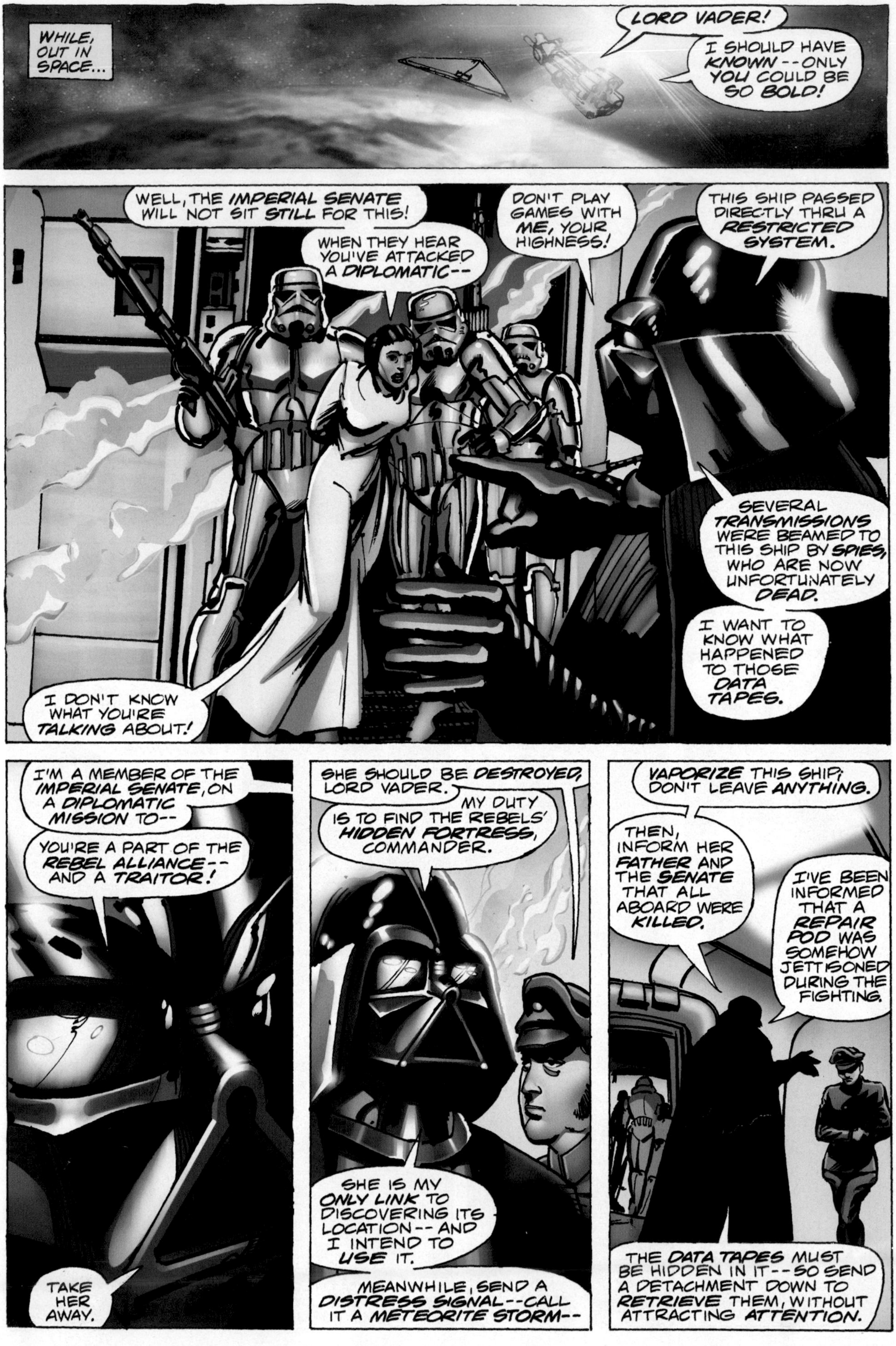
WHILE, OUT IN SPACE...
LORD VADER!
I SHOULD HAVE KNOWN--ONLY YOU COULD BE SO BOLD!
WELL, THE IMPERIAL SENATE WILL NOT SIT STILL FOR THIS!
WHEN THEY HEAR YOU'VE ATTACKED A DIPLOMATIC--
DON'T PLAY GAMES WITH ME, YOUR HIGHNESS!
THIS SHIP PASSED DIRECTLY THRU A RESTRICTED SYSTEM.
SEVERAL TRANSMISSIONS WERE BEAMED TO THIS SHIP BY SPIES, WHO ARE NOW UNFORTUNATELY DEAD.
I WANT TO KNOW WHAT HAPPENED TO THOSE DATA TAPES.
I DON'T KNOW WHAT YOU'RE TALKING ABOUT!
I'M A MEMBER OF THE IMPERIAL SENATE, ON A DIPLOMATIC MISSION TO--
YOU'RE A PART OF THE REBEL ALLIANCE--AND A TRAITOR!
TAKE HER AWAY.
SHE SHOULD BE DESTROYED, LORD VADER.
MY DUTY IS TO FIND THE REBELS' HIDDEN FORTRESS, COMMANDER.
SHE IS MY ONLY LINK TO DISCOVERING ITS LOCATION--AND I INTEND TO USE IT.
MEANWHILE, SEND A DISTRESS SIGNAL--CALL IT A METEORITE STORM--
VAPORIZE THIS SHIP; DON'T LEAVE ANYTHING.
THEN, INFORM HER FATHER AND THE SENATE THAT ALL ABOARD WERE KILLED.
I'VE BEEN INFORMED THAT A REPAIR POD WAS SOMEHOW JETTISONED DURING THE FIGHTING.
THE DATA TAPES MUST BE HIDDEN IN IT--SO SEND A DETACHMENT DOWN TO RETRIEVE THEM, WITHOUT ATTRACTING ATTENTION.

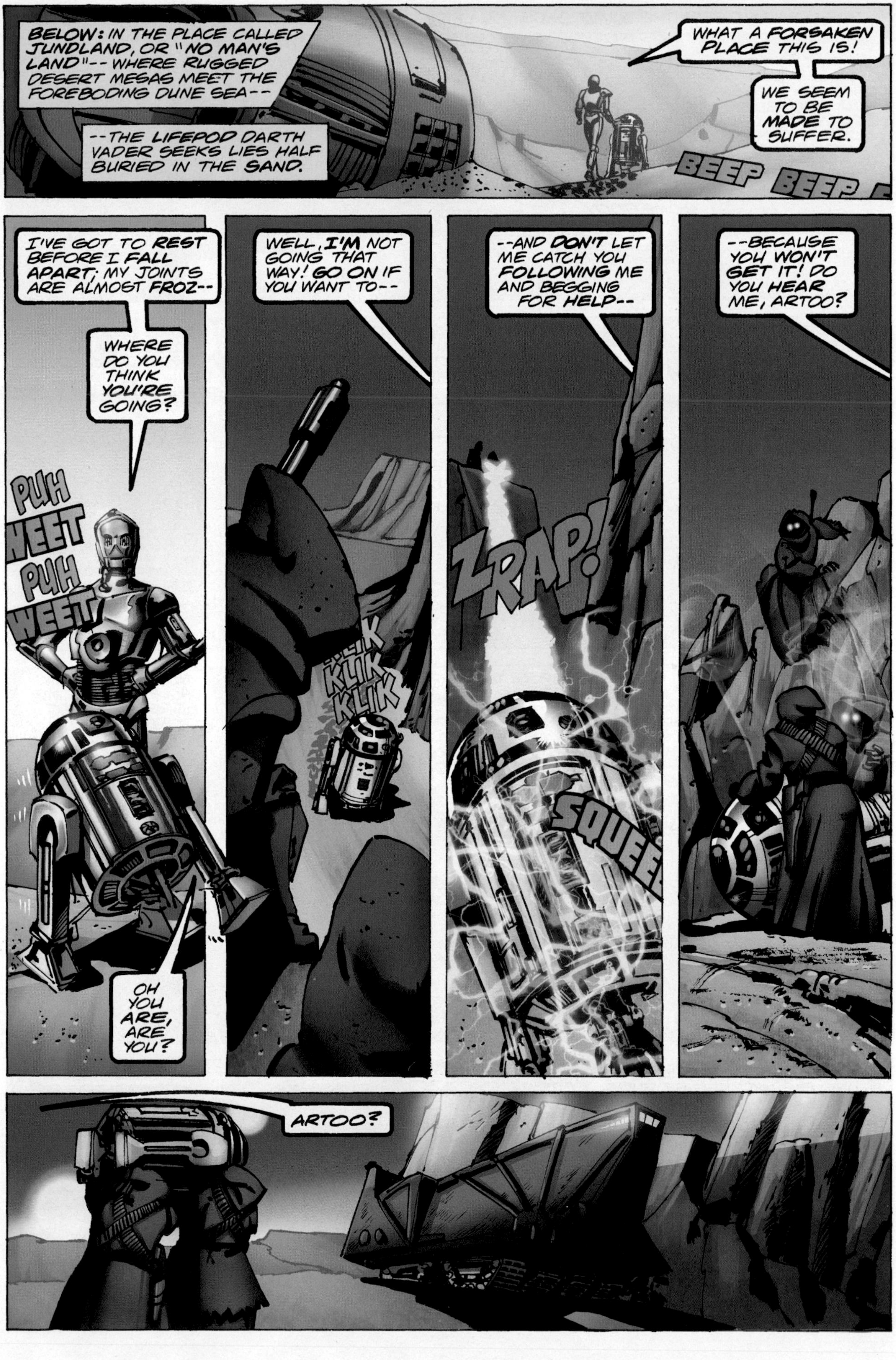

BELOW: IN THE PLACE CALLED JUNDLAND, OR "NO MAN'S LAND"-- WHERE RUGGED DESERT MESAS MEET THE FOREBODING DUNE SEA--
--THE LIFEPOD DARTH VADER SEEKS LIES HALF BURIED IN THE SAND.
WHAT A FORSAKEN PLACE THIS IS!
WE SEEM TO BE MADE TO SUFFER.
BEEP BEEP
I'VE GOT TO REST BEFORE I FALL APART; MY JOINTS ARE ALMOST FROZ--
WHERE DO YOU THINK YOU'RE GOING?
PUH WEET PUH WEET
OH YOU ARE, ARE YOU?
WELL, I'M NOT GOING THAT WAY! GO ON IF YOU WANT TO--
KLIK KLIK KLIK
--AND DON'T LET ME CATCH YOU FOLLOWING ME AND BEGGING FOR HELP--
ZRAP!
SQUEE
--BECAUSE YOU WON'T GET IT! DO YOU HEAR ME, ARTOO?
ARTOO?

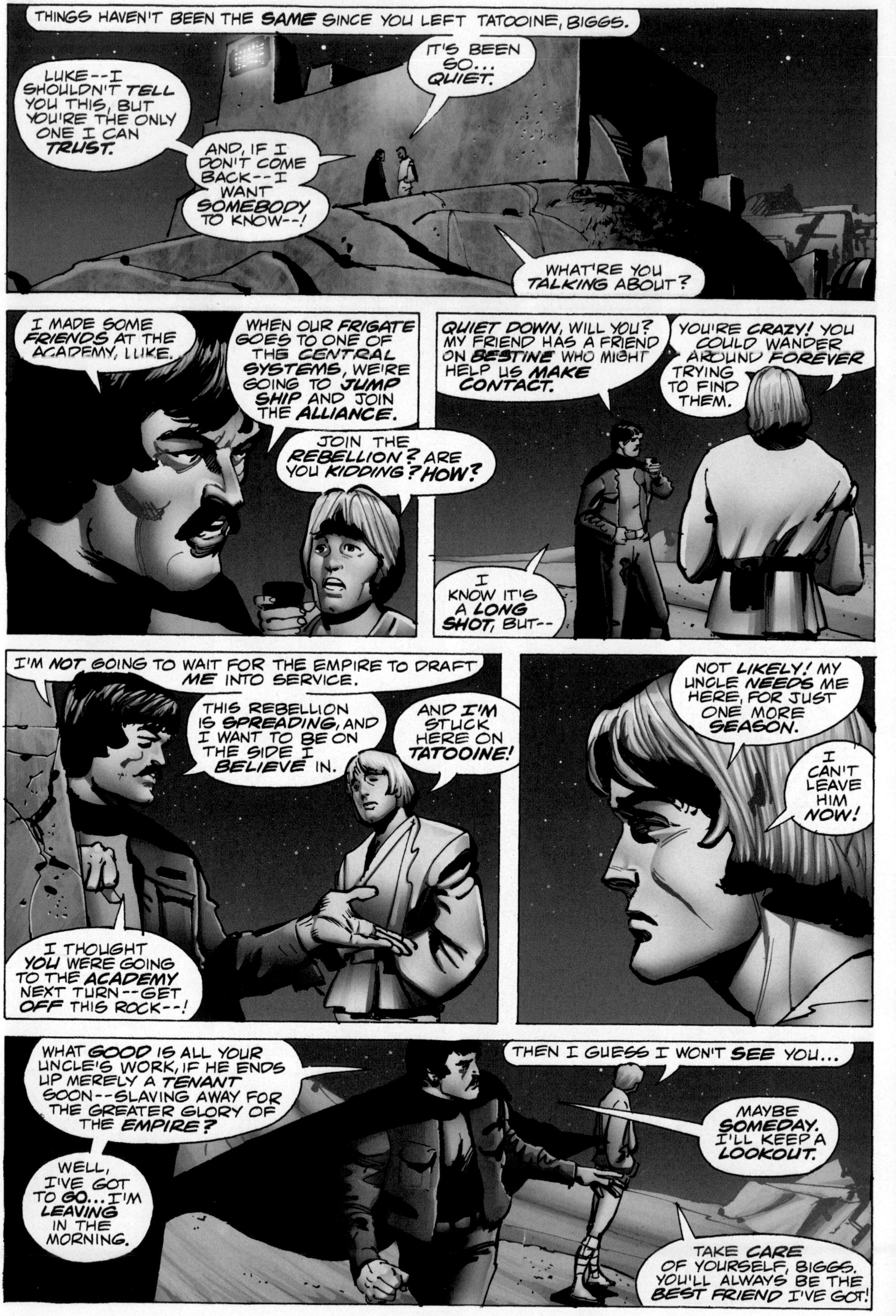

THINGS HAVEN'T BEEN THE SAME SINCE YOU LEFT TATOOINE, BIGGS.
IT'S BEEN SO... QUIET.
LUKE--I SHOULDN'T TELL YOU THIS, BUT YOU'RE THE ONLY ONE I CAN TRUST.
AND, IF I DON'T COME BACK--I WANT SOMEBODY TO KNOW--!
WHAT'RE YOU TALKING ABOUT?
I MADE SOME FRIENDS AT THE ACADEMY, LUKE.
WHEN OUR FRIGATE GOES TO ONE OF THE CENTRAL SYSTEMS, WE'RE GOING TO JUMP SHIP AND JOIN THE ALLIANCE.
JOIN THE REBELLION? ARE YOU KIDDING? HOW?
QUIET DOWN, WILL YOU? MY FRIEND HAS A FRIEND ON BESTINE WHO MIGHT HELP US MAKE CONTACT.
YOU'RE CRAZY! YOU COULD WANDER AROUND FOREVER TRYING TO FIND THEM.
I KNOW IT'S A LONG SHOT, BUT--
I'M NOT GOING TO WAIT FOR THE EMPIRE TO DRAFT ME INTO SERVICE.
THIS REBELLION IS SPREADING, AND I WANT TO BE ON THE SIDE I BELIEVE IN.
AND I'M STUCK HERE ON TATOOINE!
I THOUGHT YOU WERE GOING TO THE ACADEMY NEXT TURN--GET OFF THIS ROCK--!
NOT LIKELY! MY UNCLE NEEDS ME HERE, FOR JUST ONE MORE SEASON.
I CAN'T LEAVE HIM NOW!
WHAT GOOD IS ALL YOUR UNCLE'S WORK, IF HE ENDS UP MERELY A TENANT SOON--SLAVING AWAY FOR THE GREATER GLORY OF THE EMPIRE?
WELL, I'VE GOT TO GO... I'M LEAVING IN THE MORNING.
THEN I GUESS I WON'T SEE YOU...
MAYBE SOMEDAY. I'LL KEEP A LOOKOUT.
TAKE CARE OF YOURSELF, BIGGS. YOU'LL ALWAYS BE THE BEST FRIEND I'VE GOT!

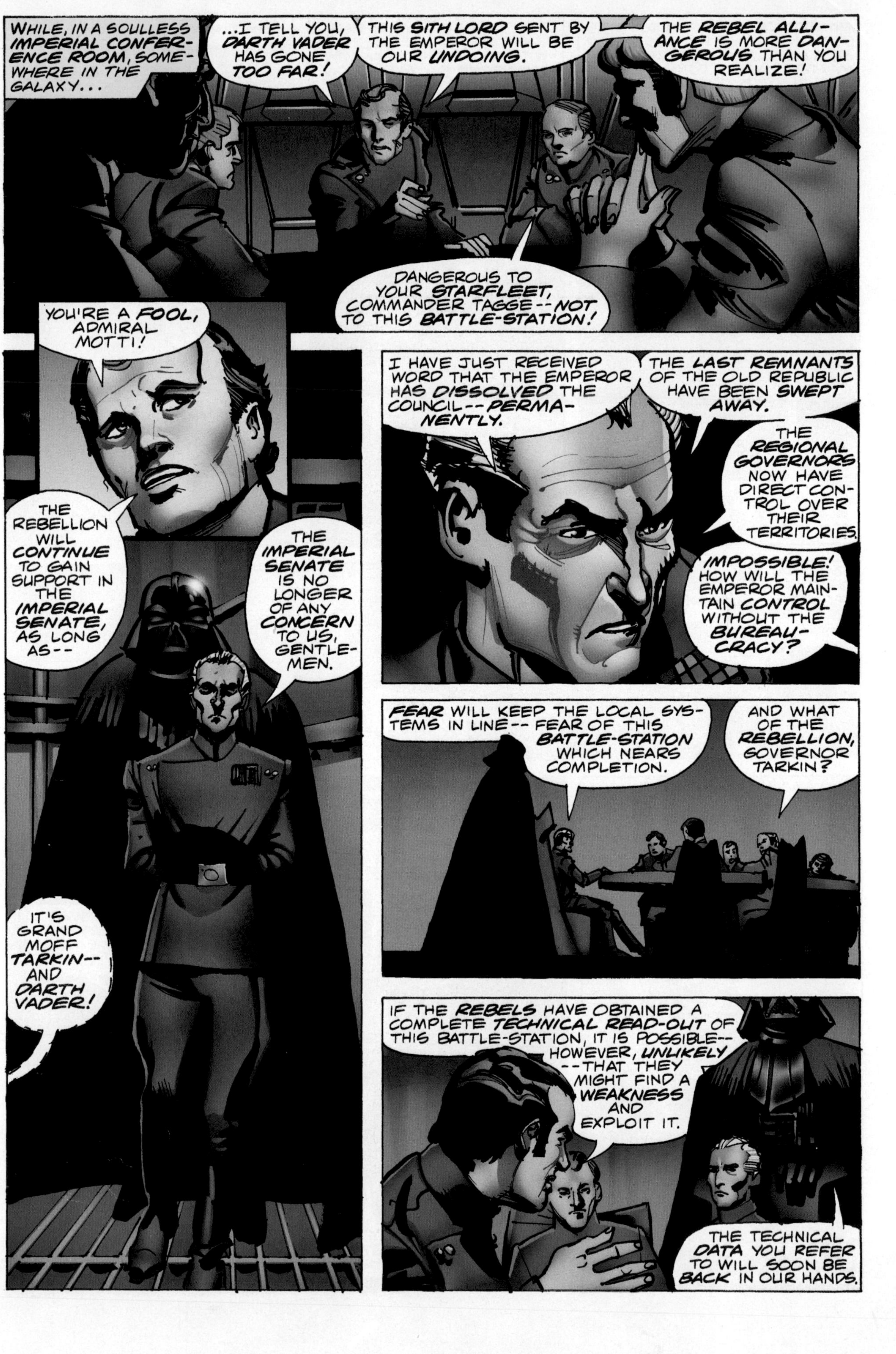

WHILE, IN A SOULLESS IMPERIAL CONFERENCE ROOM, SOMEWHERE IN THE GALAXY...
...I TELL YOU, DARTH VADER HAS GONE TOO FAR!
THIS SITH LORD SENT BY THE EMPEROR WILL BE OUR UNDOING.
THE REBEL ALLIANCE IS MORE DANGEROUS THAN YOU REALIZE!
DANGEROUS TO YOUR STARFLEET, COMMANDER TAGGE--NOT TO THIS BATTLE-STATION!
YOU'RE A FOOL, ADMIRAL MOTTI!
THE REBELLION WILL CONTINUE TO GAIN SUPPORT IN THE IMPERIAL SENATE, AS LONG AS--
THE IMPERIAL SENATE IS NO LONGER OF ANY CONCERN TO US, GENTLEMEN.
IT'S GRAND MOFF TARKIN--AND DARTH VADER!
I HAVE JUST RECEIVED WORD THAT THE EMPEROR HAS DISSOLVED THE COUNCIL--PERMANENTLY.
THE LAST REMNANTS OF THE OLD REPUBLIC HAVE BEEN SWEPT AWAY.
THE REGIONAL GOVERNORS NOW HAVE DIRECT CONTROL OVER THEIR TERRITORIES.
IMPOSSIBLE! HOW WILL THE EMPEROR MAINTAIN CONTROL WITHOUT THE BUREAUCRACY?
FEAR WILL KEEP THE LOCAL SYSTEMS IN LINE--FEAR OF THIS BATTLE-STATION WHICH NEARS COMPLETION.
AND WHAT OF THE REBELLION, GOVERNOR TARKIN?
IF THE REBELS HAVE OBTAINED A COMPLETE TECHNICAL READ-OUT OF THIS BATTLE-STATION, IT IS POSSIBLE--HOWEVER, UNLIKELY--THAT THEY MIGHT FIND A WEAKNESS AND EXPLOIT IT.
THE TECHNICAL DATA YOU REFER TO WILL SOON BE BACK IN OUR HANDS.

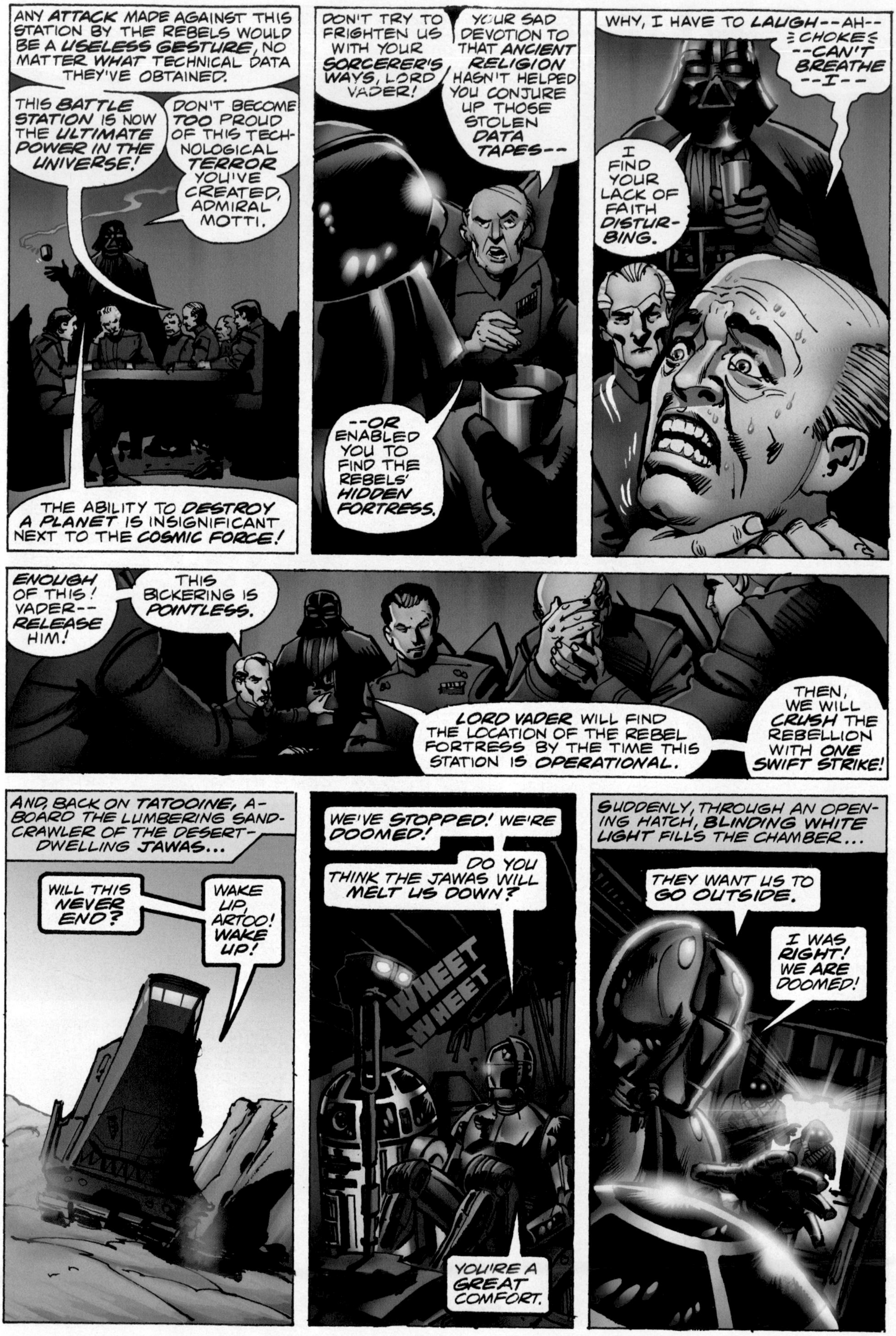

ANY ATTACK MADE AGAINST THIS STATION BY THE REBELS WOULD BE A USELESS GESTURE, NO MATTER WHAT TECHNICAL DATA THEY'VE OBTAINED.
THIS BATTLE STATION IS NOW THE ULTIMATE POWER IN THE UNIVERSE!
DON'T BECOME TOO PROUD OF THIS TECHNOLOGICAL TERROR YOU'VE CREATED, ADMIRAL MOTTI.
THE ABILITY TO DESTROY A PLANET IS INSIGNIFICANT NEXT TO THE COSMIC FORCE!
DON'T TRY TO FRIGHTEN US WITH YOUR SORCERER'S WAYS, LORD VADER!
YOUR SAD DEVOTION TO THAT ANCIENT RELIGION HASN'T HELPED YOU CONJURE UP THOSE STOLEN DATA TAPES--
--OR ENABLED YOU TO FIND THE REBELS' HIDDEN FORTRESS.
WHY, I HAVE TO LAUGH--AH--
CHOKE
--CAN'T BREATHE --I--
I FIND YOUR LACK OF FAITH DISTURBING.
ENOUGH OF THIS! VADER--RELEASE HIM!
THIS BICKERING IS POINTLESS.
LORD VADER WILL FIND THE LOCATION OF THE REBEL FORTRESS BY THE TIME THIS STATION IS OPERATIONAL.
THEN, WE WILL CRUSH THE REBELLION WITH ONE SWIFT STRIKE!
AND, BACK ON TATOOINE, ABOARD THE LUMBERING SANDCRAWLER OF THE DESERT-DWELLING JAWAS...
WILL THIS NEVER END?
WAKE UP, ARTOO! WAKE UP!
WE'VE STOPPED! WE'RE DOOMED!
DO YOU THINK THE JAWAS WILL MELT US DOWN?
WHEET WHEET
YOU'RE A GREAT COMFORT.
SUDDENLY, THROUGH AN OPENING HATCH, BLINDING WHITE LIGHT FILLS THE CHAMBER...
THEY WANT US TO GO OUTSIDE.
I WAS RIGHT! WE ARE DOOMED!

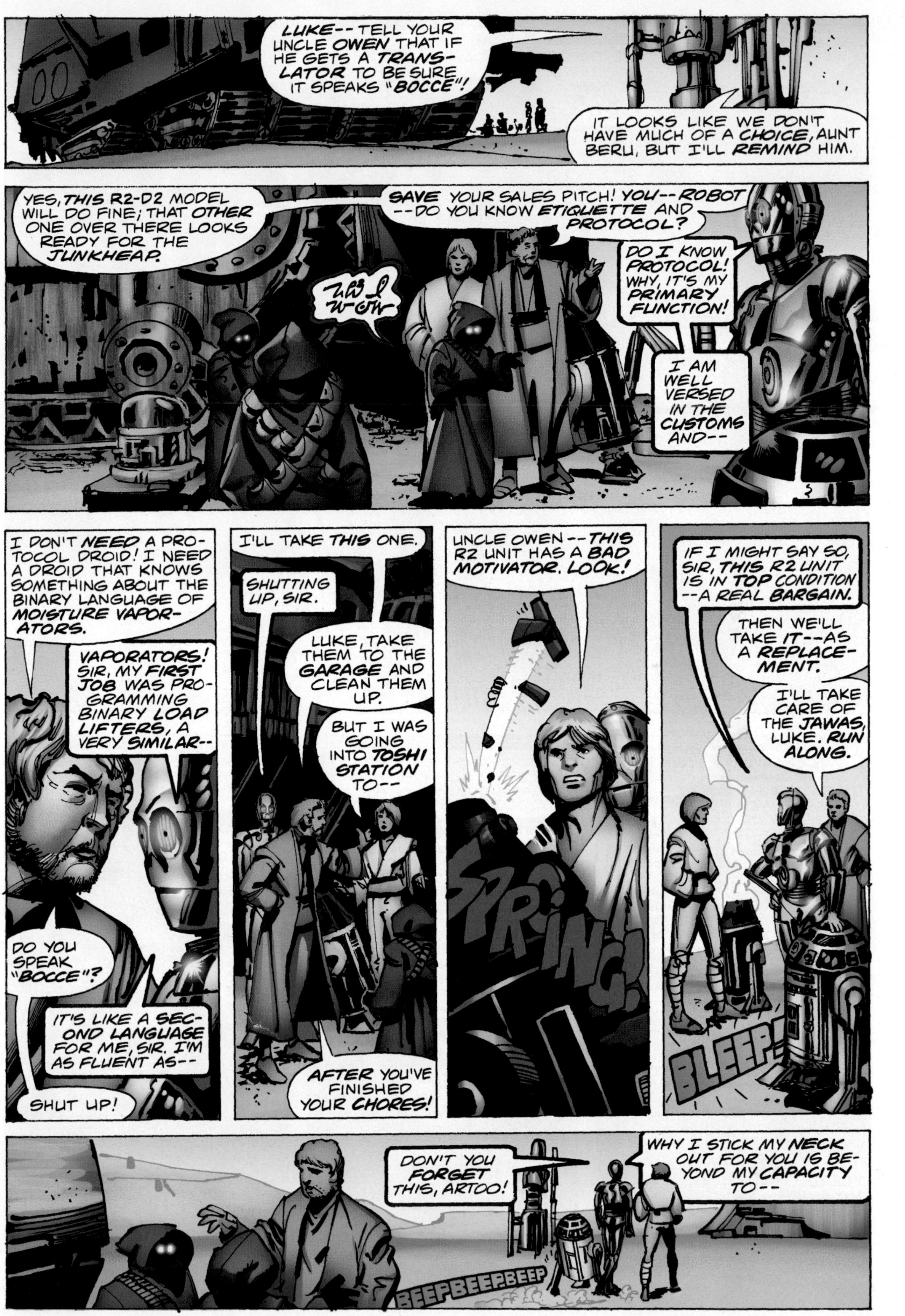
LUKE--TELL YOUR UNCLE OWEN THAT IF HE GETS A TRANSLATOR TO BE SURE IT SPEAKS "BOCCE"!
IT LOOKS LIKE WE DON'T HAVE MUCH OF A CHOICE, AUNT BERU, BUT I'LL REMIND HIM.
YES, THIS R2-D2 MODEL WILL DO FINE; THAT OTHER ONE OVER THERE LOOKS READY FOR THE JUNKHEAP.
SAVE YOUR SALES PITCH! YOU--ROBOT--DO YOU KNOW ETIQUETTE AND PROTOCOL?
DO I KNOW PROTOCOL! WHY, IT'S MY PRIMARY FUNCTION!
I AM WELL VERSED IN THE CUSTOMS AND--
I DON'T NEED A PROTOCOL DROID! I NEED A DROID THAT KNOWS SOMETHING ABOUT THE BINARY LANGUAGE OF MOISTURE VAPORATORS.
VAPORATORS! SIR, MY FIRST JOB WAS PROGRAMMING BINARY LOAD LIFTERS, A VERY SIMILAR--
DO YOU SPEAK "BOCCE"?
IT'S LIKE A SECOND LANGUAGE FOR ME, SIR. I'M AS FLUENT AS--
SHUT UP!
I'LL TAKE THIS ONE.
SHUTTING UP, SIR.
LUKE, TAKE THEM TO THE GARAGE AND CLEAN THEM UP.
BUT I WAS GOING INTO TOSHI STATION TO--
AFTER YOU'VE FINISHED YOUR CHORES!
UNCLE OWEN--THIS R2 UNIT HAS A BAD MOTIVATOR. LOOK!
SPROING!
IF I MIGHT SAY SO, SIR, THIS R2 UNIT IS IN TOP CONDITION--A REAL BARGAIN.
THEN WE'LL TAKE IT--AS A REPLACEMENT.
I'LL TAKE CARE OF THE JAWAS, LUKE. RUN ALONG.
BLEEP!
DON'T YOU FORGET THIS, ARTOO!
WHY I STICK MY NECK OUT FOR YOU IS BEYOND MY CAPACITY TO--
BEEPBEEPBEEP

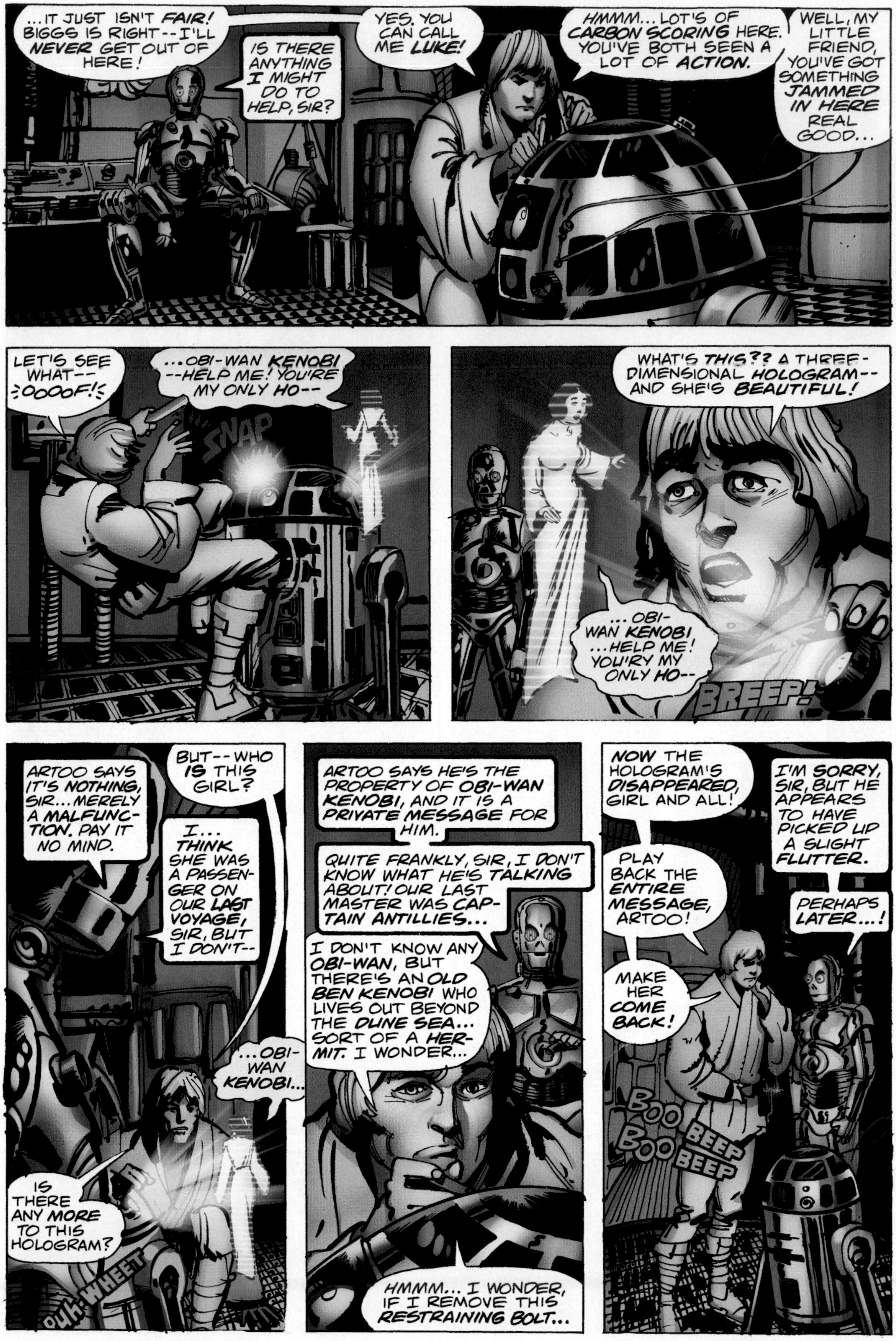
...IT JUST ISN'T FAIR! BIGGS IS RIGHT--I'LL NEVER GET OUT OF HERE!
IS THERE ANYTHING I MIGHT DO TO HELP, SIR?
YES, YOU CAN CALL ME LUKE!
HMMM... LOT'S OF CARBON SCORING HERE. YOU'VE BOTH SEEN A LOT OF ACTION.
WELL, MY LITTLE FRIEND, YOU'VE GOT SOMETHING JAMMED IN HERE REAL GOOD...
LET'S SEE WHAT-- OOOOF!
SNAP
...OBI-WAN KENOBI --HELP ME! YOU'RE MY ONLY HO--
WHAT'S THIS?? A THREE-DIMENSIONAL HOLOGRAM--AND SHE'S BEAUTIFUL!
...OBI-WAN KENOBI ...HELP ME! YOU'RY MY ONLY HO--
BREEP!
ARTOO SAYS IT'S NOTHING, SIR... MERELY A MALFUNCTION. PAY IT NO MIND.
BUT--WHO IS THIS GIRL?
I... THINK SHE WAS A PASSENGER ON OUR LAST VOYAGE, SIR, BUT I DON'T--
...OBI-WAN KENOBI...
IS THERE ANY MORE TO THIS HOLOGRAM?
WHEET
ARTOO SAYS HE'S THE PROPERTY OF OBI-WAN KENOBI, AND IT IS A PRIVATE MESSAGE FOR HIM.
QUITE FRANKLY, SIR, I DON'T KNOW WHAT HE'S TALKING ABOUT! OUR LAST MASTER WAS CAPTAIN ANTILLIES...
I DON'T KNOW ANY OBI-WAN, BUT THERE'S AN OLD BEN KENOBI WHO LIVES OUT BEYOND THE DUNE SEA... SORT OF A HERMIT. I WONDER...
HMMM... I WONDER, IF I REMOVE THIS RESTRAINING BOLT...
NOW THE HOLOGRAM'S DISAPPEARED, GIRL AND ALL!
I'M SORRY, SIR, BUT HE APPEARS TO HAVE PICKED UP A SLIGHT FLUTTER.
PLAY BACK THE ENTIRE MESSAGE, ARTOO!
PERHAPS LATER...!
MAKE HER COME BACK!
BOO BEEP
BOO BEEP

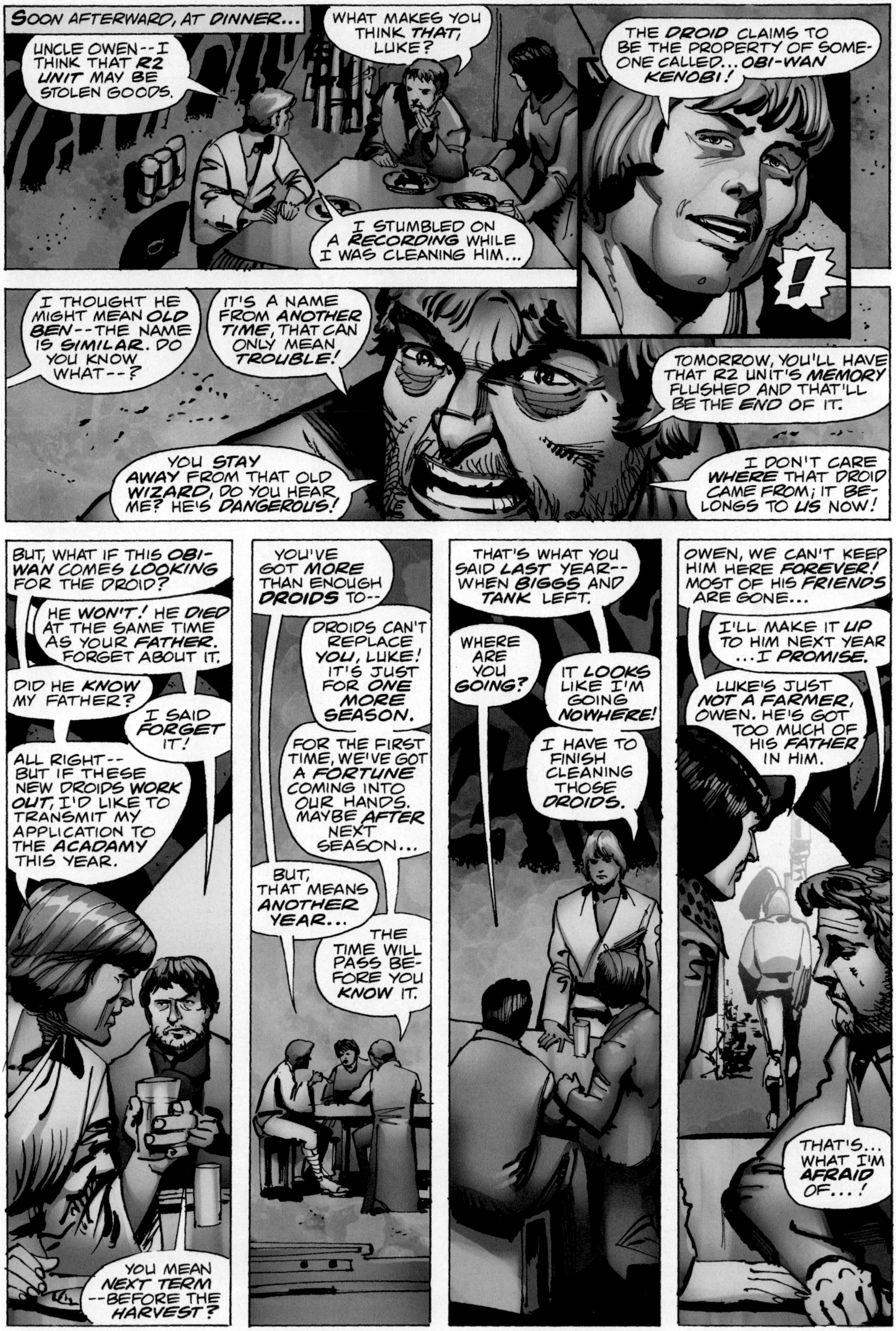
SOON AFTERWARD, AT DINNER...
UNCLE OWEN--I THINK THAT R2 UNIT MAY BE STOLEN GOODS.
WHAT MAKES YOU THINK THAT, LUKE?
I STUMBLED ON A RECORDING WHILE I WAS CLEANING HIM...
THE DROID CLAIMS TO BE THE PROPERTY OF SOMEONE CALLED... OBI-WAN KENOBI!
!
I THOUGHT HE MIGHT MEAN OLD BEN--THE NAME IS SIMILAR. DO YOU KNOW WHAT--?
IT'S A NAME FROM ANOTHER TIME, THAT CAN ONLY MEAN TROUBLE!
TOMORROW, YOU'LL HAVE THAT R2 UNIT'S MEMORY FLUSHED AND THAT'LL BE THE END OF IT.
YOU STAY AWAY FROM THAT OLD WIZARD, DO YOU HEAR ME? HE'S DANGEROUS!
I DON'T CARE WHERE THAT DROID CAME FROM; IT BELONGS TO US NOW!
BUT, WHAT IF THIS OBI-WAN COMES LOOKING FOR THE DROID?
HE WON'T! HE DIED AT THE SAME TIME AS YOUR FATHER. FORGET ABOUT IT.
DID HE KNOW MY FATHER?
I SAID FORGET IT!
ALL RIGHT--BUT IF THESE NEW DROIDS WORK OUT, I'D LIKE TO TRANSMIT MY APPLICATION TO THE ACADAMY THIS YEAR.
YOU MEAN NEXT TERM --BEFORE THE HARVEST?
YOU'VE GOT MORE THAN ENOUGH DROIDS TO--
DROIDS CAN'T REPLACE YOU, LUKE! IT'S JUST FOR ONE MORE SEASON.
FOR THE FIRST TIME, WE'VE GOT A FORTUNE COMING INTO OUR HANDS. MAYBE AFTER NEXT SEASON...
BUT, THAT MEANS ANOTHER YEAR...
THE TIME WILL PASS BEFORE YOU KNOW IT.
THAT'S WHAT YOU SAID LAST YEAR--WHEN BIGGS AND TANK LEFT.
WHERE ARE YOU GOING?
IT LOOKS LIKE I'M GOING NOWHERE!
I HAVE TO FINISH CLEANING THOSE DROIDS.
OWEN, WE CAN'T KEEP HIM HERE FOREVER! MOST OF HIS FRIENDS ARE GONE...
I'LL MAKE IT UP TO HIM NEXT YEAR ...I PROMISE.
LUKE'S JUST NOT A FARMER, OWEN. HE'S GOT TOO MUCH OF HIS FATHER IN HIM.
THAT'S... WHAT I'M AFRAID OF...!

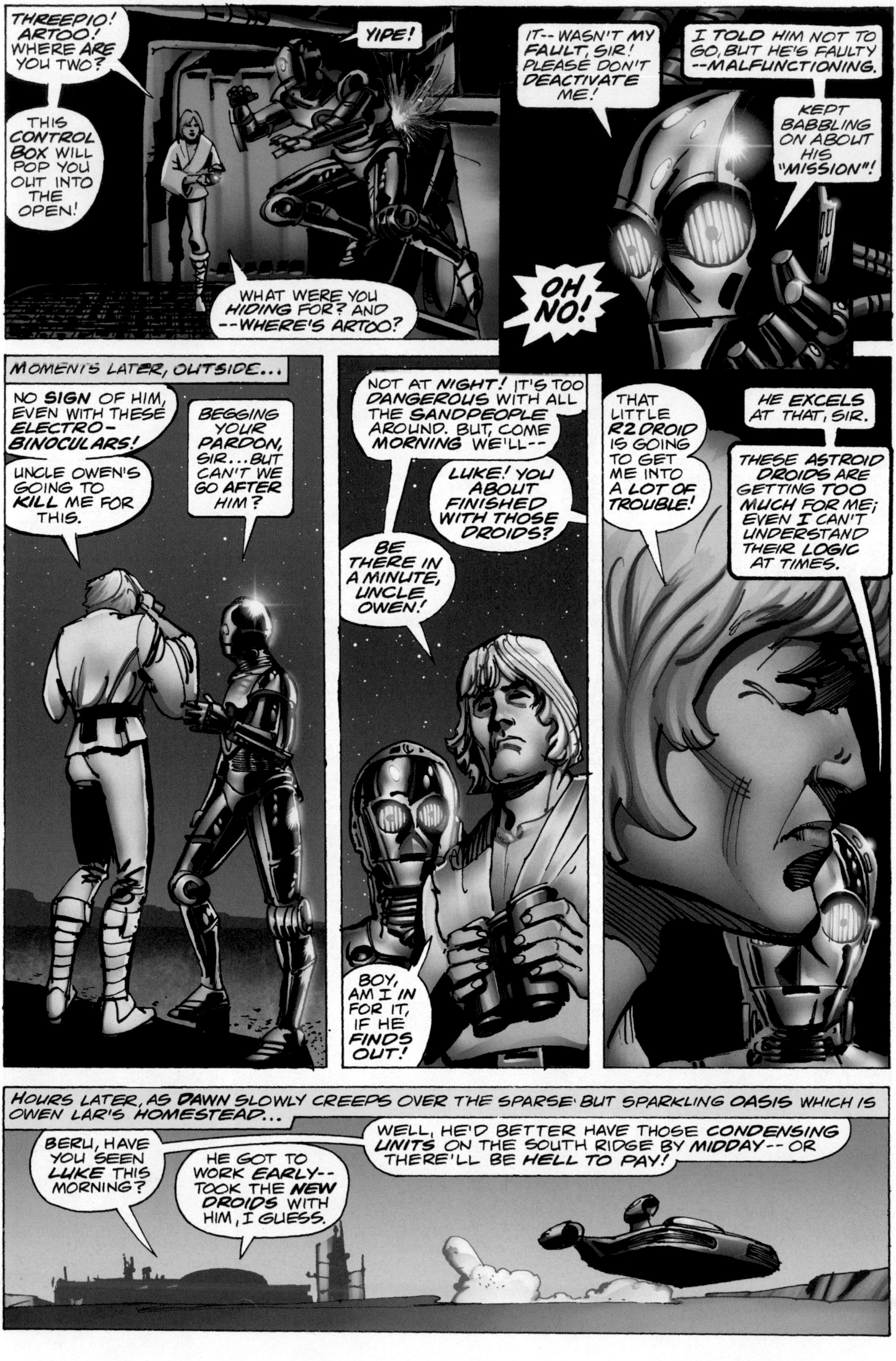
THREEPIO! ARTOO! WHERE ARE YOU TWO?
THIS CONTROL BOX WILL POP YOU OUT INTO THE OPEN!
YIPE!
WHAT WERE YOU HIDING FOR? AND --WHERE'S ARTOO?
IT-- WASN'T MY FAULT, SIR! PLEASE DON'T DEACTIVATE ME!
I TOLD HIM NOT TO GO, BUT HE'S FAULTY --MALFUNCTIONING.
KEPT BABBLING ON ABOUT HIS "MISSION"!
OH NO!
MOMENTS LATER, OUTSIDE...
NO SIGN OF HIM, EVEN WITH THESE ELECTRO-BINOCULARS!
UNCLE OWEN'S GOING TO KILL ME FOR THIS.
BEGGING YOUR PARDON, SIR... BUT CAN'T WE GO AFTER HIM?
NOT AT NIGHT! IT'S TOO DANGEROUS WITH ALL THE SANDPEOPLE AROUND. BUT, COME MORNING WE'LL--
LUKE! YOU ABOUT FINISHED WITH THOSE DROIDS?
BE THERE IN A MINUTE, UNCLE OWEN!
BOY, AM I IN FOR IT, IF HE FINDS OUT!
THAT LITTLE R2 DROID IS GOING TO GET ME INTO A LOT OF TROUBLE!
HE EXCELS AT THAT, SIR.
THESE ASTROID DROIDS ARE GETTING TOO MUCH FOR ME; EVEN I CAN'T UNDERSTAND THEIR LOGIC AT TIMES.
HOURS LATER, AS DAWN SLOWLY CREEPS OVER THE SPARSE BUT SPARKLING OASIS WHICH IS OWEN LAR'S HOMESTEAD...
BERU, HAVE YOU SEEN LUKE THIS MORNING?
HE GOT TO WORK EARLY-- TOOK THE NEW DROIDS WITH HIM, I GUESS.
WELL, HE'D BETTER HAVE THOSE CONDENSING UNITS ON THE SOUTH RIDGE BY MIDDAY-- OR THERE'LL BE HELL TO PAY!

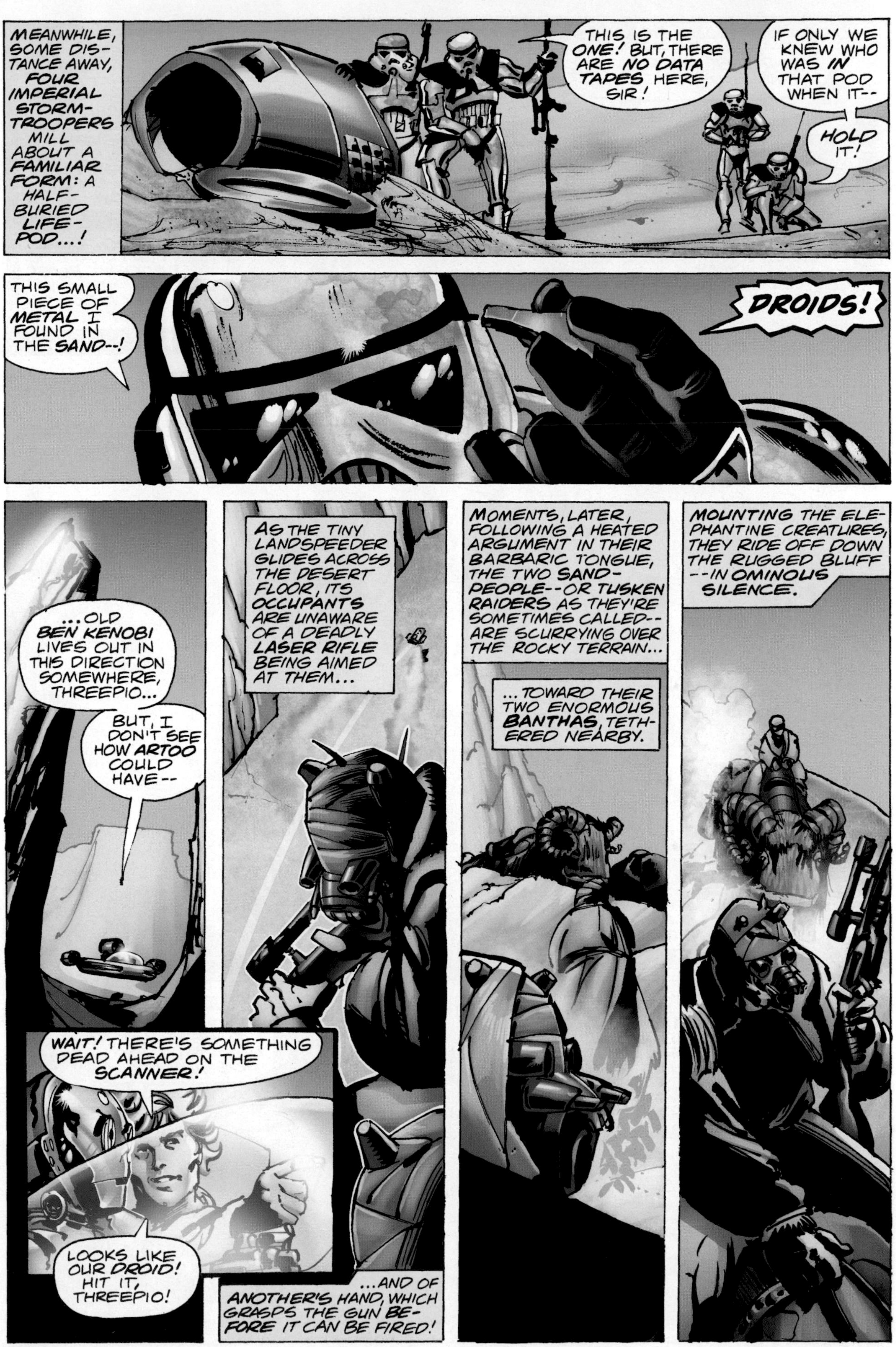
MEANWHILE, SOME DISTANCE AWAY, FOUR IMPERIAL STORM-TROOPERS MILL ABOUT A FAMILIAR FORM: A HALF-BURIED LIFE-POD...!
THIS IS THE ONE! BUT, THERE ARE NO DATA TAPES HERE, SIR!
IF ONLY WE KNEW WHO WAS IN THAT POD WHEN IT--
HOLD IT!
THIS SMALL PIECE OF METAL I FOUND IN THE SAND--!
DROIDS!
...OLD BEN KENOBI LIVES OUT IN THIS DIRECTION SOMEWHERE, THREEPIO...
BUT, I DON'T SEE HOW ARTOO COULD HAVE--
WAIT! THERE'S SOMETHING DEAD AHEAD ON THE SCANNER!
LOOKS LIKE OUR DROID! HIT IT, THREEPIO!
AS THE TINY LANDSPEEDER GLIDES ACROSS THE DESERT FLOOR, ITS OCCUPANTS ARE UNAWARE OF A DEADLY LASER RIFLE BEING AIMED AT THEM...
...AND OF ANOTHER'S HAND, WHICH GRASPS THE GUN BEFORE IT CAN BE FIRED!
MOMENTS, LATER, FOLLOWING A HEATED ARGUMENT IN THEIR BARBARIC TONGUE, THE TWO SAND-PEOPLE--OR TUSKEN RAIDERS AS THEY'RE SOMETIMES CALLED--ARE SCURRYING OVER THE ROCKY TERRAIN...
...TOWARD THEIR TWO ENORMOUS BANTHAS, TETHERED NEARBY.
MOUNTING THE ELEPHANTINE CREATURES, THEY RIDE OFF DOWN THE RUGGED BLUFF --IN OMINOUS SILENCE.

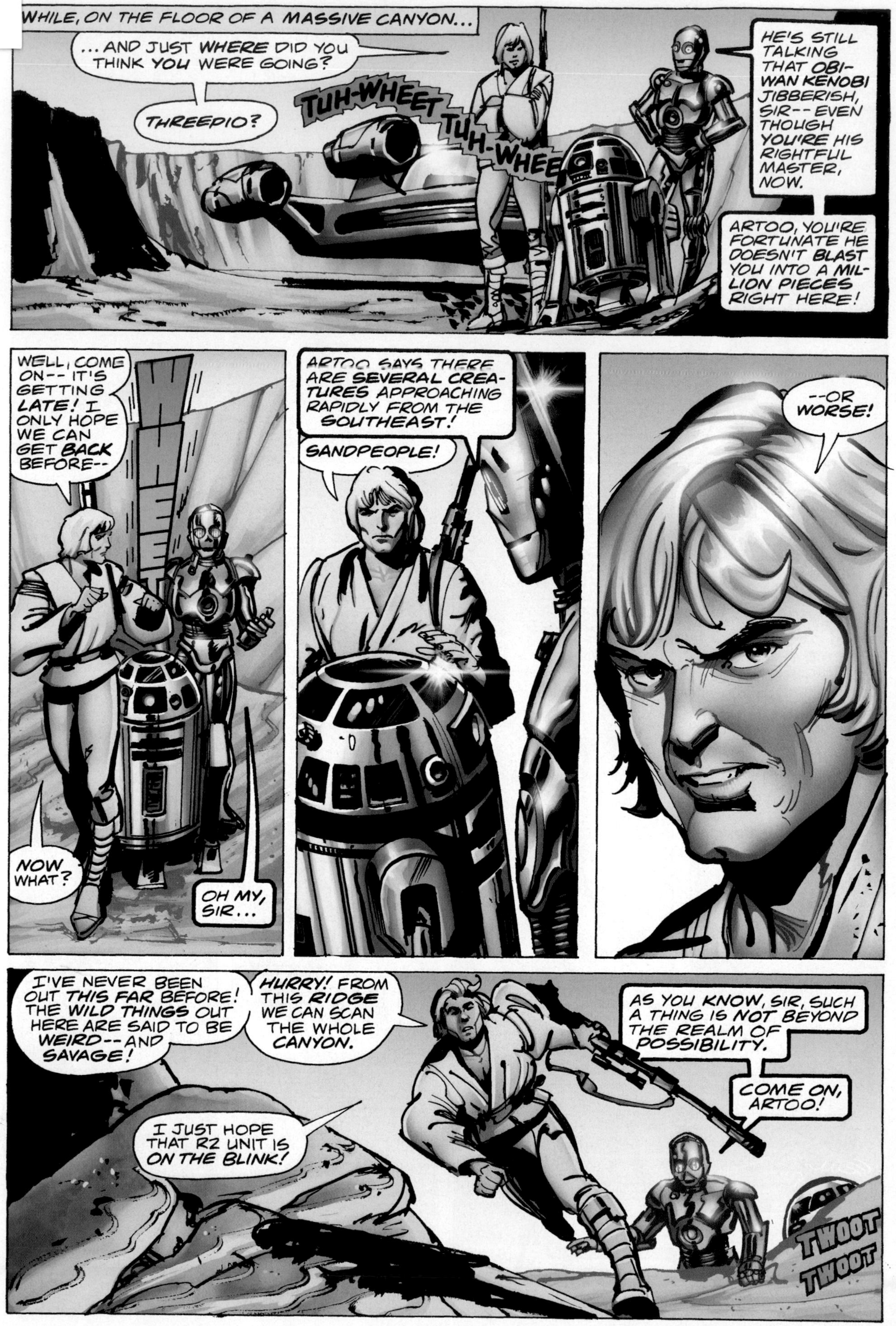
WHILE, ON THE FLOOR OF A MASSIVE CANYON...
...AND JUST WHERE DID YOU THINK YOU WERE GOING?
THREEPIO?
TUH-WHEET TUH-WHEE
HE'S STILL TALKING THAT OBI-WAN KENOBI JIBBERISH, SIR-- EVEN THOUGH YOU'RE HIS RIGHTFUL MASTER, NOW.
ARTOO, YOU'RE FORTUNATE HE DOESN'T BLAST YOU INTO A MILLION PIECES RIGHT HERE!
WELL, COME ON-- IT'S GETTING LATE! I ONLY HOPE WE CAN GET BACK BEFORE--
WHEET
NOW WHAT?
OH MY, SIR...
ARTOO SAYS THERE ARE SEVERAL CREATURES APPROACHING RAPIDLY FROM THE SOUTHEAST!
SANDPEOPLE!
--OR WORSE!
I'VE NEVER BEEN OUT THIS FAR BEFORE! THE WILD THINGS OUT HERE ARE SAID TO BE WEIRD-- AND SAVAGE!
HURRY! FROM THIS RIDGE WE CAN SCAN THE WHOLE CANYON.
AS YOU KNOW, SIR, SUCH A THING IS NOT BEYOND THE REALM OF POSSIBILITY.
COME ON, ARTOO!
I JUST HOPE THAT R2 UNIT IS ON THE BLINK!
TWOOT TWOOT

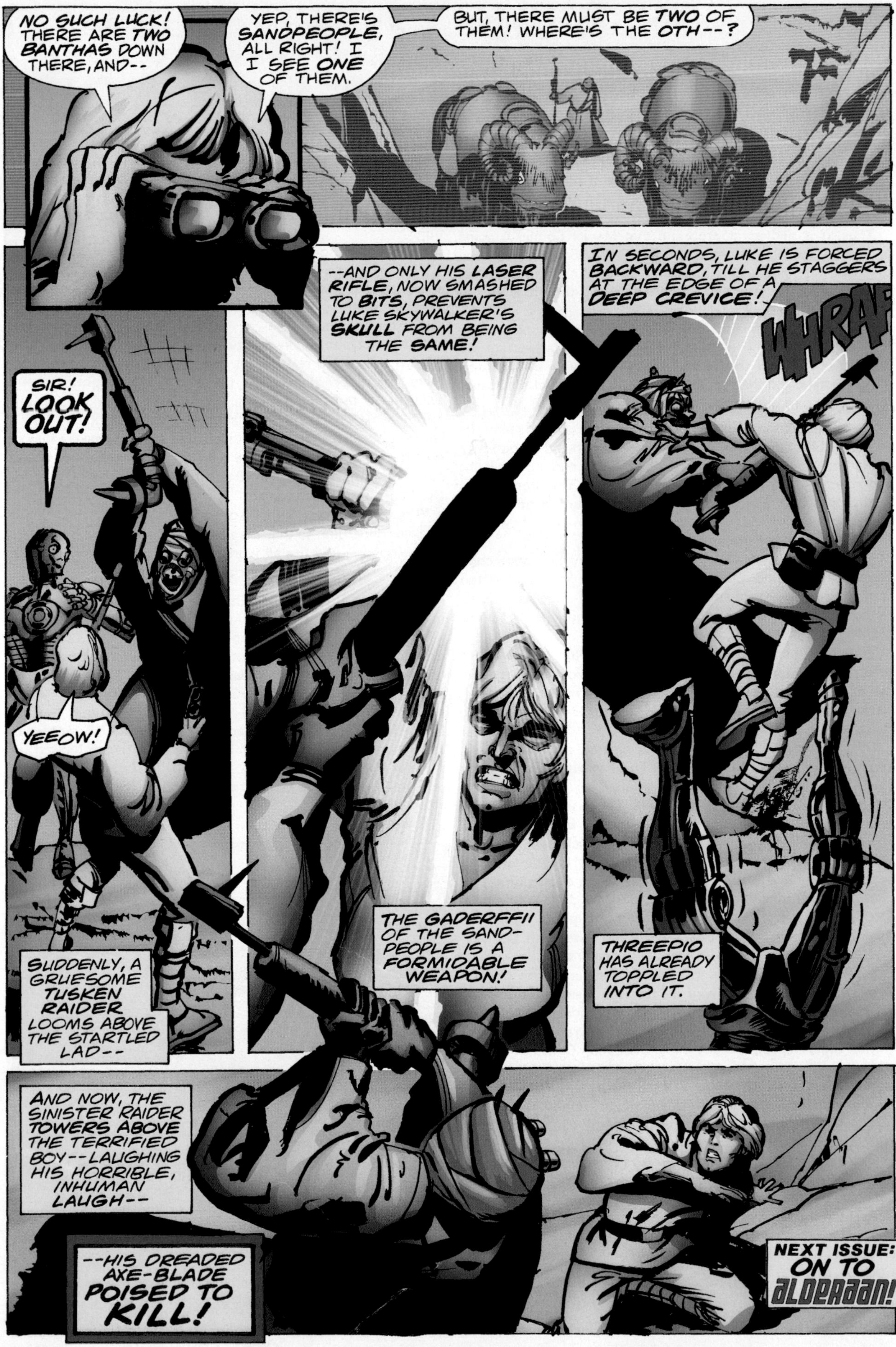
NO SUCH LUCK! THERE ARE TWO BANTHAS DOWN THERE, AND--
YEP, THERE'S SANDPEOPLE, ALL RIGHT! I SEE ONE OF THEM.
BUT, THERE MUST BE TWO OF THEM! WHERE'S THE OTH--?
SIR! LOOK OUT!
YEEOW!
SUDDENLY, A GRUESOME TUSKEN RAIDER LOOMS ABOVE THE STARTLED LAD--
--AND ONLY HIS LASER RIFLE, NOW SMASHED TO BITS, PREVENTS LUKE SKYWALKER'S SKULL FROM BEING THE SAME!
THE GADERFFII OF THE SAND-PEOPLE IS A FORMIDABLE WEAPON!
IN SECONDS, LUKE IS FORCED BACKWARD, TILL HE STAGGERS AT THE EDGE OF A DEEP CREVICE!
WHRAF
THREEPIO HAS ALREADY TOPPLED INTO IT.
AND NOW, THE SINISTER RAIDER TOWERS ABOVE THE TERRIFIED BOY--LAUGHING HIS HORRIBLE, INHUMAN LAUGH--
--HIS DREADED AXE-BLADE POISED TO KILL!
NEXT ISSUE: ON TO ALDERAAN!

STAR WARS™: THE ULTIMATE SPACE-FANTASY

A Six-Issue Prospectus On A Startling Piece of Cinema

Six years ago, George Lucas, the creator of *American Graffiti*, began his first draft of the script of a film that is certain to become a milestone in the space fantasy genre.

Thus, it is perhaps appropriate that Marvel Comics is going to take six monthly issues of this STAR WARS comic-magazine to adapt the movie into illustrated form. Anything less than approximately a hundred pages would be too little to do it justice.

Still, just to familiarize you with the territory, including a few terms new to those unfamiliar with interstellar warfare, we thought it'd be best to give you this brief overview of the story, the characters, and the people behind it. Read it carefully, 'cause there might be a quiz at the end of the sixth issue:

Through thousands of light-years come the amazing exploits of hero Luke Skywalker and his friends, flesh-and-blood space pilots and mechanical robots, as they battle numerous villains and creatures in a massive Galactic Civil War. This story has no relationship to Earth time and space. It occurs in other solar systems in another galaxy and could be happening in the future, the past, or even the present.

Young Luke Skywalker is accompanied by his robot companions R2-D2 and C-3PO (more familiarly known as Artoo and Threepio)—the tough starpilot Han Solo—the seven-foot, fur-covered Wookiee named Chewbacca—and the venerable old warrior, Ben Kenobi.

Three different worlds become settings for the series of fabulous adventures and thrills. They travel from the large arid planet Tatooine to the huge man-made planet destroyer, Death Star, and finally arrive on the dense jungle-covered fourth moon of Yavin.

Director/writer George Lucas has created a majestic visual experience of extraordinary worlds. This Panavision Technicolor motion picture, to be released in late May of this year, is produced by Gary Kurtz for Twentieth Century-Fox release and was made on locations in Tunisia and at EMI Elstree and Shepperton Studios, London, over a 17-week schedule.

Lucas and Kurtz, the successful duo of the fantastically popular *American Graffiti*, have acquired an outstanding production team, including production designer John Barry of *A Clockwork Orange* fame and director of photography Gil Taylor of Alfred Hitchcock's *Frenzy* and Twentieth Century-Fox's 1976 hit, *The Omen*. A team with credentials!

John Stears, production special-effects supervisor in London (and Academy Award winner for the James Bond film *Thunderball*) designed the robots and land vehicles and planned the cataclysmic explosions. At a hidden warehouse in the United States, special-effects miniaturist John Dykstra took full advantage of new advances in computer-controlled stop-motion animation. Matte artist Peter Ellenshaw, Jr., carried on a great family tradition in a relatively unknown motion picture art form. John Barry was production designer, while veteran John Williams scored the music.

Other important production members include make-up expert Stuart Freeborn, who designed and made the ape costumes for *2001*, and editors Marcia Lucas, Richard Chew, and Paul Hirsch.

And the *stars* of Star Wars?

Sir Alec Guinness stars as Ben (Obi-wan) Kenobi, Mark Hamill as Luke Skywalker, Harrison Ford (a featured player in *Graffiti*) as Han Solo, Carrie Fisher as Princess Leia Organa, and Peter Cushing (of Frankenstein fame and infamy) as Governor Moff Tarkin.

Others in the cast include Anthony Daniels, Kenny Baker, Peter Mayhew, and Dave Prowse—though it's doubtful even their own families would recognize them in their alien get-ups.

Now the question: *"Why did filmmaker George Lucas follow up a movie like American Graffiti with such a totally different film?"*

Here's the reason, in his own words:

"I think that anyone who goes to the movies loves to have an emotional experience. It's basic—whether you're seven, seventeen, or seventy. The more intense the experience, the more successful the film.

"I've always loved adventure films. After I finished *American Graffiti*, I came to realize that since the demise of the western, there hasn't been much in the mythological fantasy genre available to the film audience. So, instead of making 'isn't-it-terrible-what's-happening-to-mankind' movies, which is how I began, I decided that I'd try to fill that gap. I'd make a film so rooted in imagination that the grimness of everyday life would not follow the audience into the theatre. In other words, for two hours, they could forget.

"I'm trying to reconstruct a genre that's been lost and bring it to a new dimension so that the elements of space, fantasy, adventure, suspense, and fun all work and feed off each other. So, in a way, *Star Wars* is a movie for the kid in all of us."

With this multi-million-dollar Fox release slated to open in major theatres across the country in just a few short weeks—with a *Star Wars* novelization from Ballantine Books already rushing toward a second printing—and now, with the beginning of Marvel Comics' official adaptation by Roy Thomas (late of UNKNOWN WORLDS OF SCIENCE FICTION and a Skrull/Kree War or two himself) and Howard Chaykin (whose MONARK STARSTALKER and SOLOMON KANE for Marvel have shown he knows how to buckle a mean swash himself, in space or elsewhere)—

—well, it looks as if the time *has* come for STAR WARS, after all!

And it's *about* time!

STAR WARRIORS

c/o MARVEL COMICS GROUP, 575 MADISON AVE. N.Y.C. 10022

THE STORY BEHIND *STAR WARS*
The Movie and the Comic-Mag
by Roy Thomas

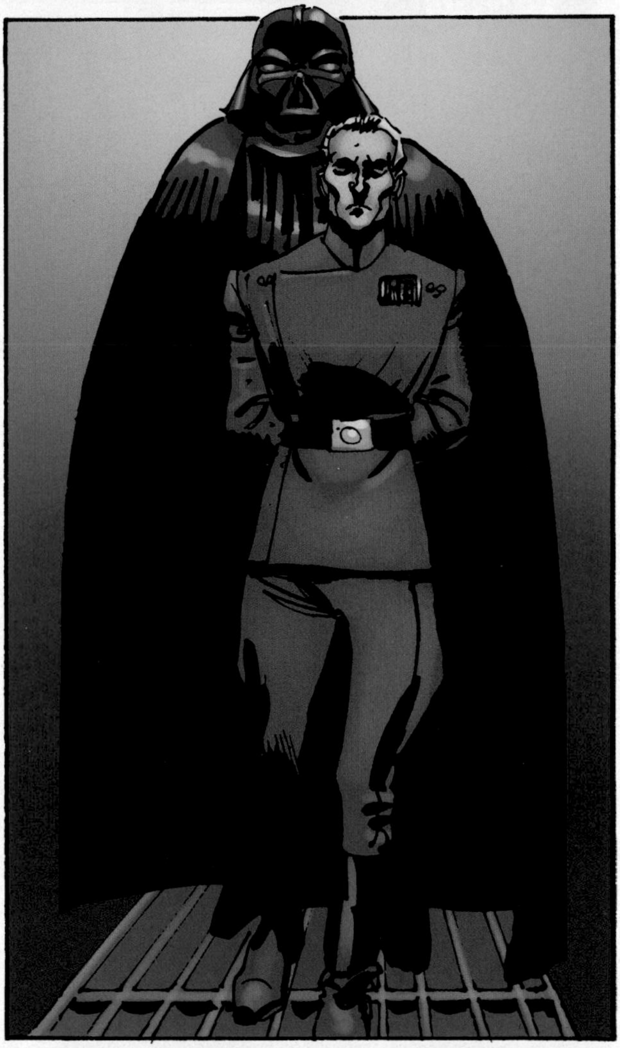

It started slowly, this *Star Wars* project. Both for George Lucas and even for Marvel Comics.

It's a couple of years now since I met George Lucas, already celebrated as the film-maker behind the blockbuster *American Graffiti.* I was an ardent admirer of that film (and had also been intrigued by his earlier, science-fiction feature *THX 1138*). George, in turn, had expressed a desire to see the Carl Barks/ Uncle Scrooge McDuck painting which hangs proudly in my living room, and was enthusiastic about another pride and joy of mine, our late lamented $1 magazine UNKNOWN WORLDS OF SCIENCE FICTION. We met, shared a dinner and a few anecdotes, and that was it.

Or so it seemed.

For, a few months later, a friend of George's looked me up. His name was Charlie Lippincott, and he was (for lack of a better term, he said) media projects director of George Lucas' new film, *Star Wars,* about which I knew nothing but the name.

Fairly understandable, since at that stage filming hadn't even been started.

Charlie informed me, after a spaghetti dinner and some more swapped anecdotes, that he and George would like Marvel Comics in general and me in particular to handle the comic-book adaptation of *Star Wars.* I was, of course, both flattered and flabbergasted. And, when Charlie brought out stats of a dozen or so beautiful paintings of projected scenes from the movie ("sketches," they're called in the trade, but they were painstakingly detailed and breathtakingly beautiful), I was definitely hooked.

Within a couple of days, Smilin' Stan Lee had seen my enthusiasm and figured, I guess, that "What the heck, it'll give the Kid something to do." STAR WARS was tentatively added to the hectic Marvel schedule, after some slight debate about whether it should be a color or black-and-white mag, about whether it should be adapted in one issue or twenty, etc. I wanted to adapt George's script in about a half dozen issues, in full color—and I guess I was fairly persuasive that particular day.

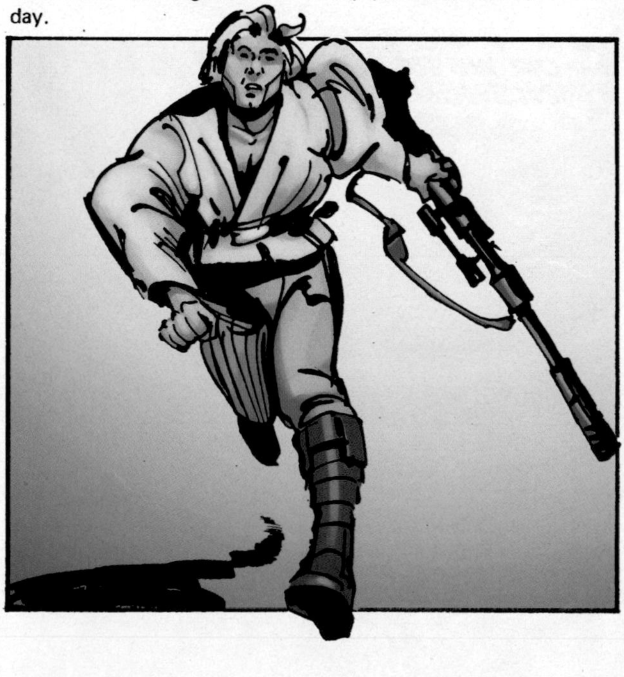

By that time, reading over the script and having perused the illustrations which would soon become filmic reality, I had already chosen the artist I would give first crack at STAR-WARS, Marvel version.

Howard Chaykin's drawn space fantasy (or space opera, if you will) for just about every market over the past couple of years. For our competition, for underground-type mags, and even for *us,* as witness last year's MARVEL PREMIERE issue featuring one MONARK STARSTALKER. Howie took one look at the script and the "production sketches," and his only question was—"When do we start?"

He's got top-notch help, too, to help the two of us produce the STAR WARS comic on a monthly basis. This issue's cover, for instance, based on a poster by the talented Mr. C., was inked by Tom Palmer, a favorite of Marveldom Assembled. And, starting with issue #2, the inking chores (if you can call such an enjoyable assignment a "chore") will be done by Steve Leialoha, in between encounters with HOWARD THE DUCK. We think Chaykin and Leialoha are gonna be a duo to remember.

And STAR WARS, both as film and as comic-book, is going to be just what it says out there on the first page:

"The Greatest Space-Fantasy of All!"

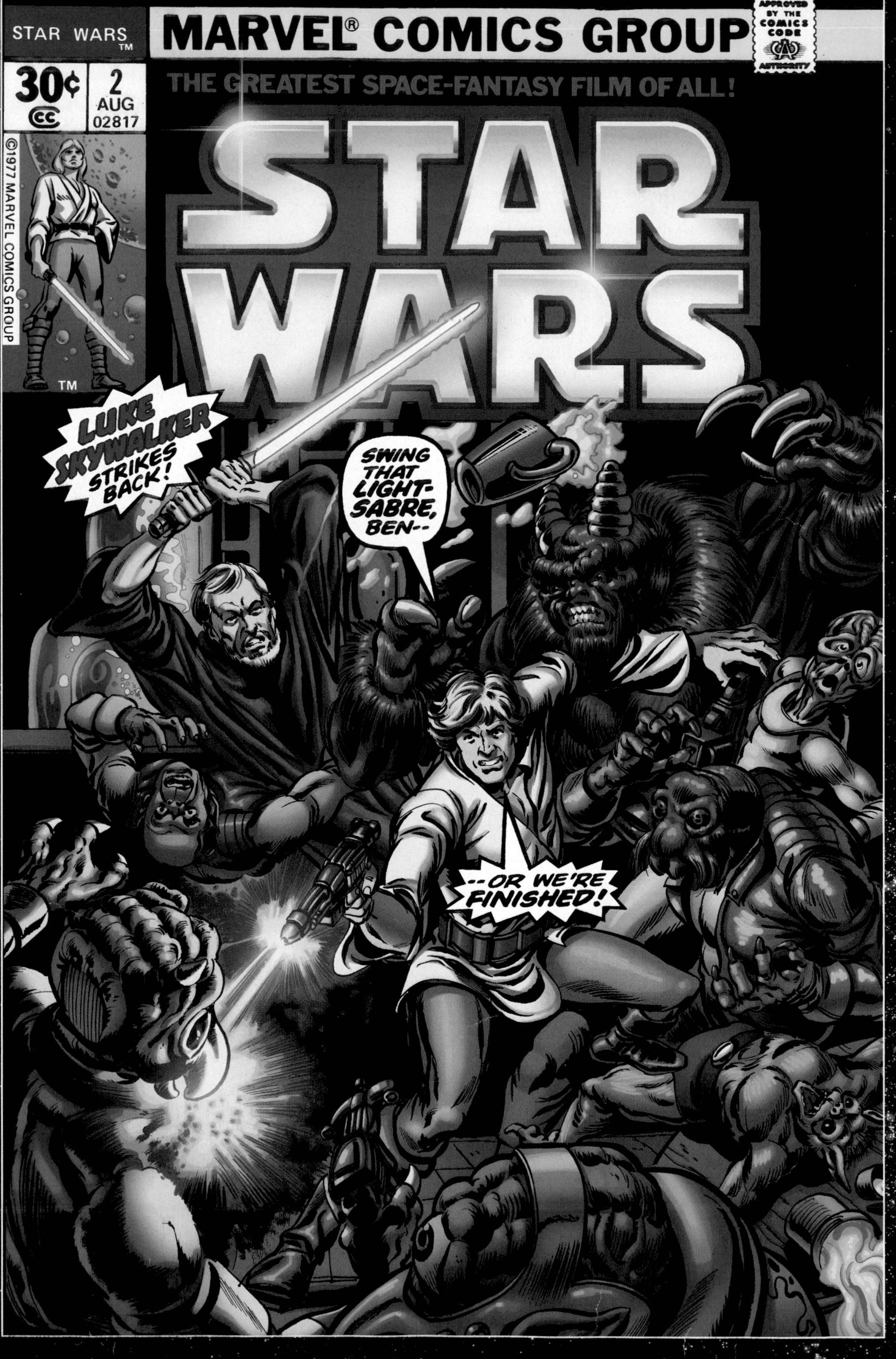
STAR WARS TM
MARVEL® COMICS GROUP
APPROVED BY THE COMICS CODE AUTHORITY
30¢ CC
2 AUG 02817
THE GREATEST SPACE-FANTASY FILM OF ALL!
STAR WARS
©1977 MARVEL COMICS GROUP
TM
LUKE SKYWALKER STRIKES BACK!
SWING THAT LIGHT-SABRE, BEN--
--OR WE'RE FINISHED!

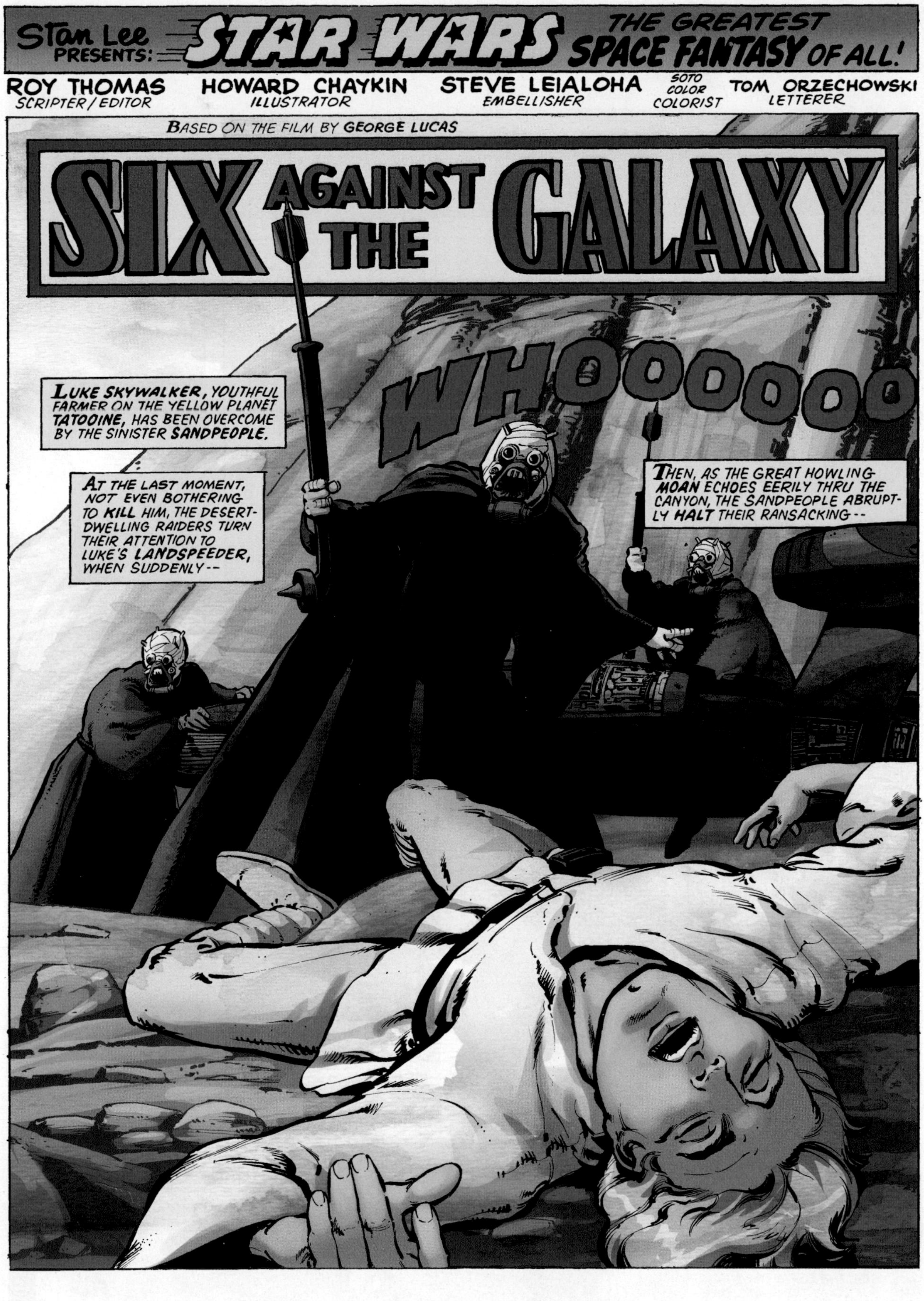
Stan Lee PRESENTS: STAR WARS THE GREATEST SPACE FANTASY OF ALL!
ROY THOMAS SCRIPTER/EDITOR
HOWARD CHAYKIN ILLUSTRATOR
STEVE LEIALOHA EMBELLISHER
SOTO COLOR COLORIST
TOM ORZECHOWSKI LETTERER
BASED ON THE FILM BY GEORGE LUCAS
SIX AGAINST THE GALAXY
LUKE SKYWALKER, YOUTHFUL FARMER ON THE YELLOW PLANET TATOOINE, HAS BEEN OVERCOME BY THE SINISTER SANDPEOPLE.
AT THE LAST MOMENT, NOT EVEN BOTHERING TO KILL HIM, THE DESERT-DWELLING RAIDERS TURN THEIR ATTENTION TO LUKE'S LANDSPEEDER, WHEN SUDDENLY--
WHOOOOOO
THEN, AS THE GREAT HOWLING MOAN ECHOES EERILY THRU THE CANYON, THE SANDPEOPLE ABRUPTLY HALT THEIR RANSACKING--

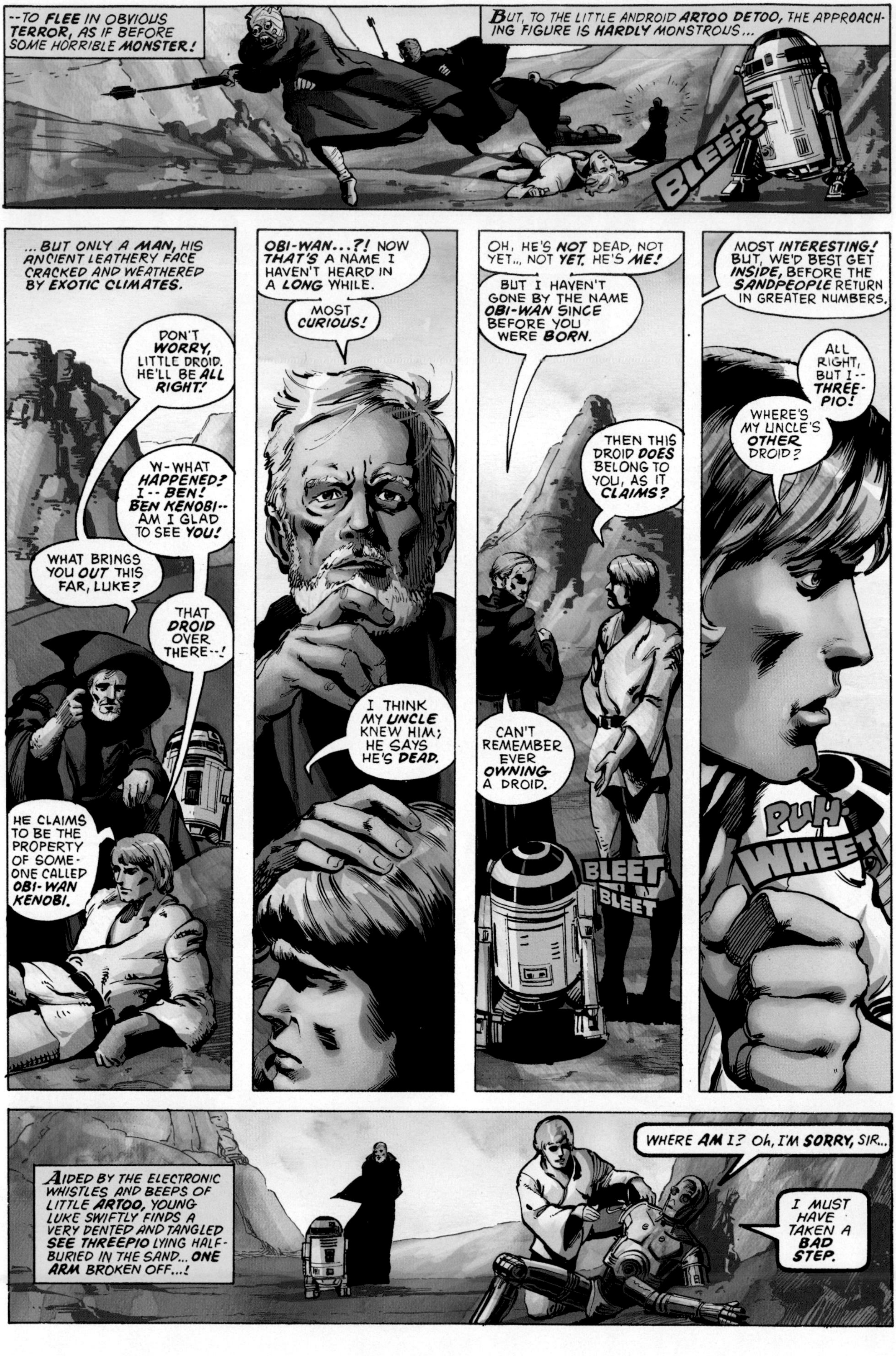

--TO FLEE IN OBVIOUS TERROR, AS IF BEFORE SOME HORRIBLE MONSTER!
BUT, TO THE LITTLE ANDROID ARTOO DETOO, THE APPROACHING FIGURE IS HARDLY MONSTROUS...
BLEEP?
...BUT ONLY A MAN, HIS ANCIENT LEATHERY FACE CRACKED AND WEATHERED BY EXOTIC CLIMATES.
DON'T WORRY, LITTLE DROID. HE'LL BE ALL RIGHT!
W-WHAT HAPPENED? I--BEN! BEN KENOBI--AM I GLAD TO SEE YOU!
WHAT BRINGS YOU OUT THIS FAR, LUKE?
THAT DROID OVER THERE--!
HE CLAIMS TO BE THE PROPERTY OF SOMEONE CALLED OBI-WAN KENOBI.
OBI-WAN...?! NOW THAT'S A NAME I HAVEN'T HEARD IN A LONG WHILE.
MOST CURIOUS!
I THINK MY UNCLE KNEW HIM; HE SAYS HE'S DEAD.
OH, HE'S NOT DEAD, NOT YET.. NOT YET. HE'S ME!
BUT I HAVEN'T GONE BY THE NAME OBI-WAN SINCE BEFORE YOU WERE BORN.
THEN THIS DROID DOES BELONG TO YOU, AS IT CLAIMS?
CAN'T REMEMBER EVER OWNING A DROID.
BLEET BLEET
MOST INTERESTING! BUT, WE'D BEST GET INSIDE, BEFORE THE SANDPEOPLE RETURN IN GREATER NUMBERS.
ALL RIGHT, BUT I--THREEPIO!
WHERE'S MY UNCLE'S OTHER DROID?
PUH-WHEET
AIDED BY THE ELECTRONIC WHISTLES AND BEEPS OF LITTLE ARTOO, YOUNG LUKE SWIFTLY FINDS A VERY DENTED AND TANGLED SEE THREEPIO LYING HALF-BURIED IN THE SAND... ONE ARM BROKEN OFF...!
WHERE AM I? Oh, I'M SORRY, SIR...
I MUST HAVE TAKEN A BAD STEP.

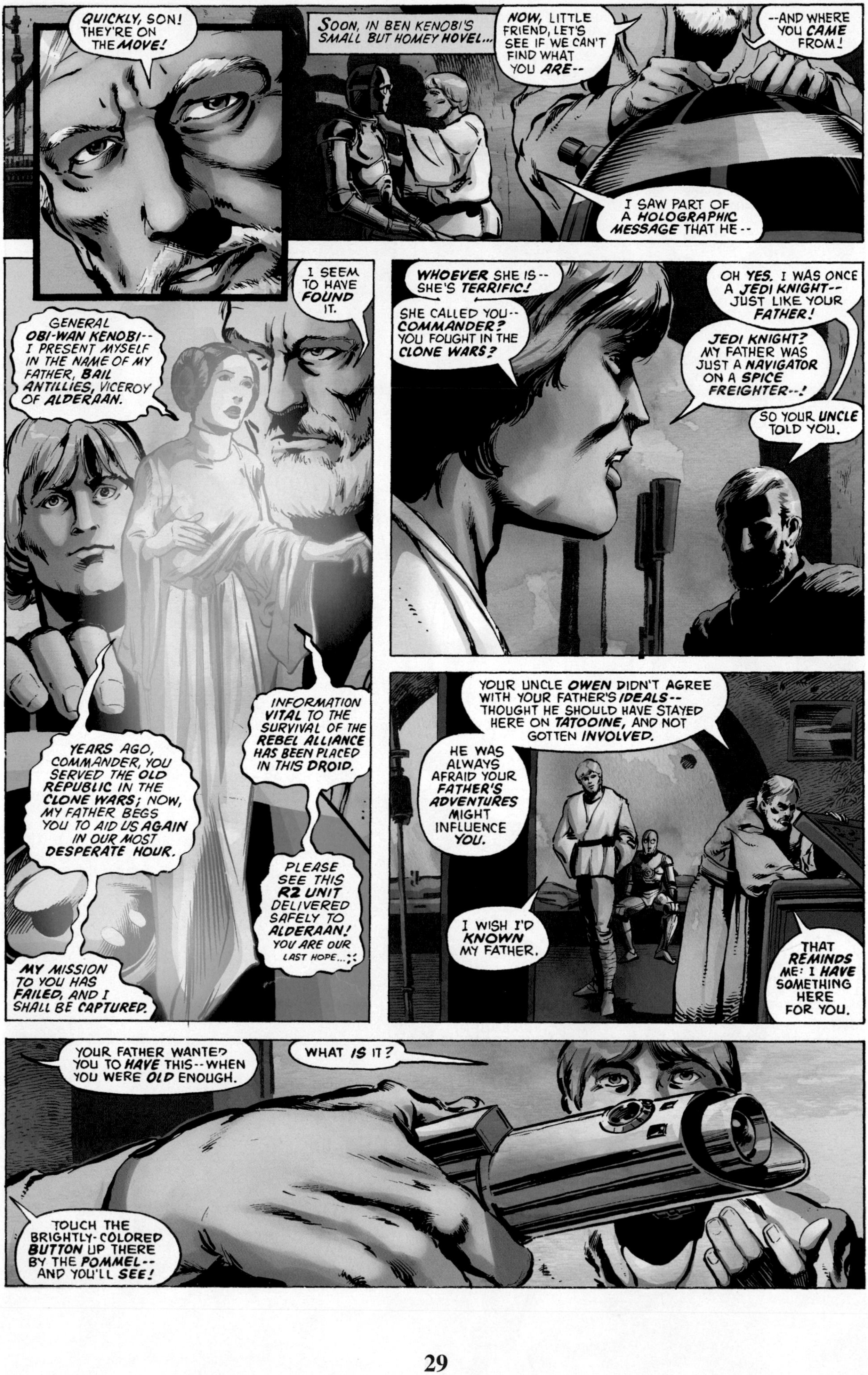
QUICKLY, SON! THEY'RE ON THE MOVE!
SOON, IN BEN KENOBI'S SMALL BUT HOMEY HOVEL...
NOW, LITTLE FRIEND, LET'S SEE IF WE CAN'T FIND WHAT YOU ARE--
--AND WHERE YOU CAME FROM!
I SAW PART OF A HOLOGRAPHIC MESSAGE THAT HE--
I SEEM TO HAVE FOUND IT.
GENERAL OBI-WAN KENOBI-- I PRESENT MYSELF IN THE NAME OF MY FATHER, BAIL ANTILLIES, VICEROY OF ALDERAAN.
YEARS AGO, COMMANDER, YOU SERVED THE OLD REPUBLIC IN THE CLONE WARS; NOW, MY FATHER BEGS YOU TO AID US AGAIN IN OUR MOST DESPERATE HOUR.
INFORMATION VITAL TO THE SURVIVAL OF THE REBEL ALLIANCE HAS BEEN PLACED IN THIS DROID.
PLEASE SEE THIS R2 UNIT DELIVERED SAFELY TO ALDERAAN! YOU ARE OUR LAST HOPE...
MY MISSION TO YOU HAS FAILED, AND I SHALL BE CAPTURED.
WHOEVER SHE IS-- SHE'S TERRIFIC!
SHE CALLED YOU-- COMMANDER? YOU FOUGHT IN THE CLONE WARS?
OH YES. I WAS ONCE A JEDI KNIGHT-- JUST LIKE YOUR FATHER!
JEDI KNIGHT? MY FATHER WAS JUST A NAVIGATOR ON A SPICE FREIGHTER--!
SO YOUR UNCLE TOLD YOU.
YOUR UNCLE OWEN DIDN'T AGREE WITH YOUR FATHER'S IDEALS-- THOUGHT HE SHOULD HAVE STAYED HERE ON TATOOINE, AND NOT GOTTEN INVOLVED.
HE WAS ALWAYS AFRAID YOUR FATHER'S ADVENTURES MIGHT INFLUENCE YOU.
I WISH I'D KNOWN MY FATHER.
THAT REMINDS ME: I HAVE SOMETHING HERE FOR YOU.
YOUR FATHER WANTED YOU TO HAVE THIS--WHEN YOU WERE OLD ENOUGH.
WHAT IS IT?
TOUCH THE BRIGHTLY-COLORED BUTTON UP THERE BY THE POMMEL-- AND YOU'LL SEE!

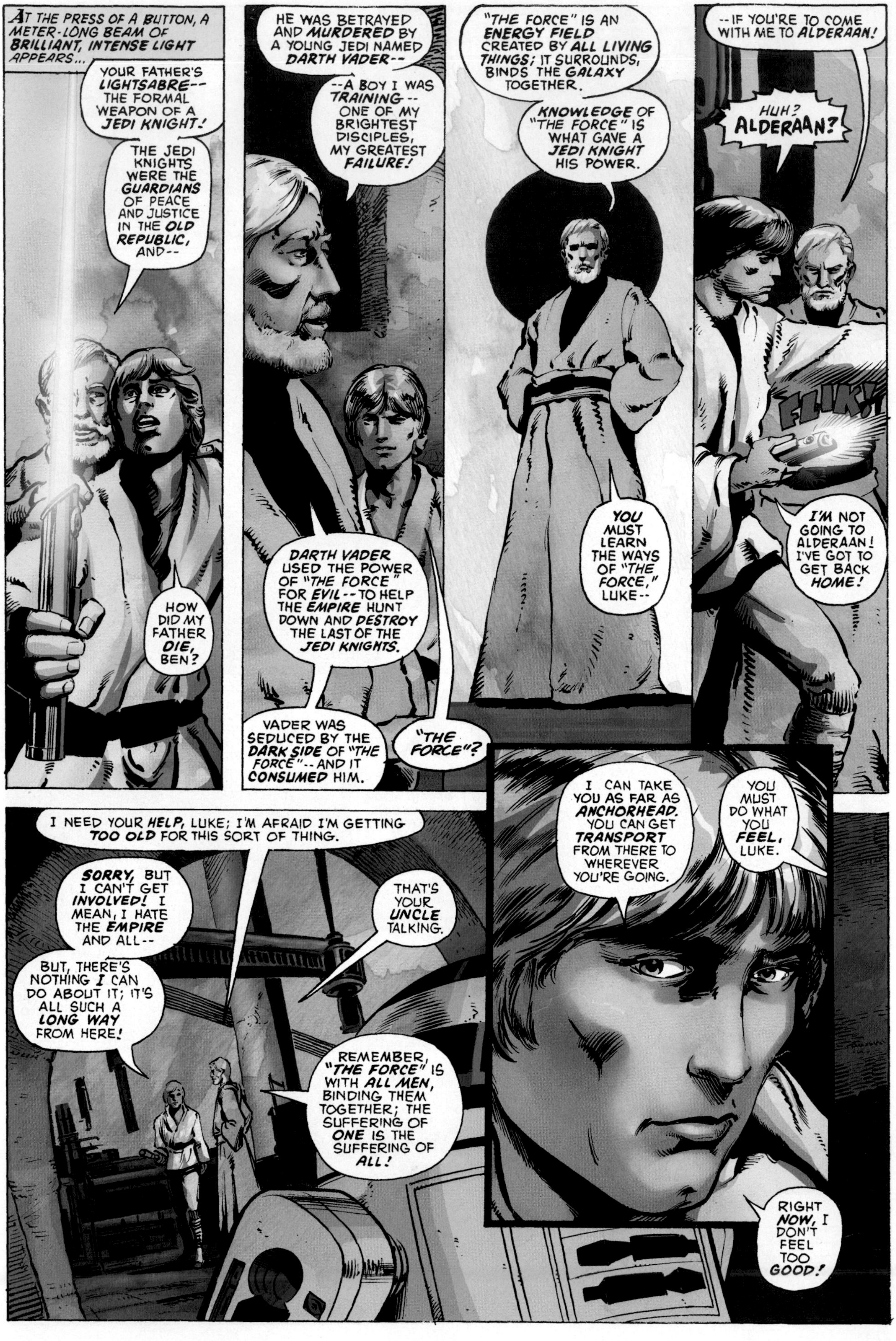
AT THE PRESS OF A BUTTON, A METER-LONG BEAM OF BRILLIANT, INTENSE LIGHT APPEARS...
YOUR FATHER'S LIGHTSABRE-- THE FORMAL WEAPON OF A JEDI KNIGHT!
THE JEDI KNIGHTS WERE THE GUARDIANS OF PEACE AND JUSTICE IN THE OLD REPUBLIC, AND--
HOW DID MY FATHER DIE, BEN?
HE WAS BETRAYED AND MURDERED BY A YOUNG JEDI NAMED DARTH VADER--
--A BOY I WAS TRAINING -- ONE OF MY BRIGHTEST DISCIPLES, MY GREATEST FAILURE!
DARTH VADER USED THE POWER OF "THE FORCE" FOR EVIL -- TO HELP THE EMPIRE HUNT DOWN AND DESTROY THE LAST OF THE JEDI KNIGHTS.
VADER WAS SEDUCED BY THE DARK SIDE OF "THE FORCE" -- AND IT CONSUMED HIM.
"THE FORCE"?
"THE FORCE" IS AN ENERGY FIELD CREATED BY ALL LIVING THINGS; IT SURROUNDS, BINDS THE GALAXY TOGETHER.
KNOWLEDGE OF "THE FORCE" IS WHAT GAVE A JEDI KNIGHT HIS POWER.
YOU MUST LEARN THE WAYS OF "THE FORCE," LUKE--
-- IF YOU'RE TO COME WITH ME TO ALDERAAN!
HUH? ALDERAAN?
FLIK!
I'M NOT GOING TO ALDERAAN! I'VE GOT TO GET BACK HOME!
I NEED YOUR HELP, LUKE; I'M AFRAID I'M GETTING TOO OLD FOR THIS SORT OF THING.
SORRY, BUT I CAN'T GET INVOLVED! I MEAN, I HATE THE EMPIRE AND ALL--
BUT, THERE'S NOTHING I CAN DO ABOUT IT; IT'S ALL SUCH A LONG WAY FROM HERE!
THAT'S YOUR UNCLE TALKING.
REMEMBER, "THE FORCE" IS WITH ALL MEN, BINDING THEM TOGETHER; THE SUFFERING OF ONE IS THE SUFFERING OF ALL!
I CAN TAKE YOU AS FAR AS ANCHORHEAD. YOU CAN GET TRANSPORT FROM THERE TO WHEREVER YOU'RE GOING.
YOU MUST DO WHAT YOU FEEL, LUKE.
RIGHT NOW, I DON'T FEEL TOO GOOD!

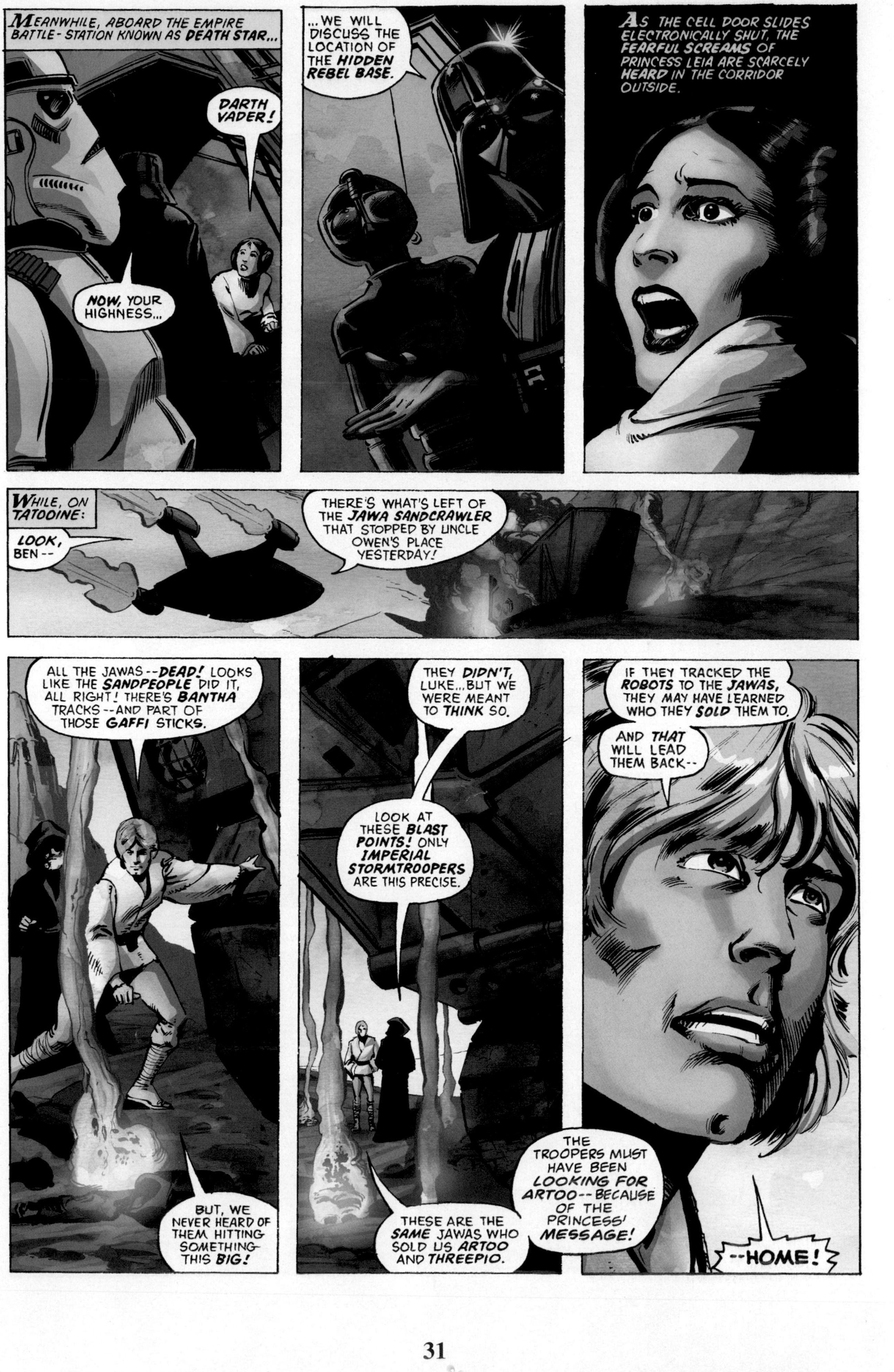
MEANWHILE, ABOARD THE EMPIRE BATTLE-STATION KNOWN AS DEATH STAR...
DARTH VADER!
NOW, YOUR HIGHNESS...
...WE WILL DISCUSS THE LOCATION OF THE HIDDEN REBEL BASE.
AS THE CELL DOOR SLIDES ELECTRONICALLY SHUT, THE FEARFUL SCREAMS OF PRINCESS LEIA ARE SCARCELY HEARD IN THE CORRIDOR OUTSIDE.
WHILE, ON TATOOINE:
LOOK, BEN--
THERE'S WHAT'S LEFT OF THE JAWA SANDCRAWLER THAT STOPPED BY UNCLE OWEN'S PLACE YESTERDAY!
ALL THE JAWAS--DEAD! LOOKS LIKE THE SANDPEOPLE DID IT, ALL RIGHT! THERE'S BANTHA TRACKS--AND PART OF THOSE GAFFI STICKS.
BUT, WE NEVER HEARD OF THEM HITTING SOMETHING THIS BIG!
THEY DIDN'T, LUKE...BUT WE WERE MEANT TO THINK SO.
LOOK AT THESE BLAST POINTS! ONLY IMPERIAL STORMTROOPERS ARE THIS PRECISE.
THESE ARE THE SAME JAWAS WHO SOLD US ARTOO AND THREEPIO.
THE TROOPERS MUST HAVE BEEN LOOKING FOR ARTOO--BECAUSE OF THE PRINCESS' MESSAGE!
IF THEY TRACKED THE ROBOTS TO THE JAWAS, THEY MAY HAVE LEARNED WHO THEY SOLD THEM TO.
AND THAT WILL LEAD THEM BACK--
--HOME!

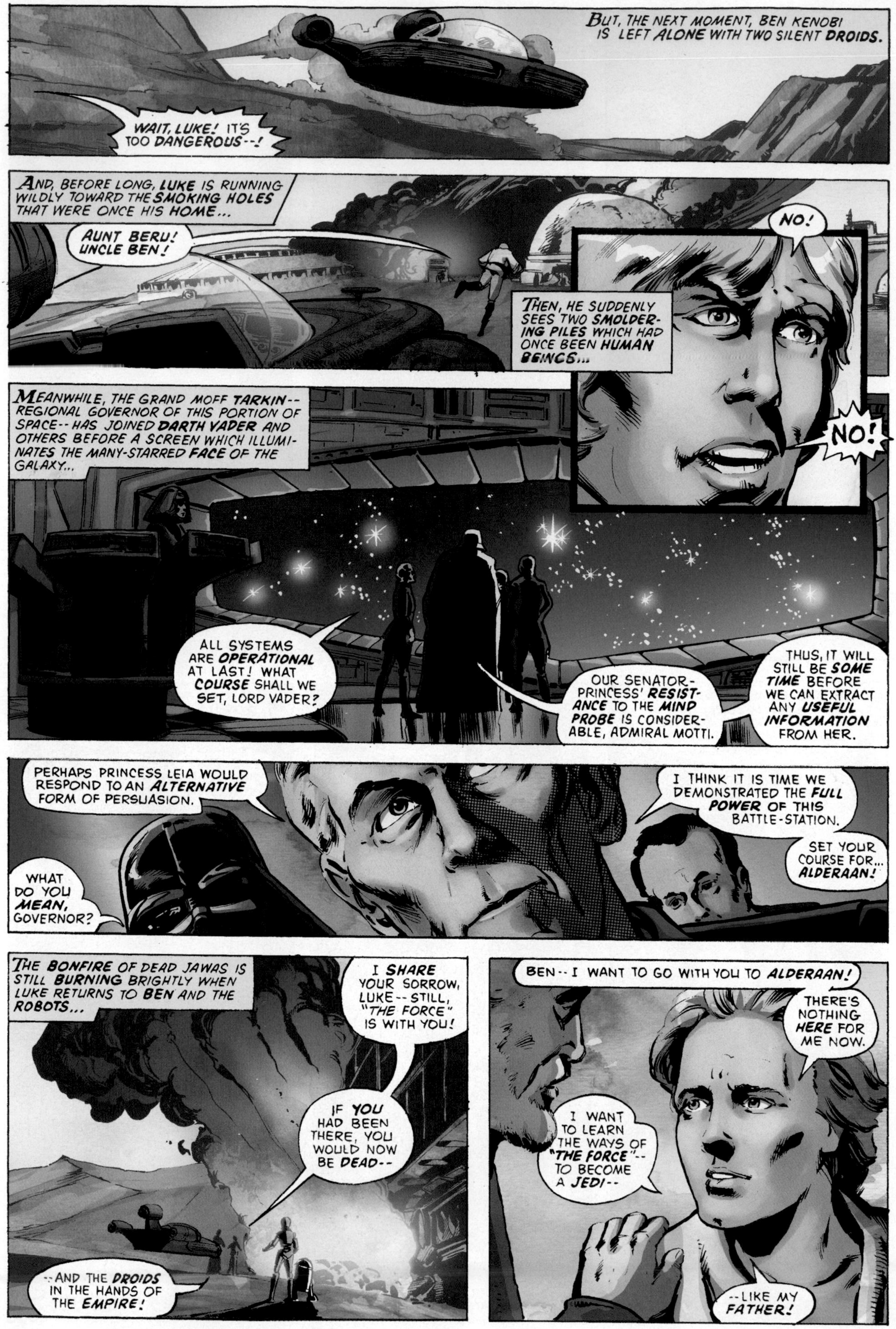
BUT, THE NEXT MOMENT, BEN KENOBI IS LEFT ALONE WITH TWO SILENT DROIDS.
WAIT, LUKE! IT'S TOO DANGEROUS--!
AND, BEFORE LONG, LUKE IS RUNNING WILDLY TOWARD THE SMOKING HOLES THAT WERE ONCE HIS HOME...
AUNT BERU! UNCLE BEN!
NO!
THEN, HE SUDDENLY SEES TWO SMOLDERING PILES WHICH HAD ONCE BEEN HUMAN BEINGS...
NO!
MEANWHILE, THE GRAND MOFF TARKIN--REGIONAL GOVERNOR OF THIS PORTION OF SPACE--HAS JOINED DARTH VADER AND OTHERS BEFORE A SCREEN WHICH ILLUMINATES THE MANY-STARRED FACE OF THE GALAXY...
ALL SYSTEMS ARE OPERATIONAL AT LAST! WHAT COURSE SHALL WE SET, LORD VADER?
OUR SENATOR-PRINCESS' RESISTANCE TO THE MIND PROBE IS CONSIDERABLE, ADMIRAL MOTTI.
THUS, IT WILL STILL BE SOME TIME BEFORE WE CAN EXTRACT ANY USEFUL INFORMATION FROM HER.
PERHAPS PRINCESS LEIA WOULD RESPOND TO AN ALTERNATIVE FORM OF PERSUASION.
WHAT DO YOU MEAN, GOVERNOR?
I THINK IT IS TIME WE DEMONSTRATED THE FULL POWER OF THIS BATTLE-STATION.
SET YOUR COURSE FOR... ALDERAAN!
THE BONFIRE OF DEAD JAWAS IS STILL BURNING BRIGHTLY WHEN LUKE RETURNS TO BEN AND THE ROBOTS...
I SHARE YOUR SORROW, LUKE--STILL, "THE FORCE" IS WITH YOU!
IF YOU HAD BEEN THERE, YOU WOULD NOW BE DEAD--
--AND THE DROIDS IN THE HANDS OF THE EMPIRE!
BEN--I WANT TO GO WITH YOU TO ALDERAAN!
THERE'S NOTHING HERE FOR ME NOW.
I WANT TO LEARN THE WAYS OF "THE FORCE"--TO BECOME A JEDI--
--LIKE MY FATHER!

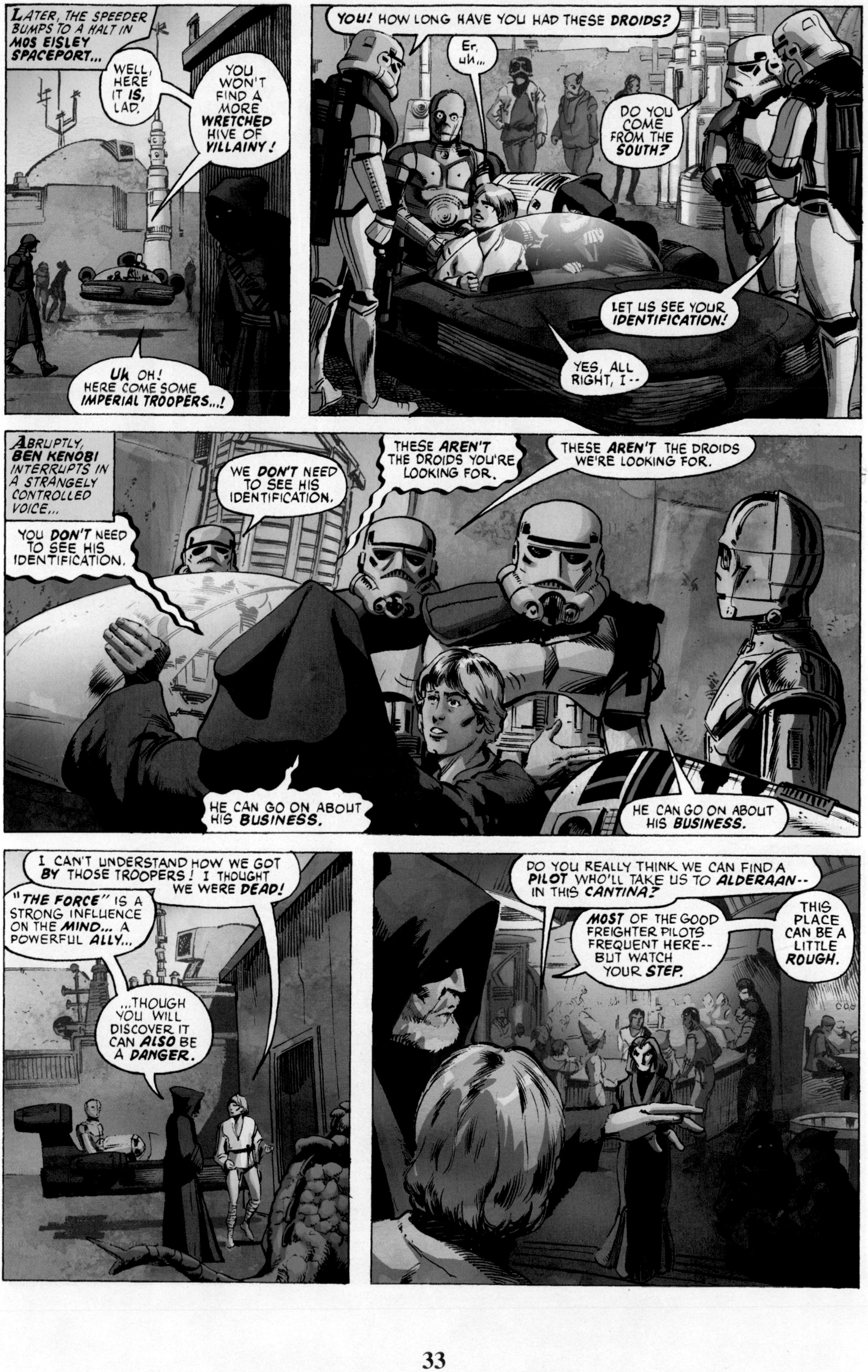
LATER, THE SPEEDER BUMPS TO A HALT IN MOS EISLEY SPACEPORT...
WELL, HERE IT IS, LAD.
YOU WON'T FIND A MORE WRETCHED HIVE OF VILLAINY!
UH OH! HERE COME SOME IMPERIAL TROOPERS...!
YOU! HOW LONG HAVE YOU HAD THESE DROIDS?
Er, uh...
DO YOU COME FROM THE SOUTH?
LET US SEE YOUR IDENTIFICATION!
YES, ALL RIGHT, I --
ABRUPTLY, BEN KENOBI INTERRUPTS IN A STRANGELY CONTROLLED VOICE...
YOU DON'T NEED TO SEE HIS IDENTIFICATION.
WE DON'T NEED TO SEE HIS IDENTIFICATION.
THESE AREN'T THE DROIDS YOU'RE LOOKING FOR.
THESE AREN'T THE DROIDS WE'RE LOOKING FOR.
HE CAN GO ON ABOUT HIS BUSINESS.
HE CAN GO ON ABOUT HIS BUSINESS.
I CAN'T UNDERSTAND HOW WE GOT BY THOSE TROOPERS! I THOUGHT WE WERE DEAD!
"THE FORCE" IS A STRONG INFLUENCE ON THE MIND... A POWERFUL ALLY...
...THOUGH YOU WILL DISCOVER IT CAN ALSO BE A DANGER.
DO YOU REALLY THINK WE CAN FIND A PILOT WHO'LL TAKE US TO ALDERAAN-- IN THIS CANTINA?
MOST OF THE GOOD FREIGHTER PILOTS FREQUENT HERE-- BUT WATCH YOUR STEP.
THIS PLACE CAN BE A LITTLE ROUGH.

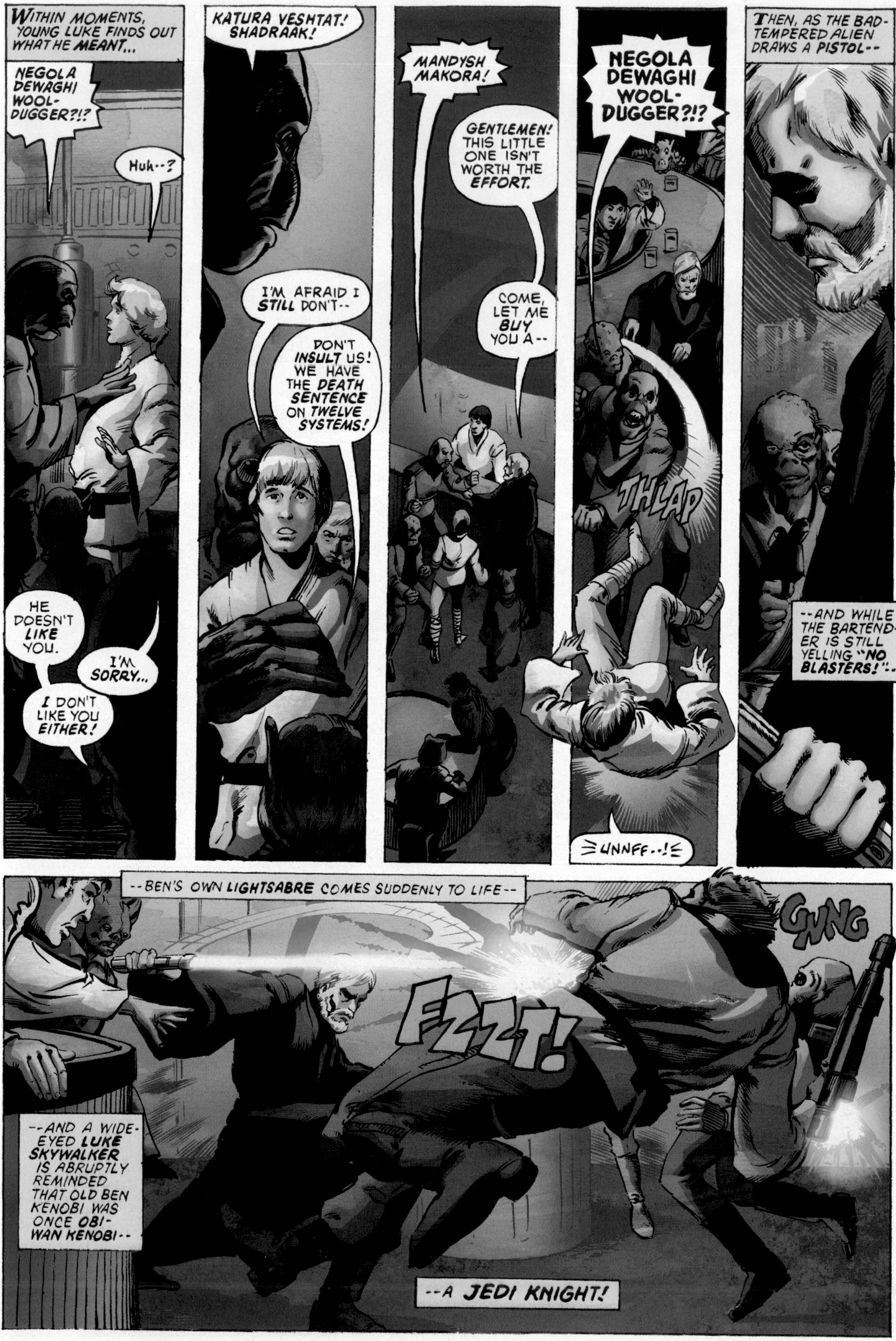
WITHIN MOMENTS, YOUNG LUKE FINDS OUT WHAT HE MEANT...
NEGOLA DEWAGHI WOOL-DUGGER?!?
HUH--?
HE DOESN'T LIKE YOU.
I'M SORRY...
I DON'T LIKE YOU EITHER!
KATURA VESHTAT! SHADRAAK!
I'M AFRAID I STILL DON'T--
DON'T INSULT US! WE HAVE THE DEATH SENTENCE ON TWELVE SYSTEMS!
MANDYSH MAKORA!
GENTLEMEN! THIS LITTLE ONE ISN'T WORTH THE EFFORT.
COME, LET ME BUY YOU A--
NEGOLA DEWAGHI WOOL-DUGGER?!?
THLAP
UNNFF--!
THEN, AS THE BAD-TEMPERED ALIEN DRAWS A PISTOL--
--AND WHILE THE BARTENDER IS STILL YELLING "NO BLASTERS!"--
--BEN'S OWN LIGHTSABRE COMES SUDDENLY TO LIFE--
GNNG
FZZZT!
--AND A WIDE-EYED LUKE SKYWALKER IS ABRUPTLY REMINDED THAT OLD BEN KENOBI WAS ONCE OBI-WAN KENOBI--
--A JEDI KNIGHT!

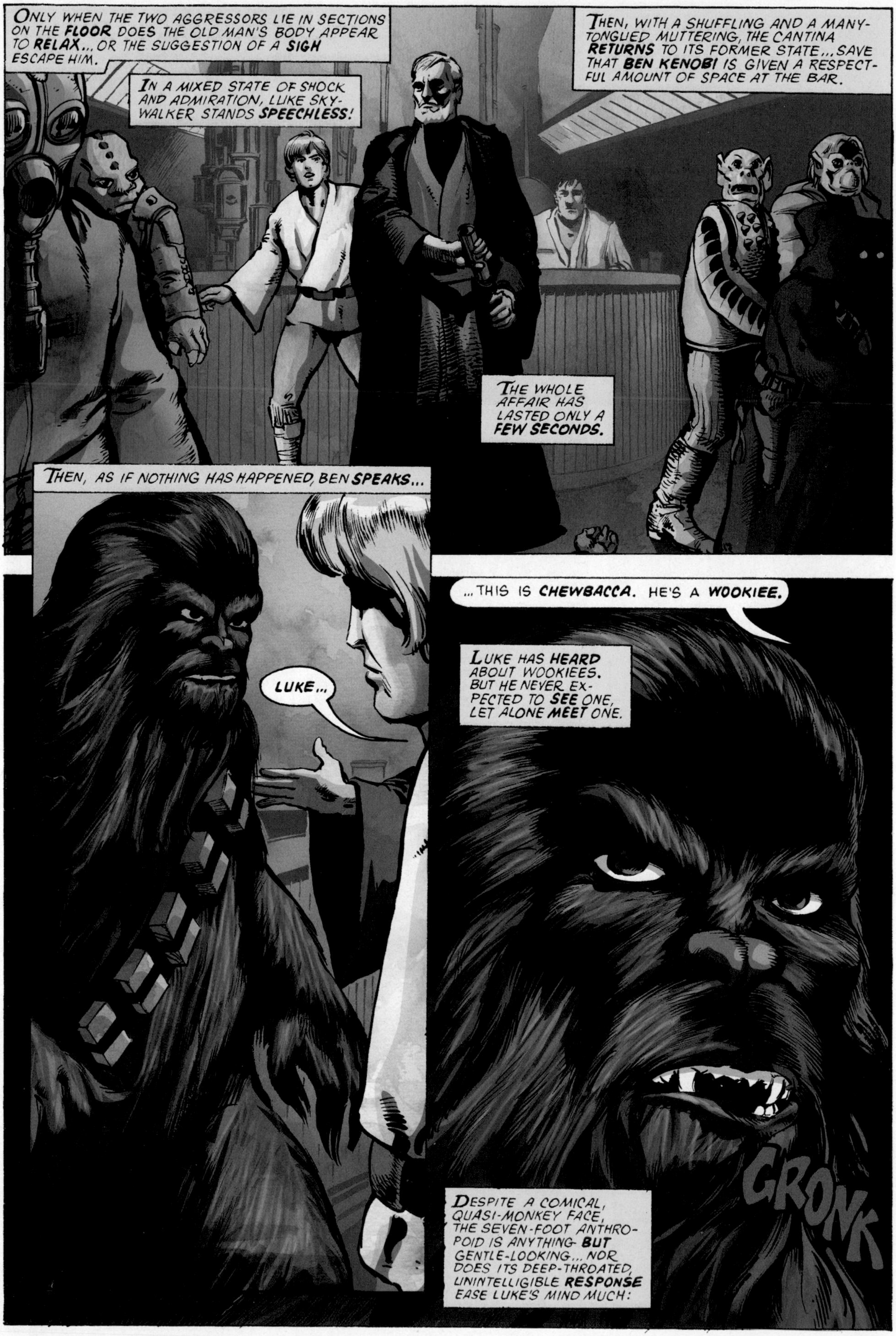
ONLY WHEN THE TWO AGGRESSORS LIE IN SECTIONS ON THE FLOOR DOES THE OLD MAN'S BODY APPEAR TO RELAX... OR THE SUGGESTION OF A SIGH ESCAPE HIM.
IN A MIXED STATE OF SHOCK AND ADMIRATION, LUKE SKYWALKER STANDS SPEECHLESS!
THEN, WITH A SHUFFLING AND A MANY-TONGUED MUTTERING, THE CANTINA RETURNS TO ITS FORMER STATE... SAVE THAT BEN KENOBI IS GIVEN A RESPECTFUL AMOUNT OF SPACE AT THE BAR.
THE WHOLE AFFAIR HAS LASTED ONLY A FEW SECONDS.
THEN, AS IF NOTHING HAS HAPPENED, BEN SPEAKS...
LUKE...
...THIS IS CHEWBACCA. HE'S A WOOKIEE.
LUKE HAS HEARD ABOUT WOOKIEES. BUT HE NEVER EXPECTED TO SEE ONE, LET ALONE MEET ONE.
DESPITE A COMICAL, QUASI-MONKEY FACE, THE SEVEN-FOOT ANTHROPOID IS ANYTHING BUT GENTLE-LOOKING... NOR DOES ITS DEEP-THROATED, UNINTELLIGIBLE RESPONSE EASE LUKE'S MIND MUCH:
GRONK

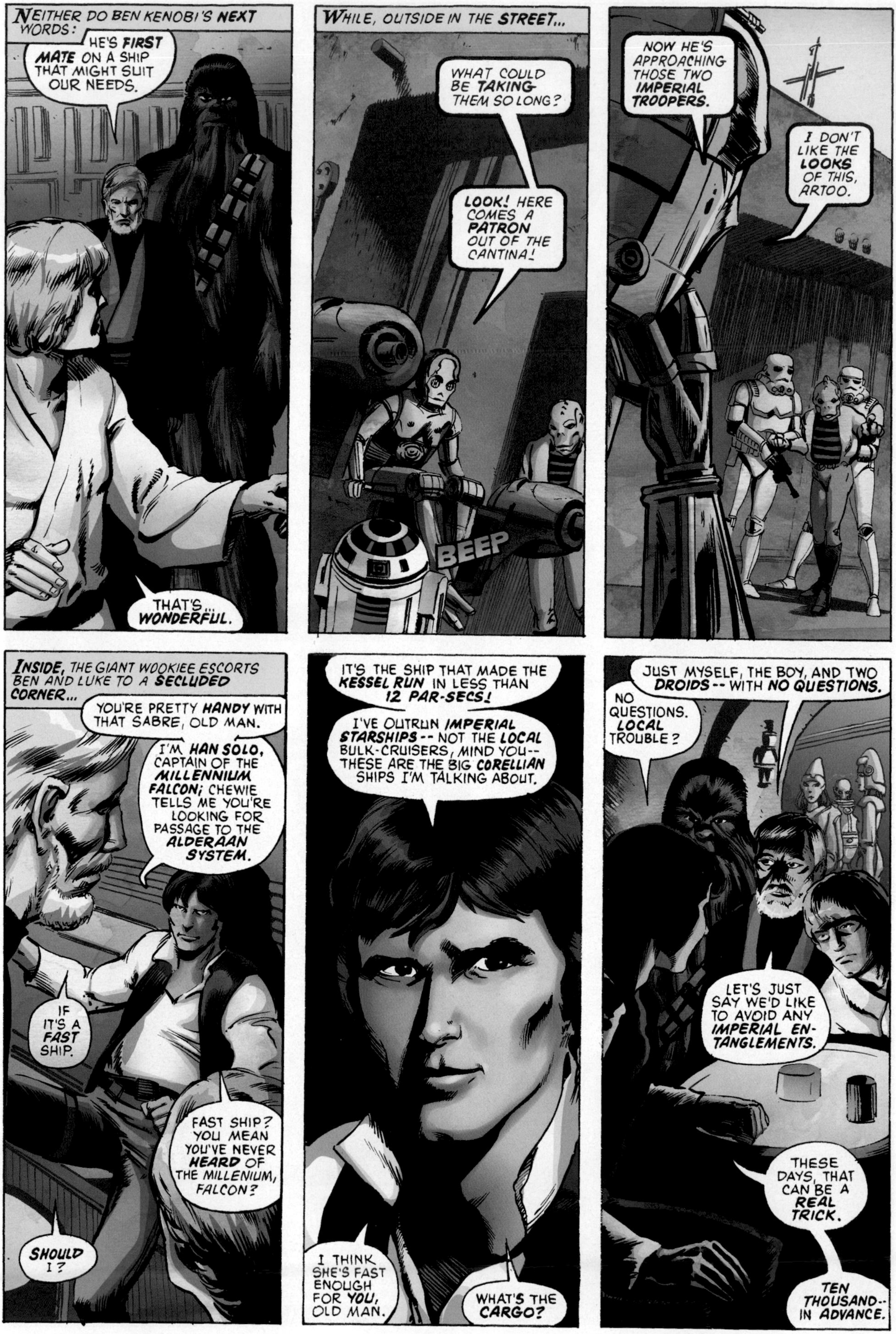
NEITHER DO BEN KENOBI'S NEXT WORDS:
HE'S FIRST MATE ON A SHIP THAT MIGHT SUIT OUR NEEDS.
THAT'S... WONDERFUL.
WHILE, OUTSIDE IN THE STREET...
WHAT COULD BE TAKING THEM SO LONG?
LOOK! HERE COMES A PATRON OUT OF THE CANTINA!
BEEP
NOW HE'S APPROACHING THOSE TWO IMPERIAL TROOPERS.
I DON'T LIKE THE LOOKS OF THIS, ARTOO.
INSIDE, THE GIANT WOOKIEE ESCORTS BEN AND LUKE TO A SECLUDED CORNER...
YOU'RE PRETTY HANDY WITH THAT SABRE, OLD MAN.
I'M HAN SOLO, CAPTAIN OF THE MILLENNIUM FALCON; CHEWIE TELLS ME YOU'RE LOOKING FOR PASSAGE TO THE ALDERAAN SYSTEM.
IF IT'S A FAST SHIP.
FAST SHIP? YOU MEAN YOU'VE NEVER HEARD OF THE MILLENIUM FALCON?
SHOULD I?
IT'S THE SHIP THAT MADE THE KESSEL RUN IN LESS THAN 12 PAR-SECS!
I'VE OUTRUN IMPERIAL STARSHIPS -- NOT THE LOCAL BULK-CRUISERS, MIND YOU-- THESE ARE THE BIG CORELLIAN SHIPS I'M TALKING ABOUT.
I THINK SHE'S FAST ENOUGH FOR YOU, OLD MAN.
WHAT'S THE CARGO?
JUST MYSELF, THE BOY, AND TWO DROIDS -- WITH NO QUESTIONS.
NO QUESTIONS. LOCAL TROUBLE?
LET'S JUST SAY WE'D LIKE TO AVOID ANY IMPERIAL ENTANGLEMENTS.
THESE DAYS, THAT CAN BE A REAL TRICK.
TEN THOUSAND-- IN ADVANCE.

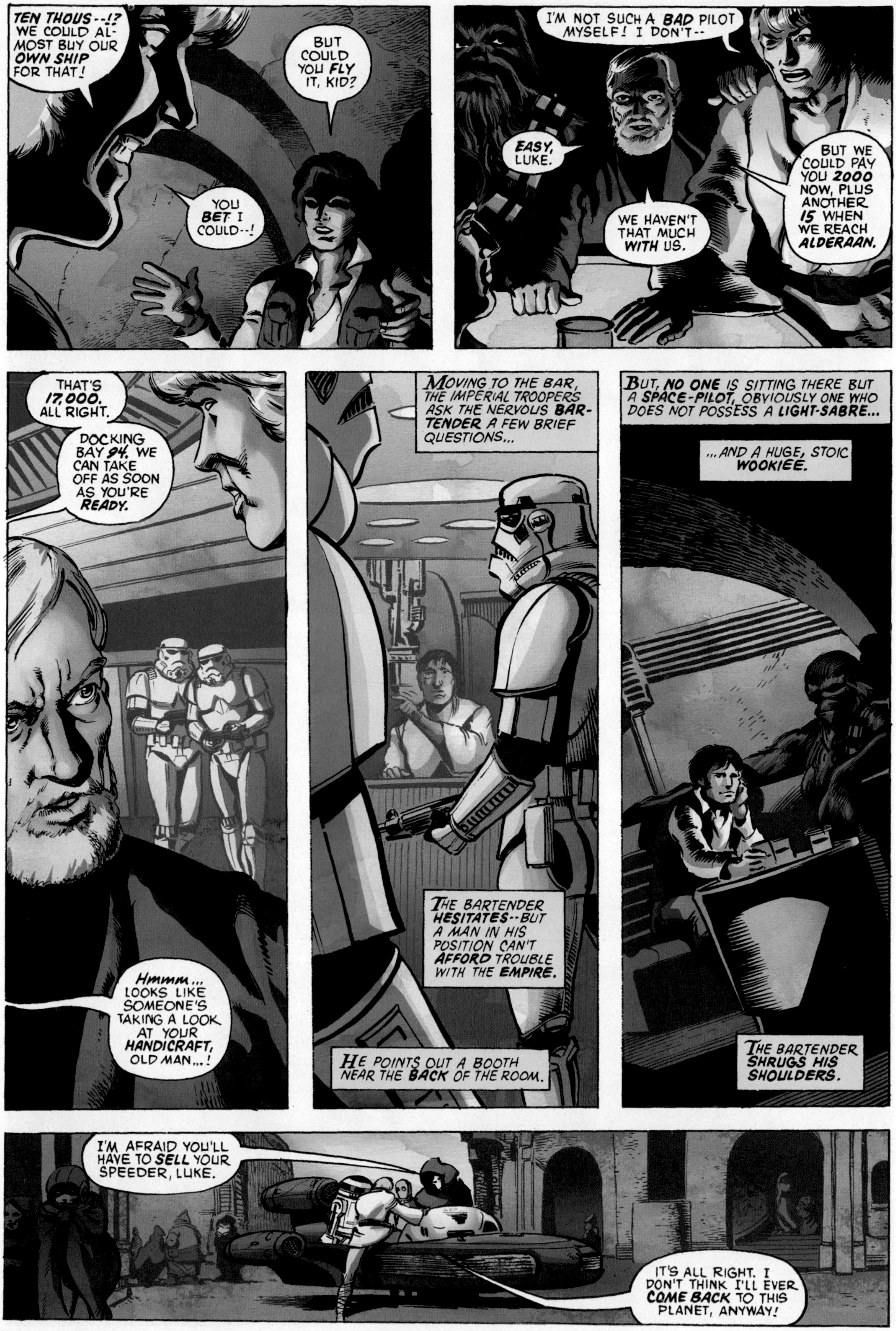
TEN THOUS--!? WE COULD ALMOST BUY OUR OWN SHIP FOR THAT!
BUT COULD YOU FLY IT, KID?
YOU BET I COULD--!
I'M NOT SUCH A BAD PILOT MYSELF! I DON'T--
EASY, LUKE.
WE HAVEN'T THAT MUCH WITH US.
BUT WE COULD PAY YOU 2000 NOW, PLUS ANOTHER 15 WHEN WE REACH ALDERAAN.
THAT'S 17,000. ALL RIGHT.
DOCKING BAY 94. WE CAN TAKE OFF AS SOON AS YOU'RE READY.
Hmmm... LOOKS LIKE SOMEONE'S TAKING A LOOK AT YOUR HANDICRAFT, OLD MAN...!
MOVING TO THE BAR, THE IMPERIAL TROOPERS ASK THE NERVOUS BARTENDER A FEW BRIEF QUESTIONS...
THE BARTENDER HESITATES--BUT A MAN IN HIS POSITION CAN'T AFFORD TROUBLE WITH THE EMPIRE.
HE POINTS OUT A BOOTH NEAR THE BACK OF THE ROOM.
BUT, NO ONE IS SITTING THERE BUT A SPACE-PILOT, OBVIOUSLY ONE WHO DOES NOT POSSESS A LIGHT-SABRE...
...AND A HUGE, STOIC WOOKIEE.
THE BARTENDER SHRUGS HIS SHOULDERS.
I'M AFRAID YOU'LL HAVE TO SELL YOUR SPEEDER, LUKE.
IT'S ALL RIGHT. I DON'T THINK I'LL EVER COME BACK TO THIS PLANET, ANYWAY!

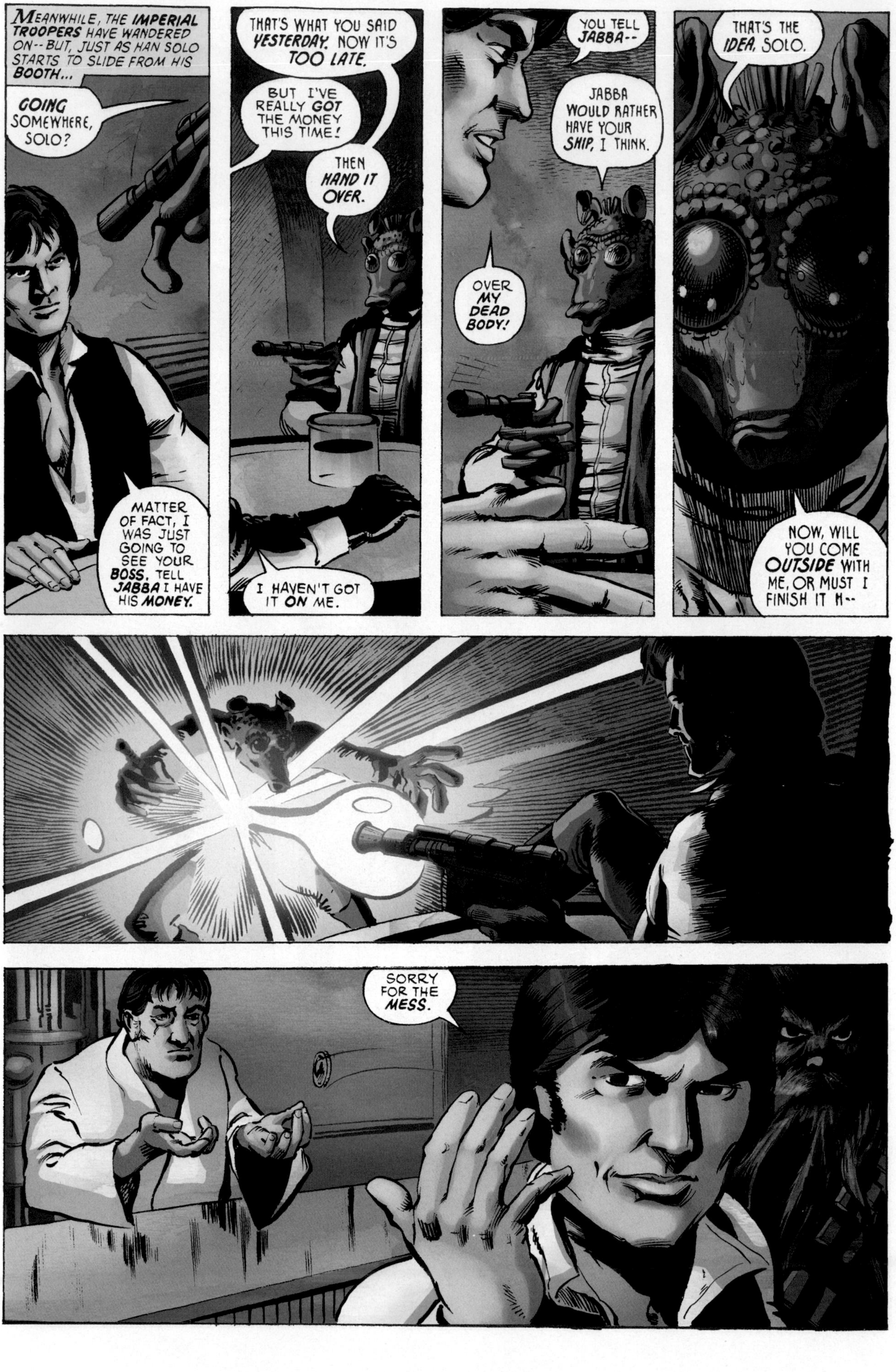
MEANWHILE, THE IMPERIAL TROOPERS HAVE WANDERED ON-- BUT, JUST AS HAN SOLO STARTS TO SLIDE FROM HIS BOOTH...
GOING SOMEWHERE, SOLO?
MATTER OF FACT, I WAS JUST GOING TO SEE YOUR BOSS. TELL JABBA I HAVE HIS MONEY.
THAT'S WHAT YOU SAID YESTERDAY. NOW IT'S TOO LATE.
BUT I'VE REALLY GOT THE MONEY THIS TIME!
THEN HAND IT OVER.
I HAVEN'T GOT IT ON ME.
YOU TELL JABBA--
JABBA WOULD RATHER HAVE YOUR SHIP, I THINK.
OVER MY DEAD BODY!
THAT'S THE IDEA, SOLO.
NOW, WILL YOU COME OUTSIDE WITH ME, OR MUST I FINISH IT H--
SORRY FOR THE MESS.

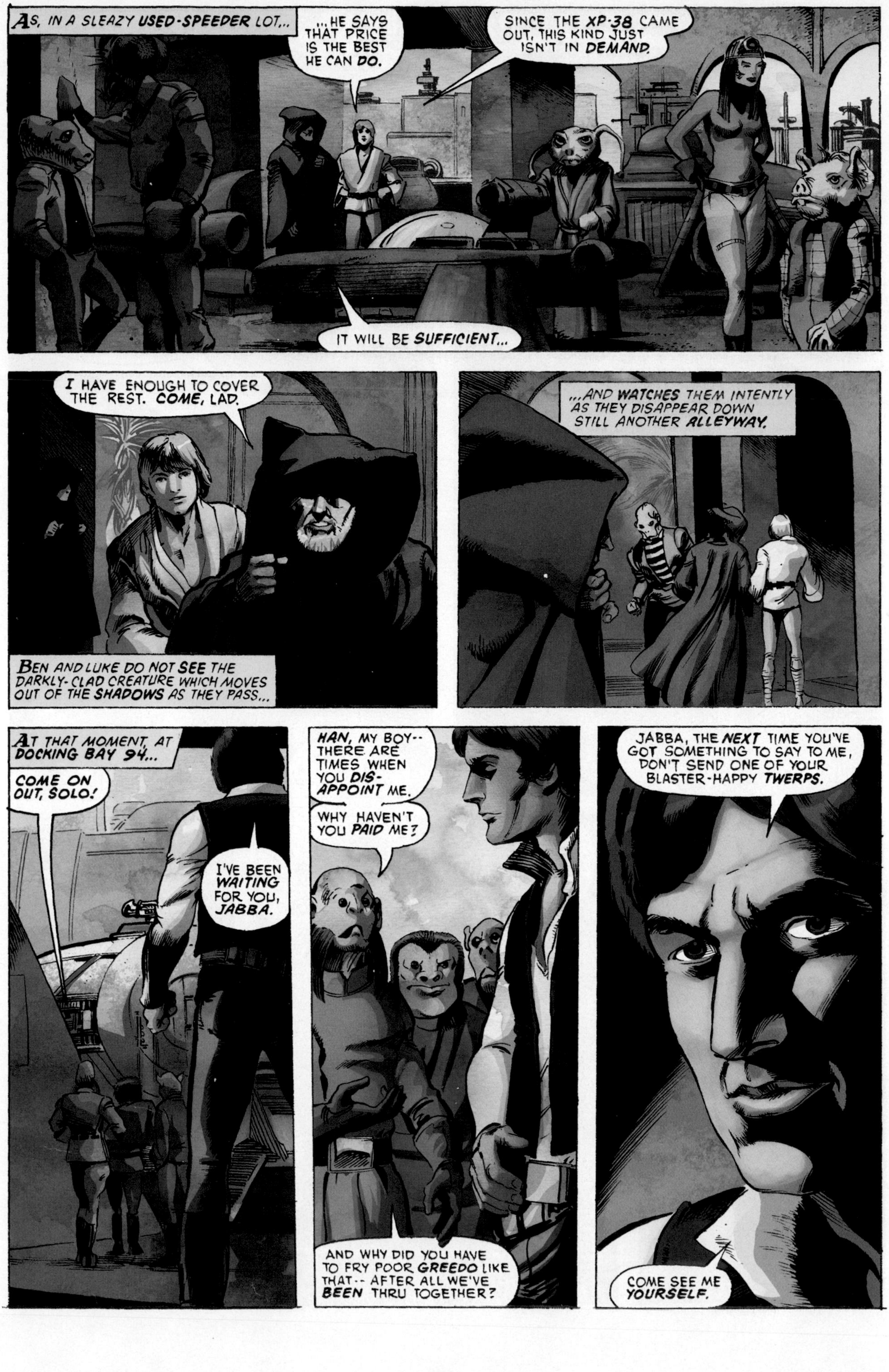

AS, IN A SLEAZY USED-SPEEDER LOT...
...HE SAYS THAT PRICE IS THE BEST HE CAN DO.
SINCE THE XP-38 CAME OUT, THIS KIND JUST ISN'T IN DEMAND.
IT WILL BE SUFFICIENT...
I HAVE ENOUGH TO COVER THE REST. COME, LAD.
BEN AND LUKE DO NOT SEE THE DARKLY-CLAD CREATURE WHICH MOVES OUT OF THE SHADOWS AS THEY PASS...
...AND WATCHES THEM INTENTLY AS THEY DISAPPEAR DOWN STILL ANOTHER ALLEYWAY.
AT THAT MOMENT, AT DOCKING BAY 94...
COME ON OUT, SOLO!
I'VE BEEN WAITING FOR YOU, JABBA.
HAN, MY BOY-- THERE ARE TIMES WHEN YOU DIS-APPOINT ME.
WHY HAVEN'T YOU PAID ME?
AND WHY DID YOU HAVE TO FRY POOR GREEDO LIKE THAT-- AFTER ALL WE'VE BEEN THRU TOGETHER?
JABBA, THE NEXT TIME YOU'VE GOT SOMETHING TO SAY TO ME, DON'T SEND ONE OF YOUR BLASTER-HAPPY TWERPS.
COME SEE ME YOURSELF.

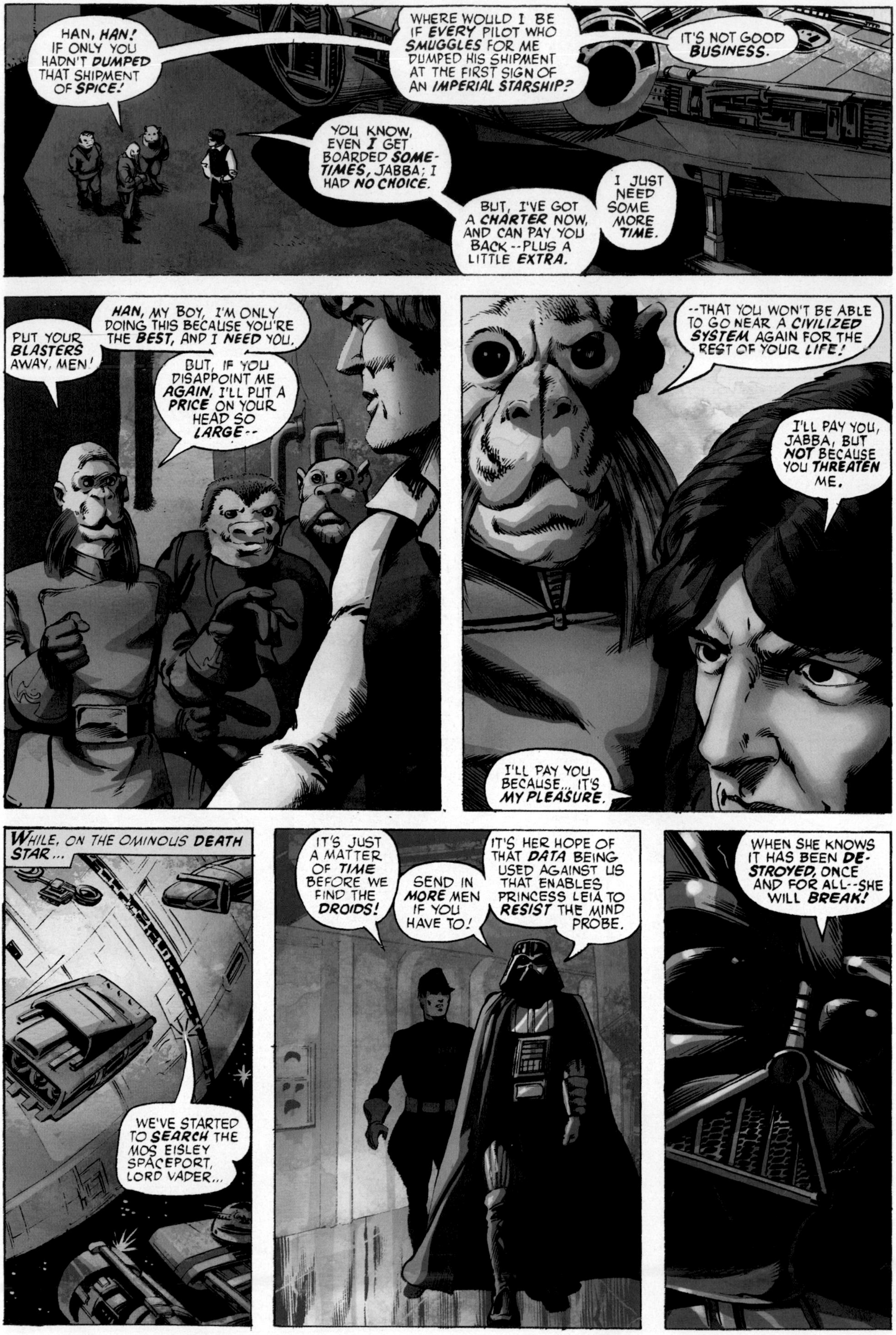
HAN, HAN! IF ONLY YOU HADN'T DUMPED THAT SHIPMENT OF SPICE!
WHERE WOULD I BE IF EVERY PILOT WHO SMUGGLES FOR ME DUMPED HIS SHIPMENT AT THE FIRST SIGN OF AN IMPERIAL STARSHIP?
IT'S NOT GOOD BUSINESS.
YOU KNOW, EVEN I GET BOARDED SOME-TIMES, JABBA; I HAD NO CHOICE.
BUT, I'VE GOT A CHARTER NOW, AND CAN PAY YOU BACK--PLUS A LITTLE EXTRA.
I JUST NEED SOME MORE TIME.
PUT YOUR BLASTERS AWAY, MEN!
HAN, MY BOY, I'M ONLY DOING THIS BECAUSE YOU'RE THE BEST, AND I NEED YOU.
BUT, IF YOU DISAPPOINT ME AGAIN, I'LL PUT A PRICE ON YOUR HEAD SO LARGE--
--THAT YOU WON'T BE ABLE TO GO NEAR A CIVILIZED SYSTEM AGAIN FOR THE REST OF YOUR LIFE!
I'LL PAY YOU, JABBA, BUT NOT BECAUSE YOU THREATEN ME.
I'LL PAY YOU BECAUSE... IT'S MY PLEASURE.
WHILE, ON THE OMINOUS DEATH STAR...
WE'VE STARTED TO SEARCH THE MOS EISLEY SPACEPORT, LORD VADER...
IT'S JUST A MATTER OF TIME BEFORE WE FIND THE DROIDS!
SEND IN MORE MEN IF YOU HAVE TO!
IT'S HER HOPE OF THAT DATA BEING USED AGAINST US THAT ENABLES PRINCESS LEIA TO RESIST THE MIND PROBE.
WHEN SHE KNOWS IT HAS BEEN DE-STROYED, ONCE AND FOR ALL--SHE WILL BREAK!

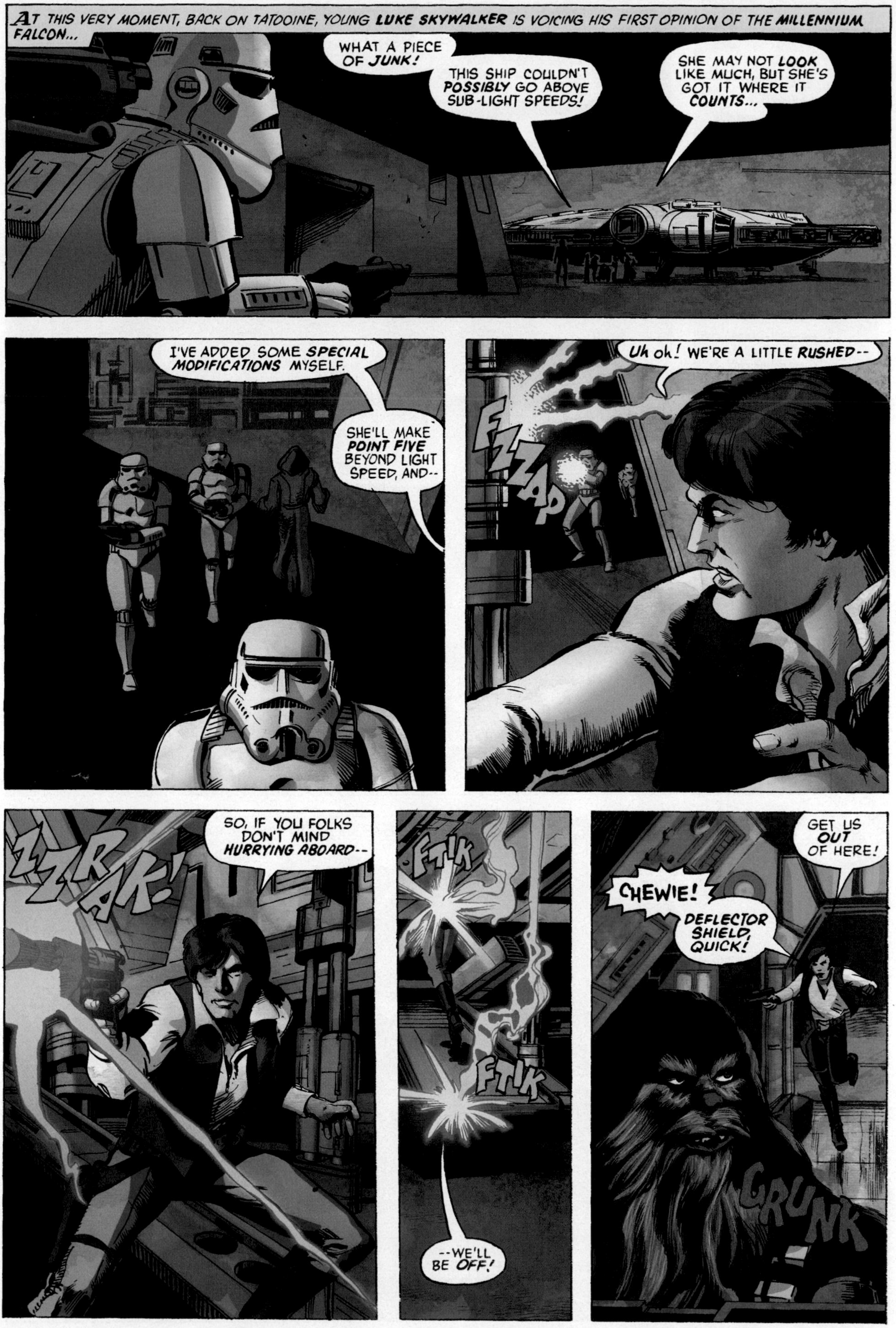
AT THIS VERY MOMENT, BACK ON TATOOINE, YOUNG LUKE SKYWALKER IS VOICING HIS FIRST OPINION OF THE MILLENNIUM FALCON...
WHAT A PIECE OF JUNK!
THIS SHIP COULDN'T POSSIBLY GO ABOVE SUB-LIGHT SPEEDS!
SHE MAY NOT LOOK LIKE MUCH, BUT SHE'S GOT IT WHERE IT COUNTS...
I'VE ADDED SOME SPECIAL MODIFICATIONS MYSELF.
SHE'LL MAKE POINT FIVE BEYOND LIGHT SPEED, AND--
Uh oh! WE'RE A LITTLE RUSHED--
FZZAP
ZZRAK!
SO, IF YOU FOLKS DON'T MIND HURRYING ABOARD--
FTIK
FTIK
--WE'LL BE OFF!
GET US OUT OF HERE!
CHEWIE!
DEFLECTOR SHIELD, QUICK!
GRUNK

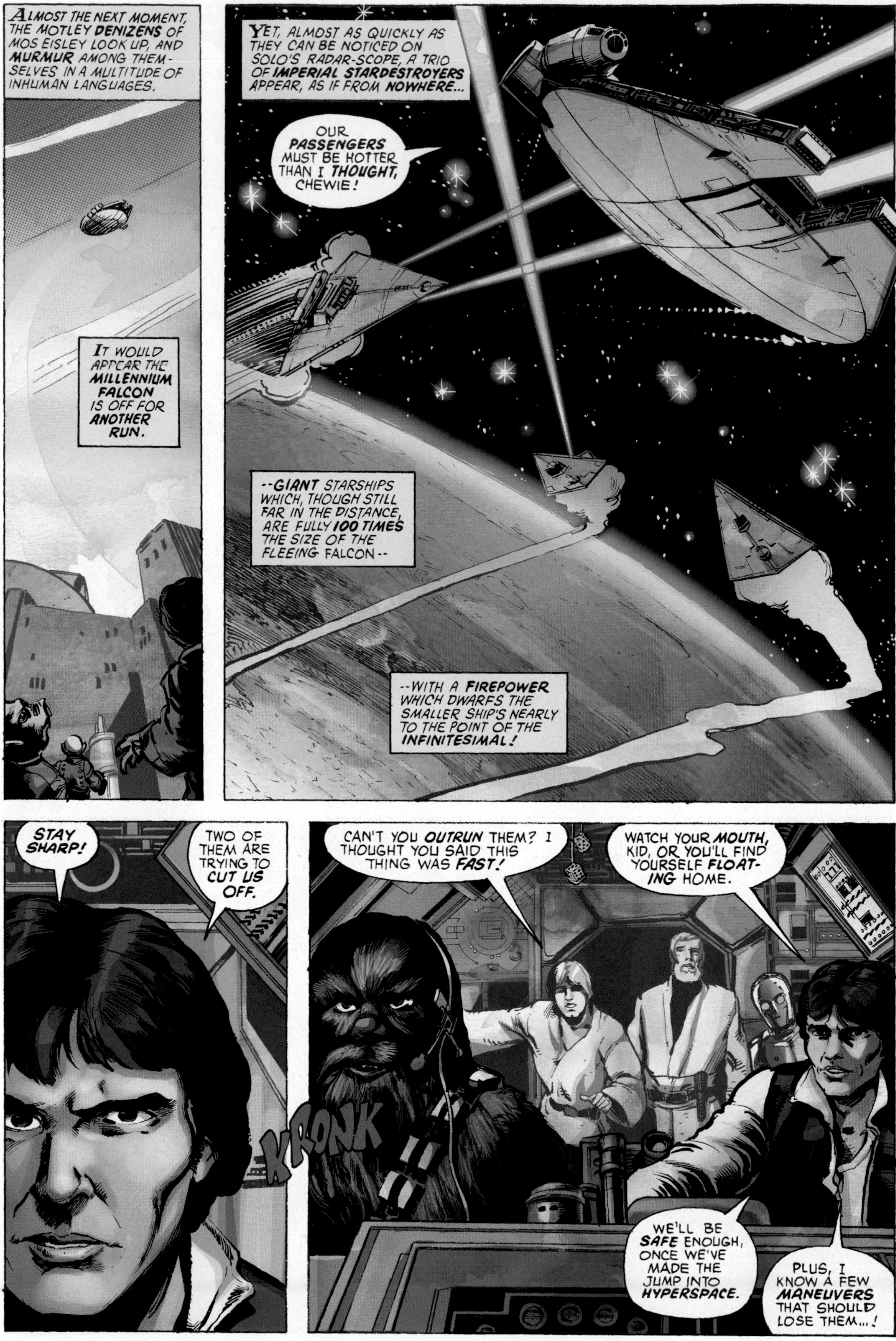

ALMOST THE NEXT MOMENT, THE MOTLEY DENIZENS OF MOS EISLEY LOOK UP, AND MURMUR AMONG THEMSELVES IN A MULTITUDE OF INHUMAN LANGUAGES.
IT WOULD APPEAR THE MILLENNIUM FALCON IS OFF FOR ANOTHER RUN.
YET, ALMOST AS QUICKLY AS THEY CAN BE NOTICED ON SOLO'S RADAR-SCOPE, A TRIO OF IMPERIAL STARDESTROYERS APPEAR, AS IF FROM NOWHERE...
OUR PASSENGERS MUST BE HOTTER THAN I THOUGHT, CHEWIE!
--GIANT STARSHIPS WHICH, THOUGH STILL FAR IN THE DISTANCE, ARE FULLY 100 TIMES THE SIZE OF THE FLEEING FALCON--
--WITH A FIREPOWER WHICH DWARFS THE SMALLER SHIP'S NEARLY TO THE POINT OF THE INFINITESIMAL!
STAY SHARP!
TWO OF THEM ARE TRYING TO CUT US OFF.
CAN'T YOU OUTRUN THEM? I THOUGHT YOU SAID THIS THING WAS FAST!
WATCH YOUR MOUTH, KID, OR YOU'LL FIND YOURSELF FLOATING HOME.
KRONK
WE'LL BE SAFE ENOUGH, ONCE WE'VE MADE THE JUMP INTO HYPERSPACE.
PLUS, I KNOW A FEW MANEUVERS THAT SHOULD LOSE THEM...!

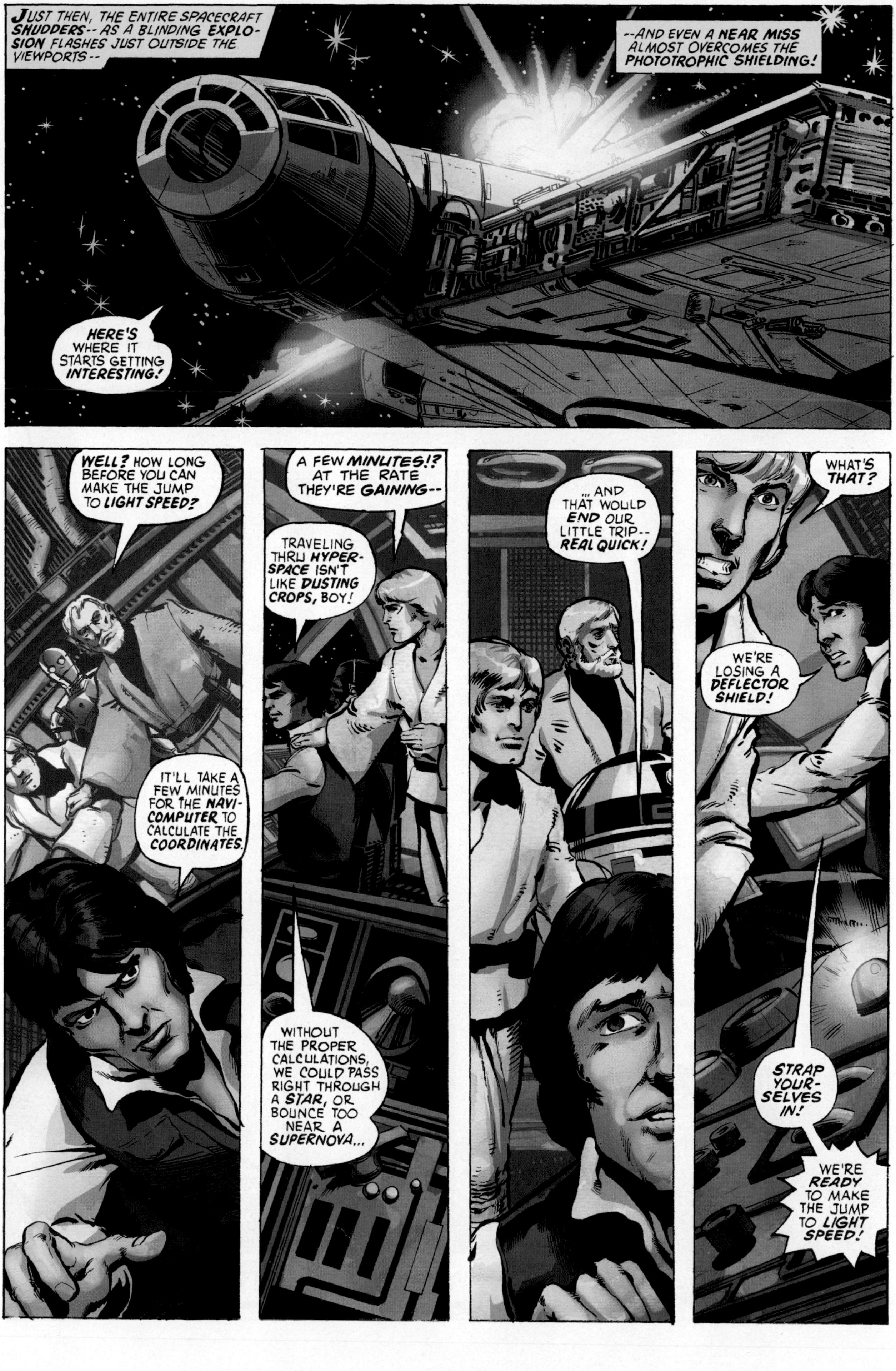
JUST THEN, THE ENTIRE SPACECRAFT SHUDDERS-- AS A BLINDING EXPLOSION FLASHES JUST OUTSIDE THE VIEWPORTS--
--AND EVEN A NEAR MISS ALMOST OVERCOMES THE PHOTOTROPHIC SHIELDING!
HERE'S WHERE IT STARTS GETTING INTERESTING!
WELL? HOW LONG BEFORE YOU CAN MAKE THE JUMP TO LIGHT SPEED?
IT'LL TAKE A FEW MINUTES FOR THE NAVI-COMPUTER TO CALCULATE THE COORDINATES.
A FEW MINUTES!? AT THE RATE THEY'RE GAINING--
TRAVELING THRU HYPER-SPACE ISN'T LIKE DUSTING CROPS, BOY!
WITHOUT THE PROPER CALCULATIONS, WE COULD PASS RIGHT THROUGH A STAR, OR BOUNCE TOO NEAR A SUPERNOVA...
... AND THAT WOULD END OUR LITTLE TRIP-- REAL QUICK!
WHAT'S THAT?
WE'RE LOSING A DEFLECTOR SHIELD!
STRAP YOURSELVES IN!
WE'RE READY TO MAKE THE JUMP TO LIGHT SPEED!

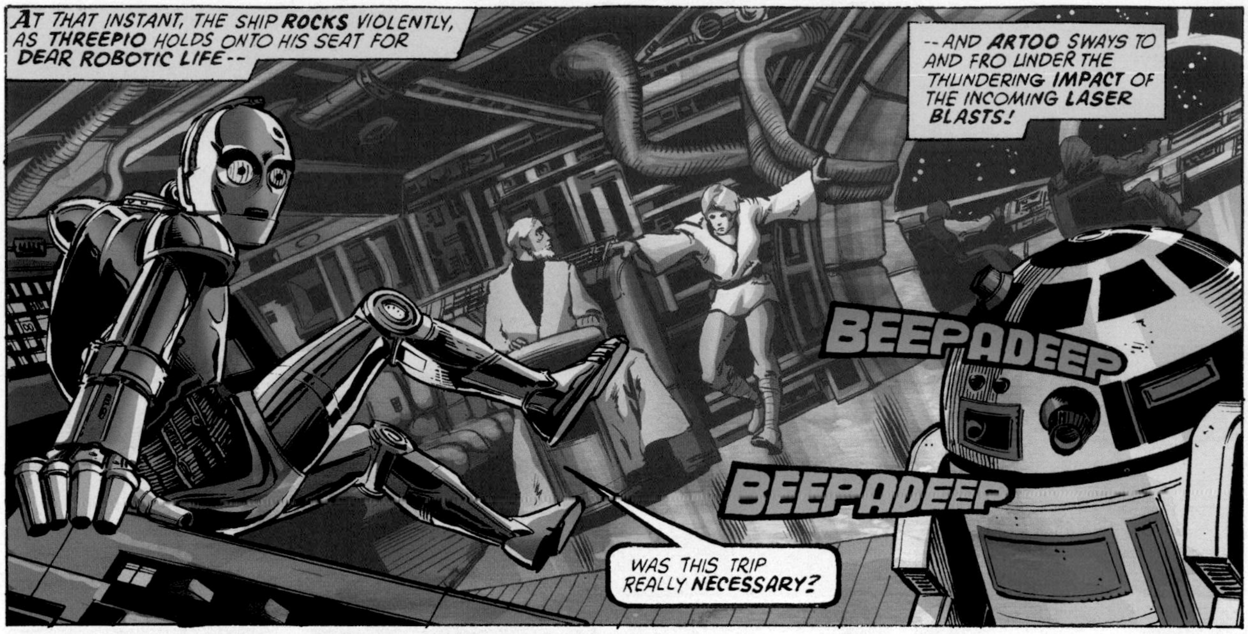
AT THAT INSTANT, THE SHIP ROCKS VIOLENTLY, AS THREEPIO HOLDS ONTO HIS SEAT FOR DEAR ROBOTIC LIFE--
--AND ARTOO SWAYS TO AND FRO UNDER THE THUNDERING IMPACT OF THE INCOMING LASER BLASTS!
BEEPADEEP
BEEPADEEP
WAS THIS TRIP REALLY NECESSARY?

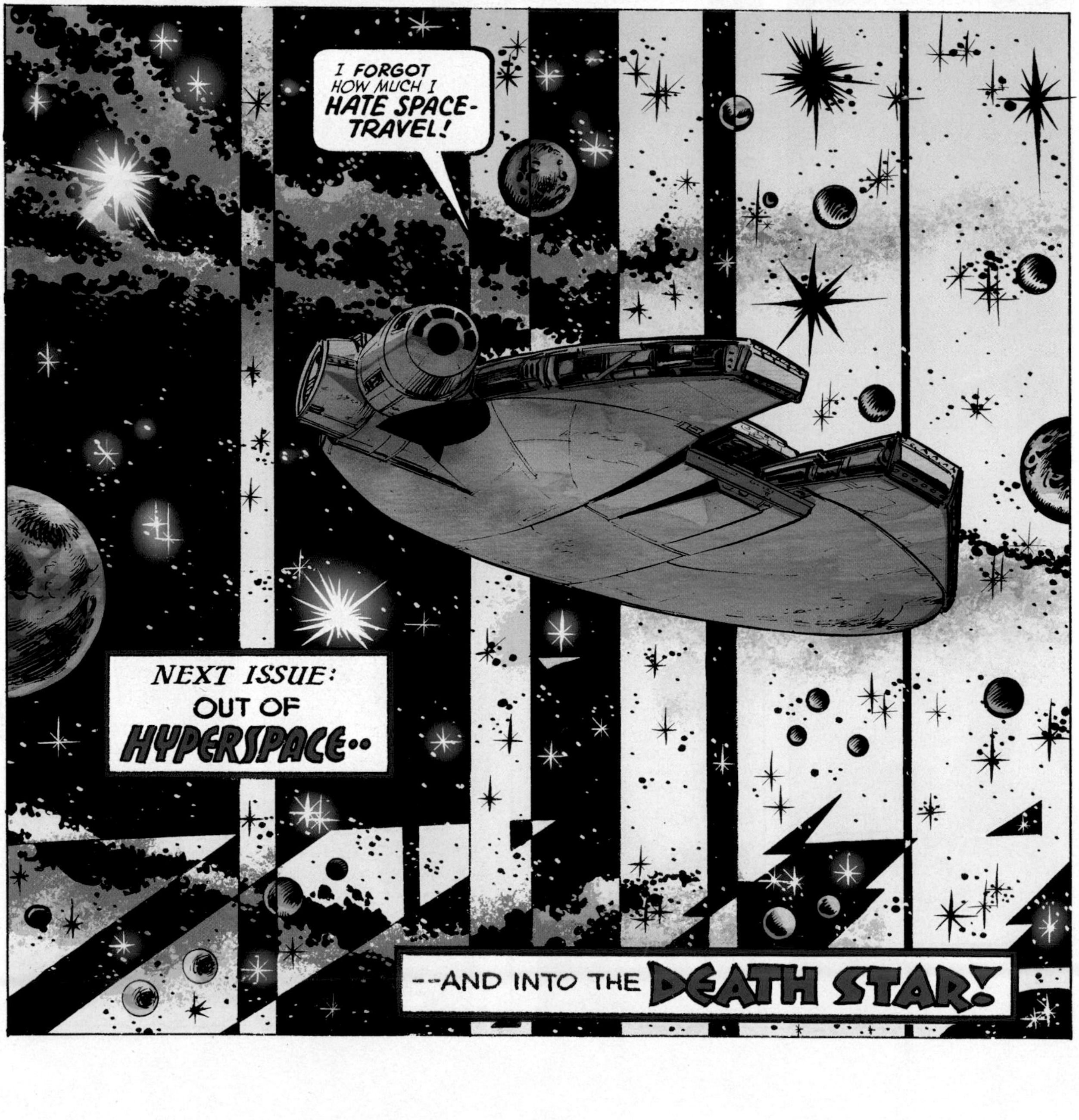
I FORGOT HOW MUCH I HATE SPACE-TRAVEL!
NEXT ISSUE: OUT OF HYPERSPACE..
--AND INTO THE DEATH STAR!

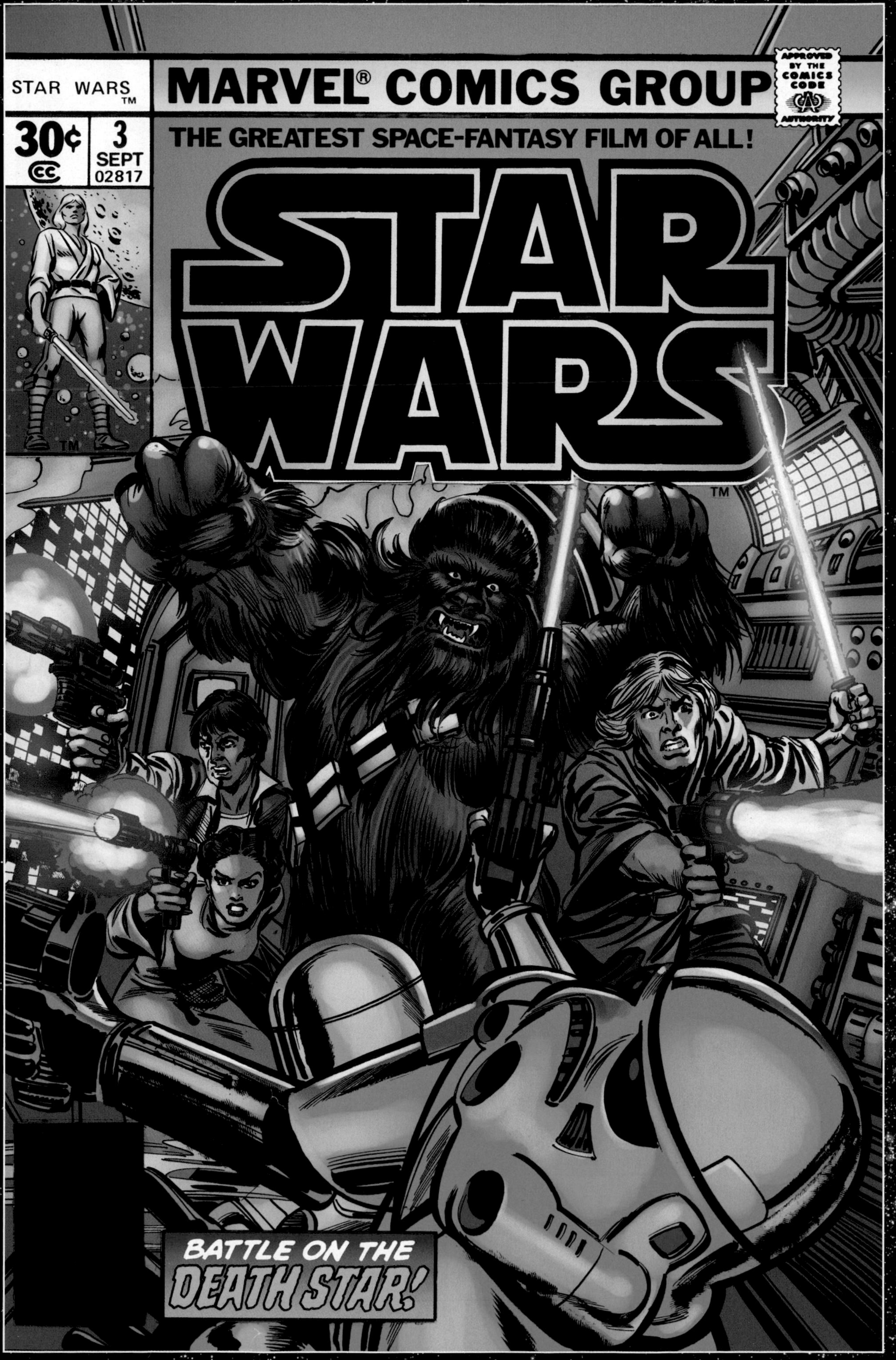
STAR WARS TM
MARVEL® COMICS GROUP
APPROVED BY THE COMICS CODE AUTHORITY
30¢ CC
3 SEPT 02817
THE GREATEST SPACE-FANTASY FILM OF ALL!
STAR WARS TM
BATTLE ON THE DEATH STAR!

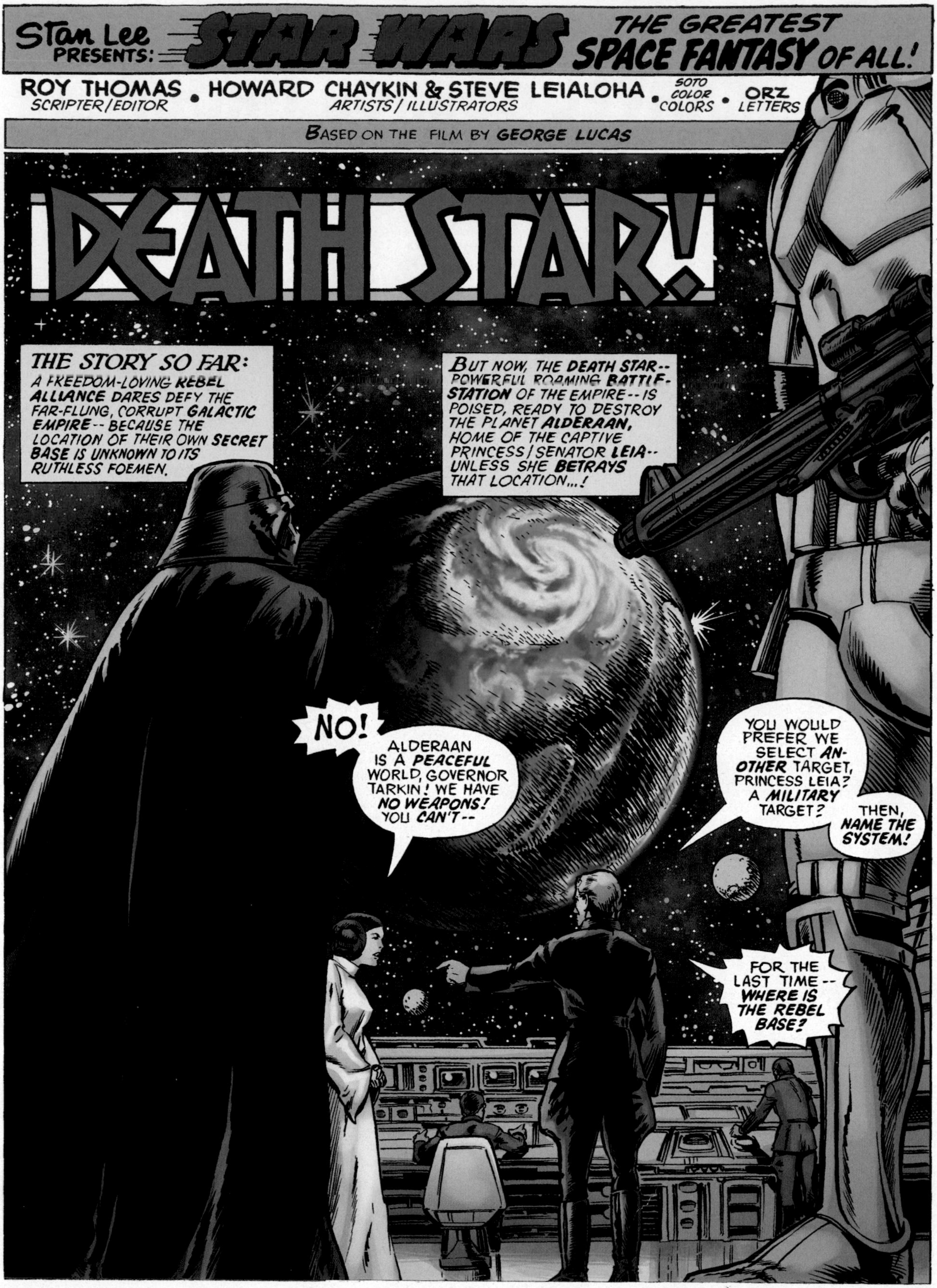
Stan Lee PRESENTS: STAR WARS THE GREATEST SPACE FANTASY OF ALL!
ROY THOMAS SCRIPTER/EDITOR • HOWARD CHAYKIN & STEVE LEIALOHA ARTISTS/ILLUSTRATORS • SOTO COLOR COLORS • ORZ LETTERS
BASED ON THE FILM BY GEORGE LUCAS
DEATH STAR!
THE STORY SO FAR: A FREEDOM-LOVING REBEL ALLIANCE DARES DEFY THE FAR-FLUNG, CORRUPT GALACTIC EMPIRE-- BECAUSE THE LOCATION OF THEIR OWN SECRET BASE IS UNKNOWN TO ITS RUTHLESS FOEMEN.
BUT NOW, THE DEATH STAR-- POWERFUL ROAMING BATTLE-STATION OF THE EMPIRE-- IS POISED, READY TO DESTROY THE PLANET ALDERAAN, HOME OF THE CAPTIVE PRINCESS/SENATOR LEIA-- UNLESS SHE BETRAYS THAT LOCATION...!
NO!
ALDERAAN IS A PEACEFUL WORLD, GOVERNOR TARKIN! WE HAVE NO WEAPONS! YOU CAN'T--
YOU WOULD PREFER WE SELECT AN-OTHER TARGET, PRINCESS LEIA? A MILITARY TARGET?
THEN, NAME THE SYSTEM!
FOR THE LAST TIME-- WHERE IS THE REBEL BASE?

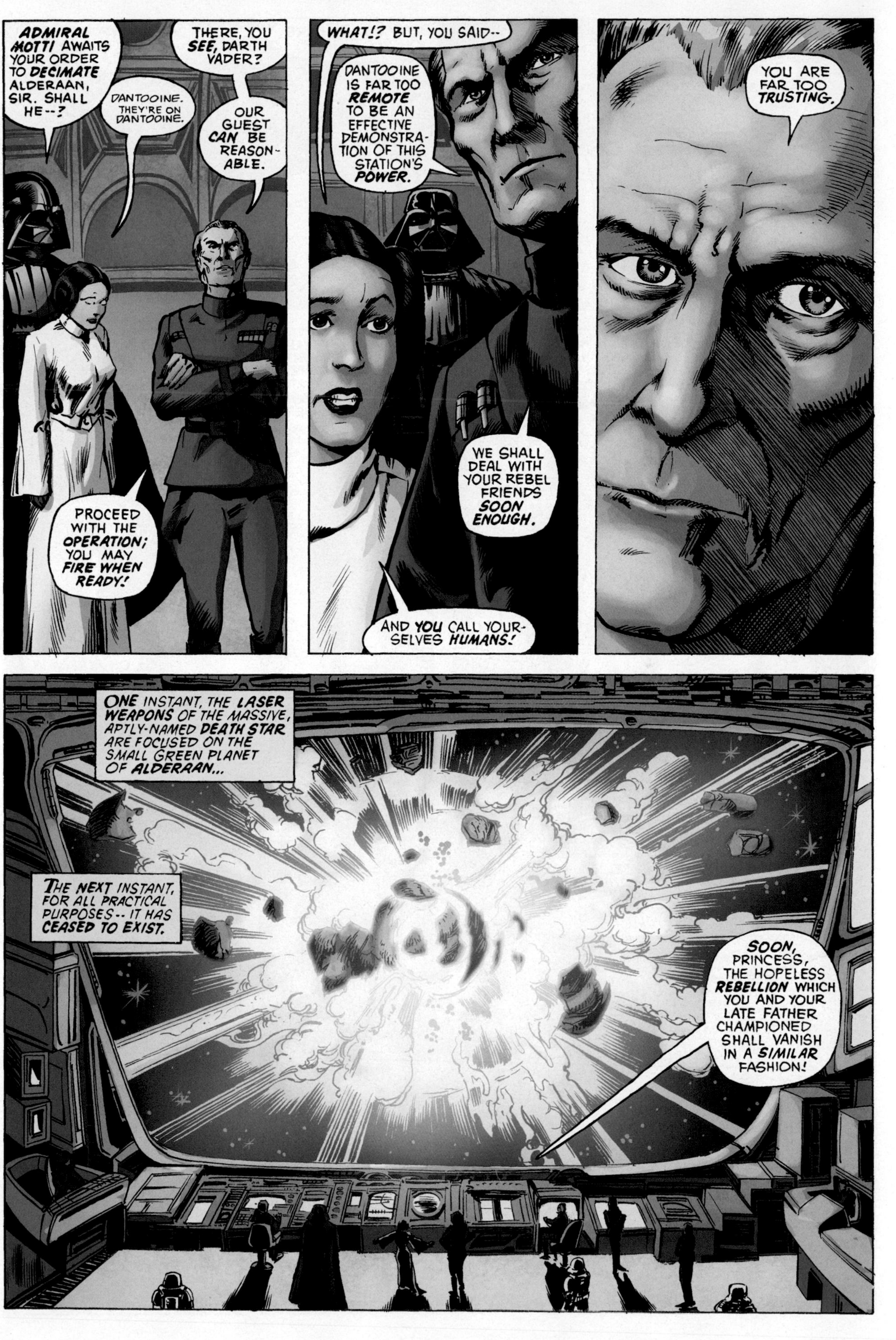
ADMIRAL MOTTI AWAITS YOUR ORDER TO DECIMATE ALDERAAN, SIR. SHALL HE--?
DANTOOINE. THEY'RE ON DANTOOINE.
THERE, YOU SEE, DARTH VADER?
OUR GUEST CAN BE REASONABLE.
PROCEED WITH THE OPERATION; YOU MAY FIRE WHEN READY!
WHAT!? BUT, YOU SAID--
DANTOOINE IS FAR TOO REMOTE TO BE AN EFFECTIVE DEMONSTRATION OF THIS STATION'S POWER.
WE SHALL DEAL WITH YOUR REBEL FRIENDS SOON ENOUGH.
AND YOU CALL YOURSELVES HUMANS!
YOU ARE FAR TOO TRUSTING.
ONE INSTANT, THE LASER WEAPONS OF THE MASSIVE, APTLY-NAMED DEATH STAR ARE FOCUSED ON THE SMALL GREEN PLANET OF ALDERAAN...
THE NEXT INSTANT, FOR ALL PRACTICAL PURPOSES-- IT HAS CEASED TO EXIST.
SOON, PRINCESS, THE HOPELESS REBELLION WHICH YOU AND YOUR LATE FATHER CHAMPIONED SHALL VANISH IN A SIMILAR FASHION!

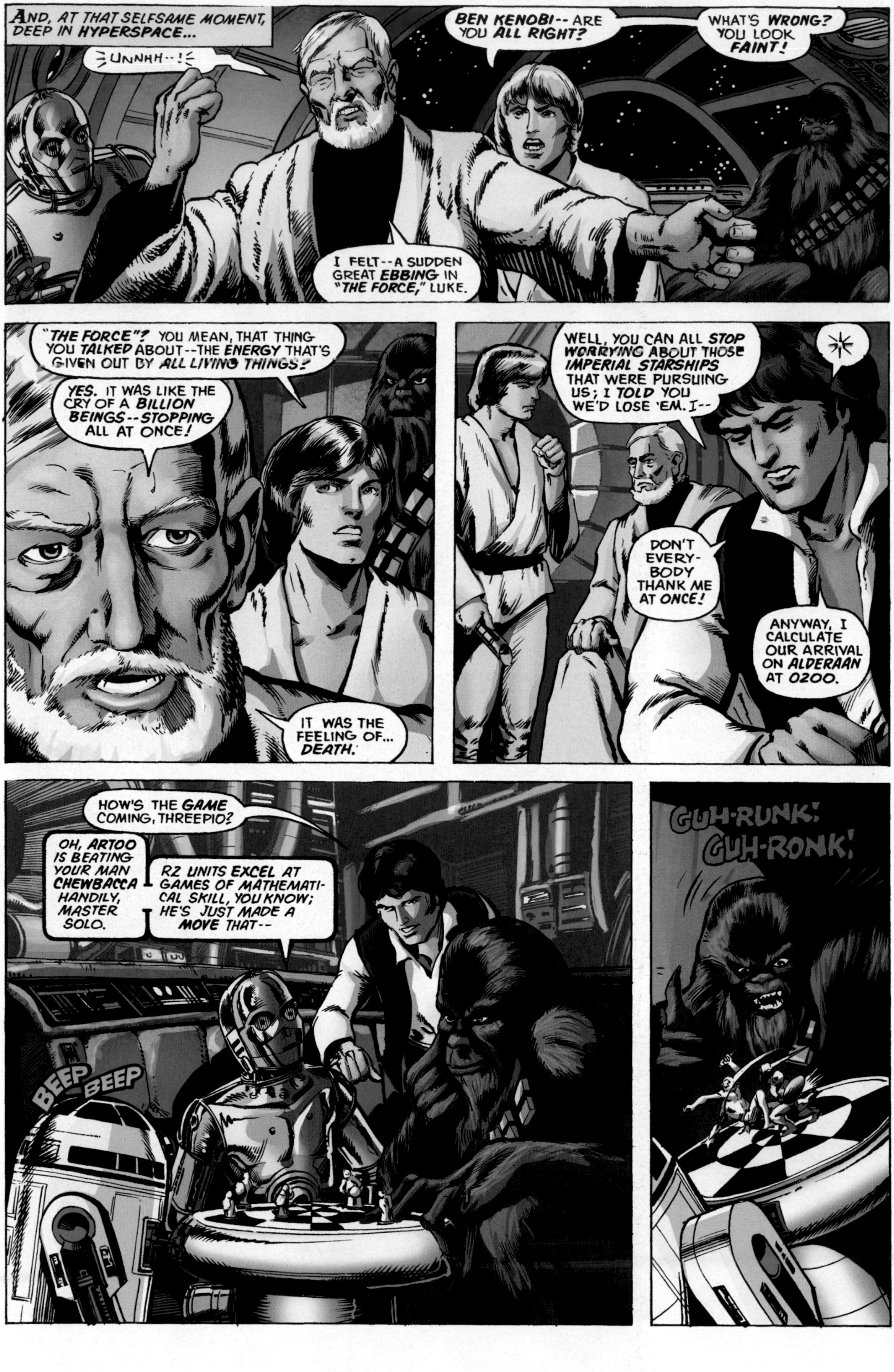
AND, AT THAT SELFSAME MOMENT, DEEP IN HYPERSPACE...
UNNHH--!
BEN KENOBI-- ARE YOU ALL RIGHT?
WHAT'S WRONG? YOU LOOK FAINT!
I FELT--A SUDDEN GREAT EBBING IN "THE FORCE," LUKE.
"THE FORCE"? YOU MEAN, THAT THING YOU TALKED ABOUT--THE ENERGY THAT'S GIVEN OUT BY ALL LIVING THINGS?
YES. IT WAS LIKE THE CRY OF A BILLION BEINGS--STOPPING ALL AT ONCE!
IT WAS THE FEELING OF... DEATH.
WELL, YOU CAN ALL STOP WORRYING ABOUT THOSE IMPERIAL STARSHIPS THAT WERE PURSUING US; I TOLD YOU WE'D LOSE 'EM. I--
DON'T EVERY-BODY THANK ME AT ONCE!
ANYWAY, I CALCULATE OUR ARRIVAL ON ALDERAAN AT 0200.
HOW'S THE GAME COMING, THREEPIO?
OH, ARTOO IS BEATING YOUR MAN CHEWBACCA HANDILY, MASTER SOLO.
R2 UNITS EXCEL AT GAMES OF MATHEMATICAL SKILL, YOU KNOW; HE'S JUST MADE A MOVE THAT--
BEEP BEEP
GUH-RUNK! GUH-RONK!

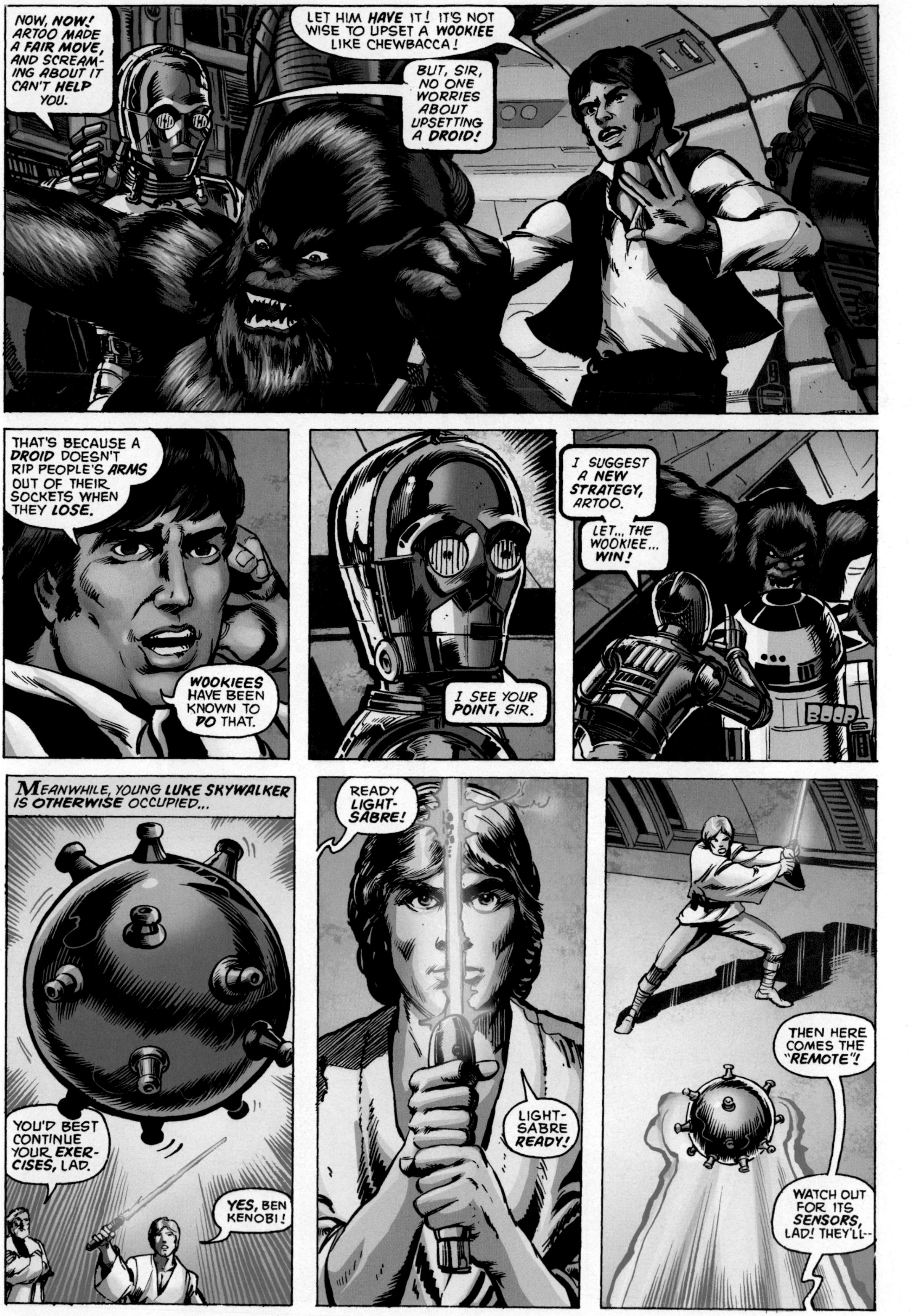
NOW, NOW! ARTOO MADE A FAIR MOVE, AND SCREAMING ABOUT IT CAN'T HELP YOU.
LET HIM HAVE IT! IT'S NOT WISE TO UPSET A WOOKIEE LIKE CHEWBACCA!
BUT, SIR, NO ONE WORRIES ABOUT UPSETTING A DROID!
THAT'S BECAUSE A DROID DOESN'T RIP PEOPLE'S ARMS OUT OF THEIR SOCKETS WHEN THEY LOSE.
WOOKIEES HAVE BEEN KNOWN TO DO THAT.
I SEE YOUR POINT, SIR.
I SUGGEST A NEW STRATEGY, ARTOO.
LET... THE WOOKIEE... WIN!
BOOP
MEANWHILE, YOUNG LUKE SKYWALKER IS OTHERWISE OCCUPIED...
YOU'D BEST CONTINUE YOUR EXERCISES, LAD.
YES, BEN KENOBI!
READY LIGHT-SABRE!
LIGHT-SABRE READY!
THEN HERE COMES THE "REMOTE"!
WATCH OUT FOR ITS SENSORS, LAD! THEY'LL--

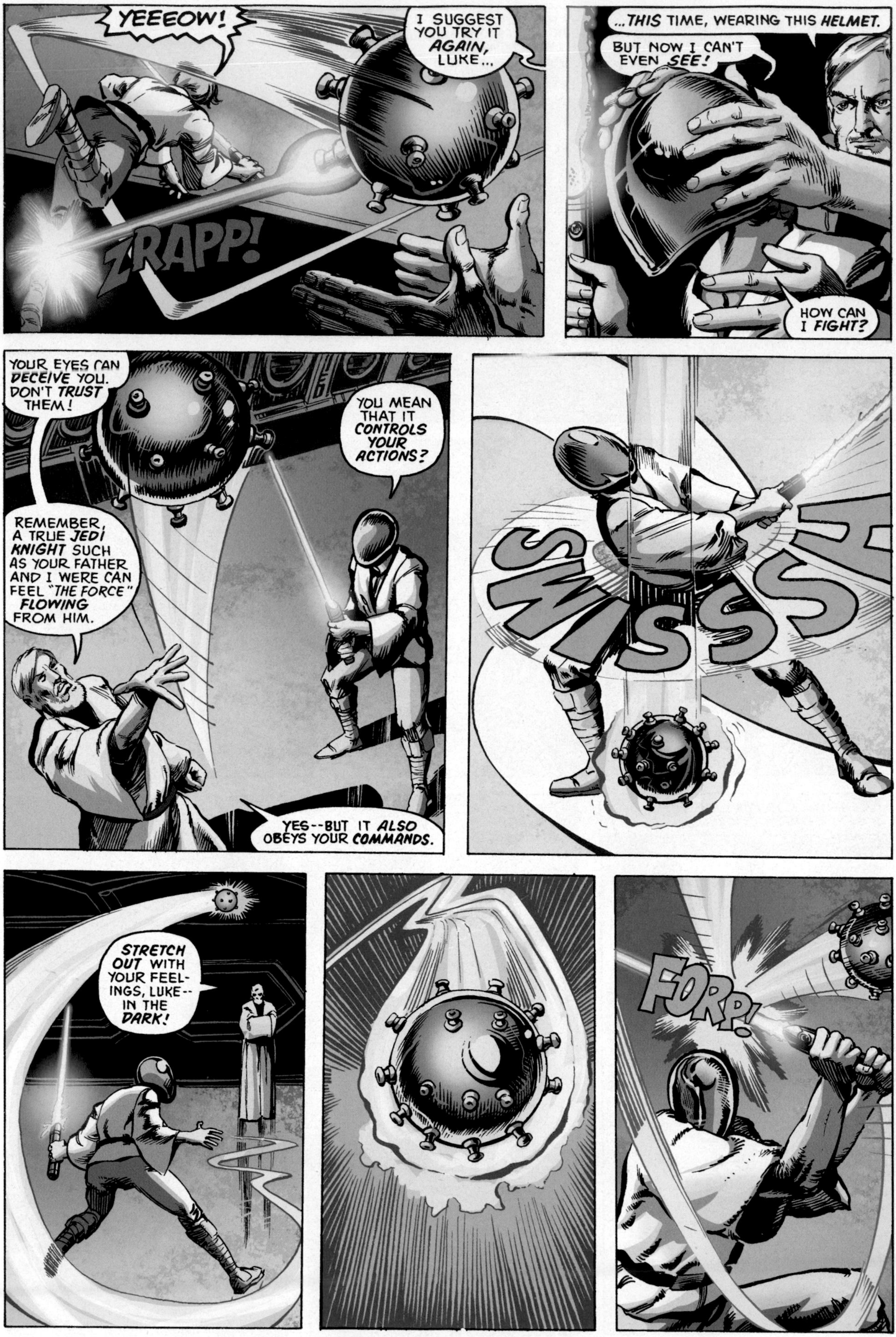
YEEEOW!
I SUGGEST YOU TRY IT AGAIN, LUKE...
ZRAPP!
...THIS TIME, WEARING THIS HELMET.
BUT NOW I CAN'T EVEN SEE!
HOW CAN I FIGHT?
YOUR EYES CAN DECEIVE YOU. DON'T TRUST THEM!
YOU MEAN THAT IT CONTROLS YOUR ACTIONS?
REMEMBER, A TRUE JEDI KNIGHT SUCH AS YOUR FATHER AND I WERE CAN FEEL "THE FORCE" FLOWING FROM HIM.
YES--BUT IT ALSO OBEYS YOUR COMMANDS.
SWISSSH
STRETCH OUT WITH YOUR FEEL-INGS, LUKE--IN THE DARK!
FORP!

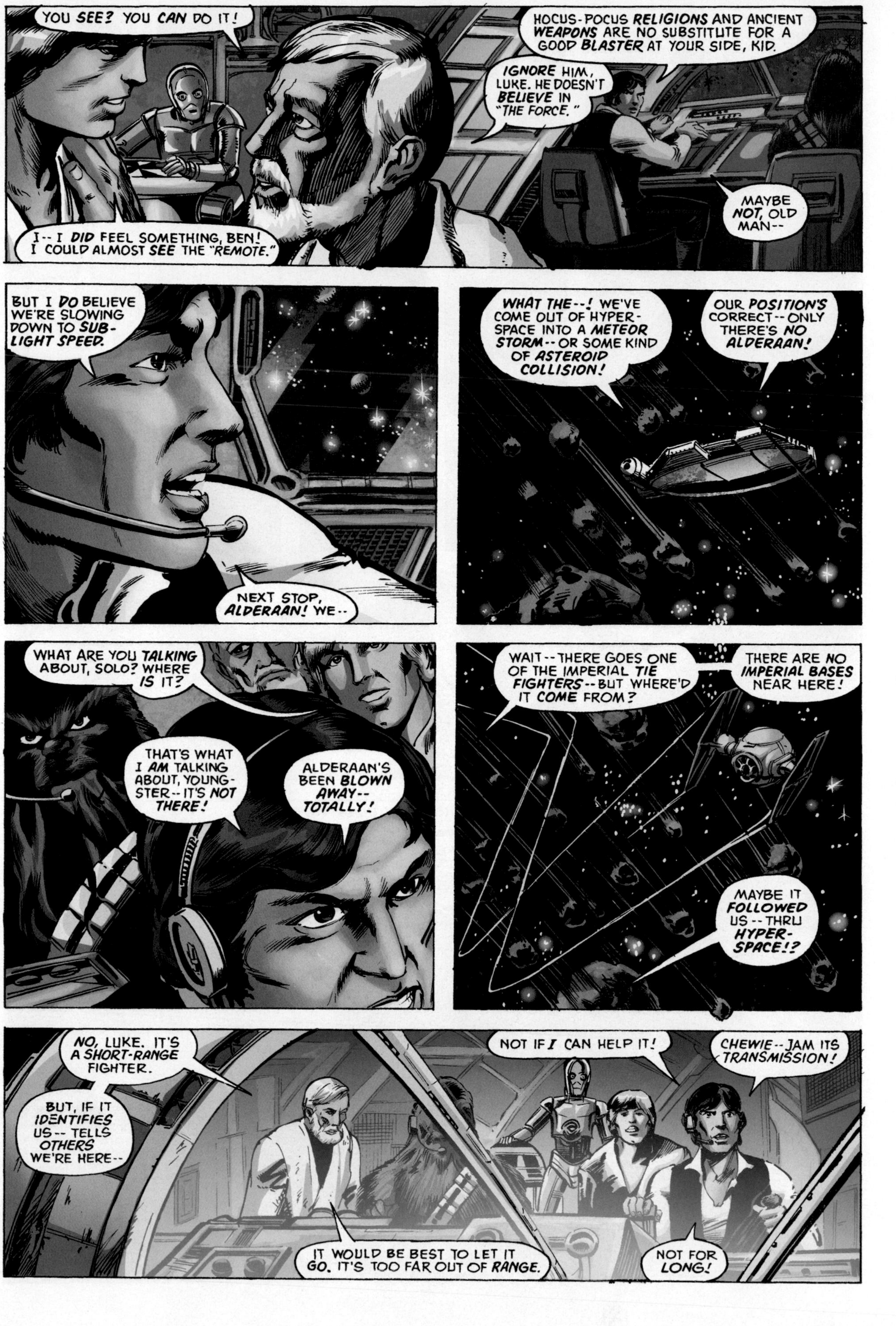
YOU SEE? YOU CAN DO IT!
HOCUS-POCUS RELIGIONS AND ANCIENT WEAPONS ARE NO SUBSTITUTE FOR A GOOD BLASTER AT YOUR SIDE, KID.
IGNORE HIM, LUKE. HE DOESN'T BELIEVE IN "THE FORCE."
I-- I DID FEEL SOMETHING, BEN! I COULD ALMOST SEE THE "REMOTE."
MAYBE NOT, OLD MAN--
BUT I DO BELIEVE WE'RE SLOWING DOWN TO SUB-LIGHT SPEED.
NEXT STOP, ALDERAAN! WE--
WHAT THE--! WE'VE COME OUT OF HYPER-SPACE INTO A METEOR STORM--OR SOME KIND OF ASTEROID COLLISION!
OUR POSITION'S CORRECT--ONLY THERE'S NO ALDERAAN!
WHAT ARE YOU TALKING ABOUT, SOLO? WHERE IS IT?
THAT'S WHAT I AM TALKING ABOUT, YOUNG-STER--IT'S NOT THERE!
ALDERAAN'S BEEN BLOWN AWAY--TOTALLY!
WAIT--THERE GOES ONE OF THE IMPERIAL TIE FIGHTERS--BUT WHERE'D IT COME FROM?
THERE ARE NO IMPERIAL BASES NEAR HERE!
MAYBE IT FOLLOWED US--THRU HYPER-SPACE!?
NO, LUKE. IT'S A SHORT-RANGE FIGHTER.
BUT, IF IT IDENTIFIES US--TELLS OTHERS WE'RE HERE--
IT WOULD BE BEST TO LET IT GO. IT'S TOO FAR OUT OF RANGE.
NOT IF I CAN HELP IT!
CHEWIE--JAM ITS TRANSMISSION!
NOT FOR LONG!

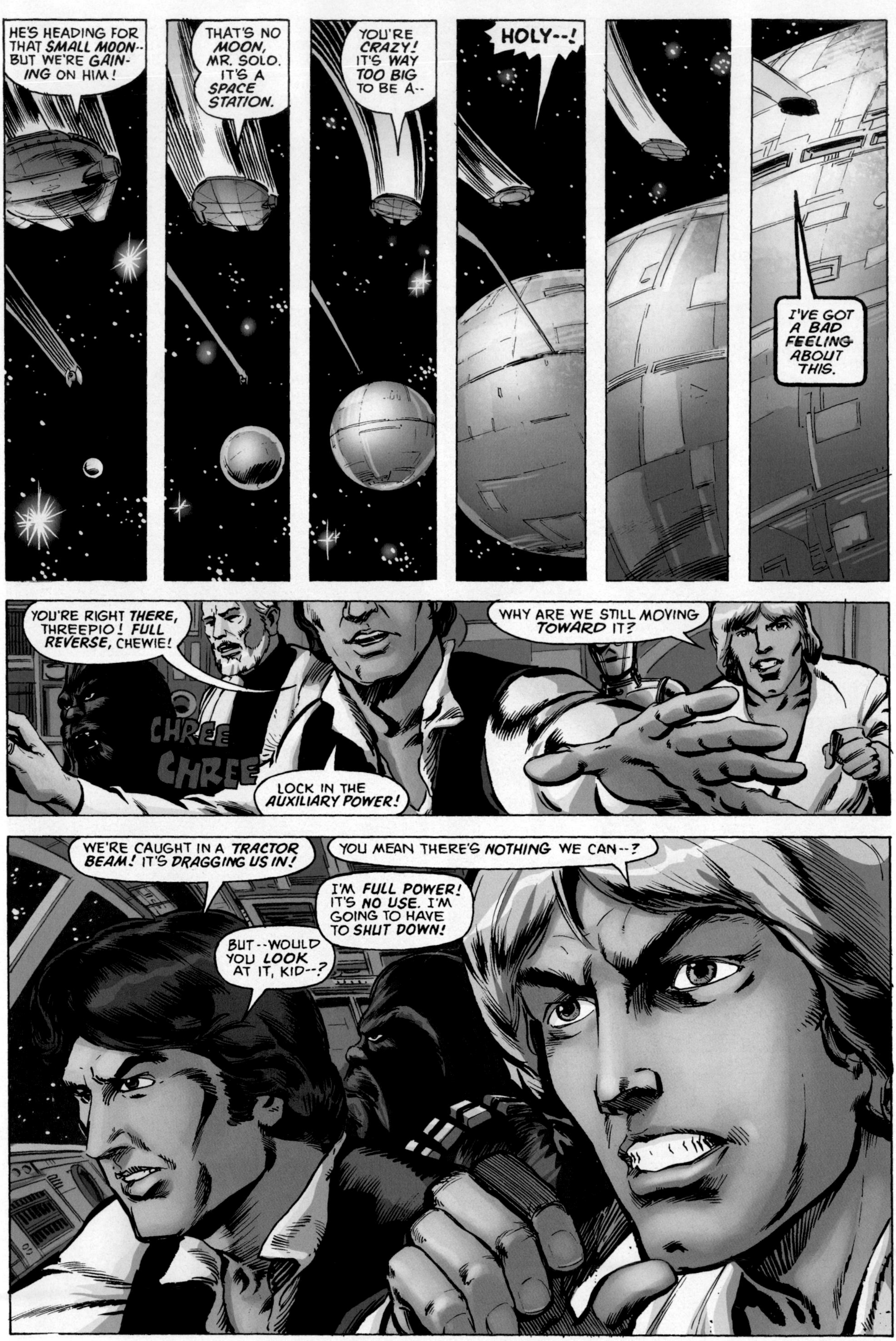
HE'S HEADING FOR THAT SMALL MOON-- BUT WE'RE GAINING ON HIM!
THAT'S NO MOON, MR. SOLO. IT'S A SPACE STATION.
YOU'RE CRAZY! IT'S WAY TOO BIG TO BE A--
HOLY--!
I'VE GOT A BAD FEELING ABOUT THIS.
YOU'RE RIGHT THERE, THREEPIO! FULL REVERSE, CHEWIE!
CHREE CHREE
LOCK IN THE AUXILIARY POWER!
WHY ARE WE STILL MOVING TOWARD IT?
WE'RE CAUGHT IN A TRACTOR BEAM! IT'S DRAGGING US IN!
YOU MEAN THERE'S NOTHING WE CAN--?
I'M FULL POWER! IT'S NO USE. I'M GOING TO HAVE TO SHUT DOWN!
BUT--WOULD YOU LOOK AT IT, KID--?

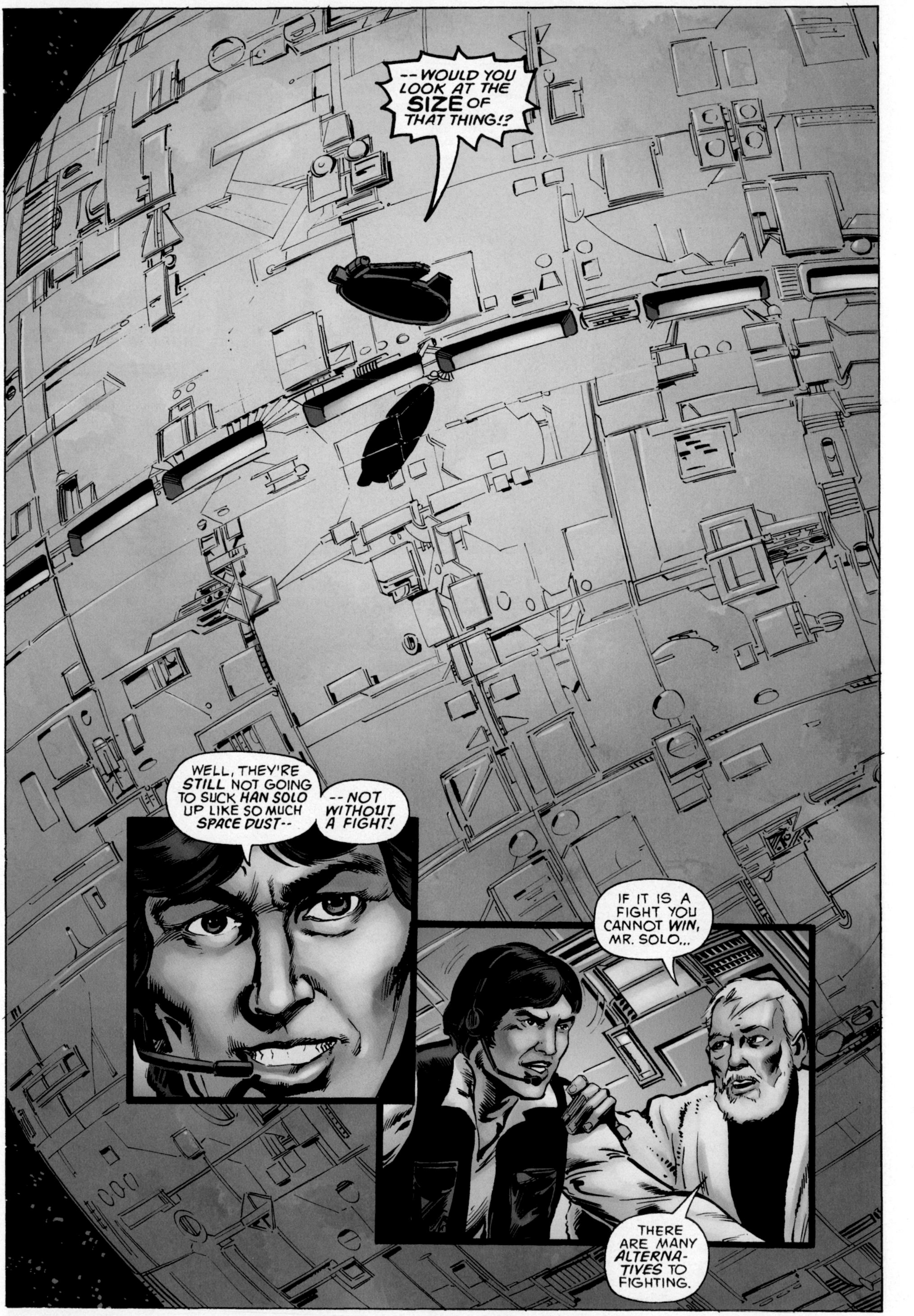
--WOULD YOU LOOK AT THE SIZE OF THAT THING!?
WELL, THEY'RE STILL NOT GOING TO SUCK HAN SOLO UP LIKE SO MUCH SPACE DUST--
--NOT WITHOUT A FIGHT!
IF IT IS A FIGHT YOU CANNOT WIN, MR. SOLO...
THERE ARE MANY ALTERNATIVES TO FIGHTING.

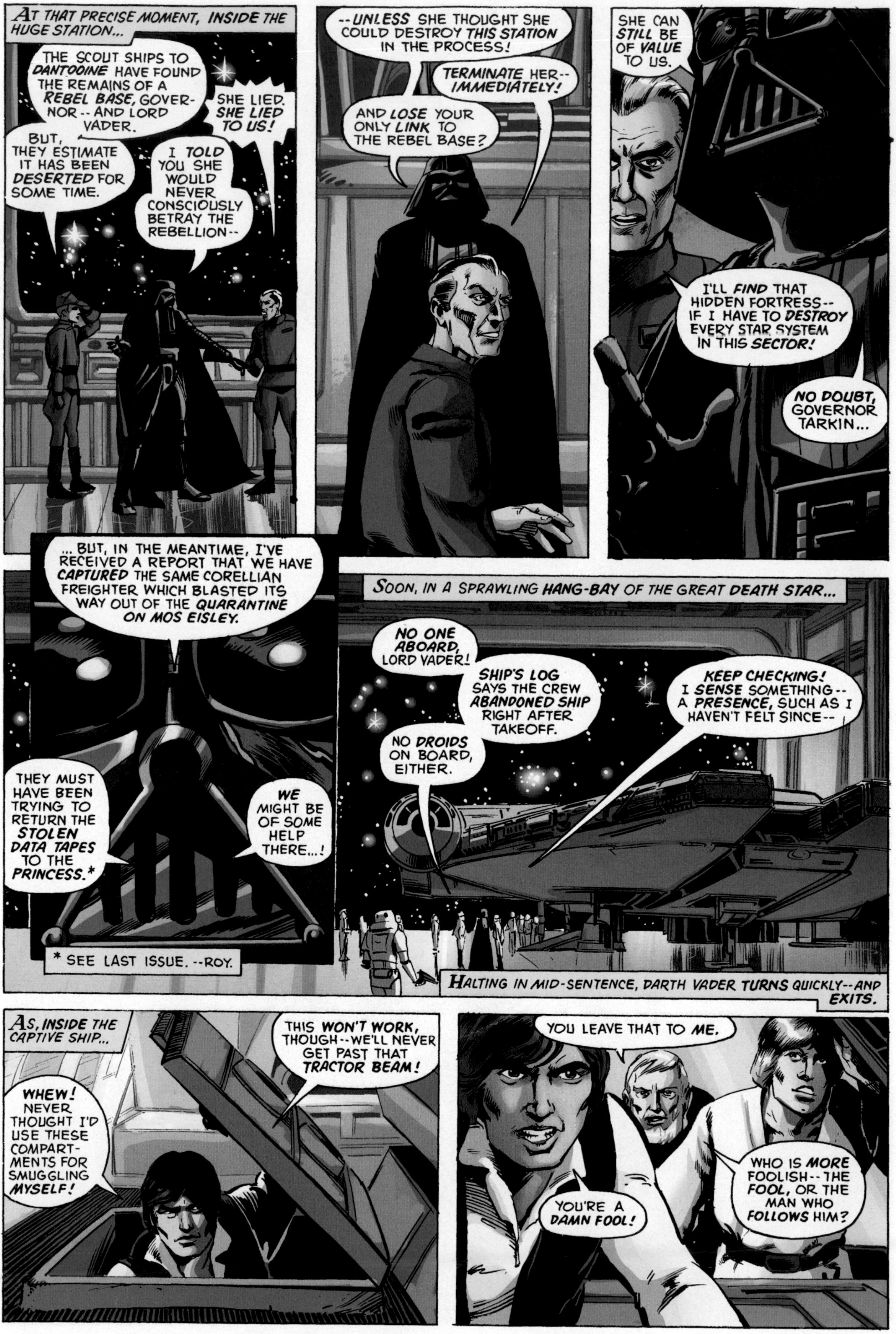
AT THAT PRECISE MOMENT, INSIDE THE HUGE STATION...
THE SCOUT SHIPS TO DANTOOINE HAVE FOUND THE REMAINS OF A REBEL BASE, GOVERNOR -- AND LORD VADER.
BUT, THEY ESTIMATE IT HAS BEEN DESERTED FOR SOME TIME.
SHE LIED. SHE LIED TO US!
I TOLD YOU SHE WOULD NEVER CONSCIOUSLY BETRAY THE REBELLION--
--UNLESS SHE THOUGHT SHE COULD DESTROY THIS STATION IN THE PROCESS!
TERMINATE HER-- IMMEDIATELY!
AND LOSE YOUR ONLY LINK TO THE REBEL BASE?
SHE CAN STILL BE OF VALUE TO US.
I'LL FIND THAT HIDDEN FORTRESS-- IF I HAVE TO DESTROY EVERY STAR SYSTEM IN THIS SECTOR!
NO DOUBT, GOVERNOR TARKIN...
... BUT, IN THE MEANTIME, I'VE RECEIVED A REPORT THAT WE HAVE CAPTURED THE SAME CORELLIAN FREIGHTER WHICH BLASTED ITS WAY OUT OF THE QUARANTINE ON MOS EISLEY.
THEY MUST HAVE BEEN TRYING TO RETURN THE STOLEN DATA TAPES TO THE PRINCESS.*
WE MIGHT BE OF SOME HELP THERE...!
* SEE LAST ISSUE. --ROY.
SOON, IN A SPRAWLING HANG-BAY OF THE GREAT DEATH STAR...
NO ONE ABOARD, LORD VADER!
SHIP'S LOG SAYS THE CREW ABANDONED SHIP RIGHT AFTER TAKEOFF.
NO DROIDS ON BOARD, EITHER.
KEEP CHECKING! I SENSE SOMETHING-- A PRESENCE, SUCH AS I HAVEN'T FELT SINCE--
HALTING IN MID-SENTENCE, DARTH VADER TURNS QUICKLY--AND EXITS.
AS, INSIDE THE CAPTIVE SHIP...
WHEW! NEVER THOUGHT I'D USE THESE COMPARTMENTS FOR SMUGGLING MYSELF!
THIS WON'T WORK, THOUGH--WE'LL NEVER GET PAST THAT TRACTOR BEAM!
YOU LEAVE THAT TO ME.
YOU'RE A DAMN FOOL!
WHO IS MORE FOOLISH-- THE FOOL, OR THE MAN WHO FOLLOWS HIM?

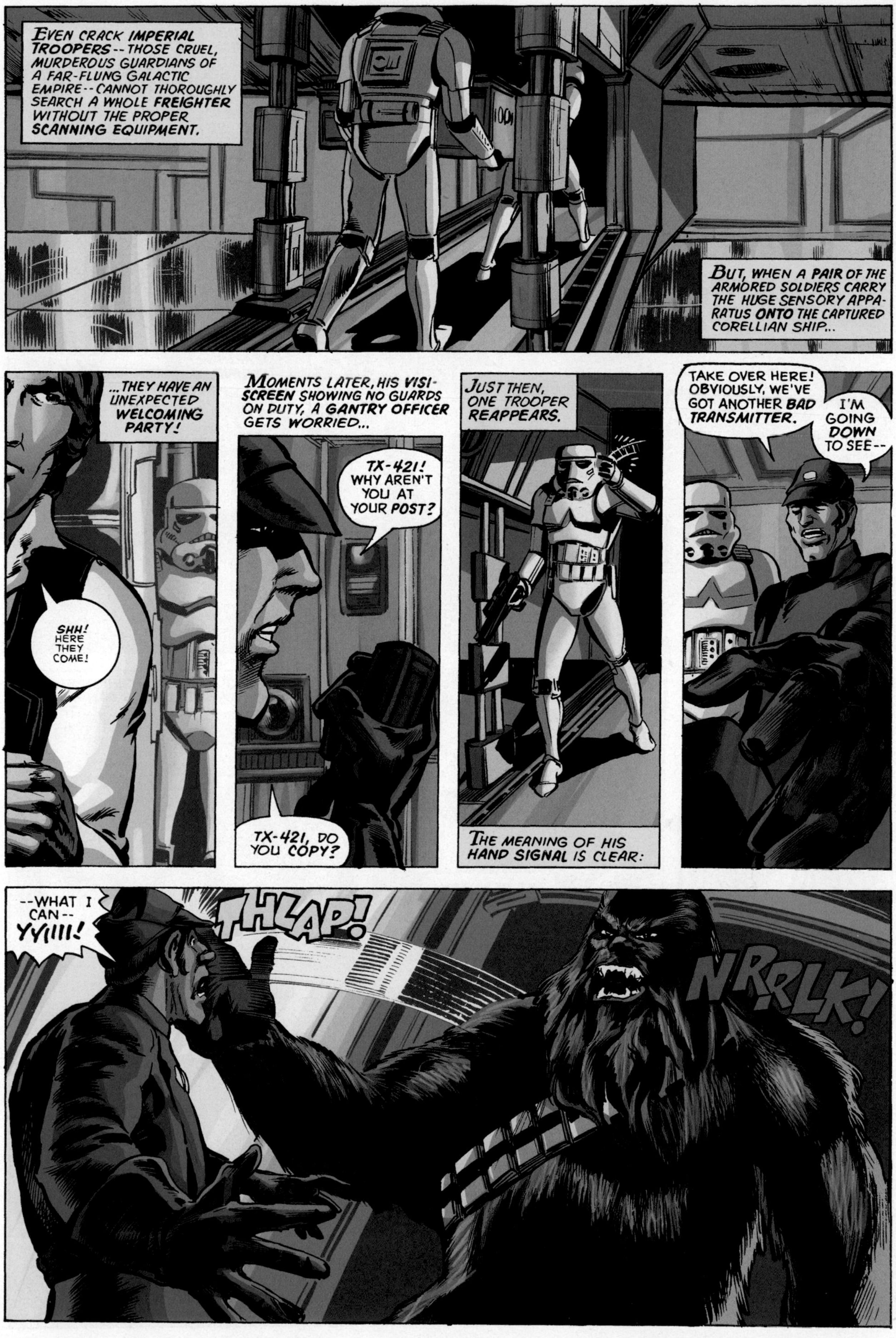
EVEN CRACK IMPERIAL TROOPERS -- THOSE CRUEL, MURDEROUS GUARDIANS OF A FAR-FLUNG GALACTIC EMPIRE -- CANNOT THOROUGHLY SEARCH A WHOLE FREIGHTER WITHOUT THE PROPER SCANNING EQUIPMENT.
BUT, WHEN A PAIR OF THE ARMORED SOLDIERS CARRY THE HUGE SENSORY APPARATUS ONTO THE CAPTURED CORELLIAN SHIP...
...THEY HAVE AN UNEXPECTED WELCOMING PARTY!
SHH! HERE THEY COME!
MOMENTS LATER, HIS VISI-SCREEN SHOWING NO GUARDS ON DUTY, A GANTRY OFFICER GETS WORRIED...
TX-421! WHY AREN'T YOU AT YOUR POST?
TX-421, DO YOU COPY?
JUST THEN, ONE TROOPER REAPPEARS.
THE MEANING OF HIS HAND SIGNAL IS CLEAR:
TAKE OVER HERE! OBVIOUSLY, WE'VE GOT ANOTHER BAD TRANSMITTER.
I'M GOING DOWN TO SEE--
--WHAT I CAN-- YYIIII!
THLAP!
NRRLK!

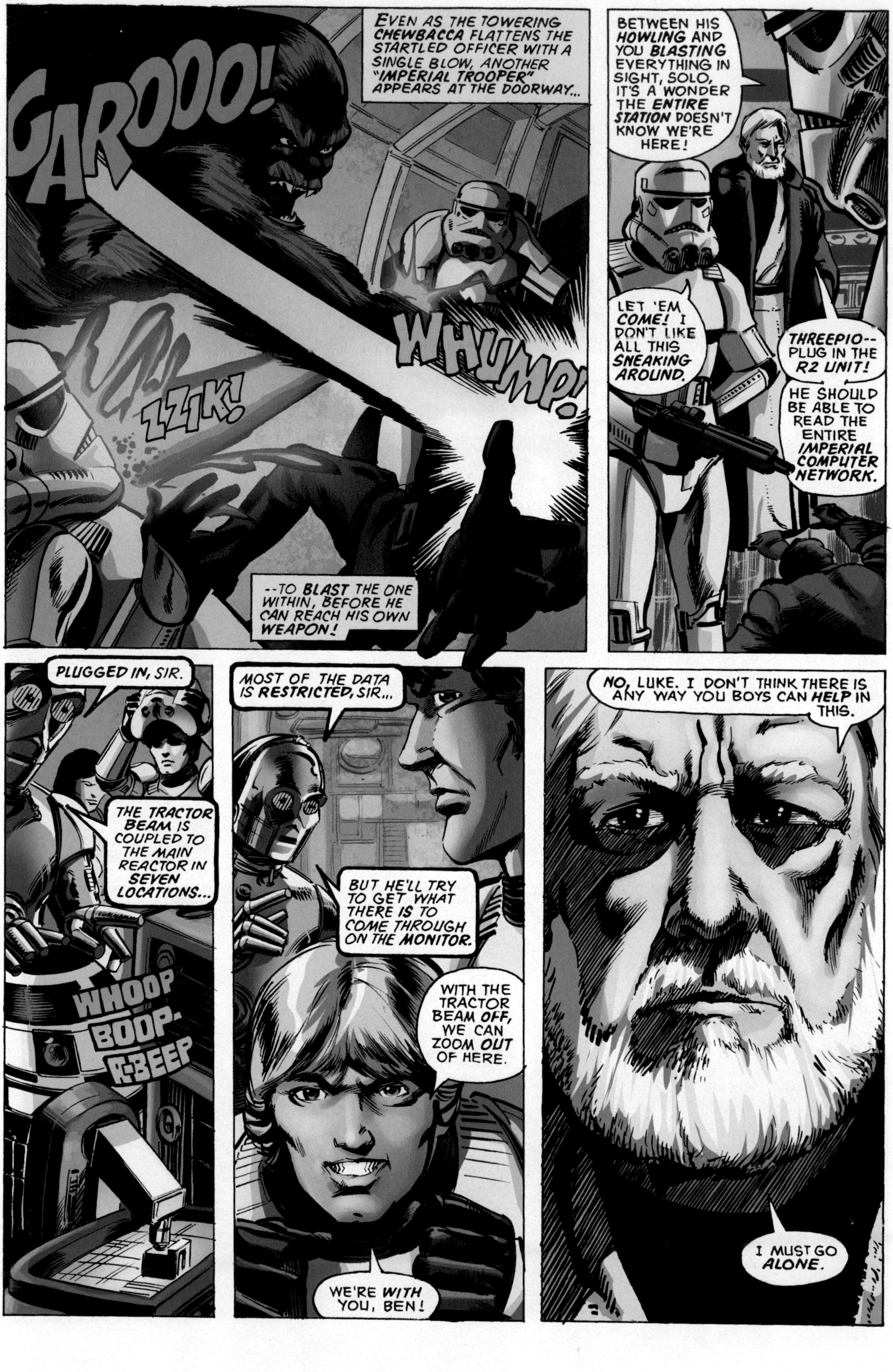
EVEN AS THE TOWERING CHEWBACCA FLATTENS THE STARTLED OFFICER WITH A SINGLE BLOW, ANOTHER "IMPERIAL TROOPER" APPEARS AT THE DOORWAY...
GAROOO!
WHUMP!
ZZIK!
--TO BLAST THE ONE WITHIN, BEFORE HE CAN REACH HIS OWN WEAPON!
BETWEEN HIS HOWLING AND YOU BLASTING EVERYTHING IN SIGHT, SOLO, IT'S A WONDER THE ENTIRE STATION DOESN'T KNOW WE'RE HERE!
LET 'EM COME! I DON'T LIKE ALL THIS SNEAKING AROUND.
THREEPIO-- PLUG IN THE R2 UNIT!
HE SHOULD BE ABLE TO READ THE ENTIRE IMPERIAL COMPUTER NETWORK.
PLUGGED IN, SIR.
THE TRACTOR BEAM IS COUPLED TO THE MAIN REACTOR IN SEVEN LOCATIONS...
WHOOP BOOP R-BEEP
MOST OF THE DATA IS RESTRICTED, SIR...
BUT HE'LL TRY TO GET WHAT THERE IS TO COME THROUGH ON THE MONITOR.
WITH THE TRACTOR BEAM OFF, WE CAN ZOOM OUT OF HERE.
WE'RE WITH YOU, BEN!
NO, LUKE. I DON'T THINK THERE IS ANY WAY YOU BOYS CAN HELP IN THIS.
I MUST GO ALONE.

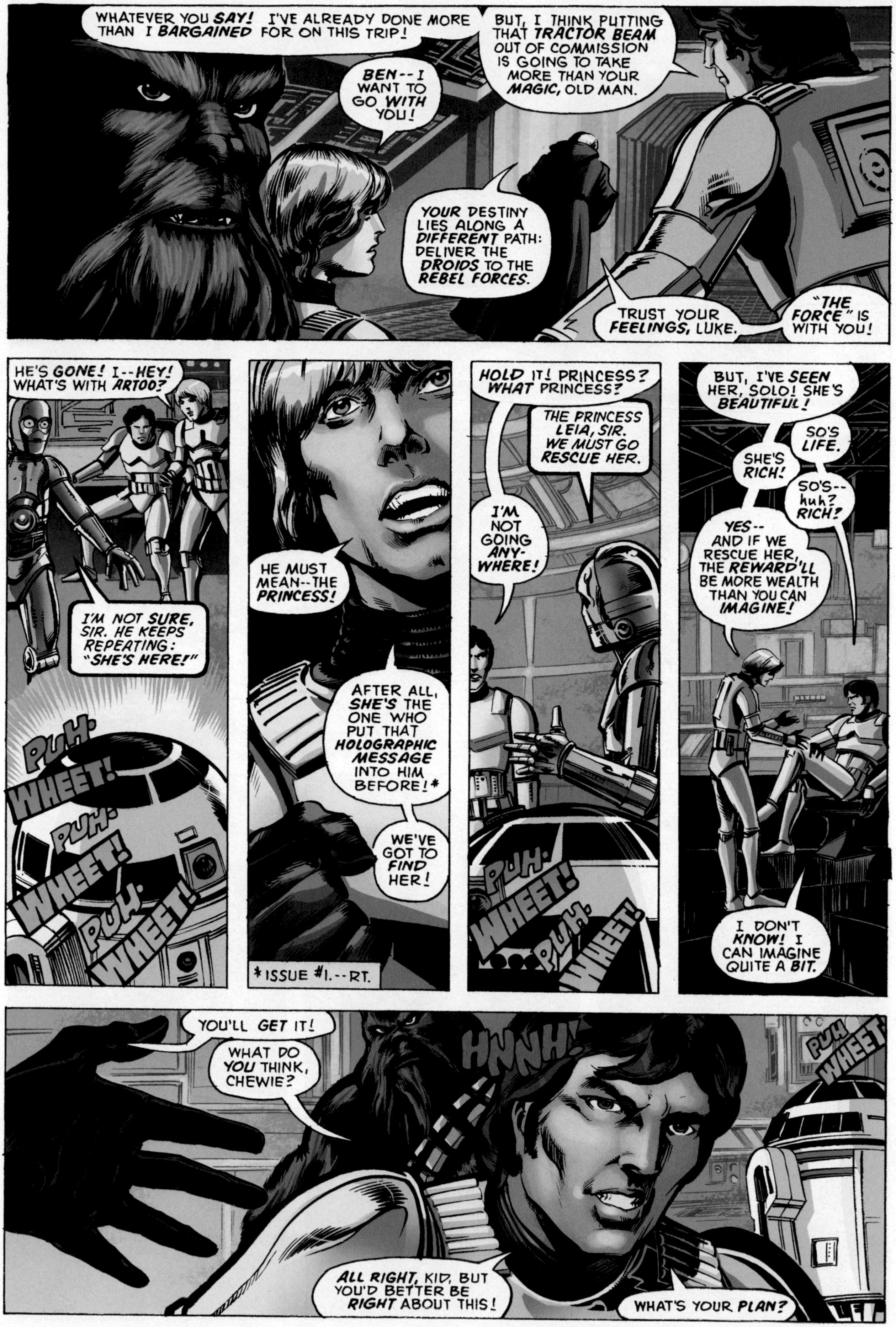
WHATEVER YOU SAY! I'VE ALREADY DONE MORE THAN I BARGAINED FOR ON THIS TRIP!
BUT, I THINK PUTTING THAT TRACTOR BEAM OUT OF COMMISSION IS GOING TO TAKE MORE THAN YOUR MAGIC, OLD MAN.
BEN--I WANT TO GO WITH YOU!
YOUR DESTINY LIES ALONG A DIFFERENT PATH: DELIVER THE DROIDS TO THE REBEL FORCES.
TRUST YOUR FEELINGS, LUKE.
"THE FORCE" IS WITH YOU!
HE'S GONE! I--HEY! WHAT'S WITH ARTOO?
I'M NOT SURE, SIR. HE KEEPS REPEATING: "SHE'S HERE!"
PUH-WHEET! PUH-WHEET! PUH-WHEET!
HE MUST MEAN--THE PRINCESS!
AFTER ALL, SHE'S THE ONE WHO PUT THAT HOLOGRAPHIC MESSAGE INTO HIM BEFORE!*
WE'VE GOT TO FIND HER!
*ISSUE #1.--RT.
HOLD IT! PRINCESS? WHAT PRINCESS?
THE PRINCESS LEIA, SIR. WE MUST GO RESCUE HER.
I'M NOT GOING ANY-WHERE!
PUH-WHEET! PUH-WHEET!
BUT, I'VE SEEN HER, SOLO! SHE'S BEAUTIFUL!
SO'S LIFE.
SHE'S RICH!
SO'S--huh? RICH?
YES--AND IF WE RESCUE HER, THE REWARD'LL BE MORE WEALTH THAN YOU CAN IMAGINE!
I DON'T KNOW! I CAN IMAGINE QUITE A BIT.
YOU'LL GET IT!
WHAT DO YOU THINK, CHEWIE?
HNNH!
PUH WHEET
ALL RIGHT, KID, BUT YOU'D BETTER BE RIGHT ABOUT THIS!
WHAT'S YOUR PLAN?

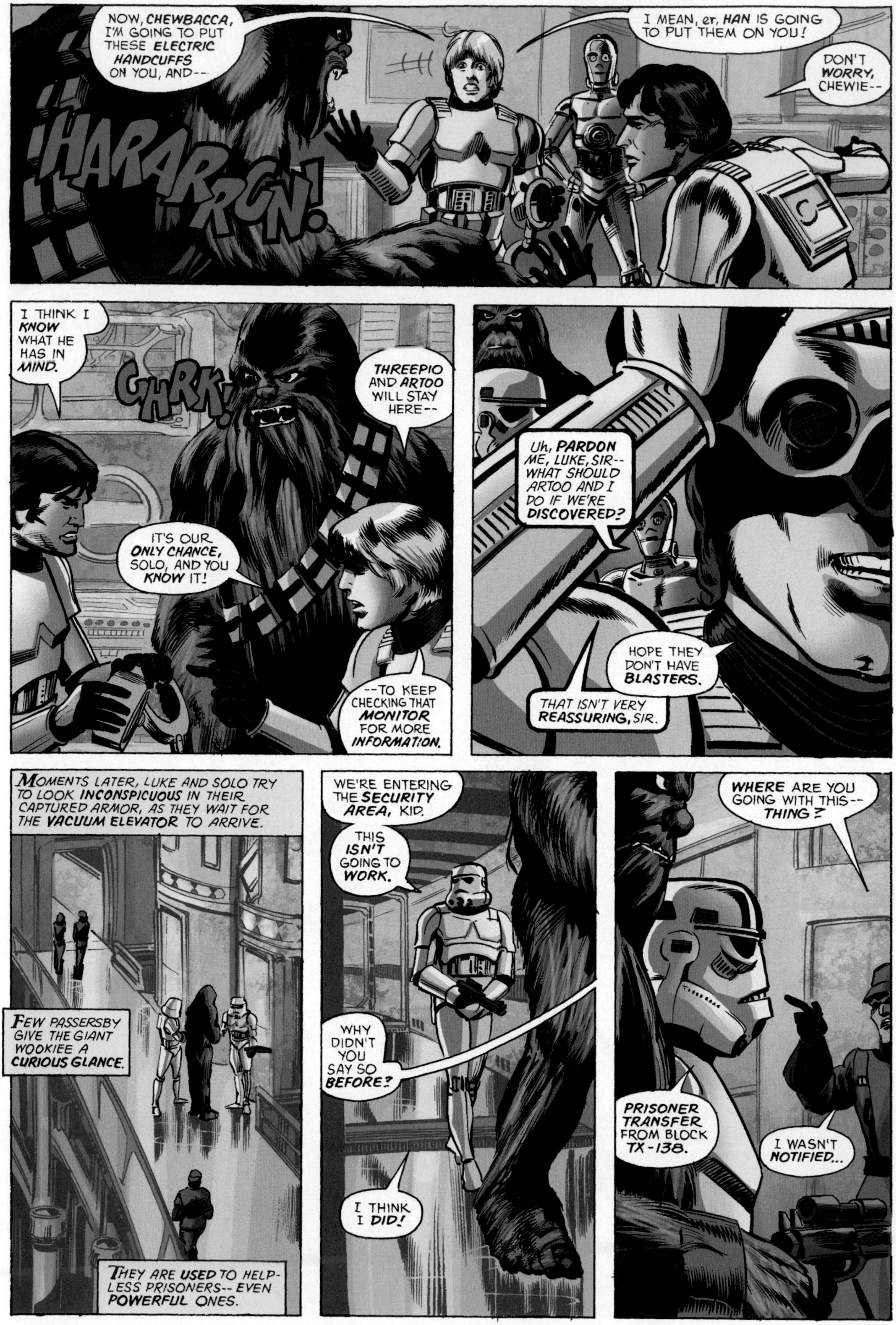
NOW, CHEWBACCA, I'M GOING TO PUT THESE ELECTRIC HANDCUFFS ON YOU, AND--
I MEAN, er, HAN IS GOING TO PUT THEM ON YOU!
DON'T WORRY, CHEWIE--
HARARRGN!
I THINK I KNOW WHAT HE HAS IN MIND.
GHRK!
THREEPIO AND ARTOO WILL STAY HERE--
IT'S OUR ONLY CHANCE, SOLO, AND YOU KNOW IT!
--TO KEEP CHECKING THAT MONITOR FOR MORE INFORMATION.
Uh, PARDON ME, LUKE, SIR-- WHAT SHOULD ARTOO AND I DO IF WE'RE DISCOVERED?
HOPE THEY DON'T HAVE BLASTERS.
THAT ISN'T VERY REASSURING, SIR.
MOMENTS LATER, LUKE AND SOLO TRY TO LOOK INCONSPICUOUS IN THEIR CAPTURED ARMOR, AS THEY WAIT FOR THE VACUUM ELEVATOR TO ARRIVE.
FEW PASSERSBY GIVE THE GIANT WOOKIEE A CURIOUS GLANCE.
THEY ARE USED TO HELPLESS PRISONERS-- EVEN POWERFUL ONES.
WE'RE ENTERING THE SECURITY AREA, KID.
THIS ISN'T GOING TO WORK.
WHY DIDN'T YOU SAY SO BEFORE?
I THINK I DID!
WHERE ARE YOU GOING WITH THIS-- THING?
PRISONER TRANSFER FROM BLOCK TX-138.
I WASN'T NOTIFIED...

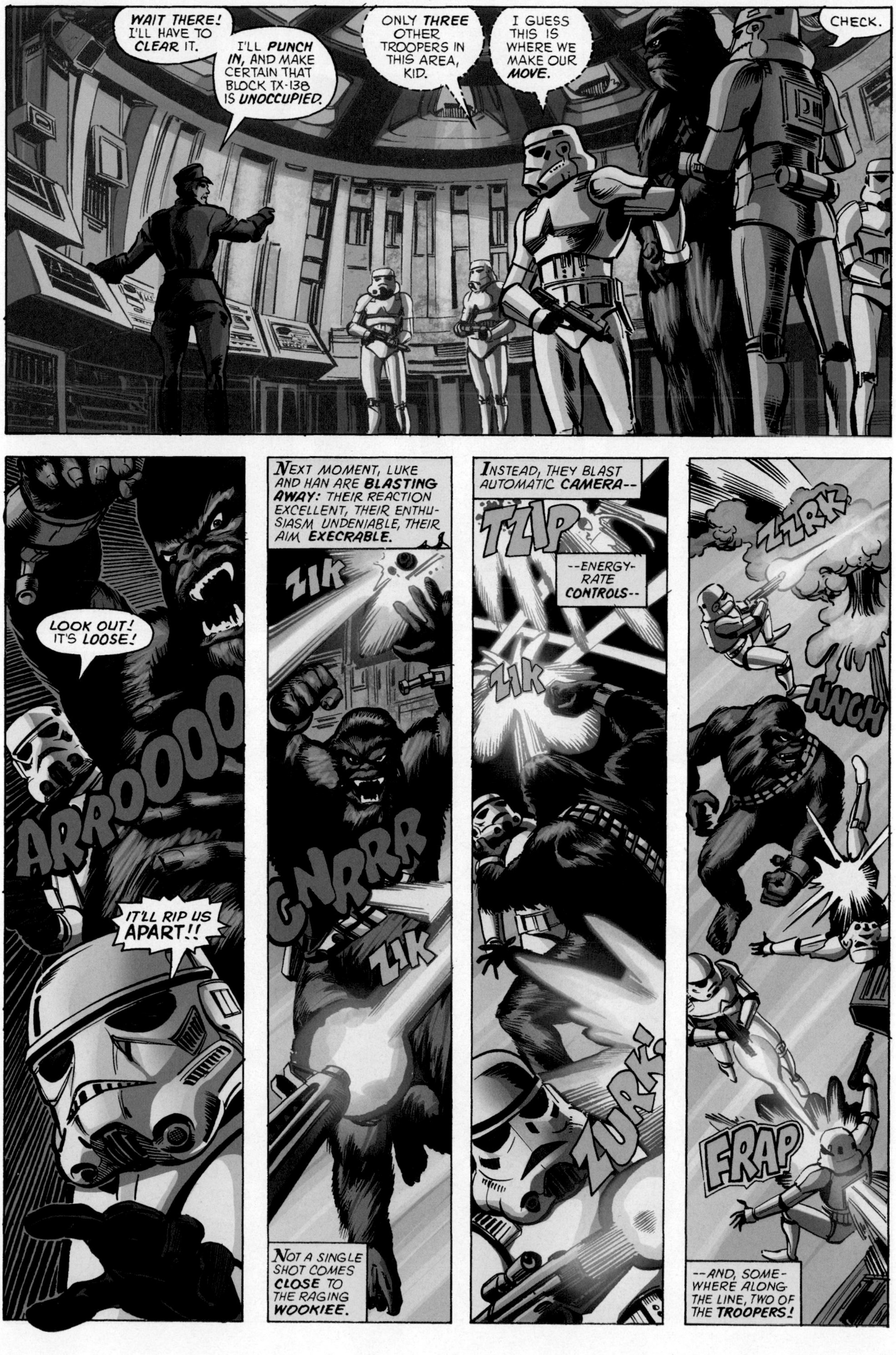
WAIT THERE! I'LL HAVE TO CLEAR IT.
I'LL PUNCH IN, AND MAKE CERTAIN THAT BLOCK TX-138 IS UNOCCUPIED.
ONLY THREE OTHER TROOPERS IN THIS AREA, KID.
I GUESS THIS IS WHERE WE MAKE OUR MOVE.
CHECK.
LOOK OUT! IT'S LOOSE!
ARROOOOO
IT'LL RIP US APART!!
NEXT MOMENT, LUKE AND HAN ARE BLASTING AWAY: THEIR REACTION EXCELLENT, THEIR ENTHUSIASM UNDENIABLE, THEIR AIM EXECRABLE.
ZIK
GNRRR
ZIK
NOT A SINGLE SHOT COMES CLOSE TO THE RAGING WOOKIEE.
INSTEAD, THEY BLAST AUTOMATIC CAMERA--
TZIP
--ENERGY-RATE CONTROLS--
ZIK
ZURK!
ZZRK
HNGH
FRAP
--AND, SOMEWHERE ALONG THE LINE, TWO OF THE TROOPERS!

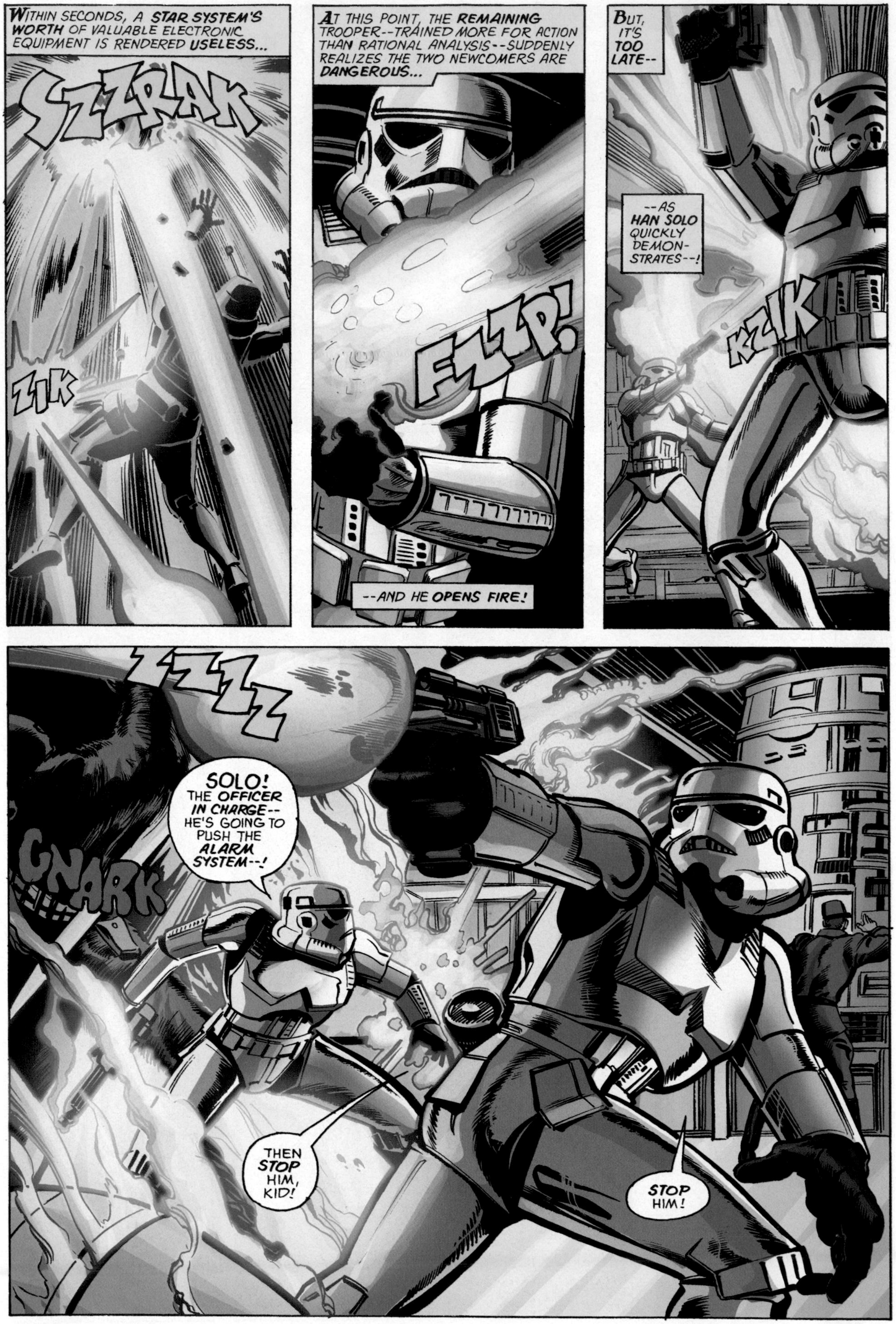
WITHIN SECONDS, A STAR SYSTEM'S WORTH OF VALUABLE ELECTRONIC EQUIPMENT IS RENDERED USELESS...
SZZRAK
ZIK
AT THIS POINT, THE REMAINING TROOPER--TRAINED MORE FOR ACTION THAN RATIONAL ANALYSIS--SUDDENLY REALIZES THE TWO NEWCOMERS ARE DANGEROUS...
FZZP!
--AND HE OPENS FIRE!
BUT, IT'S TOO LATE--
--AS HAN SOLO QUICKLY DEMON-STRATES--!
KZIK
ZZZZZ
SOLO! THE OFFICER IN CHARGE-- HE'S GOING TO PUSH THE ALARM SYSTEM--!
GNARK
THEN STOP HIM, KID!
STOP HIM!

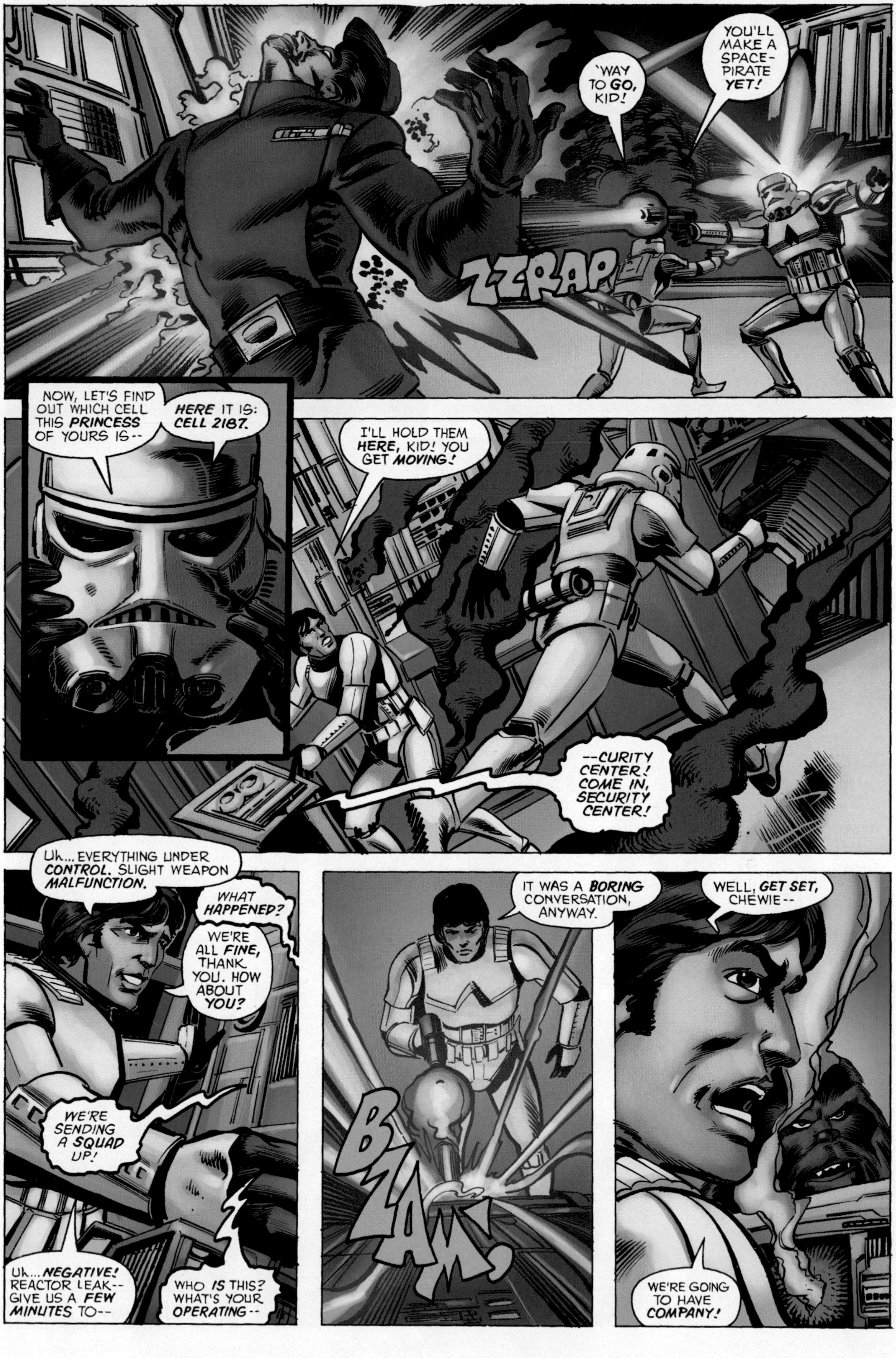
'WAY TO GO, KID!
YOU'LL MAKE A SPACE-PIRATE YET!
ZZRAP
NOW, LET'S FIND OUT WHICH CELL THIS PRINCESS OF YOURS IS--
HERE IT IS: CELL 2187.
I'LL HOLD THEM HERE, KID! YOU GET MOVING!
--CURITY CENTER! COME IN, SECURITY CENTER!
Uh... EVERYTHING UNDER CONTROL. SLIGHT WEAPON MALFUNCTION.
WHAT HAPPENED?
WE'RE ALL FINE, THANK YOU. HOW ABOUT YOU?
WE'RE SENDING A SQUAD UP!
Uh... NEGATIVE! REACTOR LEAK-- GIVE US A FEW MINUTES TO--
WHO IS THIS? WHAT'S YOUR OPERATING--
IT WAS A BORING CONVERSATION, ANYWAY.
BLAM!
WELL, GET SET, CHEWIE--
WE'RE GOING TO HAVE COMPANY!

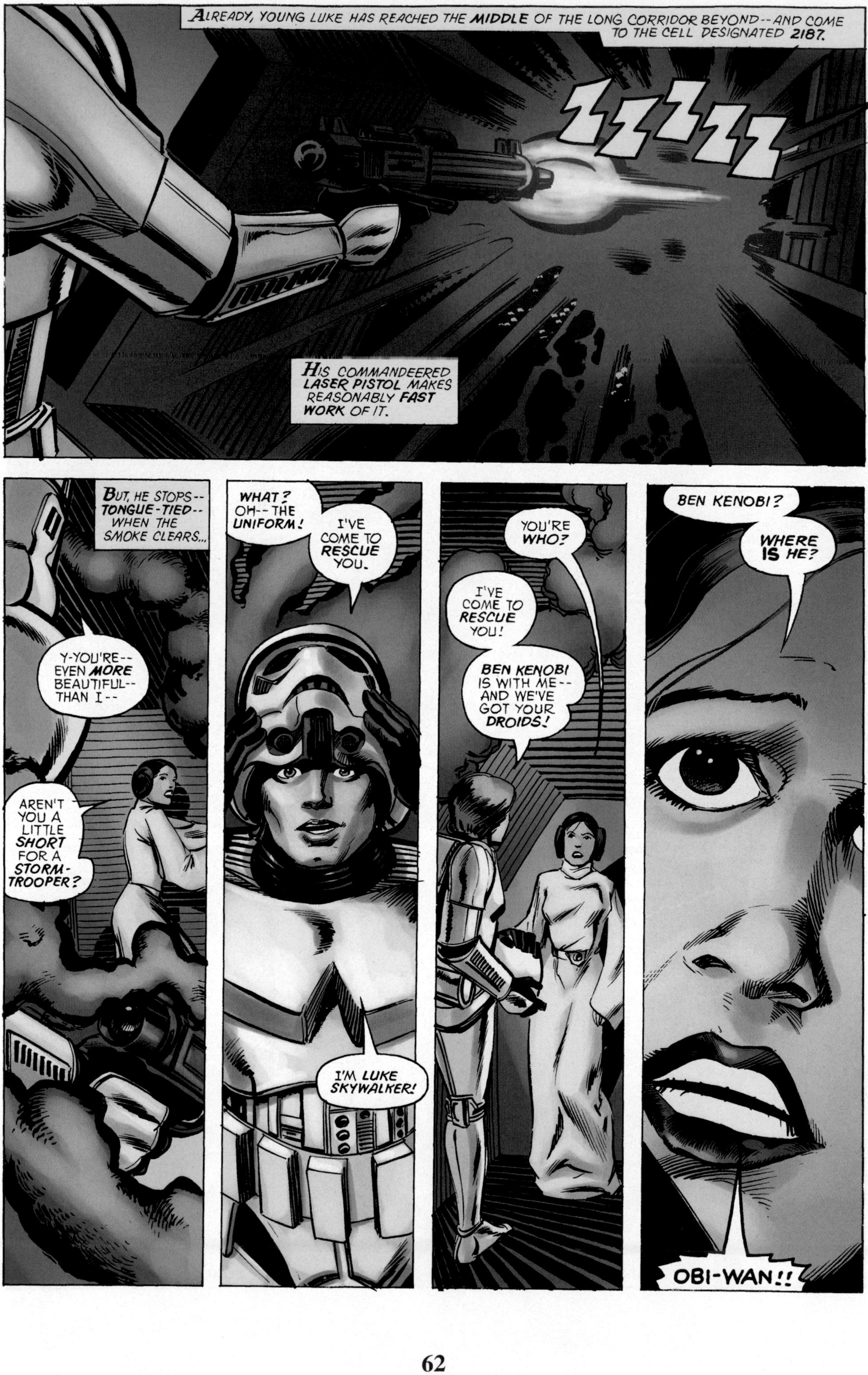
ALREADY, YOUNG LUKE HAS REACHED THE MIDDLE OF THE LONG CORRIDOR BEYOND-- AND COME TO THE CELL DESIGNATED 2187.
ZZZZZZ
HIS COMMANDEERED LASER PISTOL MAKES REASONABLY FAST WORK OF IT.
BUT, HE STOPS-- TONGUE-TIED-- WHEN THE SMOKE CLEARS...
Y-YOU'RE-- EVEN MORE BEAUTIFUL-- THAN I--
AREN'T YOU A LITTLE SHORT FOR A STORM-TROOPER?
WHAT? OH-- THE UNIFORM!
I'VE COME TO RESCUE YOU.
I'M LUKE SKYWALKER!
YOU'RE WHO?
I'VE COME TO RESCUE YOU!
BEN KENOBI IS WITH ME-- AND WE'VE GOT YOUR DROIDS!
BEN KENOBI?
WHERE IS HE?
OBI-WAN!!

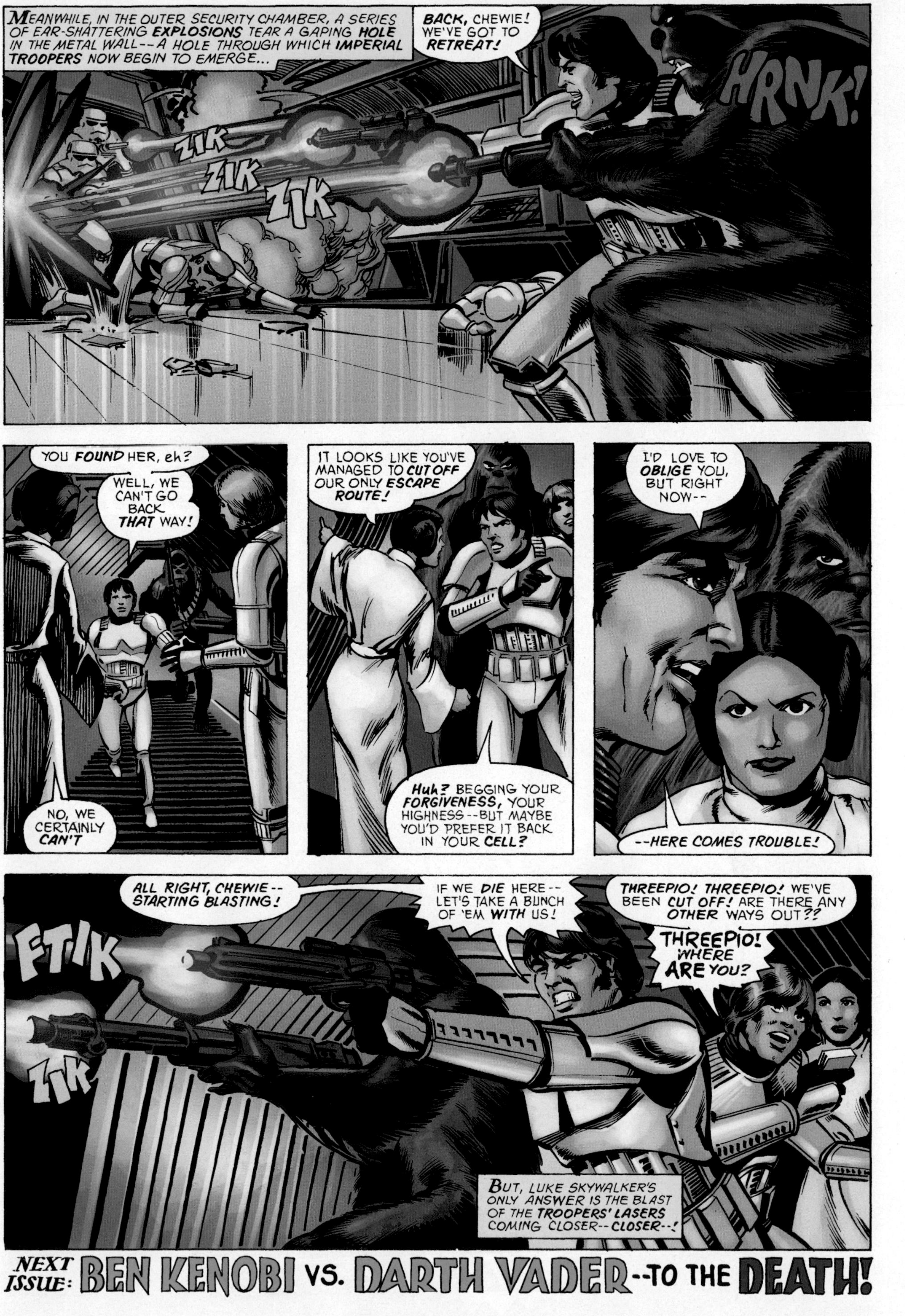
MEANWHILE, IN THE OUTER SECURITY CHAMBER, A SERIES OF EAR-SHATTERING EXPLOSIONS TEAR A GAPING HOLE IN THE METAL WALL-- A HOLE THROUGH WHICH IMPERIAL TROOPERS NOW BEGIN TO EMERGE...
BACK, CHEWIE! WE'VE GOT TO RETREAT!
HRNK!
ZIK
ZIK
ZIK
YOU FOUND HER, eh?
WELL, WE CAN'T GO BACK THAT WAY!
NO, WE CERTAINLY CAN'T
IT LOOKS LIKE YOU'VE MANAGED TO CUT OFF OUR ONLY ESCAPE ROUTE!
Huh? BEGGING YOUR FORGIVENESS, YOUR HIGHNESS--BUT MAYBE YOU'D PREFER IT BACK IN YOUR CELL?
I'D LOVE TO OBLIGE YOU, BUT RIGHT NOW--
--HERE COMES TROUBLE!
ALL RIGHT, CHEWIE-- STARTING BLASTING!
IF WE DIE HERE-- LET'S TAKE A BUNCH OF 'EM WITH US!
THREEPIO! THREEPIO! WE'VE BEEN CUT OFF! ARE THERE ANY OTHER WAYS OUT??
THREEPIO! WHERE ARE YOU?
FTIK
ZIK
BUT, LUKE SKYWALKER'S ONLY ANSWER IS THE BLAST OF THE TROOPERS' LASERS COMING CLOSER--CLOSER--!
NEXT ISSUE: BEN KENOBI VS. DARTH VADER--TO THE DEATH!

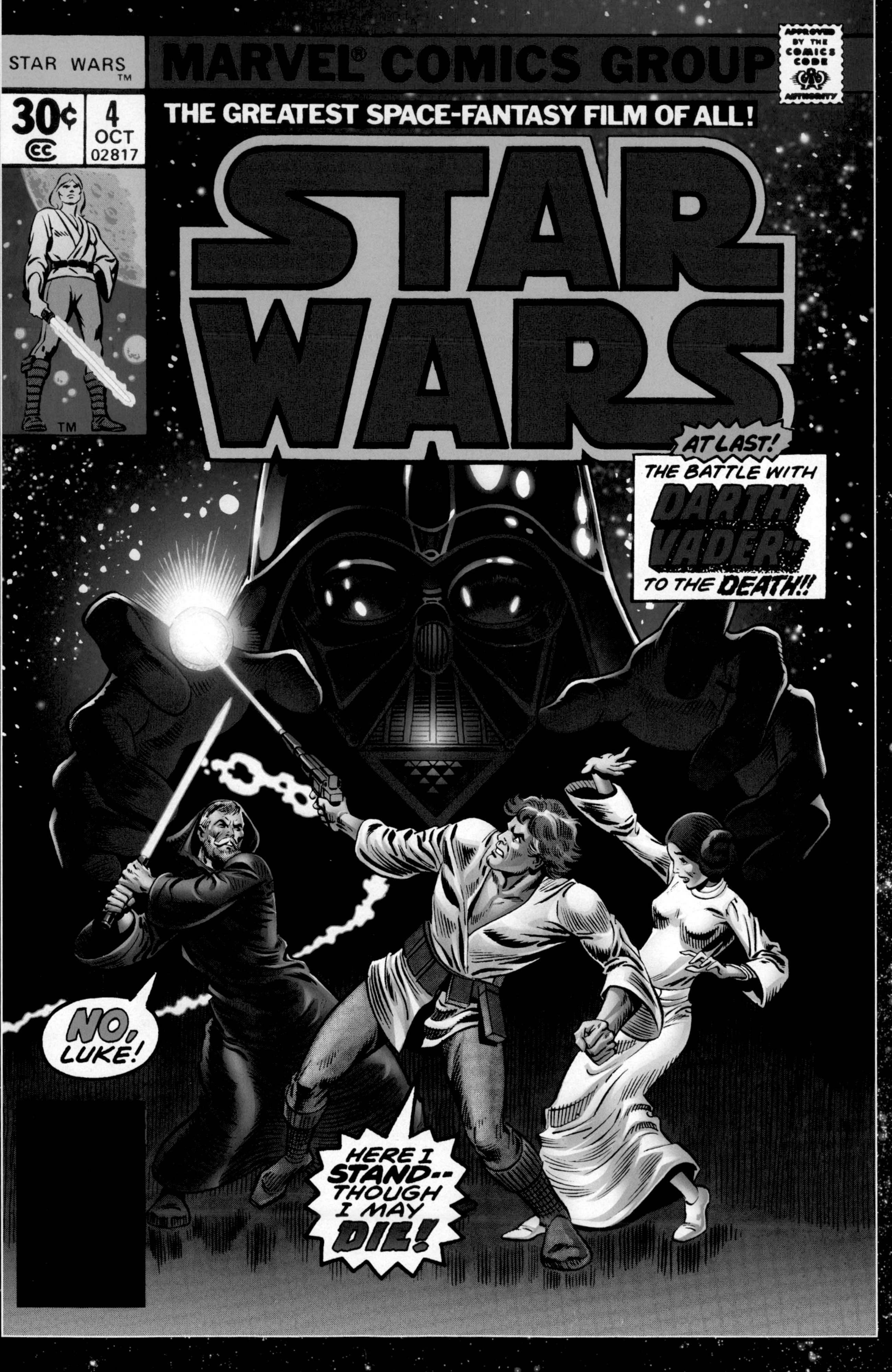
STAR WARS ™
MARVEL® COMICS GROUP
APPROVED BY THE COMICS CODE AUTHORITY
30¢
CC
4
OCT
02817
THE GREATEST SPACE-FANTASY FILM OF ALL!
STAR WARS
TM
AT LAST!
THE BATTLE WITH DARTH VADER -- TO THE DEATH!!
NO, LUKE!
HERE I STAND-- THOUGH I MAY DIE!

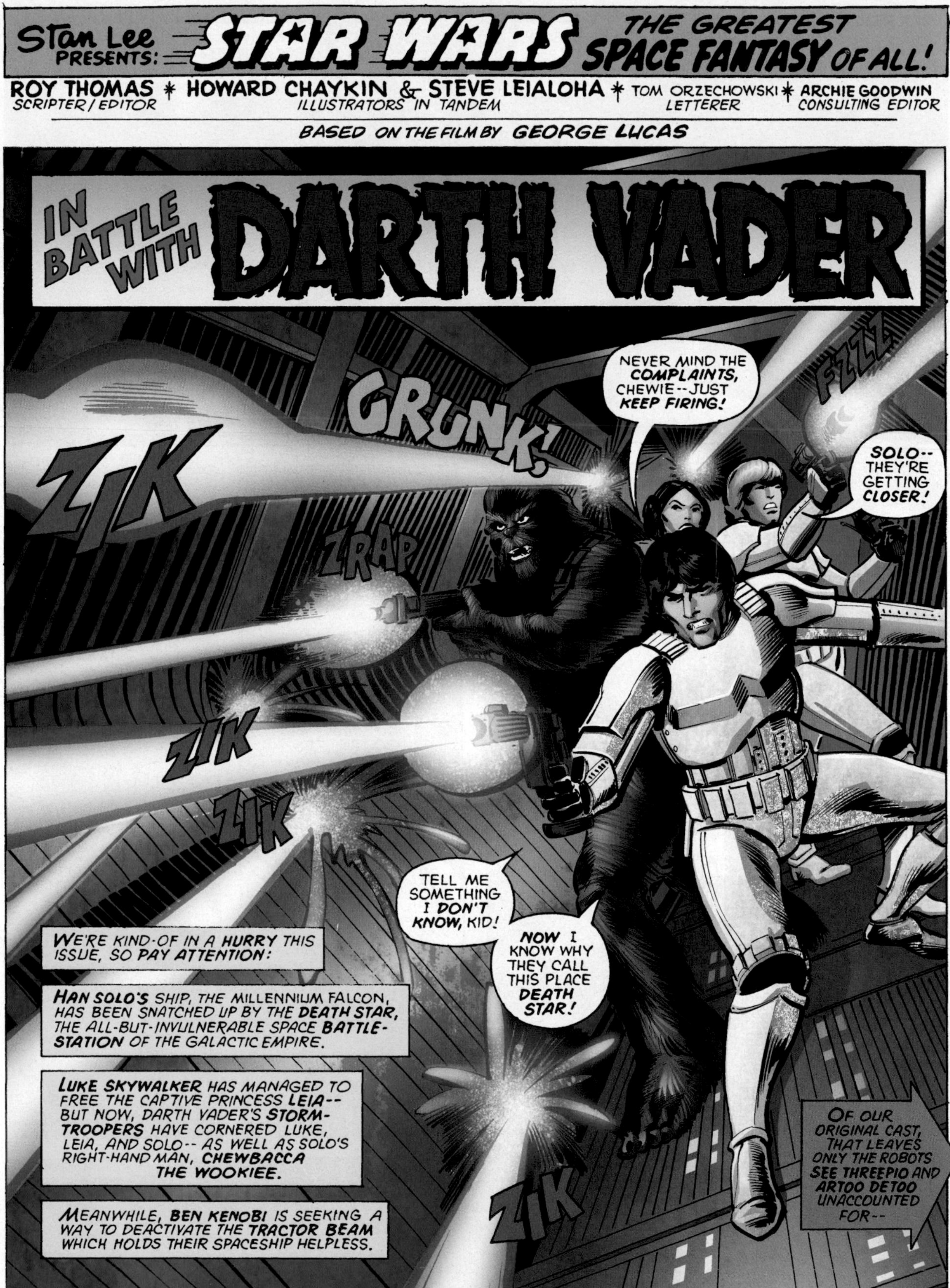

Stan Lee PRESENTS: STAR WARS THE GREATEST SPACE FANTASY OF ALL!
ROY THOMAS SCRIPTER/EDITOR * HOWARD CHAYKIN & STEVE LEIALOHA ILLUSTRATORS IN TANDEM * TOM ORZECHOWSKI LETTERER * ARCHIE GOODWIN CONSULTING EDITOR
BASED ON THE FILM BY GEORGE LUCAS
IN BATTLE WITH DARTH VADER
GRUNK!
NEVER MIND THE COMPLAINTS, CHEWIE--JUST KEEP FIRING!
FZZZZ
SOLO--THEY'RE GETTING CLOSER!
ZIK
ZRAP
ZIK
ZIK
TELL ME SOMETHING I DON'T KNOW, KID!
NOW I KNOW WHY THEY CALL THIS PLACE DEATH STAR!
WE'RE KIND-OF IN A HURRY THIS ISSUE, SO PAY ATTENTION:
HAN SOLO'S SHIP, THE MILLENNIUM FALCON, HAS BEEN SNATCHED UP BY THE DEATH STAR, THE ALL-BUT-INVULNERABLE SPACE BATTLE-STATION OF THE GALACTIC EMPIRE.
LUKE SKYWALKER HAS MANAGED TO FREE THE CAPTIVE PRINCESS LEIA--BUT NOW, DARTH VADER'S STORM-TROOPERS HAVE CORNERED LUKE, LEIA, AND SOLO--AS WELL AS SOLO'S RIGHT-HAND MAN, CHEWBACCA THE WOOKIEE.
MEANWHILE, BEN KENOBI IS SEEKING A WAY TO DEACTIVATE THE TRACTOR BEAM WHICH HOLDS THEIR SPACESHIP HELPLESS.
ZIK
OF OUR ORIGINAL CAST, THAT LEAVES ONLY THE ROBOTS SEE THREEPIO AND ARTOO DETOO UNACCOUNTED FOR--

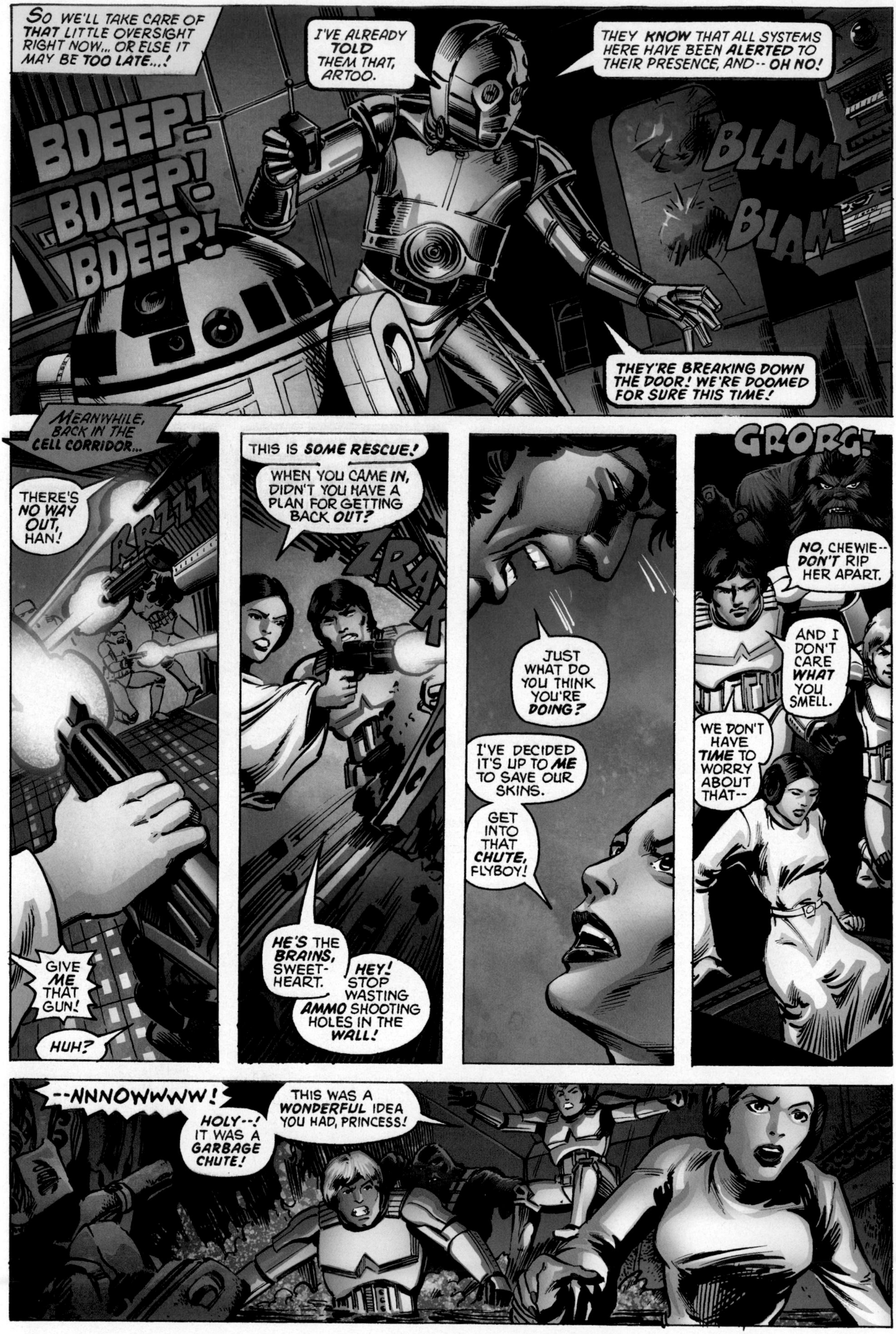

SO WE'LL TAKE CARE OF THAT LITTLE OVERSIGHT RIGHT NOW... OR ELSE IT MAY BE TOO LATE...!
BDEEP! - BDEEP! - BDEEP!
I'VE ALREADY TOLD THEM THAT, ARTOO.
THEY KNOW THAT ALL SYSTEMS HERE HAVE BEEN ALERTED TO THEIR PRESENCE, AND-- OH NO!
BLAM
BLAM
THEY'RE BREAKING DOWN THE DOOR! WE'RE DOOMED FOR SURE THIS TIME!
MEANWHILE, BACK IN THE CELL CORRIDOR...
THERE'S NO WAY OUT, HAN!
GIVE ME THAT GUN!
HUH?
THIS IS SOME RESCUE!
WHEN YOU CAME IN, DIDN'T YOU HAVE A PLAN FOR GETTING BACK OUT?
ZRAK
HE'S THE BRAINS, SWEETHEART.
HEY! STOP WASTING AMMO SHOOTING HOLES IN THE WALL!
JUST WHAT DO YOU THINK YOU'RE DOING?
I'VE DECIDED IT'S UP TO ME TO SAVE OUR SKINS.
GET INTO THAT CHUTE, FLYBOY!
GRORG!
NO, CHEWIE-- DON'T RIP HER APART.
AND I DON'T CARE WHAT YOU SMELL.
WE DON'T HAVE TIME TO WORRY ABOUT THAT--
--NNNOWWWW!
HOLY--! IT WAS A GARBAGE CHUTE!
THIS WAS A WONDERFUL IDEA YOU HAD, PRINCESS!

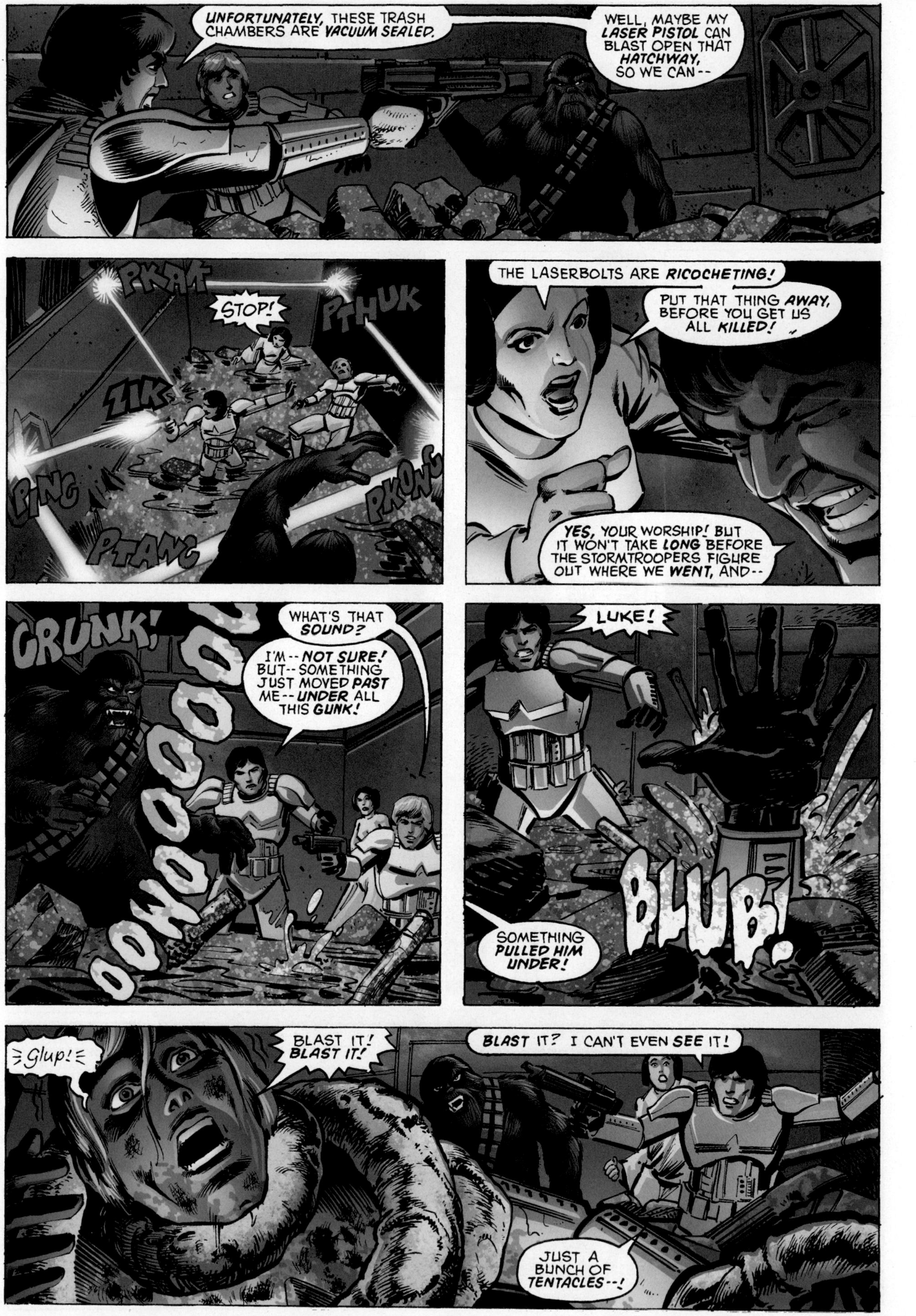
UNFORTUNATELY, THESE TRASH CHAMBERS ARE VACUUM SEALED.
WELL, MAYBE MY LASER PISTOL CAN BLAST OPEN THAT HATCHWAY, SO WE CAN--
PKAK
STOP!
PTHUK
ZIK
PING
PTANG
PKONG
THE LASERBOLTS ARE RICOCHETING!
PUT THAT THING AWAY, BEFORE YOU GET US ALL KILLED!
YES, YOUR WORSHIP! BUT IT WON'T TAKE LONG BEFORE THE STORMTROOPERS FIGURE OUT WHERE WE WENT, AND--
CRUNK!
WHAT'S THAT SOUND?
I'M--NOT SURE! BUT--SOMETHING JUST MOVED PAST ME--UNDER ALL THIS GUNK!
LUKE!
BLUB!
SOMETHING PULLED HIM UNDER!
Glup!
BLAST IT! BLAST IT!
BLAST IT? I CAN'T EVEN SEE IT!
JUST A BUNCH OF TENTACLES--!

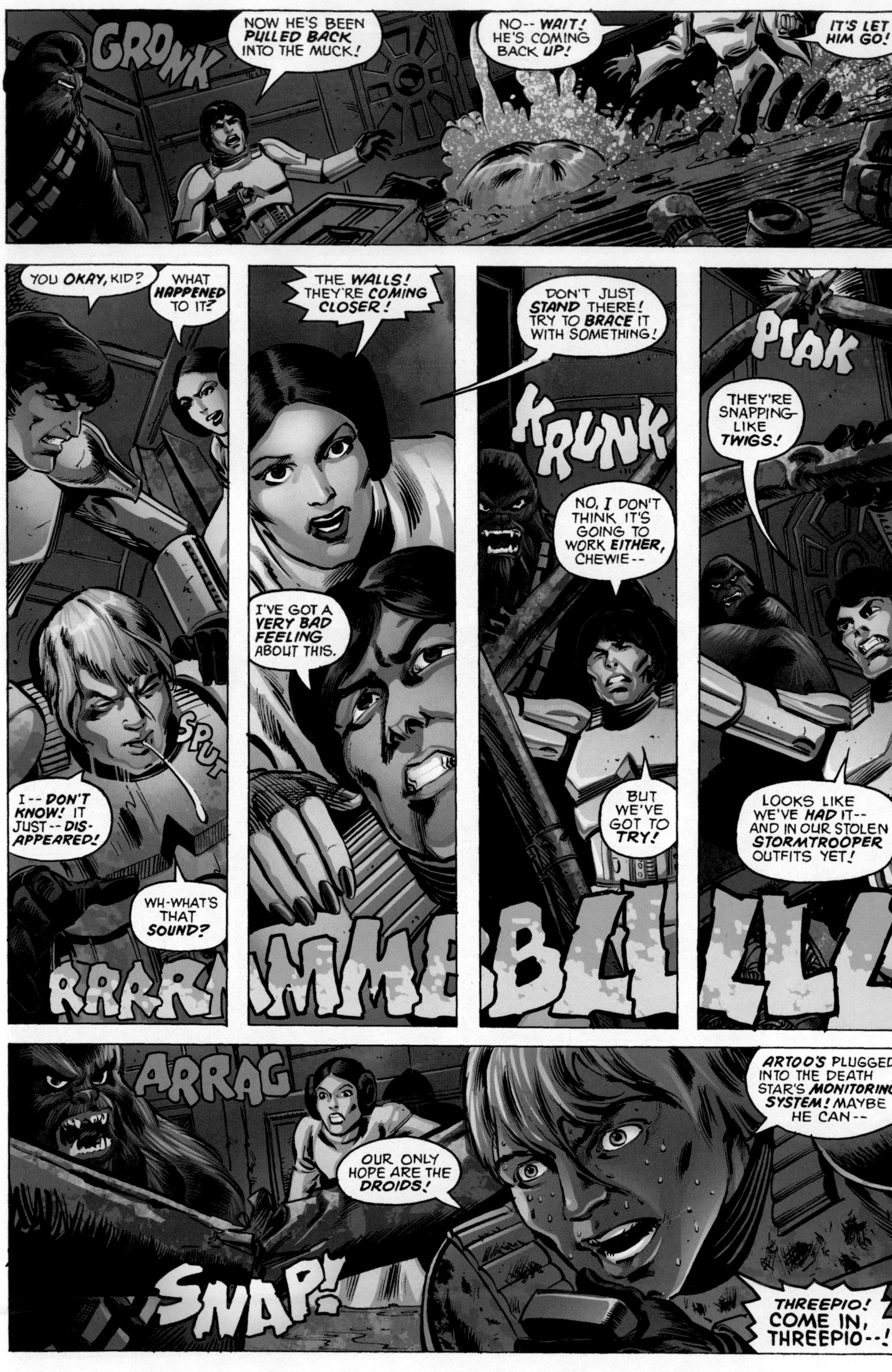
GRONK
NOW HE'S BEEN PULLED BACK INTO THE MUCK!
NO-- WAIT! HE'S COMING BACK UP!
IT'S LET HIM GO!
YOU OKAY, KID?
WHAT HAPPENED TO IT?
I -- DON'T KNOW! IT JUST -- DIS-APPEARED!
SPUT
WH-WHAT'S THAT SOUND?
THE WALLS! THEY'RE COMING CLOSER!
I'VE GOT A VERY BAD FEELING ABOUT THIS.
DON'T JUST STAND THERE! TRY TO BRACE IT WITH SOMETHING!
KRUNK
NO, I DON'T THINK IT'S GOING TO WORK EITHER, CHEWIE--
BUT WE'VE GOT TO TRY!
PTAK
THEY'RE SNAPPING-- LIKE TWIGS!
LOOKS LIKE WE'VE HAD IT-- AND IN OUR STOLEN STORMTROOPER OUTFITS YET!
RRRRMMBBLLL
ARRAG
OUR ONLY HOPE ARE THE DROIDS!
ARTOO'S PLUGGED INTO THE DEATH STAR'S MONITORING SYSTEM! MAYBE HE CAN--
SNAP!
THREEPIO! COME IN, THREEPIO--!

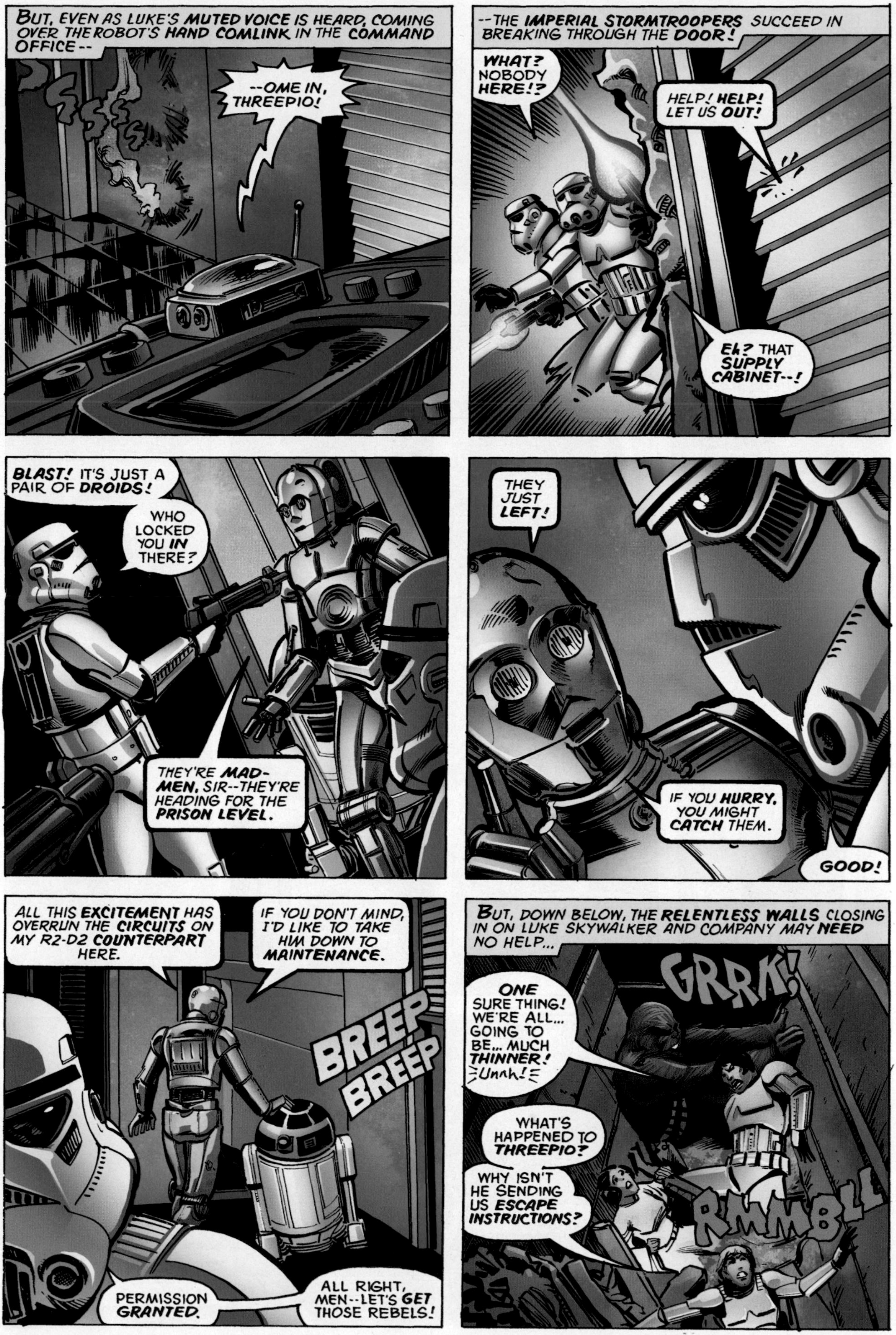

BUT, EVEN AS LUKE'S MUTED VOICE IS HEARD, COMING OVER THE ROBOT'S HAND COMLINK IN THE COMMAND OFFICE--
SSSSS
--OME IN, THREEPIO!
--THE IMPERIAL STORMTROOPERS SUCCEED IN BREAKING THROUGH THE DOOR!
WHAT? NOBODY HERE!?
HELP! HELP! LET US OUT!
Eh? THAT SUPPLY CABINET--!
BLAST! IT'S JUST A PAIR OF DROIDS!
WHO LOCKED YOU IN THERE?
THEY'RE MAD-MEN, SIR--THEY'RE HEADING FOR THE PRISON LEVEL.
THEY JUST LEFT!
IF YOU HURRY, YOU MIGHT CATCH THEM.
GOOD!
ALL THIS EXCITEMENT HAS OVERRUN THE CIRCUITS ON MY R2-D2 COUNTERPART HERE.
IF YOU DON'T MIND, I'D LIKE TO TAKE HIM DOWN TO MAINTENANCE.
BREEP BREEP
PERMISSION GRANTED.
ALL RIGHT, MEN--LET'S GET THOSE REBELS!
BUT, DOWN BELOW, THE RELENTLESS WALLS CLOSING IN ON LUKE SKYWALKER AND COMPANY MAY NEED NO HELP...
GRRK!
ONE SURE THING! WE'RE ALL... GOING TO BE... MUCH THINNER! Unnh!
WHAT'S HAPPENED TO THREEPIO?
WHY ISN'T HE SENDING US ESCAPE INSTRUCTIONS?
RMMBLL

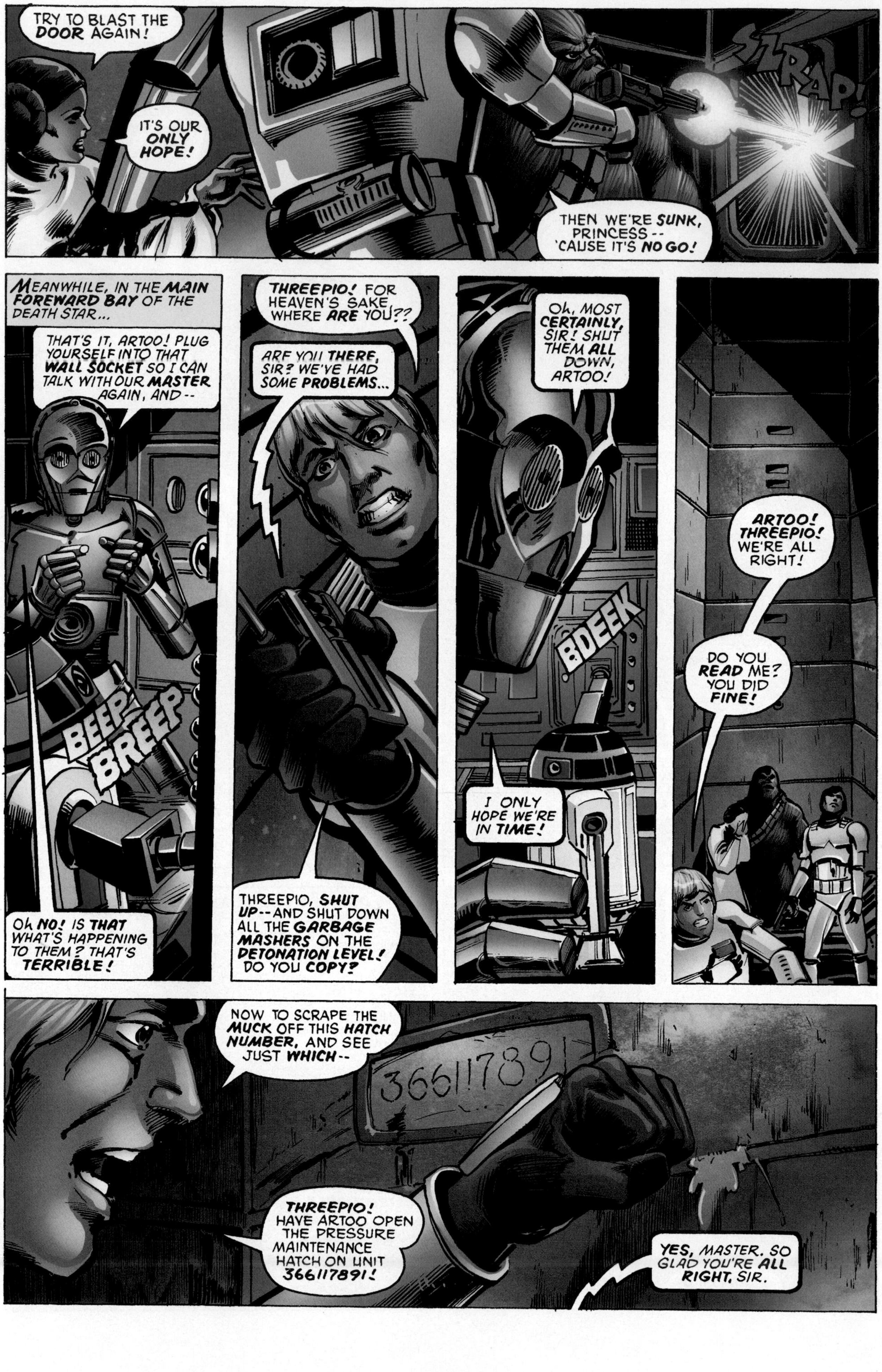
TRY TO BLAST THE DOOR AGAIN!
IT'S OUR ONLY HOPE!
SKRAP!
THEN WE'RE SUNK, PRINCESS -- 'CAUSE IT'S NO GO!
MEANWHILE, IN THE MAIN FOREWARD BAY OF THE DEATH STAR...
THAT'S IT, ARTOO! PLUG YOURSELF INTO THAT WALL SOCKET SO I CAN TALK WITH OUR MASTER AGAIN, AND --
BEEP BREEP
Oh NO! IS THAT WHAT'S HAPPENING TO THEM? THAT'S TERRIBLE!
THREEPIO! FOR HEAVEN'S SAKE WHERE ARE YOU??
ARE YOU THERE, SIR? WE'VE HAD SOME PROBLEMS...
THREEPIO, SHUT UP-- AND SHUT DOWN ALL THE GARBAGE MASHERS ON THE DETONATION LEVEL! DO YOU COPY?
Oh, MOST CERTAINLY, SIR! SHUT THEM ALL DOWN, ARTOO!
BDEEK
I ONLY HOPE WE'RE IN TIME!
ARTOO! THREEPIO! WE'RE ALL RIGHT!
DO YOU READ ME? YOU DID FINE!
NOW TO SCRAPE THE MUCK OFF THIS HATCH NUMBER, AND SEE JUST WHICH --
3661789
THREEPIO! HAVE ARTOO OPEN THE PRESSURE MAINTENANCE HATCH ON UNIT 366117891!
YES, MASTER. SO GLAD YOU'RE ALL RIGHT, SIR.

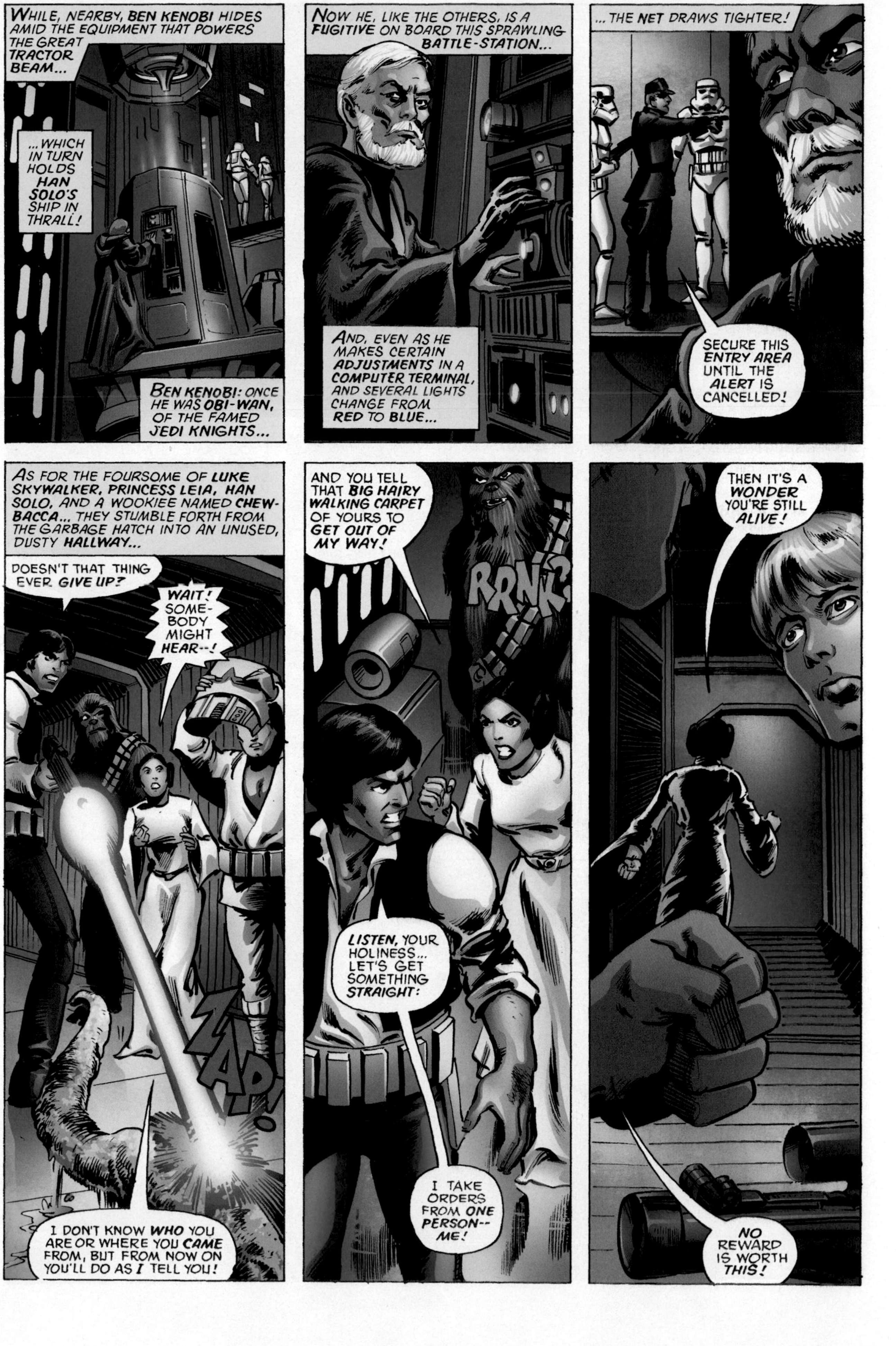
WHILE, NEARBY, BEN KENOBI HIDES AMID THE EQUIPMENT THAT POWERS THE GREAT TRACTOR BEAM...
...WHICH IN TURN HOLDS HAN SOLO'S SHIP IN THRALL!
BEN KENOBI: ONCE HE WAS OBI-WAN, OF THE FAMED JEDI KNIGHTS...
NOW HE, LIKE THE OTHERS, IS A FUGITIVE ON BOARD THIS SPRAWLING BATTLE-STATION...
AND, EVEN AS HE MAKES CERTAIN ADJUSTMENTS IN A COMPUTER TERMINAL, AND SEVERAL LIGHTS CHANGE FROM RED TO BLUE...
...THE NET DRAWS TIGHTER!
SECURE THIS ENTRY AREA UNTIL THE ALERT IS CANCELLED!
AS FOR THE FOURSOME OF LUKE SKYWALKER, PRINCESS LEIA, HAN SOLO, AND A WOOKIEE NAMED CHEWBACCA... THEY STUMBLE FORTH FROM THE GARBAGE HATCH INTO AN UNUSED, DUSTY HALLWAY...
DOESN'T THAT THING EVER GIVE UP?
WAIT! SOMEBODY MIGHT HEAR--!
ZAP!
I DON'T KNOW WHO YOU ARE OR WHERE YOU CAME FROM, BUT FROM NOW ON YOU'LL DO AS I TELL YOU!
AND YOU TELL THAT BIG HAIRY WALKING CARPET OF YOURS TO GET OUT OF MY WAY!
RRNK!
LISTEN, YOUR HOLINESS... LET'S GET SOMETHING STRAIGHT:
I TAKE ORDERS FROM ONE PERSON-- ME!
THEN IT'S A WONDER YOU'RE STILL ALIVE!
NO REWARD IS WORTH THIS!

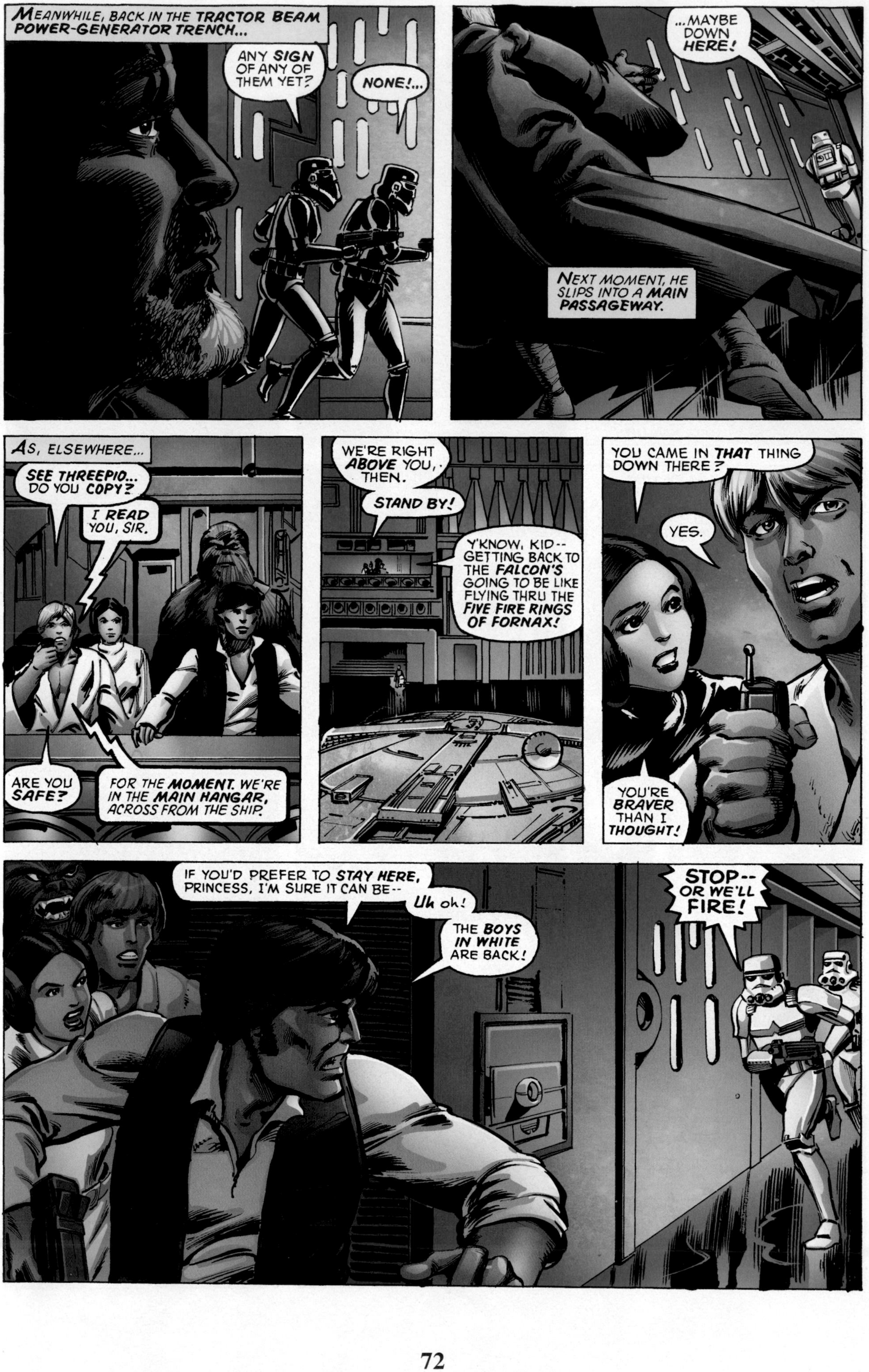
MEANWHILE, BACK IN THE TRACTOR BEAM POWER-GENERATOR TRENCH...
ANY SIGN OF ANY OF THEM YET?
NONE!...
...MAYBE DOWN HERE!
NEXT MOMENT, HE SLIPS INTO A MAIN PASSAGEWAY.
AS, ELSEWHERE...
SEE THREEPIO... DO YOU COPY?
I READ YOU, SIR.
ARE YOU SAFE?
FOR THE MOMENT. WE'RE IN THE MAIN HANGAR, ACROSS FROM THE SHIP.
WE'RE RIGHT ABOVE YOU, THEN.
STAND BY!
Y'KNOW, KID-- GETTING BACK TO THE FALCON'S GOING TO BE LIKE FLYING THRU THE FIVE FIRE RINGS OF FORNAX!
YOU CAME IN THAT THING DOWN THERE?
YES.
YOU'RE BRAVER THAN I THOUGHT!
IF YOU'D PREFER TO STAY HERE, PRINCESS, I'M SURE IT CAN BE--
Uh oh!
THE BOYS IN WHITE ARE BACK!
STOP-- OR WE'LL FIRE!

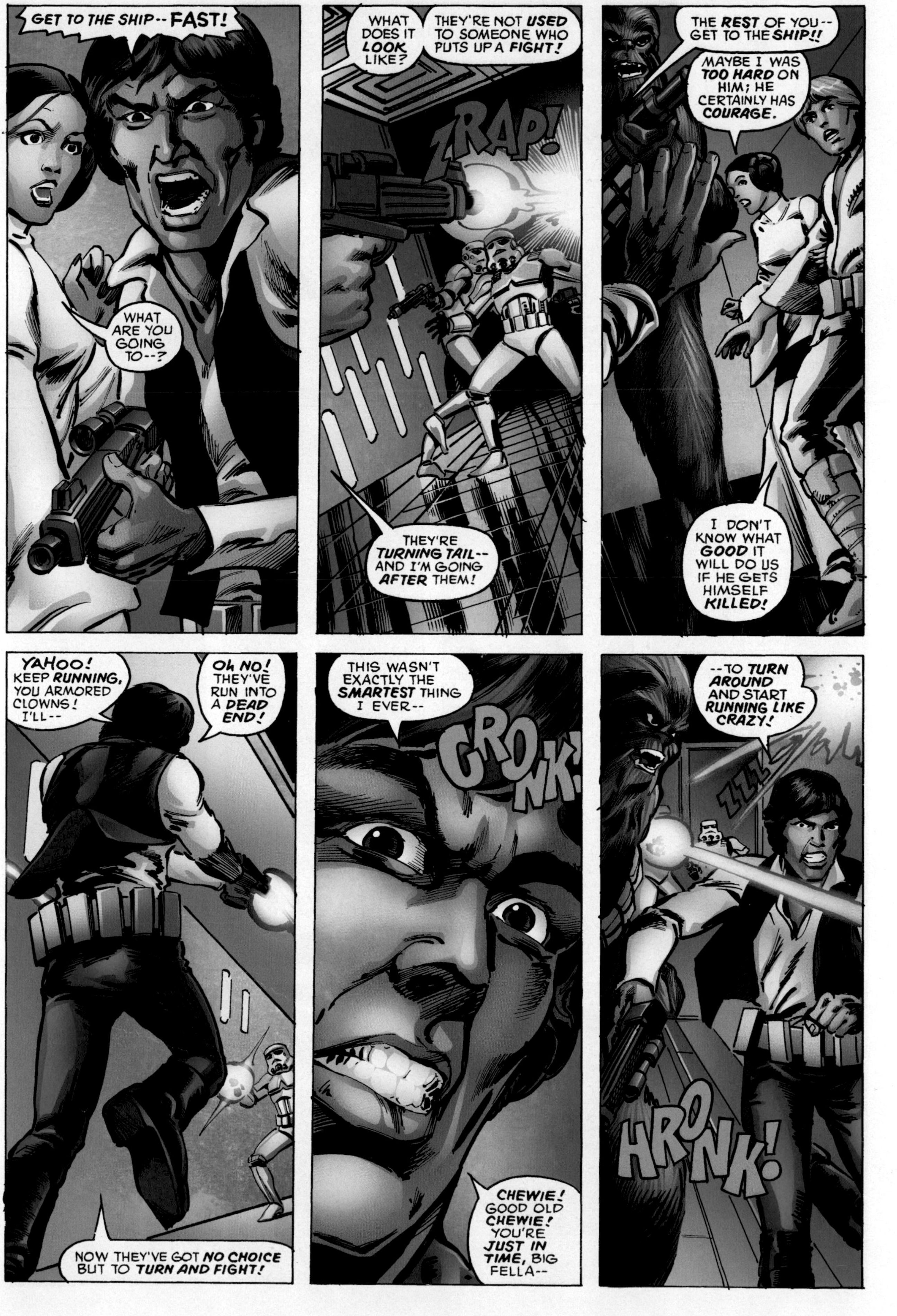
GET TO THE SHIP-- FAST!
WHAT ARE YOU GOING TO--?
WHAT DOES IT LOOK LIKE?
THEY'RE NOT USED TO SOMEONE WHO PUTS UP A FIGHT!
ZRAP!
THEY'RE TURNING TAIL-- AND I'M GOING AFTER THEM!
THE REST OF YOU-- GET TO THE SHIP!!
MAYBE I WAS TOO HARD ON HIM; HE CERTAINLY HAS COURAGE.
I DON'T KNOW WHAT GOOD IT WILL DO US IF HE GETS HIMSELF KILLED!
YAHOO! KEEP RUNNING, YOU ARMORED CLOWNS! I'LL--
Oh NO! THEY'VE RUN INTO A DEAD END!
NOW THEY'VE GOT NO CHOICE BUT TO TURN AND FIGHT!
THIS WASN'T EXACTLY THE SMARTEST THING I EVER--
CRONK!
CHEWIE! GOOD OLD CHEWIE! YOU'RE JUST IN TIME, BIG FELLA--
--TO TURN AROUND AND START RUNNING LIKE CRAZY!
HRONK!

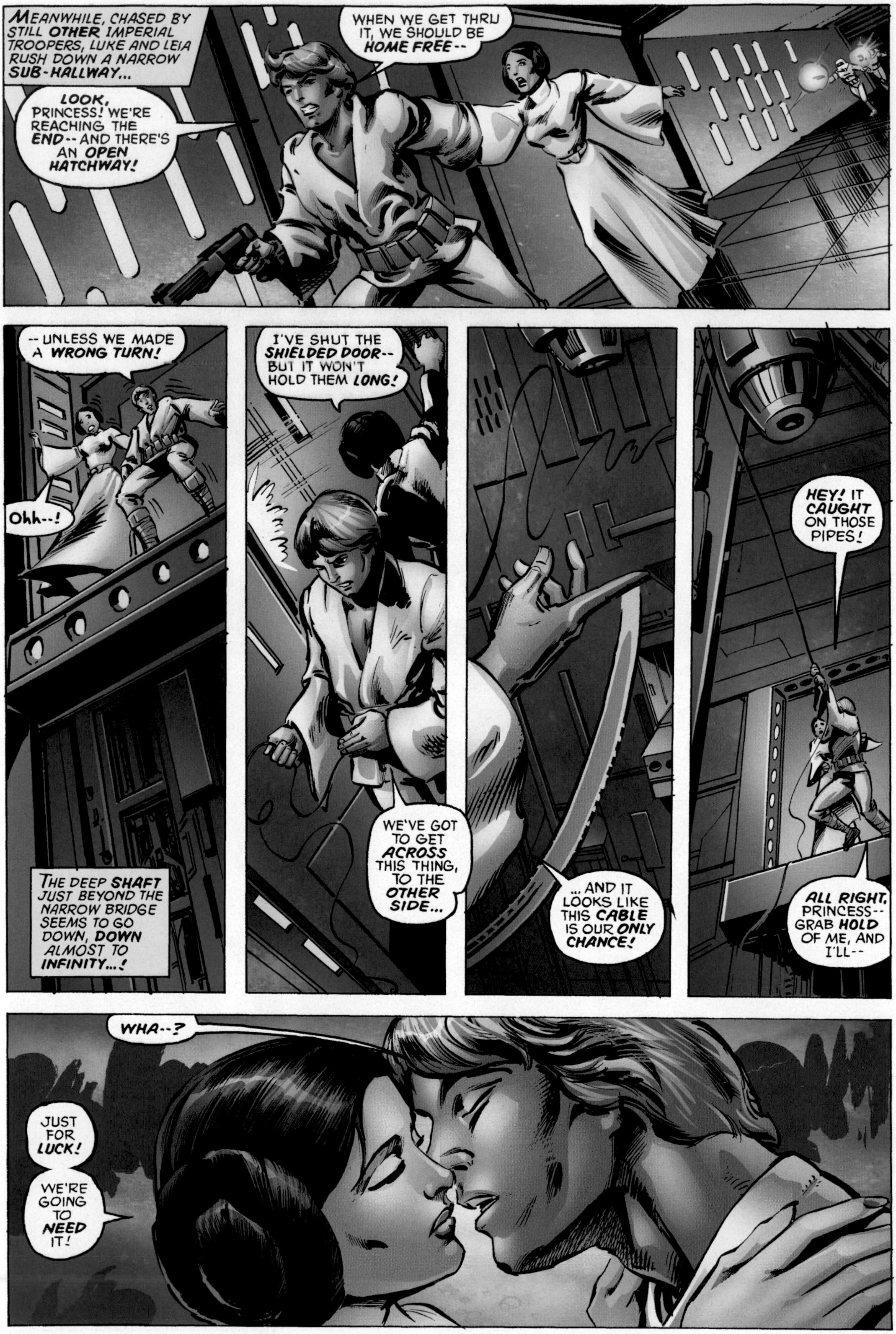

MEANWHILE, CHASED BY STILL OTHER IMPERIAL TROOPERS, LUKE AND LEIA RUSH DOWN A NARROW SUB-HALLWAY...
WHEN WE GET THRU IT, WE SHOULD BE HOME FREE--
LOOK, PRINCESS! WE'RE REACHING THE END--AND THERE'S AN OPEN HATCHWAY!
--UNLESS WE MADE A WRONG TURN!
Ohh--!
THE DEEP SHAFT JUST BEYOND THE NARROW BRIDGE SEEMS TO GO DOWN, DOWN ALMOST TO INFINITY...!
I'VE SHUT THE SHIELDED DOOR--BUT IT WON'T HOLD THEM LONG!
WE'VE GOT TO GET ACROSS THIS THING, TO THE OTHER SIDE...
...AND IT LOOKS LIKE THIS CABLE IS OUR ONLY CHANCE!
HEY! IT CAUGHT ON THOSE PIPES!
ALL RIGHT, PRINCESS--GRAB HOLD OF ME, AND I'LL--
WHA--?
JUST FOR LUCK!
WE'RE GOING TO NEED IT!

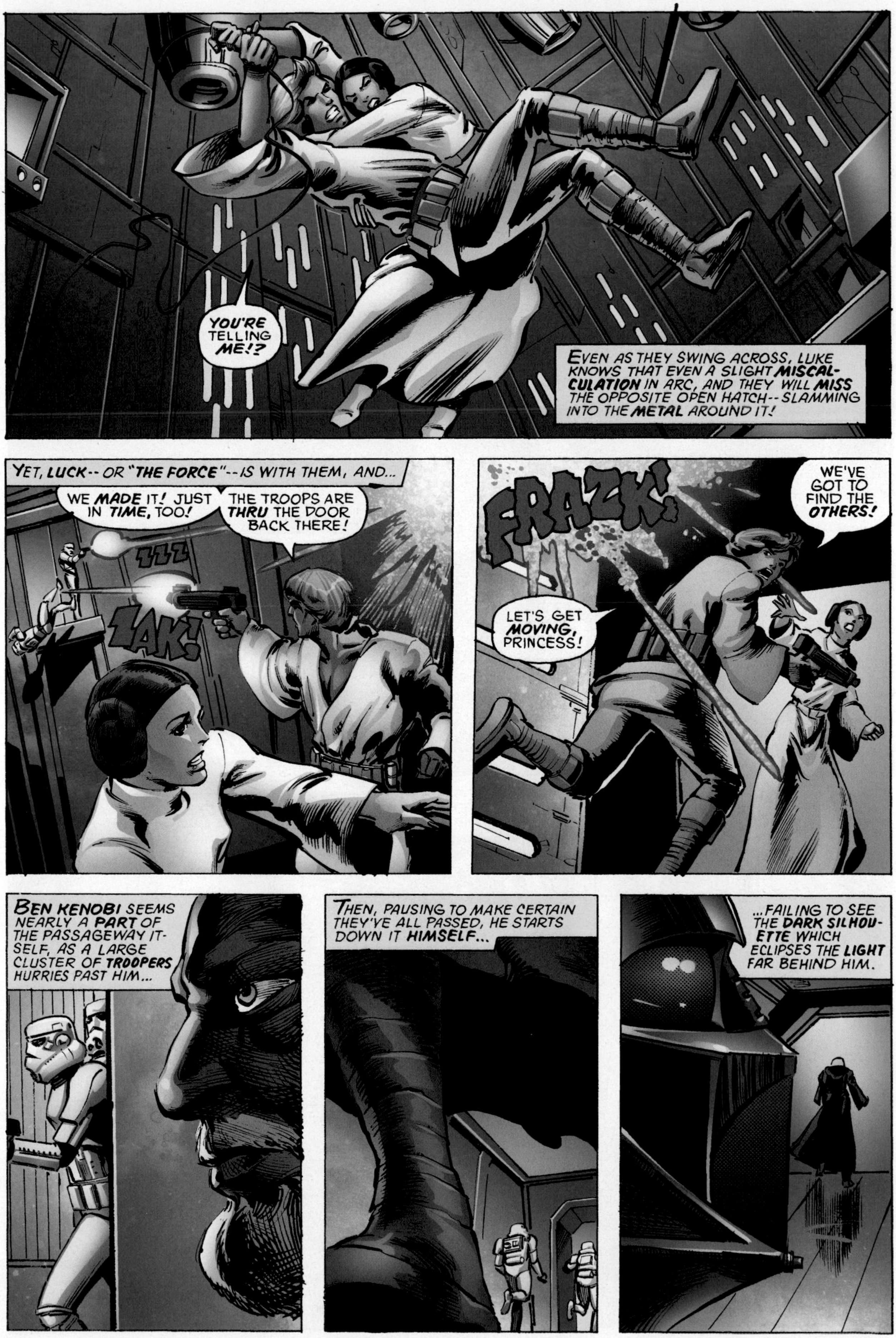
YOU'RE TELLING ME!?
EVEN AS THEY SWING ACROSS, LUKE KNOWS THAT EVEN A SLIGHT MISCALCULATION IN ARC, AND THEY WILL MISS THE OPPOSITE OPEN HATCH-- SLAMMING INTO THE METAL AROUND IT!
YET, LUCK-- OR "THE FORCE"--IS WITH THEM, AND...
WE MADE IT! JUST IN TIME, TOO!
THE TROOPS ARE THRU THE DOOR BACK THERE!
ZZZ
ZAK!
FRAZK!
WE'VE GOT TO FIND THE OTHERS!
LET'S GET MOVING, PRINCESS!
BEN KENOBI SEEMS NEARLY A PART OF THE PASSAGEWAY ITSELF, AS A LARGE CLUSTER OF TROOPERS HURRIES PAST HIM...
THEN, PAUSING TO MAKE CERTAIN THEY'VE ALL PASSED, HE STARTS DOWN IT HIMSELF...
...FAILING TO SEE THE DARK SILHOUETTE WHICH ECLIPSES THE LIGHT FAR BEHIND HIM.

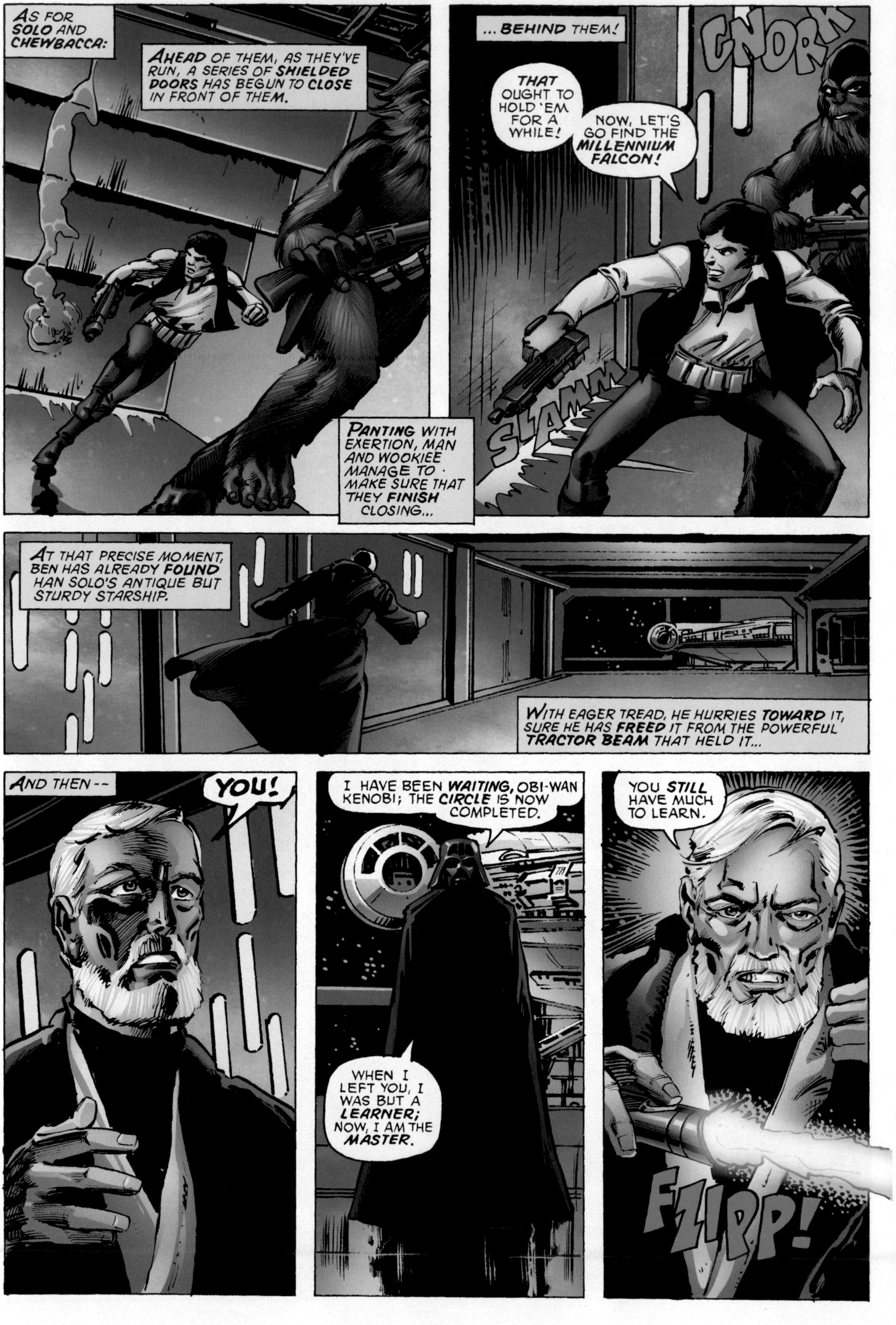
AS FOR SOLO AND CHEWBACCA:
AHEAD OF THEM, AS THEY'VE RUN, A SERIES OF SHIELDED DOORS HAS BEGUN TO CLOSE IN FRONT OF THEM.
PANTING WITH EXERTION, MAN AND WOOKIEE MANAGE TO MAKE SURE THAT THEY FINISH CLOSING...
SLAMM
...BEHIND THEM!
CNORK
THAT OUGHT TO HOLD 'EM FOR A WHILE!
NOW, LET'S GO FIND THE MILLENNIUM FALCON!
AT THAT PRECISE MOMENT, BEN HAS ALREADY FOUND HAN SOLO'S ANTIQUE BUT STURDY STARSHIP.
WITH EAGER TREAD, HE HURRIES TOWARD IT, SURE HE HAS FREED IT FROM THE POWERFUL TRACTOR BEAM THAT HELD IT...
AND THEN--
YOU!
I HAVE BEEN WAITING, OBI-WAN KENOBI; THE CIRCLE IS NOW COMPLETED.
WHEN I LEFT YOU, I WAS BUT A LEARNER; NOW, I AM THE MASTER.
YOU STILL HAVE MUCH TO LEARN.
FZIPP!

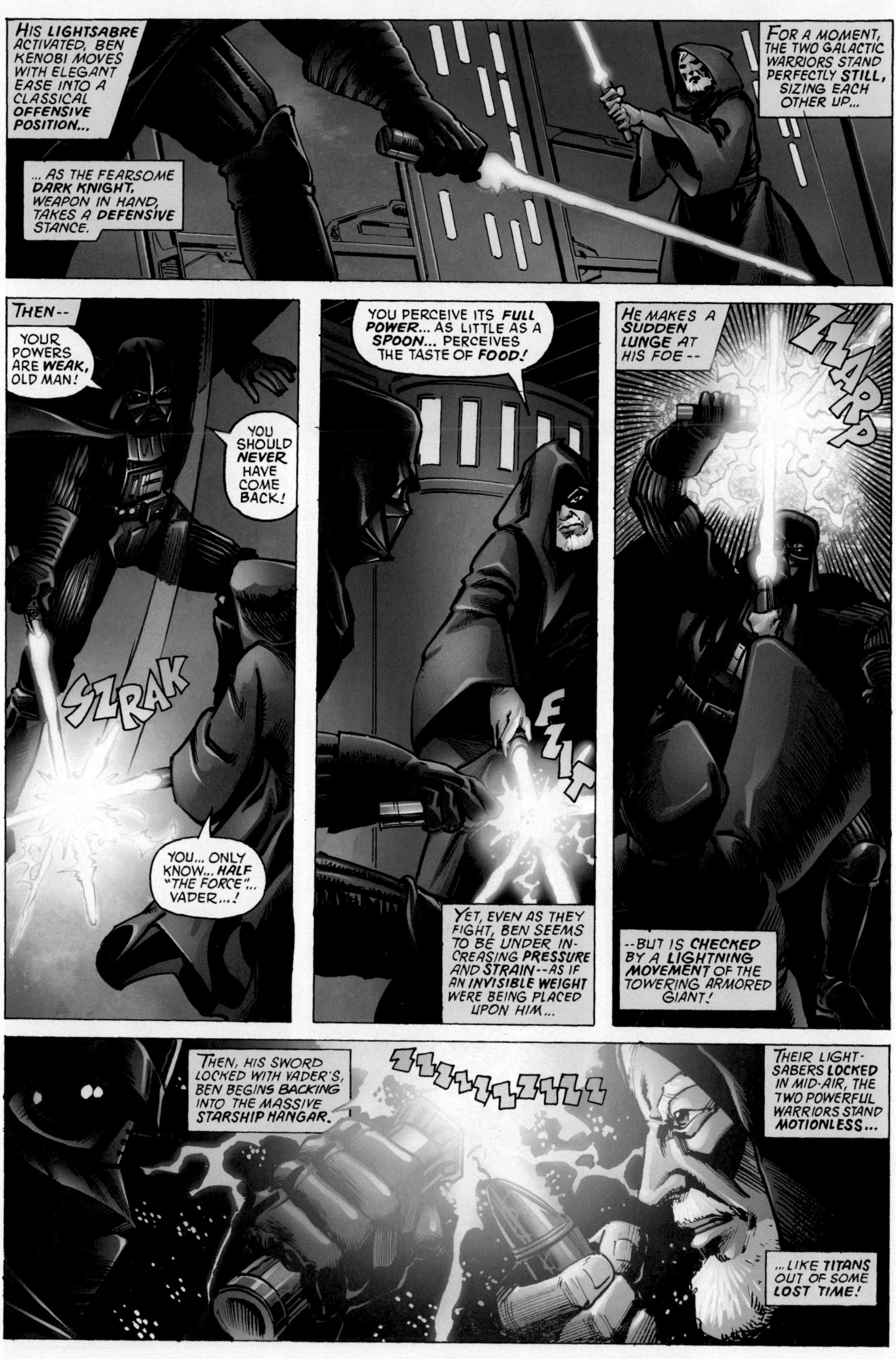
HIS LIGHTSABRE ACTIVATED, BEN KENOBI MOVES WITH ELEGANT EASE INTO A CLASSICAL OFFENSIVE POSITION...
... AS THE FEARSOME DARK KNIGHT, WEAPON IN HAND, TAKES A DEFENSIVE STANCE.
FOR A MOMENT, THE TWO GALACTIC WARRIORS STAND PERFECTLY STILL, SIZING EACH OTHER UP...
THEN--
YOUR POWERS ARE WEAK, OLD MAN!
YOU SHOULD NEVER HAVE COME BACK!
SZRAK
YOU... ONLY KNOW... HALF "THE FORCE"... VADER...!
YOU PERCEIVE ITS FULL POWER... AS LITTLE AS A SPOON... PERCEIVES THE TASTE OF FOOD!
FZZIT
YET, EVEN AS THEY FIGHT, BEN SEEMS TO BE UNDER IN-CREASING PRESSURE AND STRAIN--AS IF AN INVISIBLE WEIGHT WERE BEING PLACED UPON HIM...
HE MAKES A SUDDEN LUNGE AT HIS FOE --
ZZARP
--BUT IS CHECKED BY A LIGHTNING MOVEMENT OF THE TOWERING ARMORED GIANT!
THEN, HIS SWORD LOCKED WITH VADER'S, BEN BEGINS BACKING INTO THE MASSIVE STARSHIP HANGAR.
ZZZZZZZZZZZZZ
THEIR LIGHT-SABERS LOCKED IN MID-AIR, THE TWO POWERFUL WARRIORS STAND MOTIONLESS...
...LIKE TITANS OUT OF SOME LOST TIME!

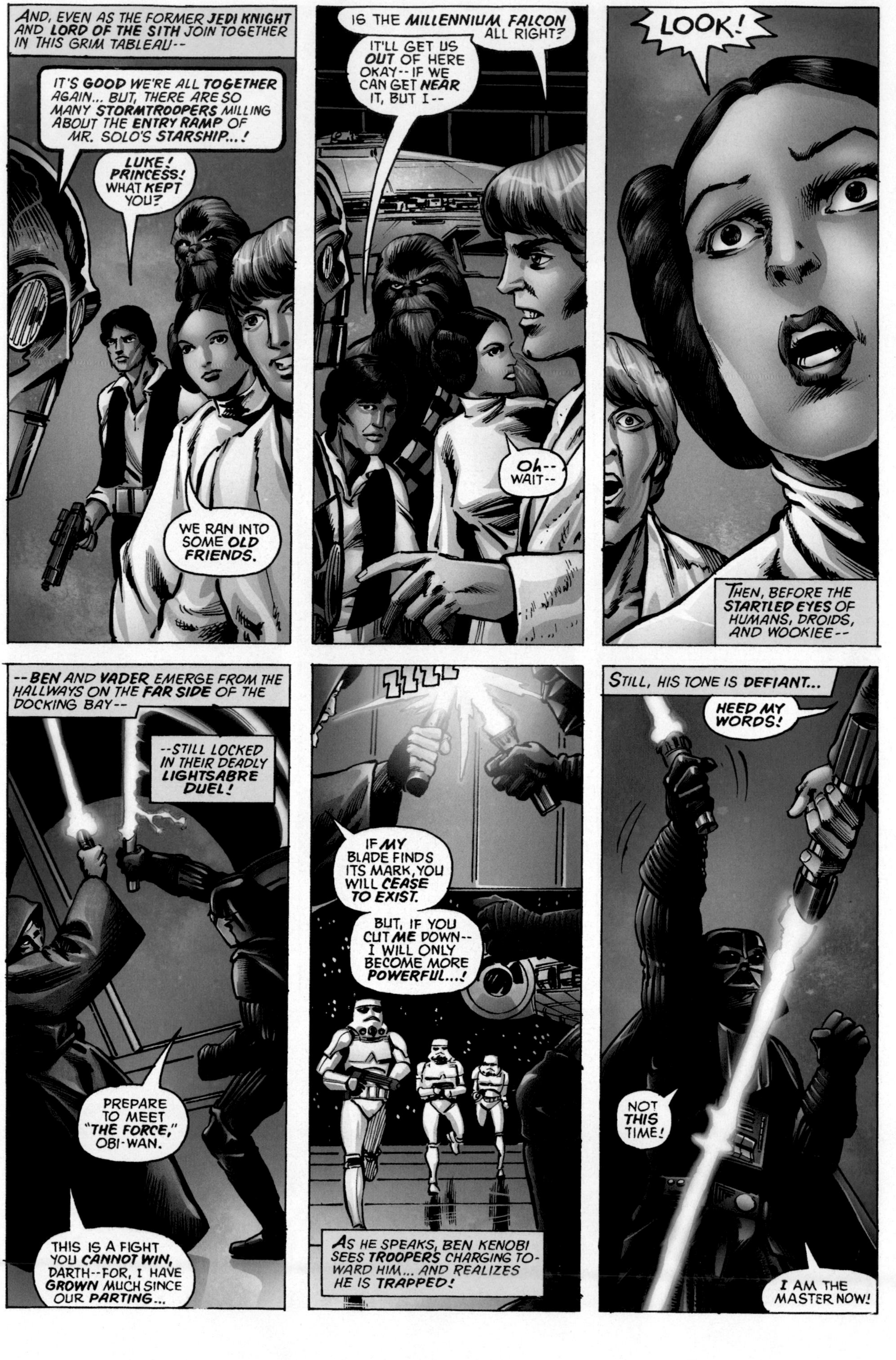

AND, EVEN AS THE FORMER JEDI KNIGHT AND LORD OF THE SITH JOIN TOGETHER IN THIS GRIM TABLEAU--
IT'S GOOD WE'RE ALL TOGETHER AGAIN... BUT, THERE ARE SO MANY STORMTROOPERS MILLING ABOUT THE ENTRY RAMP OF MR. SOLO'S STARSHIP...!
LUKE! PRINCESS! WHAT KEPT YOU?
WE RAN INTO SOME OLD FRIENDS.
IS THE MILLENNIUM FALCON ALL RIGHT?
IT'LL GET US OUT OF HERE OKAY-- IF WE CAN GET NEAR IT, BUT I--
Oh-- WAIT--
LOOK!
THEN, BEFORE THE STARTLED EYES OF HUMANS, DROIDS, AND WOOKIEE--
--BEN AND VADER EMERGE FROM THE HALLWAYS ON THE FAR SIDE OF THE DOCKING BAY--
--STILL LOCKED IN THEIR DEADLY LIGHTSABRE DUEL!
PREPARE TO MEET "THE FORCE," OBI-WAN.
THIS IS A FIGHT YOU CANNOT WIN, DARTH--FOR, I HAVE GROWN MUCH SINCE OUR PARTING...
IF MY BLADE FINDS ITS MARK, YOU WILL CEASE TO EXIST.
BUT, IF YOU CUT ME DOWN-- I WILL ONLY BECOME MORE POWERFUL...!
AS HE SPEAKS, BEN KENOBI SEES TROOPERS CHARGING TOWARD HIM... AND REALIZES HE IS TRAPPED!
STILL, HIS TONE IS DEFIANT...
HEED MY WORDS!
NOT THIS TIME!
I AM THE MASTER NOW!

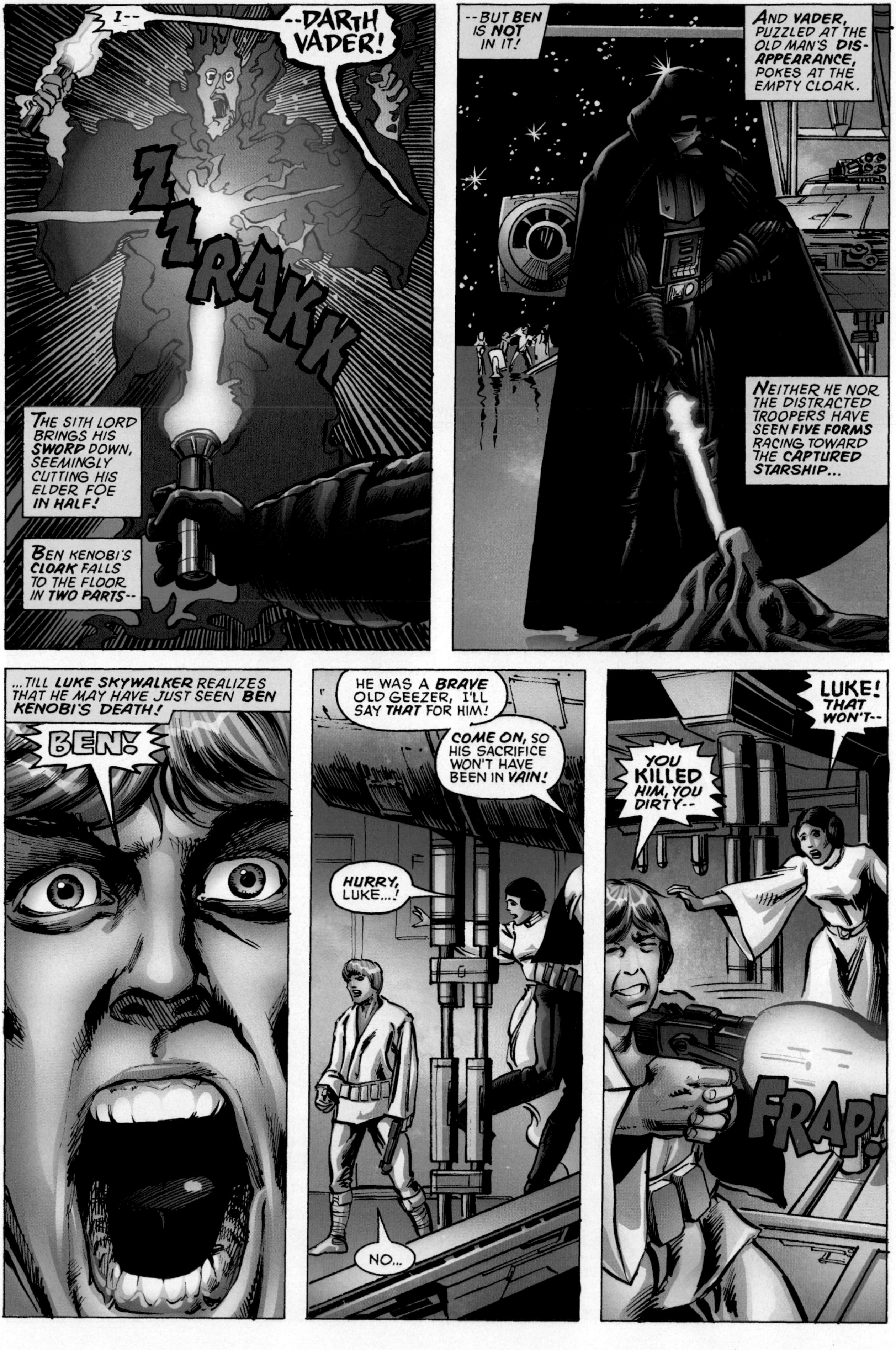
I--
--DARTH VADER!
ZZRAKK
THE SITH LORD BRINGS HIS SWORD DOWN, SEEMINGLY CUTTING HIS ELDER FOE IN HALF!
BEN KENOBI'S CLOAK FALLS TO THE FLOOR IN TWO PARTS--
--BUT BEN IS NOT IN IT!
AND VADER, PUZZLED AT THE OLD MAN'S DISAPPEARANCE, POKES AT THE EMPTY CLOAK.
NEITHER HE NOR THE DISTRACTED TROOPERS HAVE SEEN FIVE FORMS RACING TOWARD THE CAPTURED STARSHIP...
...TILL LUKE SKYWALKER REALIZES THAT HE MAY HAVE JUST SEEN BEN KENOBI'S DEATH!
BEN!
HE WAS A BRAVE OLD GEEZER, I'LL SAY THAT FOR HIM!
COME ON, SO HIS SACRIFICE WON'T HAVE BEEN IN VAIN!
HURRY, LUKE...!
NO...
LUKE! THAT WON'T--
YOU KILLED HIM, YOU DIRTY--
FRAP!

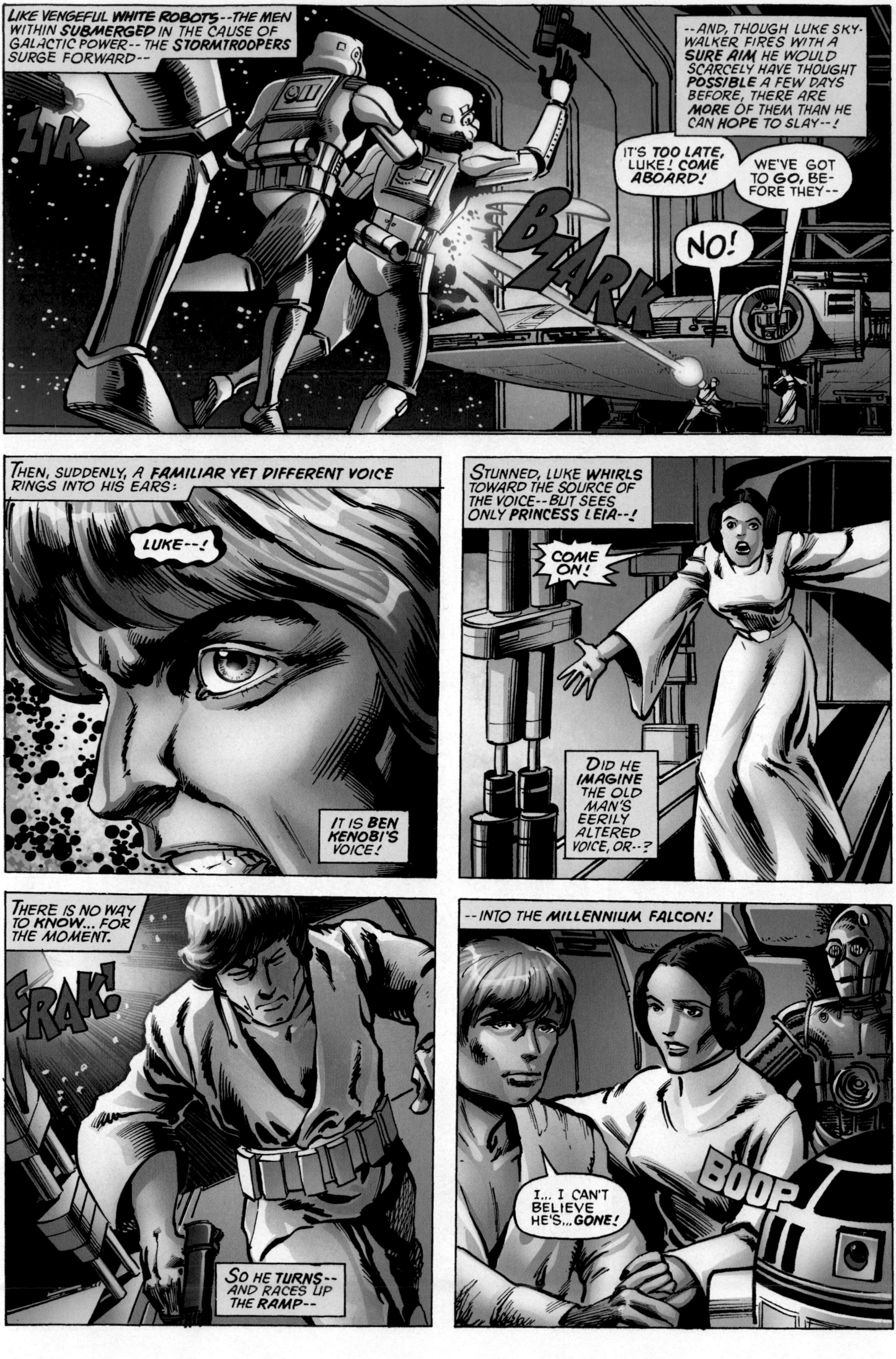
LIKE VENGEFUL WHITE ROBOTS--THE MEN WITHIN SUBMERGED IN THE CAUSE OF GALACTIC POWER--THE STORMTROOPERS SURGE FORWARD--
ZIK
--AND, THOUGH LUKE SKYWALKER FIRES WITH A SURE AIM HE WOULD SCARCELY HAVE THOUGHT POSSIBLE A FEW DAYS BEFORE, THERE ARE MORE OF THEM THAN HE CAN HOPE TO SLAY--!
IT'S TOO LATE, LUKE! COME ABOARD!
WE'VE GOT TO GO, BEFORE THEY--
BZARK
NO!
THEN, SUDDENLY, A FAMILIAR YET DIFFERENT VOICE RINGS INTO HIS EARS:
LUKE--!
IT IS BEN KENOBI'S VOICE!
STUNNED, LUKE WHIRLS TOWARD THE SOURCE OF THE VOICE--BUT SEES ONLY PRINCESS LEIA--!
COME ON!
DID HE IMAGINE THE OLD MAN'S EERILY ALTERED VOICE, OR--?
THERE IS NO WAY TO KNOW... FOR THE MOMENT.
FRAK!
SO HE TURNS--AND RACES UP THE RAMP--
--INTO THE MILLENNIUM FALCON!
BOOP
I... I CAN'T BELIEVE HE'S...GONE!

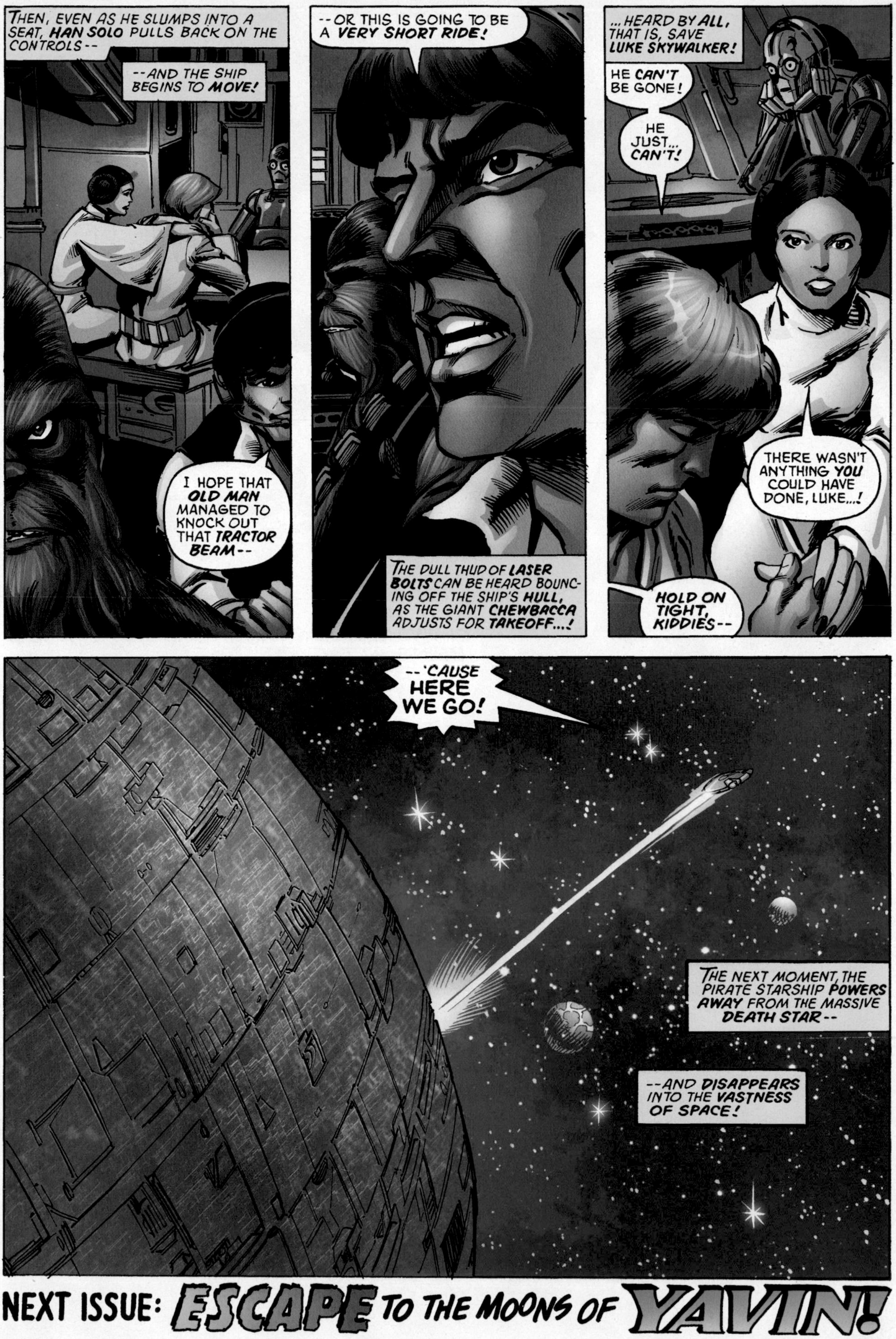
THEN, EVEN AS HE SLUMPS INTO A SEAT, HAN SOLO PULLS BACK ON THE CONTROLS--
--AND THE SHIP BEGINS TO MOVE!
I HOPE THAT OLD MAN MANAGED TO KNOCK OUT THAT TRACTOR BEAM--
--OR THIS IS GOING TO BE A VERY SHORT RIDE!
THE DULL THUD OF LASER BOLTS CAN BE HEARD BOUNCING OFF THE SHIP'S HULL, AS THE GIANT CHEWBACCA ADJUSTS FOR TAKEOFF...!
...HEARD BY ALL, THAT IS, SAVE LUKE SKYWALKER!
HE CAN'T BE GONE!
HE JUST... CAN'T!
THERE WASN'T ANYTHING YOU COULD HAVE DONE, LUKE...!
HOLD ON TIGHT, KIDDIES--
--'CAUSE HERE WE GO!
THE NEXT MOMENT, THE PIRATE STARSHIP POWERS AWAY FROM THE MASSIVE DEATH STAR--
--AND DISAPPEARS INTO THE VASTNESS OF SPACE!

NEXT ISSUE: ESCAPE TO THE MOONS OF YAVIN!

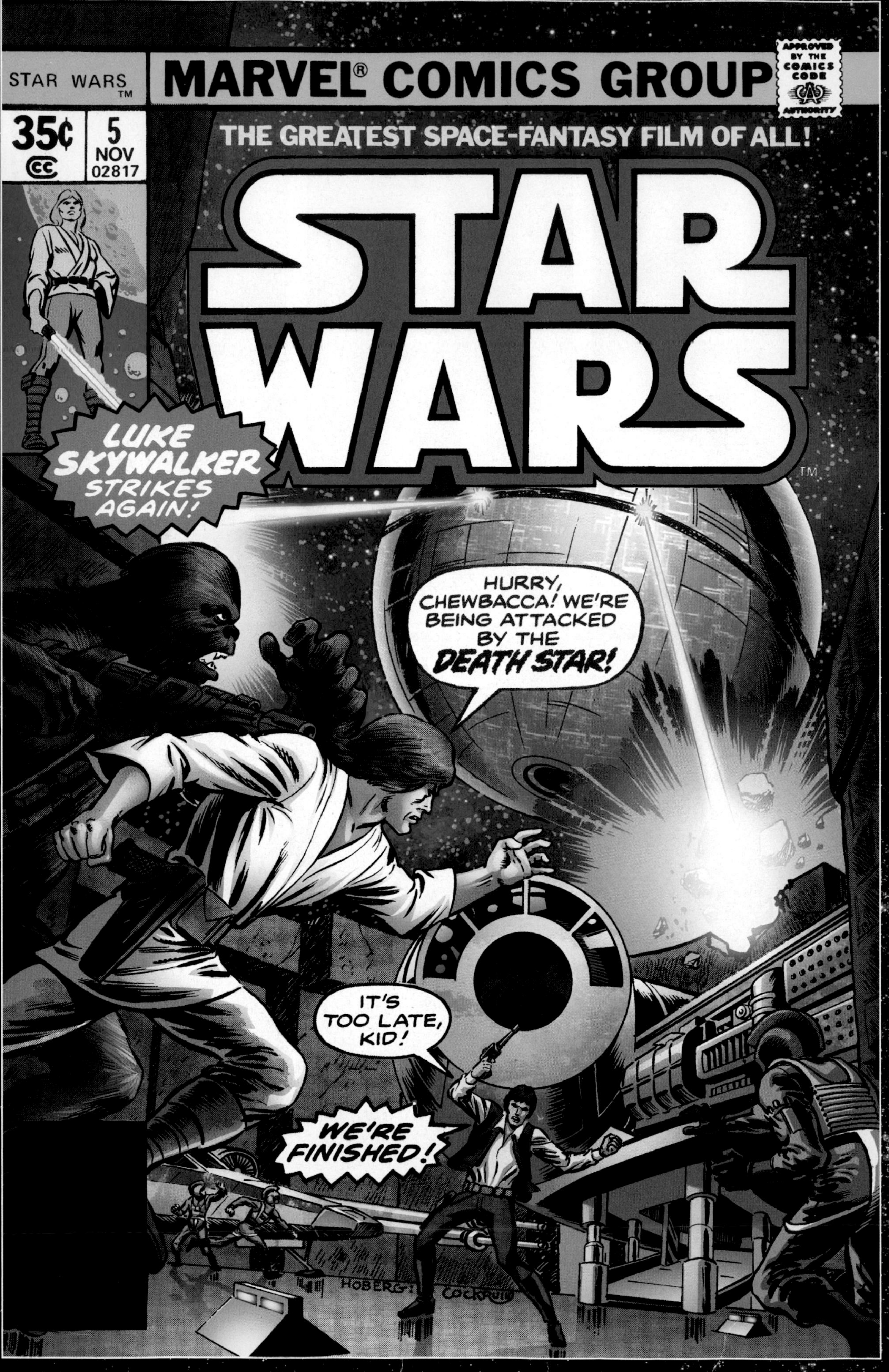

STAR WARS ™
MARVEL® COMICS GROUP
APPROVED BY THE COMICS CODE AUTHORITY
35¢
5 NOV 02817
THE GREATEST SPACE-FANTASY FILM OF ALL!
STAR WARS ™
LUKE SKYWALKER STRIKES AGAIN!
HURRY, CHEWBACCA! WE'RE BEING ATTACKED BY THE DEATH STAR!
IT'S TOO LATE, KID!
WE'RE FINISHED!
HOBERG: COCKRUM

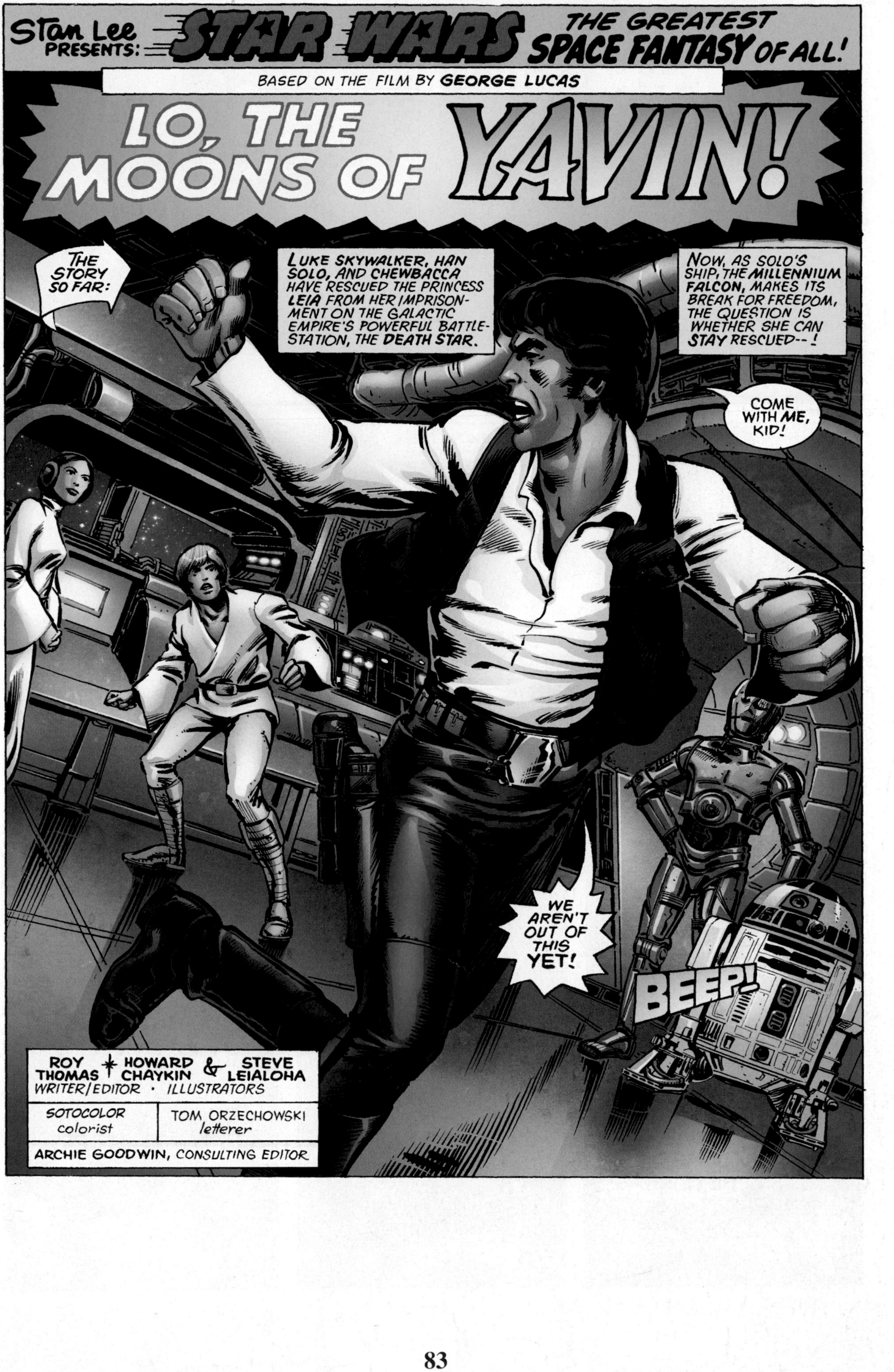
Stan Lee PRESENTS: STAR WARS THE GREATEST SPACE FANTASY OF ALL!
BASED ON THE FILM BY GEORGE LUCAS
LO, THE MOONS OF YAVIN!
THE STORY SO FAR:
LUKE SKYWALKER, HAN SOLO, AND CHEWBACCA HAVE RESCUED THE PRINCESS LEIA FROM HER IMPRISONMENT ON THE GALACTIC EMPIRE'S POWERFUL BATTLE-STATION, THE DEATH STAR.
NOW, AS SOLO'S SHIP, THE MILLENNIUM FALCON, MAKES ITS BREAK FOR FREEDOM, THE QUESTION IS WHETHER SHE CAN STAY RESCUED-- !
COME WITH ME, KID!
WE AREN'T OUT OF THIS YET!
BEEP!
ROY THOMAS WRITER/EDITOR
HOWARD CHAYKIN & STEVE LEIALOHA ILLUSTRATORS
SOTOCOLOR colorist
TOM ORZECHOWSKI letterer
ARCHIE GOODWIN, CONSULTING EDITOR

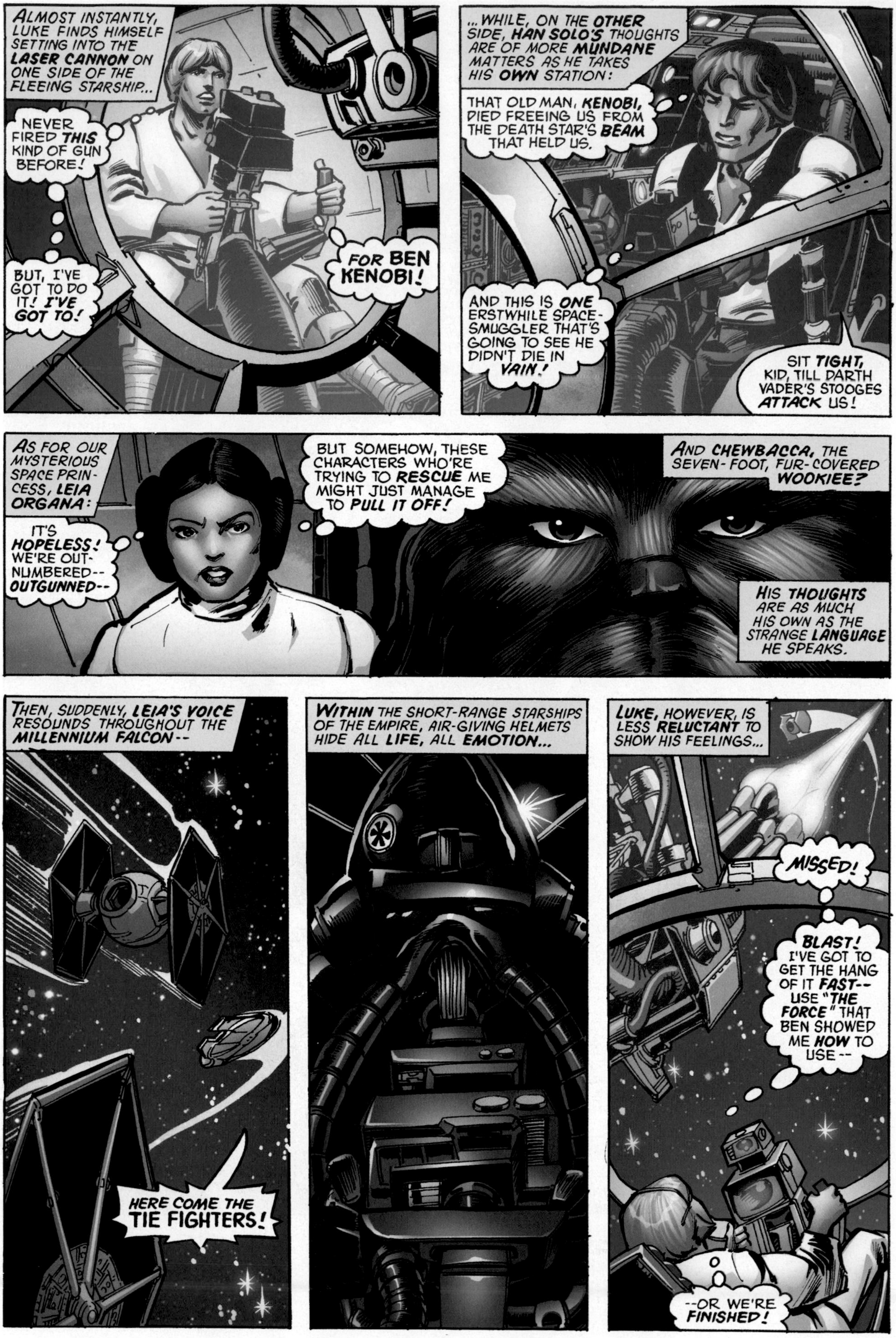

ALMOST INSTANTLY, LUKE FINDS HIMSELF SETTING INTO THE LASER CANNON ON ONE SIDE OF THE FLEEING STARSHIP...
NEVER FIRED THIS KIND OF GUN BEFORE!
BUT, I'VE GOT TO DO IT! I'VE GOT TO!
FOR BEN KENOBI!
...WHILE, ON THE OTHER SIDE, HAN SOLO'S THOUGHTS ARE OF MORE MUNDANE MATTERS AS HE TAKES HIS OWN STATION:
THAT OLD MAN, KENOBI, DIED FREEING US FROM THE DEATH STAR'S BEAM THAT HELD US.
AND THIS IS ONE ERSTWHILE SPACE-SMUGGLER THAT'S GOING TO SEE HE DIDN'T DIE IN VAIN!
SIT TIGHT, KID, TILL DARTH VADER'S STOOGES ATTACK US!
AS FOR OUR MYSTERIOUS SPACE PRINCESS, LEIA ORGANA:
IT'S HOPELESS! WE'RE OUT-NUMBERED-- OUTGUNNED--
BUT SOMEHOW, THESE CHARACTERS WHO'RE TRYING TO RESCUE ME MIGHT JUST MANAGE TO PULL IT OFF!
AND CHEWBACCA, THE SEVEN-FOOT, FUR-COVERED WOOKIEE?
HIS THOUGHTS ARE AS MUCH HIS OWN AS THE STRANGE LANGUAGE HE SPEAKS.
THEN, SUDDENLY, LEIA'S VOICE RESOUNDS THROUGHOUT THE MILLENNIUM FALCON--
HERE COME THE TIE FIGHTERS!
WITHIN THE SHORT-RANGE STARSHIPS OF THE EMPIRE, AIR-GIVING HELMETS HIDE ALL LIFE, ALL EMOTION...
LUKE, HOWEVER, IS LESS RELUCTANT TO SHOW HIS FEELINGS...
MISSED!
BLAST! I'VE GOT TO GET THE HANG OF IT FAST-- USE "THE FORCE" THAT BEN SHOWED ME HOW TO USE--
--OR WE'RE FINISHED!

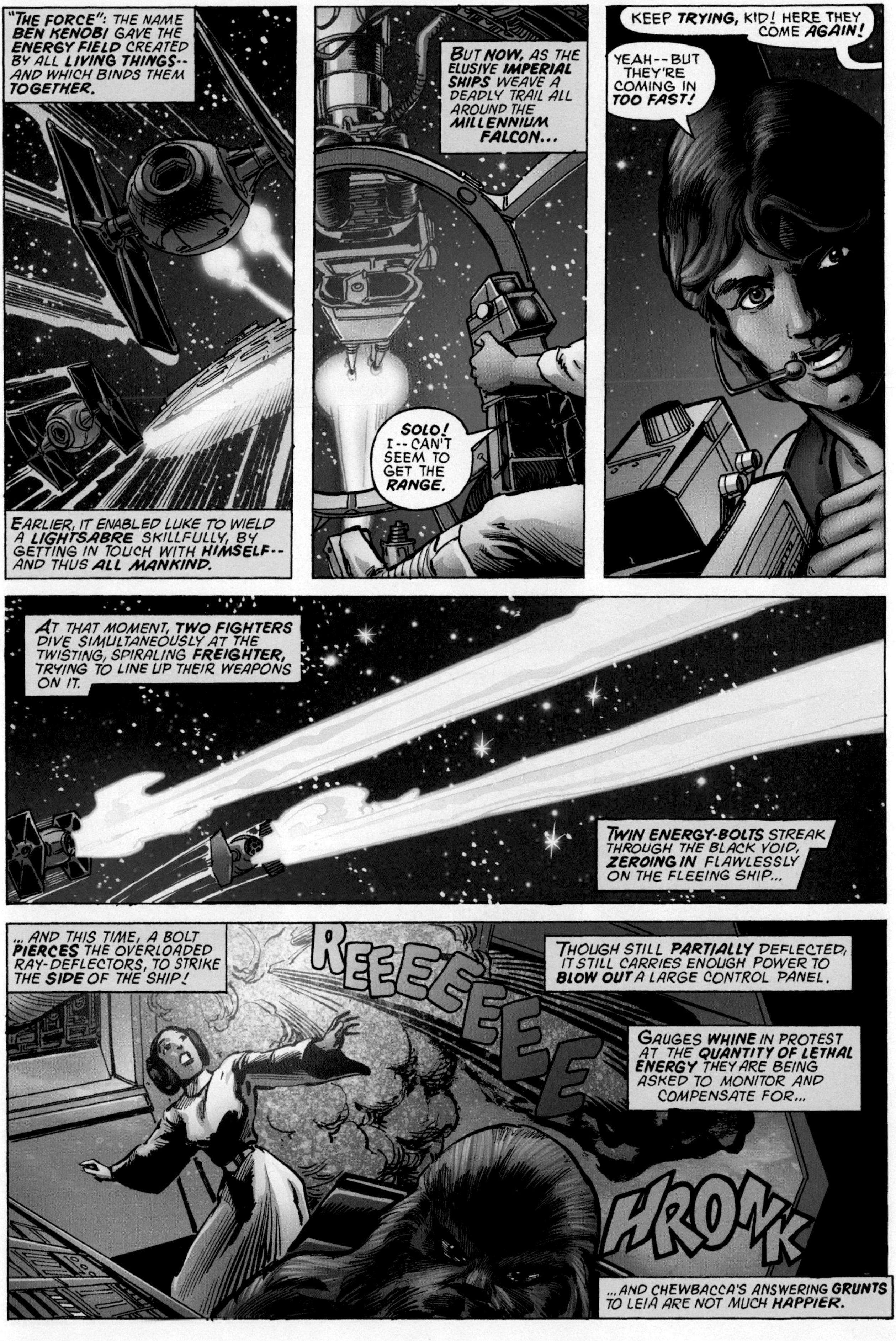
"THE FORCE": THE NAME BEN KENOBI GAVE THE ENERGY FIELD CREATED BY ALL LIVING THINGS-- AND WHICH BINDS THEM TOGETHER.
EARLIER, IT ENABLED LUKE TO WIELD A LIGHTSABRE SKILLFULLY, BY GETTING IN TOUCH WITH HIMSELF-- AND THUS ALL MANKIND.
BUT NOW, AS THE ELUSIVE IMPERIAL SHIPS WEAVE A DEADLY TRAIL ALL AROUND THE MILLENNIUM FALCON...
SOLO! I--CAN'T SEEM TO GET THE RANGE.
KEEP TRYING, KID! HERE THEY COME AGAIN!
YEAH--BUT THEY'RE COMING IN TOO FAST!
AT THAT MOMENT, TWO FIGHTERS DIVE SIMULTANEOUSLY AT THE TWISTING, SPIRALING FREIGHTER, TRYING TO LINE UP THEIR WEAPONS ON IT.
TWIN ENERGY-BOLTS STREAK THROUGH THE BLACK VOID, ZEROING IN FLAWLESSLY ON THE FLEEING SHIP...
...AND THIS TIME, A BOLT PIERCES THE OVERLOADED RAY-DEFLECTORS, TO STRIKE THE SIDE OF THE SHIP!
REEEEEEEE
THOUGH STILL PARTIALLY DEFLECTED, IT STILL CARRIES ENOUGH POWER TO BLOW OUT A LARGE CONTROL PANEL.
GAUGES WHINE IN PROTEST AT THE QUANTITY OF LETHAL ENERGY THEY ARE BEING ASKED TO MONITOR AND COMPENSATE FOR...
HRONK
...AND CHEWBACCA'S ANSWERING GRUNTS TO LEIA ARE NOT MUCH HAPPIER.

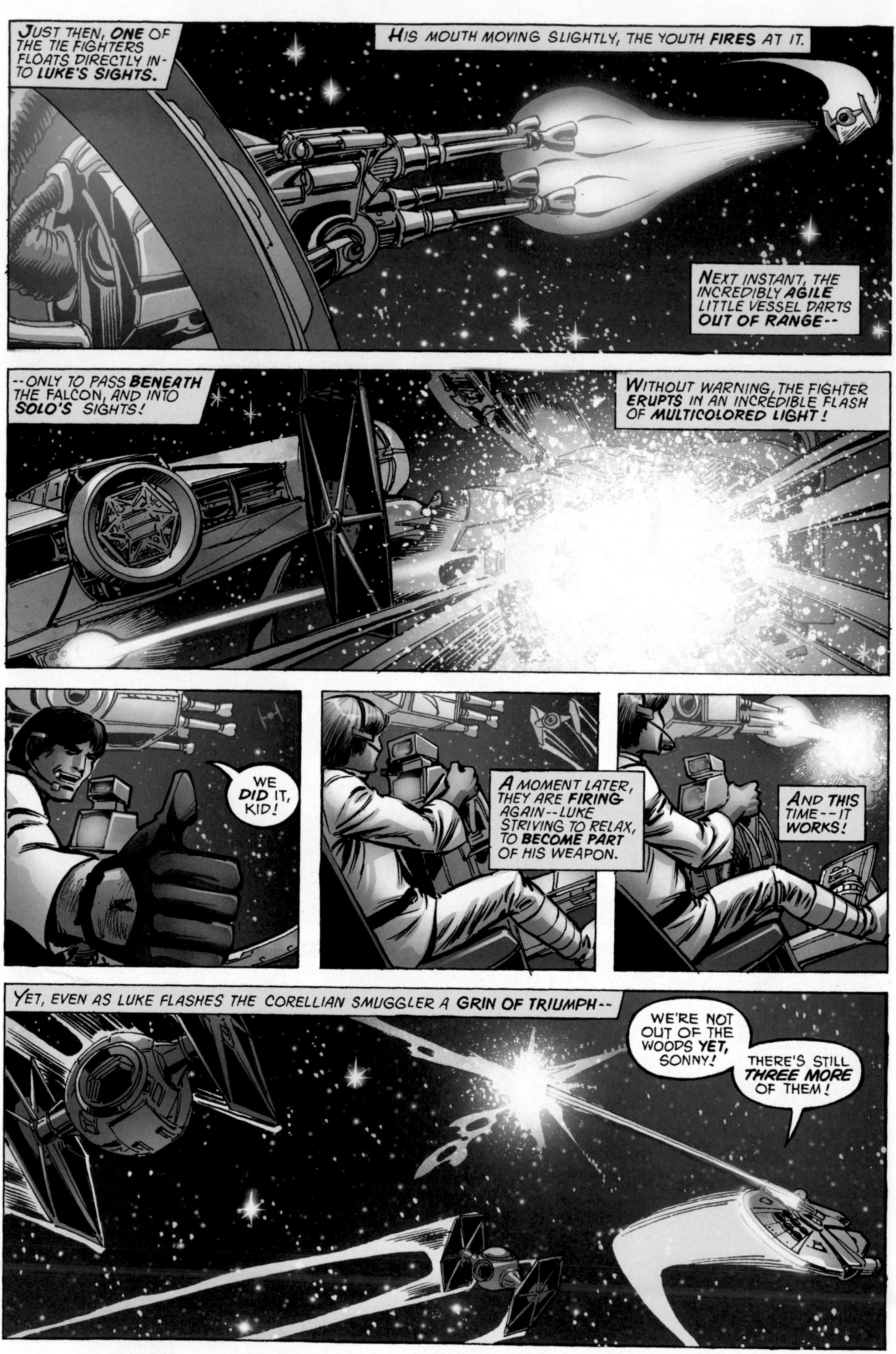
JUST THEN, ONE OF THE TIE FIGHTERS FLOATS DIRECTLY IN-TO LUKE'S SIGHTS.
HIS MOUTH MOVING SLIGHTLY, THE YOUTH FIRES AT IT.
NEXT INSTANT, THE INCREDIBLY AGILE LITTLE VESSEL DARTS OUT OF RANGE--
--ONLY TO PASS BENEATH THE FALCON, AND INTO SOLO'S SIGHTS!
WITHOUT WARNING, THE FIGHTER ERUPTS IN AN INCREDIBLE FLASH OF MULTICOLORED LIGHT!
WE DID IT, KID!
A MOMENT LATER, THEY ARE FIRING AGAIN--LUKE STRIVING TO RELAX, TO BECOME PART OF HIS WEAPON.
AND THIS TIME--IT WORKS!
YET, EVEN AS LUKE FLASHES THE CORELLIAN SMUGGLER A GRIN OF TRIUMPH--
WE'RE NOT OUT OF THE WOODS YET, SONNY!
THERE'S STILL THREE MORE OF THEM!

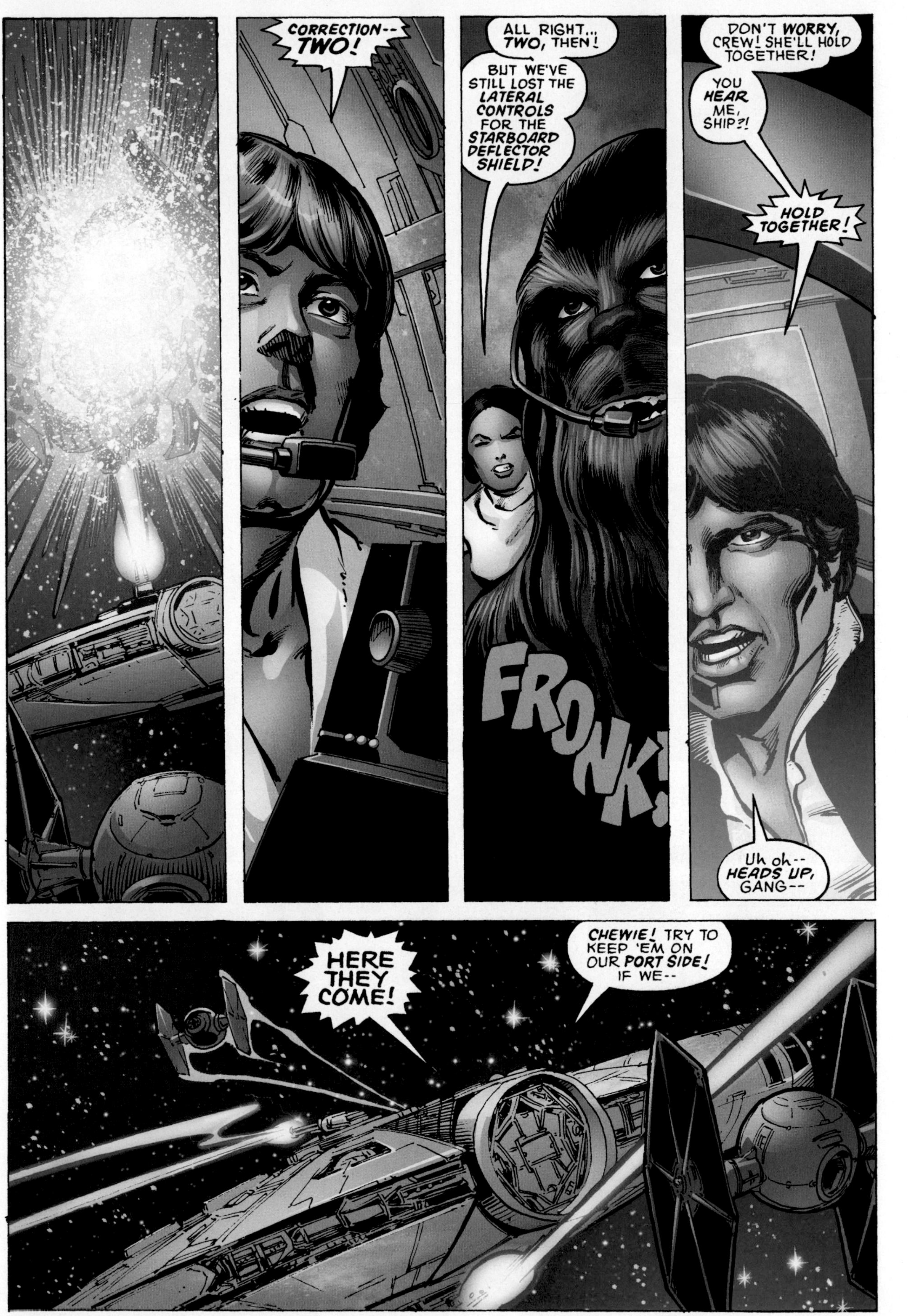

CORRECTION-- TWO!
ALL RIGHT... TWO, THEN!
BUT WE'VE STILL LOST THE LATERAL CONTROLS FOR THE STARBOARD DEFLECTOR SHIELD!
FRONK!
DON'T WORRY, CREW! SHE'LL HOLD TOGETHER!
YOU HEAR ME, SHIP?!
HOLD TOGETHER!
Uh oh-- HEADS UP, GANG--
HERE THEY COME!
CHEWIE! TRY TO KEEP 'EM ON OUR PORT SIDE! IF WE--

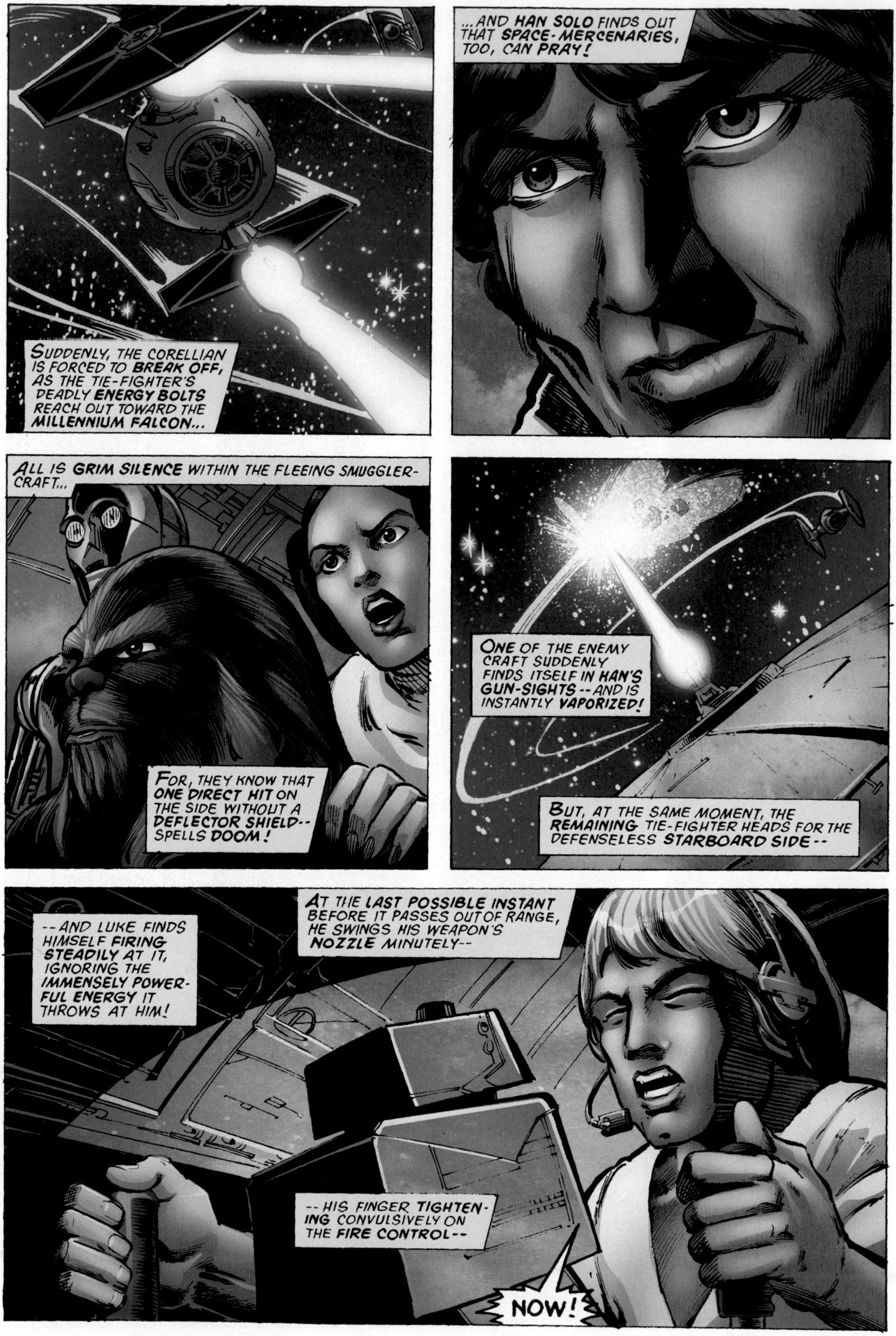
SUDDENLY, THE CORELLIAN IS FORCED TO BREAK OFF, AS THE TIE-FIGHTER'S DEADLY ENERGY BOLTS REACH OUT TOWARD THE MILLENNIUM FALCON...
...AND HAN SOLO FINDS OUT THAT SPACE-MERCENARIES, TOO, CAN PRAY!
ALL IS GRIM SILENCE WITHIN THE FLEEING SMUGGLER-CRAFT...
FOR, THEY KNOW THAT ONE DIRECT HIT ON THE SIDE WITHOUT A DEFLECTOR SHIELD-- SPELLS DOOM!
ONE OF THE ENEMY CRAFT SUDDENLY FINDS ITSELF IN HAN'S GUN-SIGHTS--AND IS INSTANTLY VAPORIZED!
BUT, AT THE SAME MOMENT, THE REMAINING TIE-FIGHTER HEADS FOR THE DEFENSELESS STARBOARD SIDE--
--AND LUKE FINDS HIMSELF FIRING STEADILY AT IT, IGNORING THE IMMENSELY POWER-FUL ENERGY IT THROWS AT HIM!
AT THE LAST POSSIBLE INSTANT BEFORE IT PASSES OUT OF RANGE, HE SWINGS HIS WEAPON'S NOZZLE MINUTELY--
--HIS FINGER TIGHTEN-ING CONVULSIVELY ON THE FIRE CONTROL--
NOW!

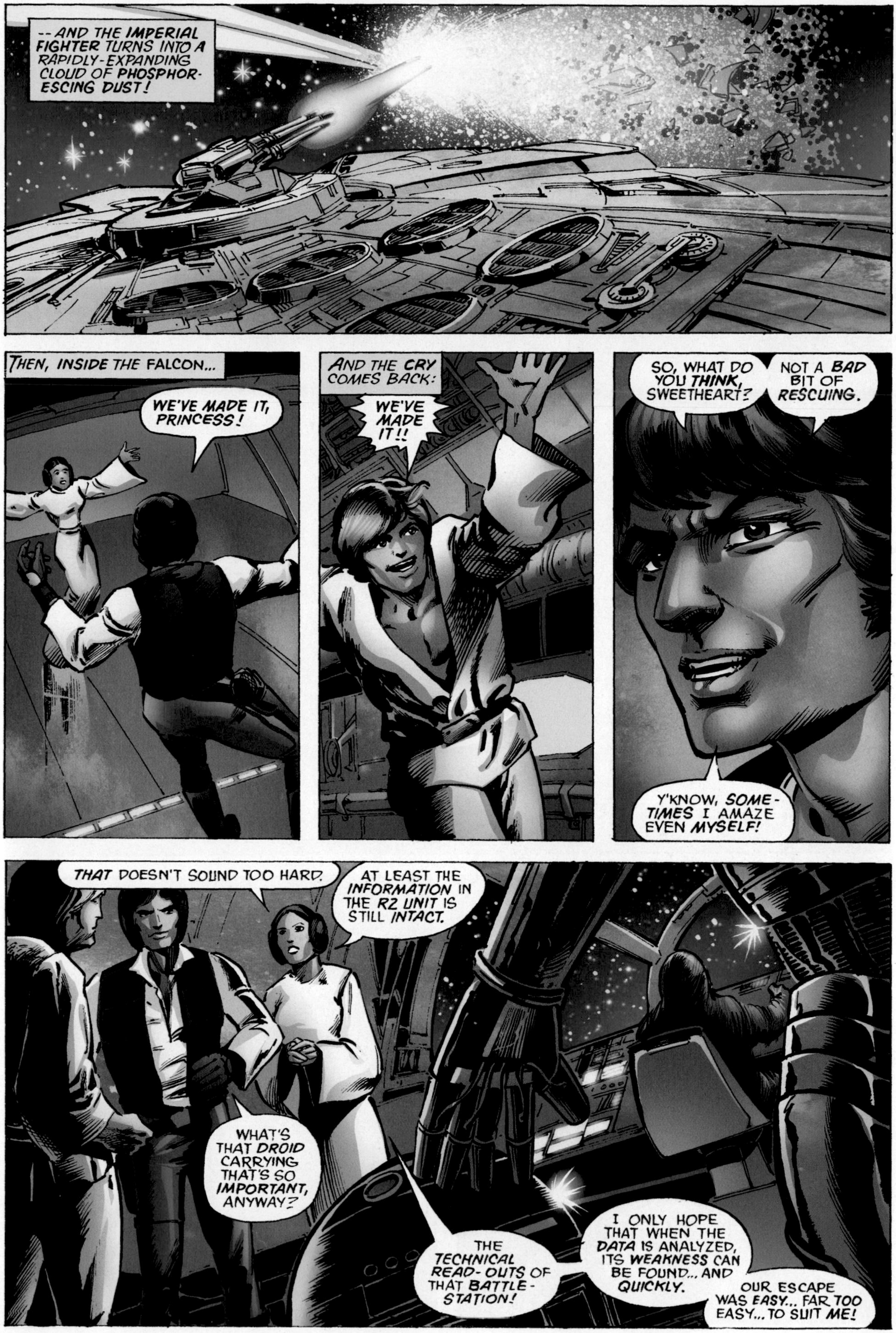
--AND THE IMPERIAL FIGHTER TURNS INTO A RAPIDLY-EXPANDING CLOUD OF PHOSPHOR-ESCING DUST!
THEN, INSIDE THE FALCON...
WE'VE MADE IT, PRINCESS!
AND THE CRY COMES BACK:
WE'VE MADE IT!!
SO, WHAT DO YOU THINK, SWEETHEART?
NOT A BAD BIT OF RESCUING.
Y'KNOW, SOME-TIMES I AMAZE EVEN MYSELF!
THAT DOESN'T SOUND TOO HARD.
AT LEAST THE INFORMATION IN THE R2 UNIT IS STILL INTACT.
WHAT'S THAT DROID CARRYING THAT'S SO IMPORTANT, ANYWAY?
THE TECHNICAL READ-OUTS OF THAT BATTLE-STATION!
I ONLY HOPE THAT WHEN THE DATA IS ANALYZED, ITS WEAKNESS CAN BE FOUND... AND QUICKLY.
OUR ESCAPE WAS EASY... FAR TOO EASY... TO SUIT ME!

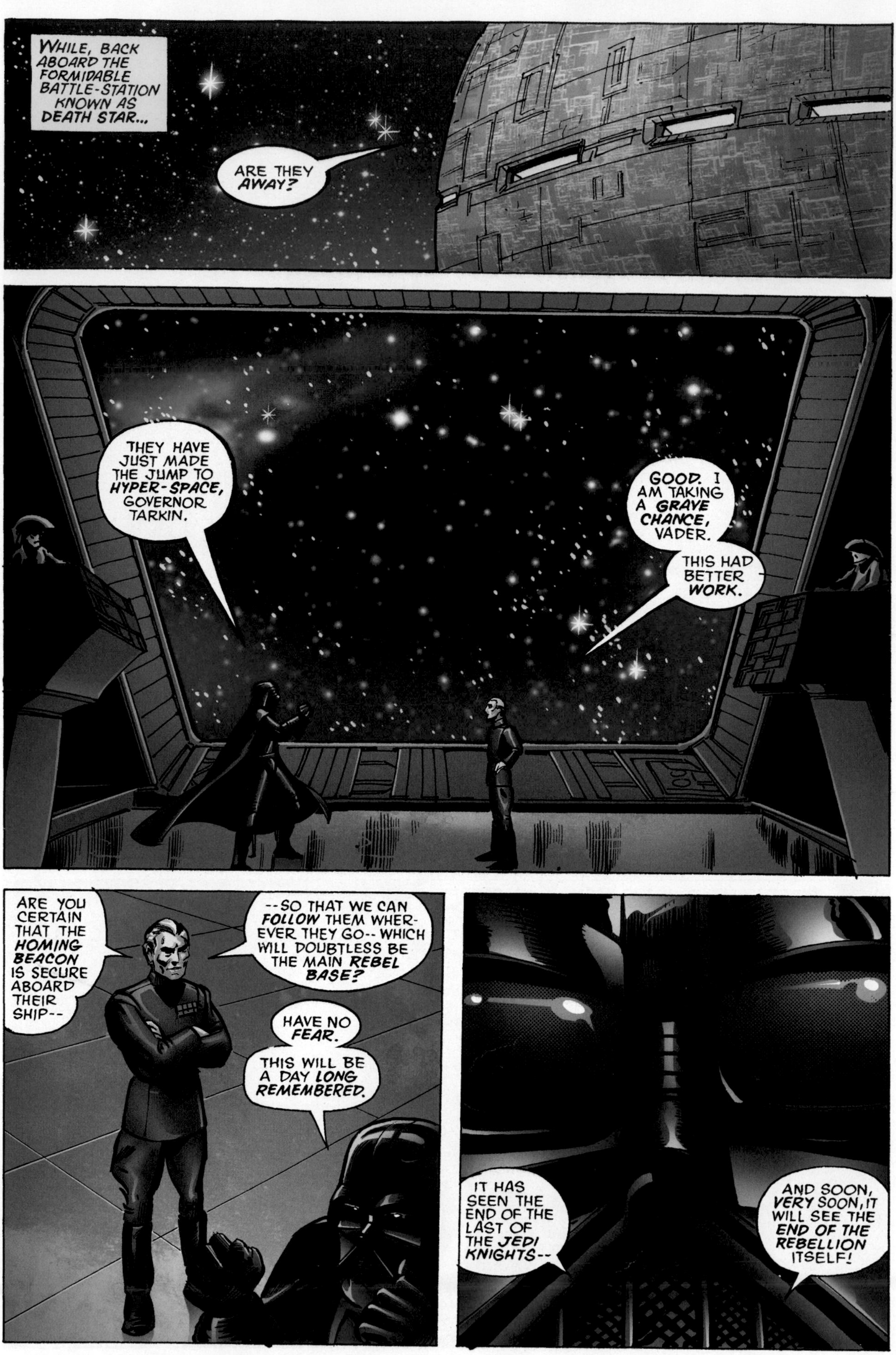

WHILE, BACK ABOARD THE FORMIDABLE BATTLE-STATION KNOWN AS DEATH STAR...
ARE THEY AWAY?
THEY HAVE JUST MADE THE JUMP TO HYPER-SPACE, GOVERNOR TARKIN.
GOOD. I AM TAKING A GRAVE CHANCE, VADER.
THIS HAD BETTER WORK.
ARE YOU CERTAIN THAT THE HOMING BEACON IS SECURE ABOARD THEIR SHIP--
--SO THAT WE CAN FOLLOW THEM WHEREVER THEY GO-- WHICH WILL DOUBTLESS BE THE MAIN REBEL BASE?
HAVE NO FEAR.
THIS WILL BE A DAY LONG REMEMBERED.
IT HAS SEEN THE END OF THE LAST OF THE JEDI KNIGHTS--
AND SOON, VERY SOON, IT WILL SEE THE END OF THE REBELLION ITSELF!

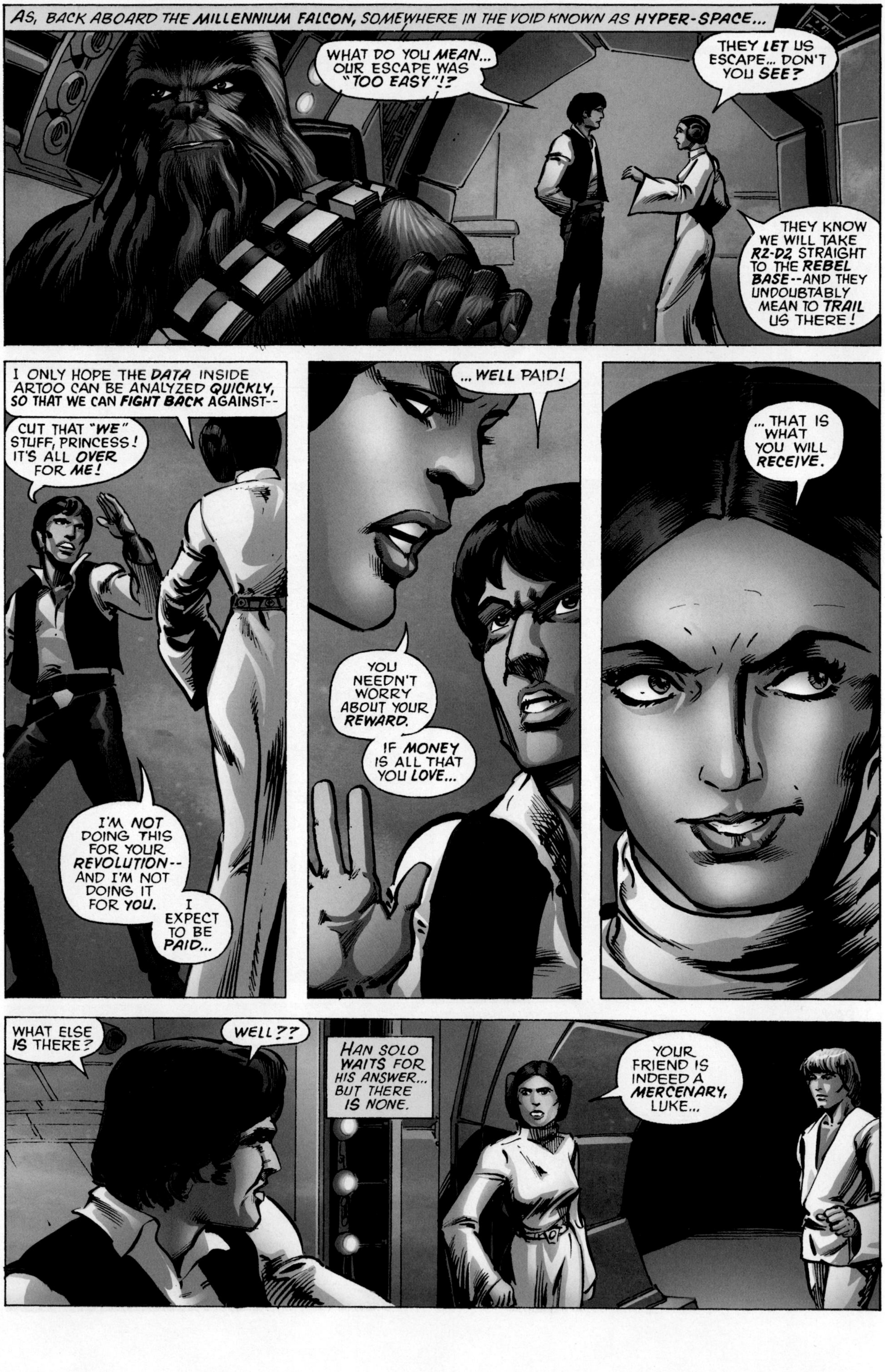

AS, BACK ABOARD THE MILLENNIUM FALCON, SOMEWHERE IN THE VOID KNOWN AS HYPER-SPACE...
WHAT DO YOU MEAN... OUR ESCAPE WAS "TOO EASY"!?
THEY LET US ESCAPE... DON'T YOU SEE?
THEY KNOW WE WILL TAKE R2-D2 STRAIGHT TO THE REBEL BASE--AND THEY UNDOUBTABLY MEAN TO TRAIL US THERE!
I ONLY HOPE THE DATA INSIDE ARTOO CAN BE ANALYZED QUICKLY, SO THAT WE CAN FIGHT BACK AGAINST--
CUT THAT "WE" STUFF, PRINCESS! IT'S ALL OVER FOR ME!
I'M NOT DOING THIS FOR YOUR REVOLUTION-- AND I'M NOT DOING IT FOR YOU.
I EXPECT TO BE PAID...
...WELL PAID!
YOU NEEDN'T WORRY ABOUT YOUR REWARD.
IF MONEY IS ALL THAT YOU LOVE...
...THAT IS WHAT YOU WILL RECEIVE.
WHAT ELSE IS THERE?
WELL??
HAN SOLO WAITS FOR HIS ANSWER... BUT THERE IS NONE.
YOUR FRIEND IS INDEED A MERCENARY, LUKE...

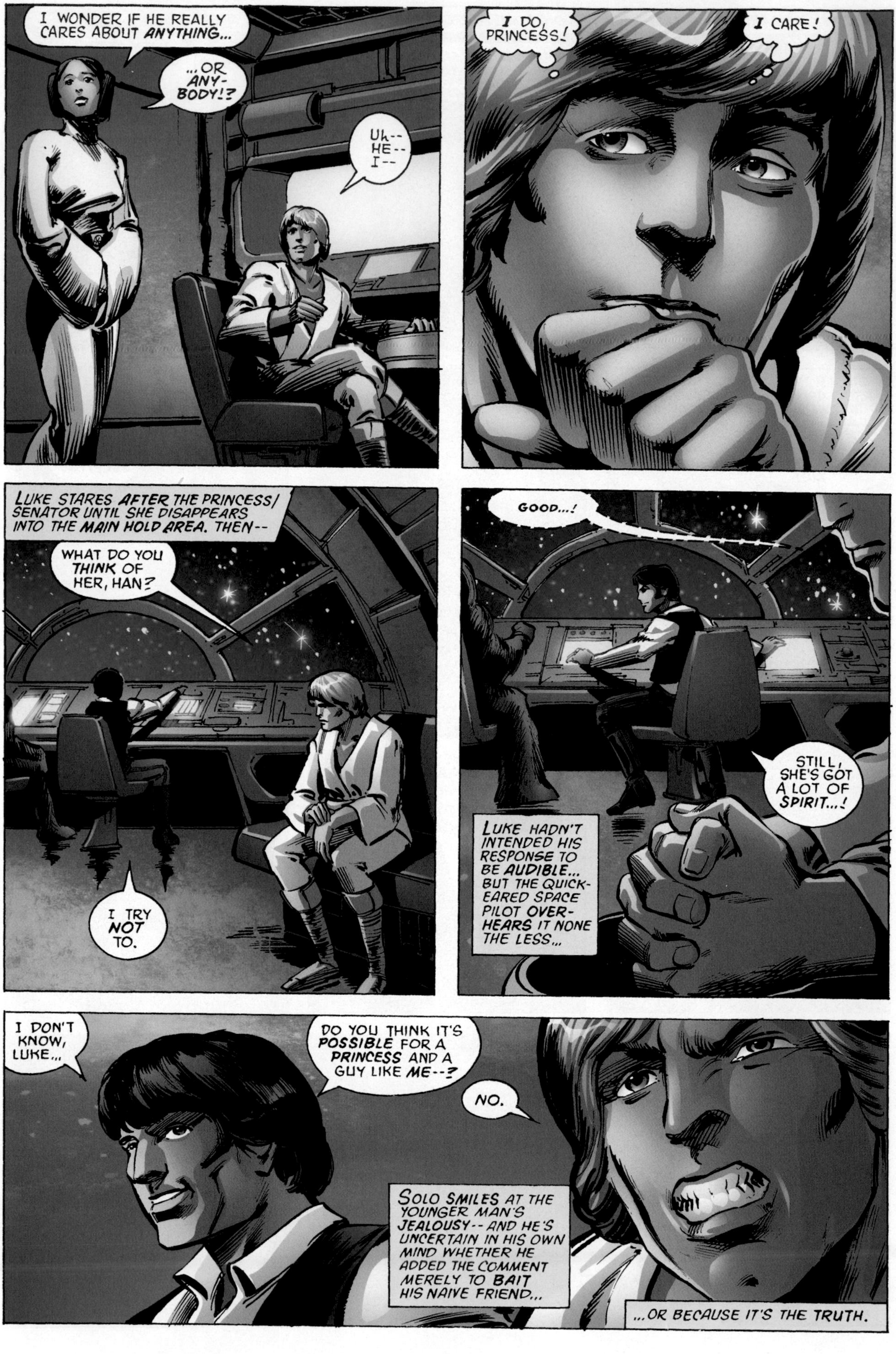

I WONDER IF HE REALLY CARES ABOUT ANYTHING...
...OR ANY-BODY!?
Uh-- HE-- I--
I DO, PRINCESS!
I CARE!
LUKE STARES AFTER THE PRINCESS/ SENATOR UNTIL SHE DISAPPEARS INTO THE MAIN HOLD AREA. THEN--
WHAT DO YOU THINK OF HER, HAN?
I TRY NOT TO.
GOOD...!
STILL, SHE'S GOT A LOT OF SPIRIT...!
LUKE HADN'T INTENDED HIS RESPONSE TO BE AUDIBLE... BUT THE QUICK-EARED SPACE PILOT OVER-HEARS IT NONE THE LESS...
I DON'T KNOW, LUKE...
DO YOU THINK IT'S POSSIBLE FOR A PRINCESS AND A GUY LIKE ME--?
NO.
SOLO SMILES AT THE YOUNGER MAN'S JEALOUSY-- AND HE'S UNCERTAIN IN HIS OWN MIND WHETHER HE ADDED THE COMMENT MERELY TO BAIT HIS NAIVE FRIEND...
...OR BECAUSE IT'S THE TRUTH.

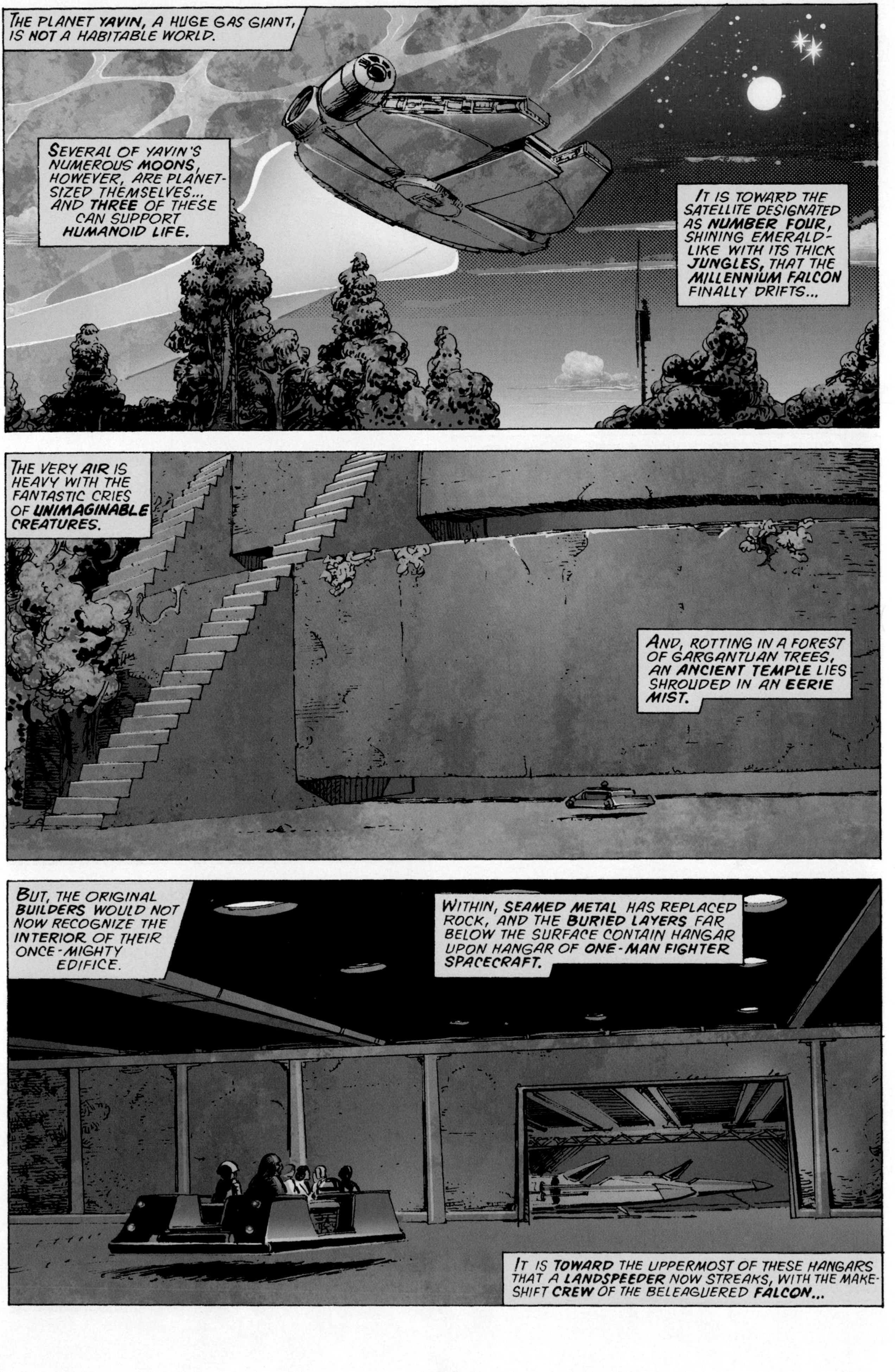
THE PLANET YAVIN, A HUGE GAS GIANT, IS NOT A HABITABLE WORLD.
SEVERAL OF YAVIN'S NUMEROUS MOONS, HOWEVER, ARE PLANET-SIZED THEMSELVES... AND THREE OF THESE CAN SUPPORT HUMANOID LIFE.
IT IS TOWARD THE SATELLITE DESIGNATED AS NUMBER FOUR, SHINING EMERALD-LIKE WITH ITS THICK JUNGLES, THAT THE MILLENNIUM FALCON FINALLY DRIFTS...
THE VERY AIR IS HEAVY WITH THE FANTASTIC CRIES OF UNIMAGINABLE CREATURES.
AND, ROTTING IN A FOREST OF GARGANTUAN TREES, AN ANCIENT TEMPLE LIES SHROUDED IN AN EERIE MIST.
BUT, THE ORIGINAL BUILDERS WOULD NOT NOW RECOGNIZE THE INTERIOR OF THEIR ONCE-MIGHTY EDIFICE.
WITHIN, SEAMED METAL HAS REPLACED ROCK, AND THE BURIED LAYERS FAR BELOW THE SURFACE CONTAIN HANGAR UPON HANGAR OF ONE-MAN FIGHTER SPACECRAFT.
IT IS TOWARD THE UPPERMOST OF THESE HANGARS THAT A LANDSPEEDER NOW STREAKS, WITH THE MAKE-SHIFT CREW OF THE BELEAGUERED FALCON...

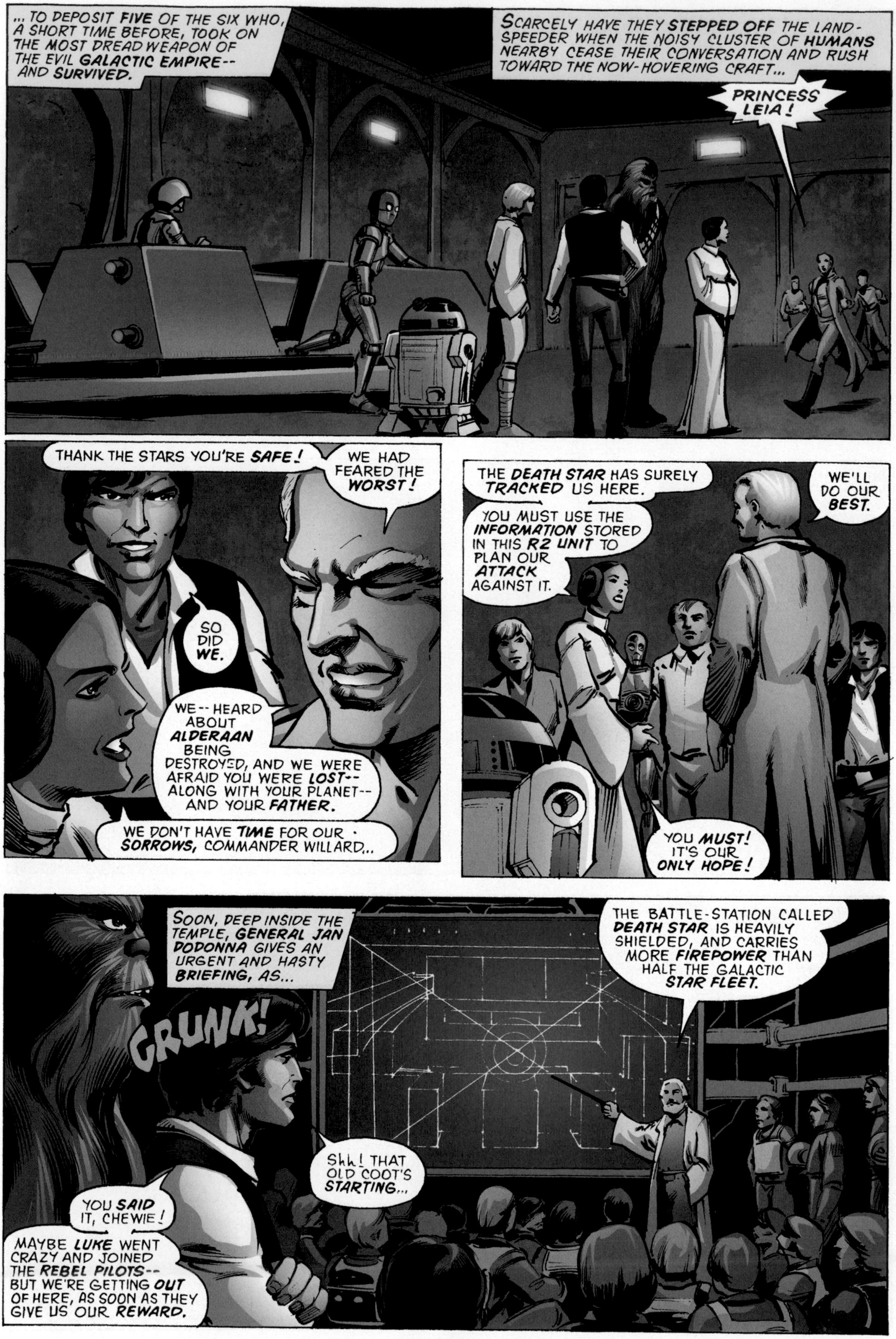
...TO DEPOSIT FIVE OF THE SIX WHO, A SHORT TIME BEFORE, TOOK ON THE MOST DREAD WEAPON OF THE EVIL GALACTIC EMPIRE-- AND SURVIVED.
SCARCELY HAVE THEY STEPPED OFF THE LAND-SPEEDER WHEN THE NOISY CLUSTER OF HUMANS NEARBY CEASE THEIR CONVERSATION AND RUSH TOWARD THE NOW-HOVERING CRAFT...
PRINCESS LEIA!
THANK THE STARS YOU'RE SAFE!
WE HAD FEARED THE WORST!
SO DID WE.
WE--HEARD ABOUT ALDERAAN BEING DESTROYED, AND WE WERE AFRAID YOU WERE LOST-- ALONG WITH YOUR PLANET-- AND YOUR FATHER.
WE DON'T HAVE TIME FOR OUR SORROWS, COMMANDER WILLARD...
THE DEATH STAR HAS SURELY TRACKED US HERE.
YOU MUST USE THE INFORMATION STORED IN THIS R2 UNIT TO PLAN OUR ATTACK AGAINST IT.
WE'LL DO OUR BEST.
YOU MUST! IT'S OUR ONLY HOPE!
SOON, DEEP INSIDE THE TEMPLE, GENERAL JAN DODONNA GIVES AN URGENT AND HASTY BRIEFING, AS...
THE BATTLE-STATION CALLED DEATH STAR IS HEAVILY SHIELDED, AND CARRIES MORE FIREPOWER THAN HALF THE GALACTIC STAR FLEET.
GRUNK!
SHH! THAT OLD COOT'S STARTING...
YOU SAID IT, CHEWIE!
MAYBE LUKE WENT CRAZY AND JOINED THE REBEL PILOTS-- BUT WE'RE GETTING OUT OF HERE, AS SOON AS THEY GIVE US OUR REWARD.

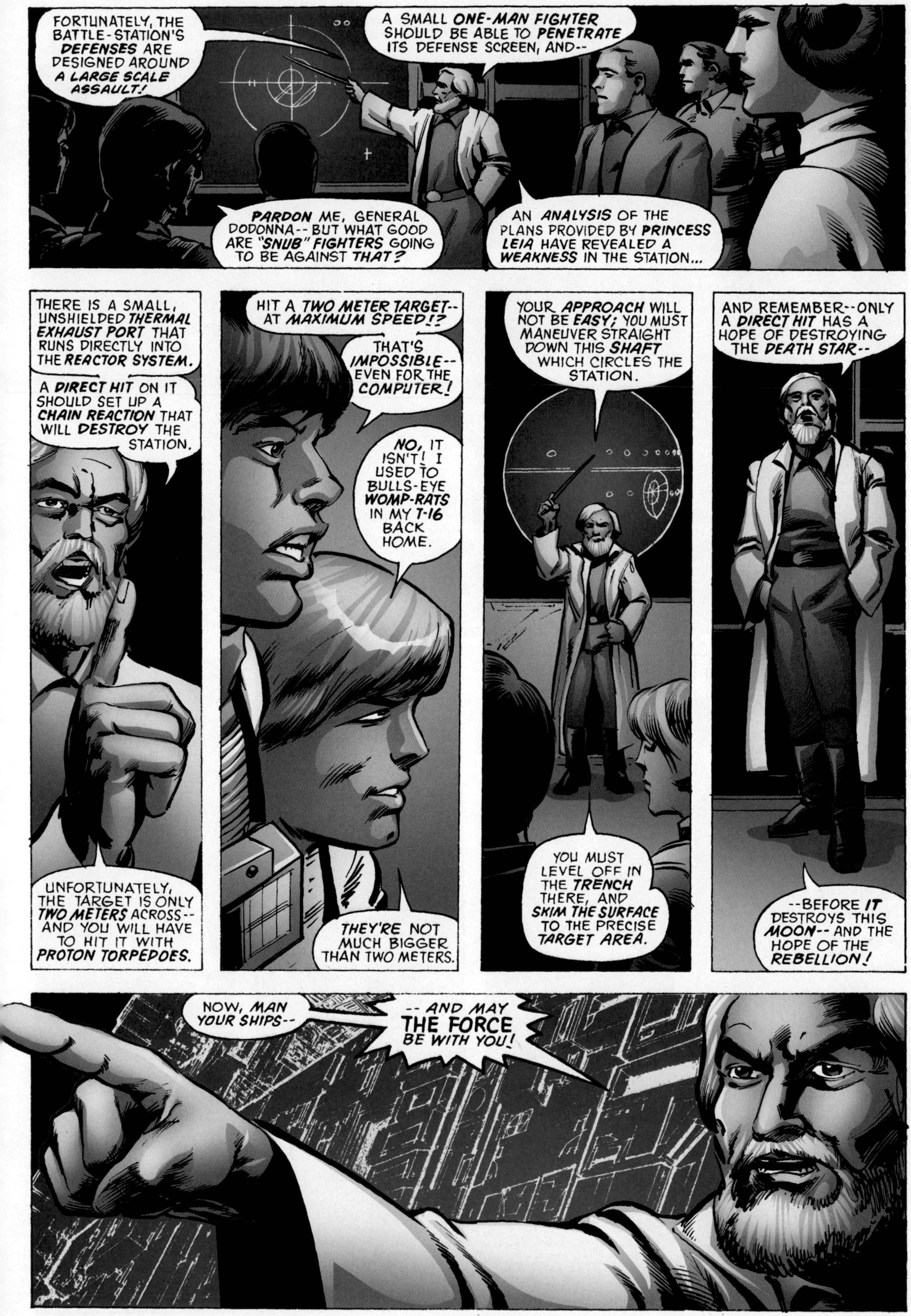
FORTUNATELY, THE BATTLE-STATION'S DEFENSES ARE DESIGNED AROUND A LARGE SCALE ASSAULT!
A SMALL ONE-MAN FIGHTER SHOULD BE ABLE TO PENETRATE ITS DEFENSE SCREEN, AND--
PARDON ME, GENERAL DODONNA-- BUT WHAT GOOD ARE "SNUB" FIGHTERS GOING TO BE AGAINST THAT?
AN ANALYSIS OF THE PLANS PROVIDED BY PRINCESS LEIA HAVE REVEALED A WEAKNESS IN THE STATION...
THERE IS A SMALL, UNSHIELDED THERMAL EXHAUST PORT THAT RUNS DIRECTLY INTO THE REACTOR SYSTEM.
A DIRECT HIT ON IT SHOULD SET UP A CHAIN REACTION THAT WILL DESTROY THE STATION.
UNFORTUNATELY, THE TARGET IS ONLY TWO METERS ACROSS-- AND YOU WILL HAVE TO HIT IT WITH PROTON TORPEDOES.
HIT A TWO METER TARGET-- AT MAXIMUM SPEED!?
THAT'S IMPOSSIBLE-- EVEN FOR THE COMPUTER!
NO, IT ISN'T! I USED TO BULLS-EYE WOMP-RATS IN MY T-16 BACK HOME.
THEY'RE NOT MUCH BIGGER THAN TWO METERS.
YOUR APPROACH WILL NOT BE EASY; YOU MUST MANEUVER STRAIGHT DOWN THIS SHAFT WHICH CIRCLES THE STATION.
YOU MUST LEVEL OFF IN THE TRENCH THERE, AND SKIM THE SURFACE TO THE PRECISE TARGET AREA.
AND REMEMBER--ONLY A DIRECT HIT HAS A HOPE OF DESTROYING THE DEATH STAR--
--BEFORE IT DESTROYS THIS MOON-- AND THE HOPE OF THE REBELLION!
NOW, MAN YOUR SHIPS--
-- AND MAY THE FORCE BE WITH YOU!

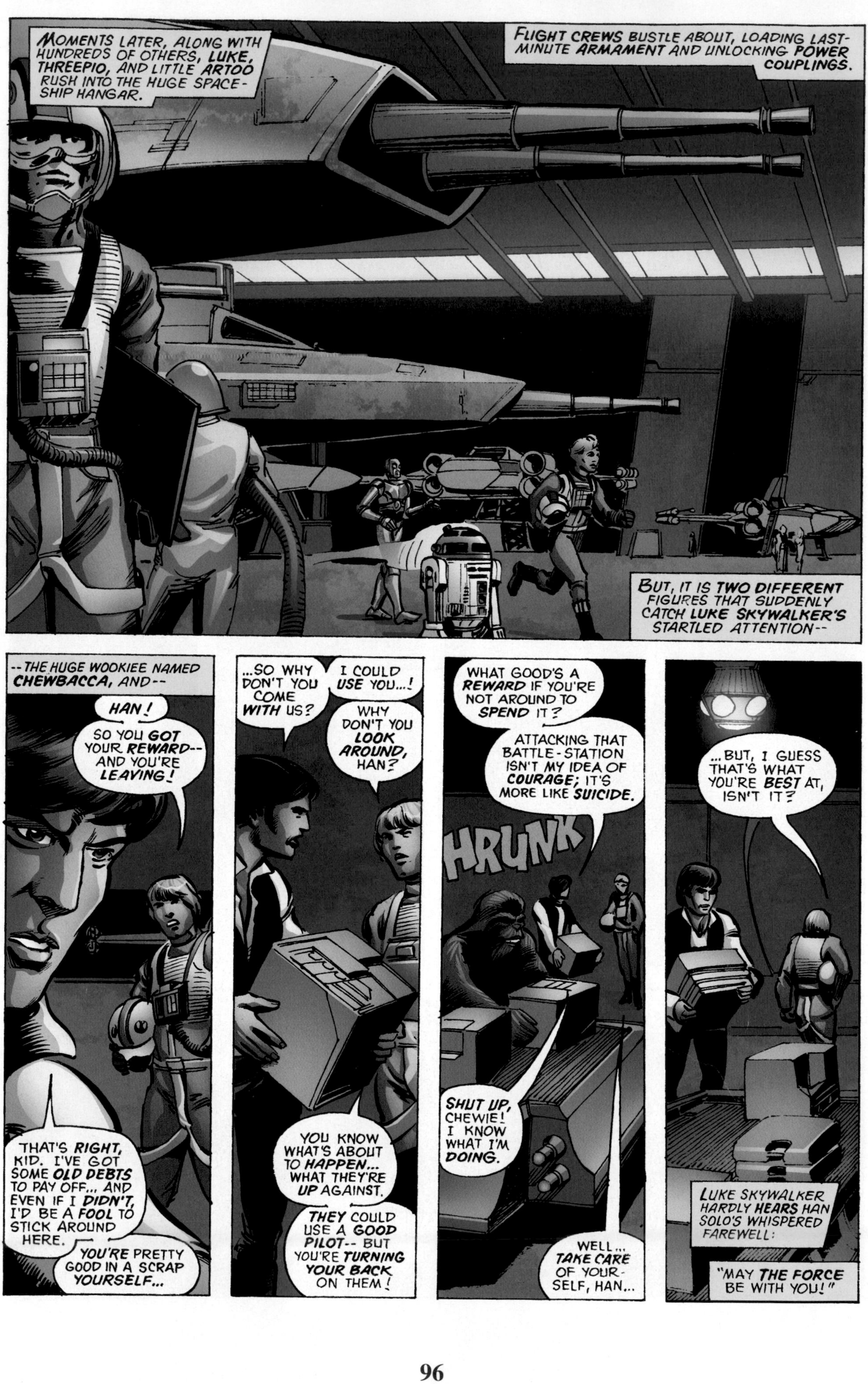
MOMENTS LATER, ALONG WITH HUNDREDS OF OTHERS, LUKE, THREEPIO, AND LITTLE ARTOO RUSH INTO THE HUGE SPACE-SHIP HANGAR.
FLIGHT CREWS BUSTLE ABOUT, LOADING LAST-MINUTE ARMAMENT AND UNLOCKING POWER COUPLINGS.
BUT, IT IS TWO DIFFERENT FIGURES THAT SUDDENLY CATCH LUKE SKYWALKER'S STARTLED ATTENTION--
--THE HUGE WOOKIEE NAMED CHEWBACCA, AND--
HAN!
SO YOU GOT YOUR REWARD-- AND YOU'RE LEAVING!
THAT'S RIGHT, KID. I'VE GOT SOME OLD DEBTS TO PAY OFF... AND EVEN IF I DIDN'T, I'D BE A FOOL TO STICK AROUND HERE.
YOU'RE PRETTY GOOD IN A SCRAP YOURSELF...
...SO WHY DON'T YOU COME WITH US?
I COULD USE YOU...!
WHY DON'T YOU LOOK AROUND, HAN?
YOU KNOW WHAT'S ABOUT TO HAPPEN... WHAT THEY'RE UP AGAINST.
THEY COULD USE A GOOD PILOT-- BUT YOU'RE TURNING YOUR BACK ON THEM!
WHAT GOOD'S A REWARD IF YOU'RE NOT AROUND TO SPEND IT?
ATTACKING THAT BATTLE-STATION ISN'T MY IDEA OF COURAGE; IT'S MORE LIKE SUICIDE.
HRUNK
SHUT UP, CHEWIE! I KNOW WHAT I'M DOING.
WELL... TAKE CARE OF YOURSELF, HAN...
...BUT, I GUESS THAT'S WHAT YOU'RE BEST AT, ISN'T IT?
LUKE SKYWALKER HARDLY HEARS HAN SOLO'S WHISPERED FAREWELL:
"MAY THE FORCE BE WITH YOU!"

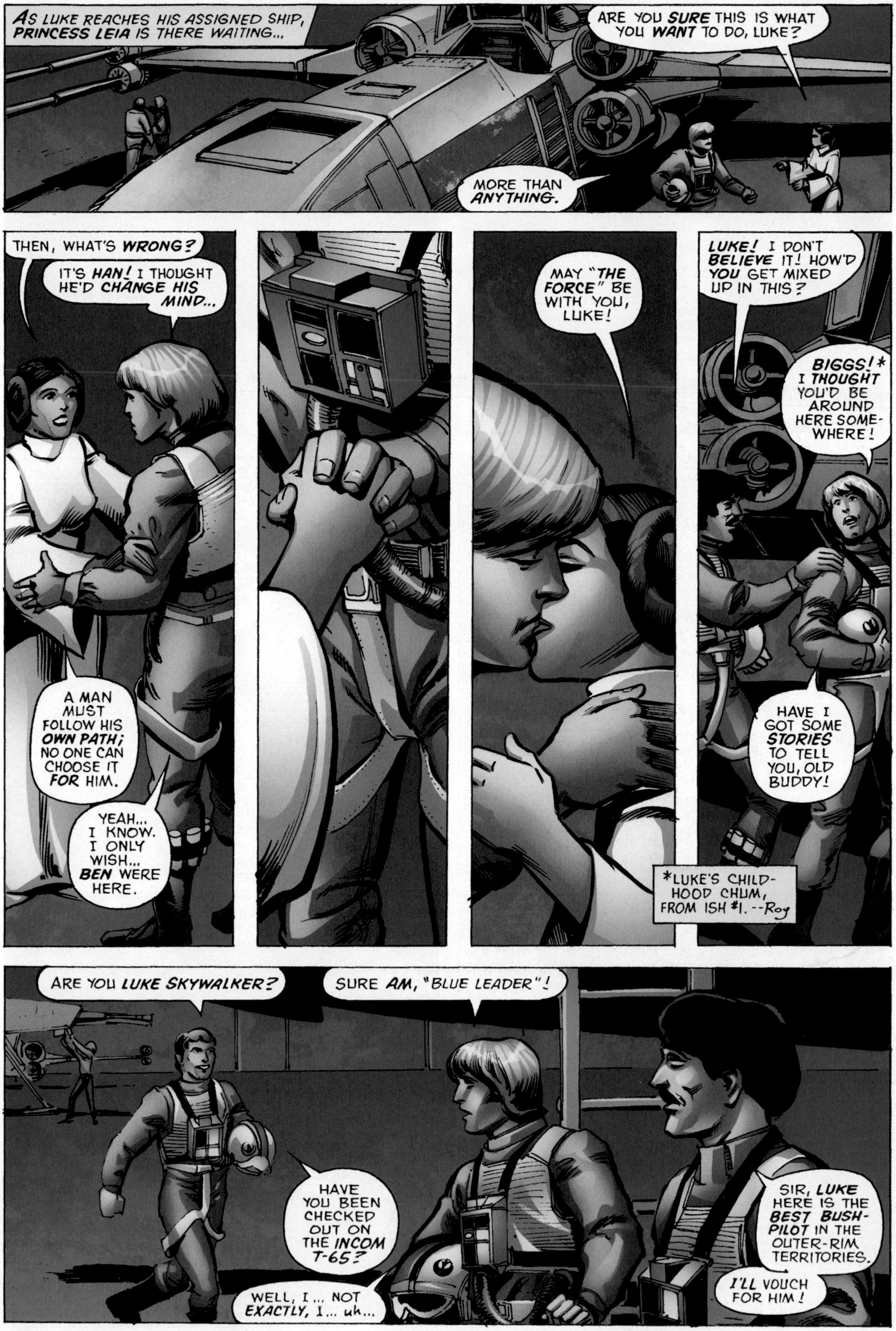
AS LUKE REACHES HIS ASSIGNED SHIP, PRINCESS LEIA IS THERE WAITING...
ARE YOU SURE THIS IS WHAT YOU WANT TO DO, LUKE?
MORE THAN ANYTHING.
THEN, WHAT'S WRONG?
IT'S HAN! I THOUGHT HE'D CHANGE HIS MIND...
A MAN MUST FOLLOW HIS OWN PATH; NO ONE CAN CHOOSE IT FOR HIM.
YEAH... I KNOW. I ONLY WISH... BEN WERE HERE.
MAY "THE FORCE" BE WITH YOU, LUKE!
LUKE! I DON'T BELIEVE IT! HOW'D YOU GET MIXED UP IN THIS?
BIGGS!* I THOUGHT YOU'D BE AROUND HERE SOMEWHERE!
HAVE I GOT SOME STORIES TO TELL YOU, OLD BUDDY!
*LUKE'S CHILDHOOD CHUM, FROM ISH #1. --Roy
ARE YOU LUKE SKYWALKER?
SURE AM, "BLUE LEADER"!
HAVE YOU BEEN CHECKED OUT ON THE INCOM T-65?
WELL, I... NOT EXACTLY, I... uh...
SIR, LUKE HERE IS THE BEST BUSH-PILOT IN THE OUTER-RIM TERRITORIES.
I'LL VOUCH FOR HIM!

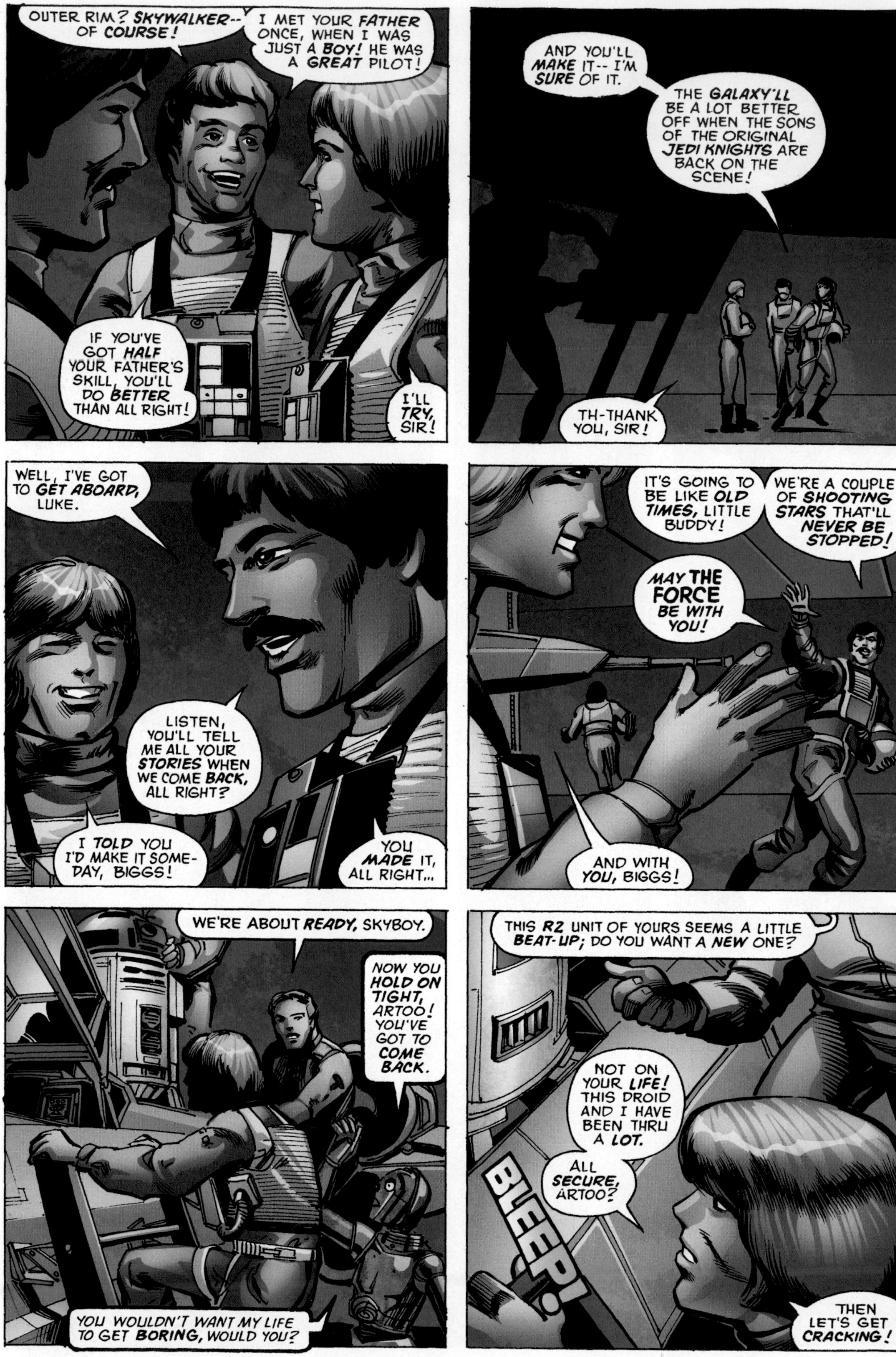
OUTER RIM? SKYWALKER-- OF COURSE!
I MET YOUR FATHER ONCE, WHEN I WAS JUST A BOY! HE WAS A GREAT PILOT!
IF YOU'VE GOT HALF YOUR FATHER'S SKILL, YOU'LL DO BETTER THAN ALL RIGHT!
I'LL TRY, SIR!
AND YOU'LL MAKE IT-- I'M SURE OF IT.
THE GALAXY'LL BE A LOT BETTER OFF WHEN THE SONS OF THE ORIGINAL JEDI KNIGHTS ARE BACK ON THE SCENE!
TH-THANK YOU, SIR!
WELL, I'VE GOT TO GET ABOARD, LUKE.
LISTEN, YOU'LL TELL ME ALL YOUR STORIES WHEN WE COME BACK, ALL RIGHT?
I TOLD YOU I'D MAKE IT SOME-DAY, BIGGS!
YOU MADE IT, ALL RIGHT...
IT'S GOING TO BE LIKE OLD TIMES, LITTLE BUDDY!
WE'RE A COUPLE OF SHOOTING STARS THAT'LL NEVER BE STOPPED!
MAY THE FORCE BE WITH YOU!
AND WITH YOU, BIGGS!
WE'RE ABOUT READY, SKYBOY.
NOW YOU HOLD ON TIGHT, ARTOO! YOU'VE GOT TO COME BACK.
YOU WOULDN'T WANT MY LIFE TO GET BORING, WOULD YOU?
THIS R2 UNIT OF YOURS SEEMS A LITTLE BEAT-UP; DO YOU WANT A NEW ONE?
NOT ON YOUR LIFE! THIS DROID AND I HAVE BEEN THRU A LOT.
ALL SECURE, ARTOO?
BLEEP!
THEN LET'S GET CRACKING!

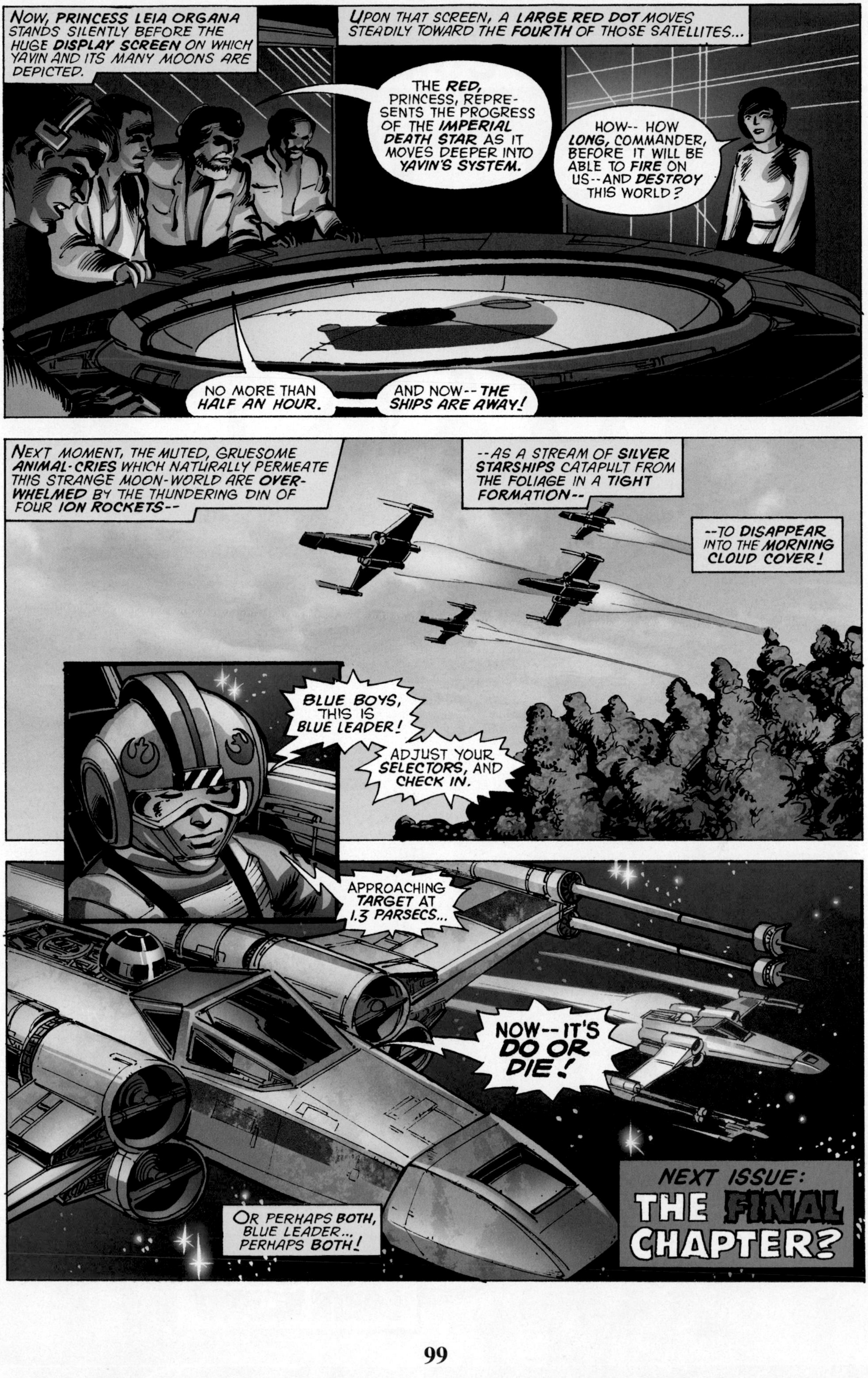
NOW, PRINCESS LEIA ORGANA STANDS SILENTLY BEFORE THE HUGE DISPLAY SCREEN ON WHICH YAVIN AND ITS MANY MOONS ARE DEPICTED.
UPON THAT SCREEN, A LARGE RED DOT MOVES STEADILY TOWARD THE FOURTH OF THOSE SATELLITES...
THE RED, PRINCESS, REPRESENTS THE PROGRESS OF THE IMPERIAL DEATH STAR AS IT MOVES DEEPER INTO YAVIN'S SYSTEM.
HOW-- HOW LONG, COMMANDER, BEFORE IT WILL BE ABLE TO FIRE ON US--AND DESTROY THIS WORLD?
NO MORE THAN HALF AN HOUR.
AND NOW--THE SHIPS ARE AWAY!
NEXT MOMENT, THE MUTED, GRUESOME ANIMAL-CRIES WHICH NATURALLY PERMEATE THIS STRANGE MOON-WORLD ARE OVERWHELMED BY THE THUNDERING DIN OF FOUR ION ROCKETS--
--AS A STREAM OF SILVER STARSHIPS CATAPULT FROM THE FOLIAGE IN A TIGHT FORMATION--
--TO DISAPPEAR INTO THE MORNING CLOUD COVER!
BLUE BOYS, THIS IS BLUE LEADER!
ADJUST YOUR SELECTORS, AND CHECK IN.
APPROACHING TARGET AT 1.3 PARSECS...
NOW--IT'S DO OR DIE!
OR PERHAPS BOTH, BLUE LEADER... PERHAPS BOTH!
NEXT ISSUE: THE FINAL CHAPTER?

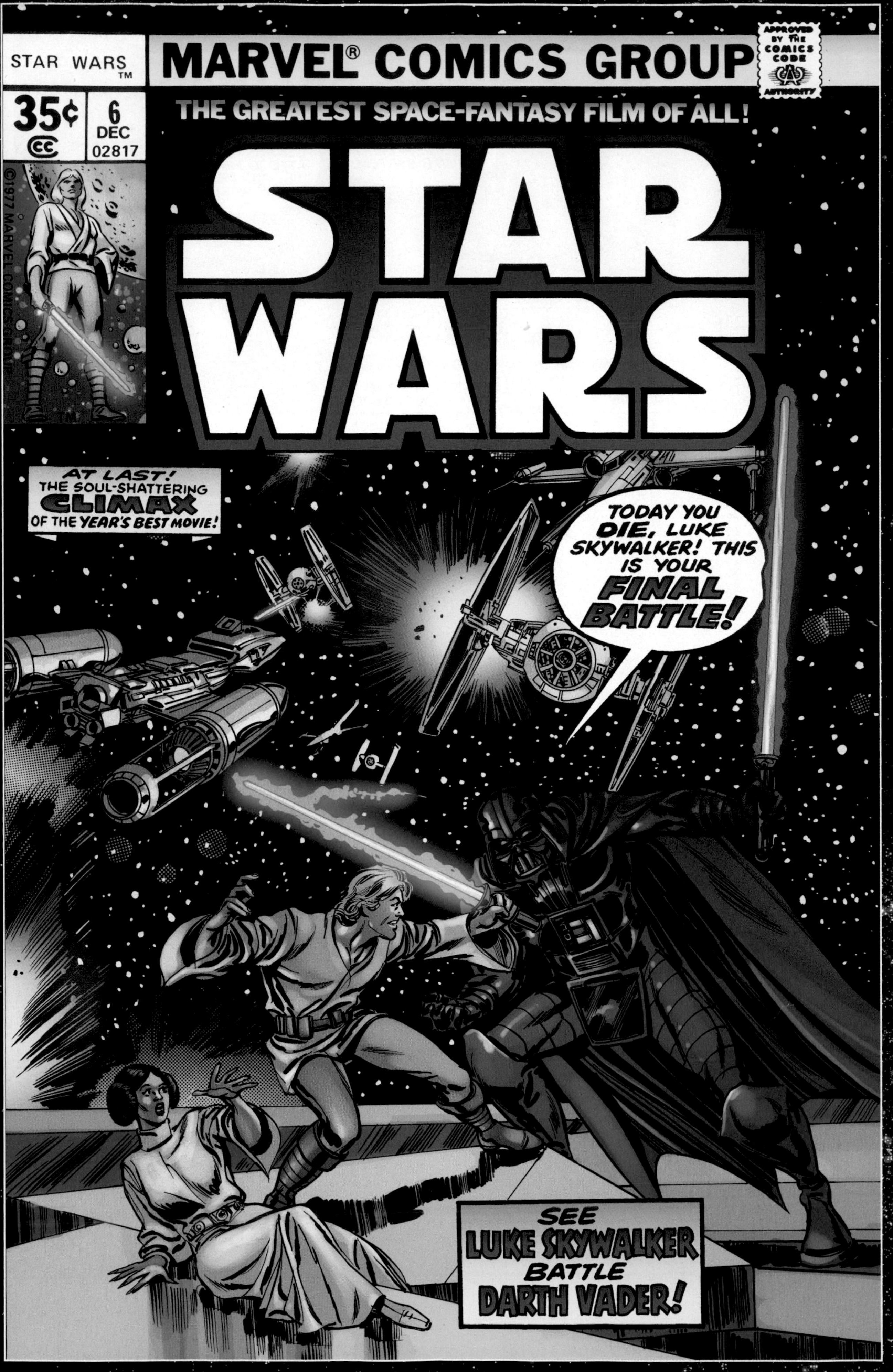
STAR WARS TM
MARVEL® COMICS GROUP
APPROVED BY THE COMICS CODE AUTHORITY
35¢ CC
6 DEC 02817
THE GREATEST SPACE-FANTASY FILM OF ALL!
©1977 MARVEL COMICS GROUP
STAR WARS
AT LAST! THE SOUL-SHATTERING CLIMAX OF THE YEAR'S BEST MOVIE!
TODAY YOU DIE, LUKE SKYWALKER! THIS IS YOUR FINAL BATTLE!
SEE LUKE SKYWALKER BATTLE DARTH VADER!

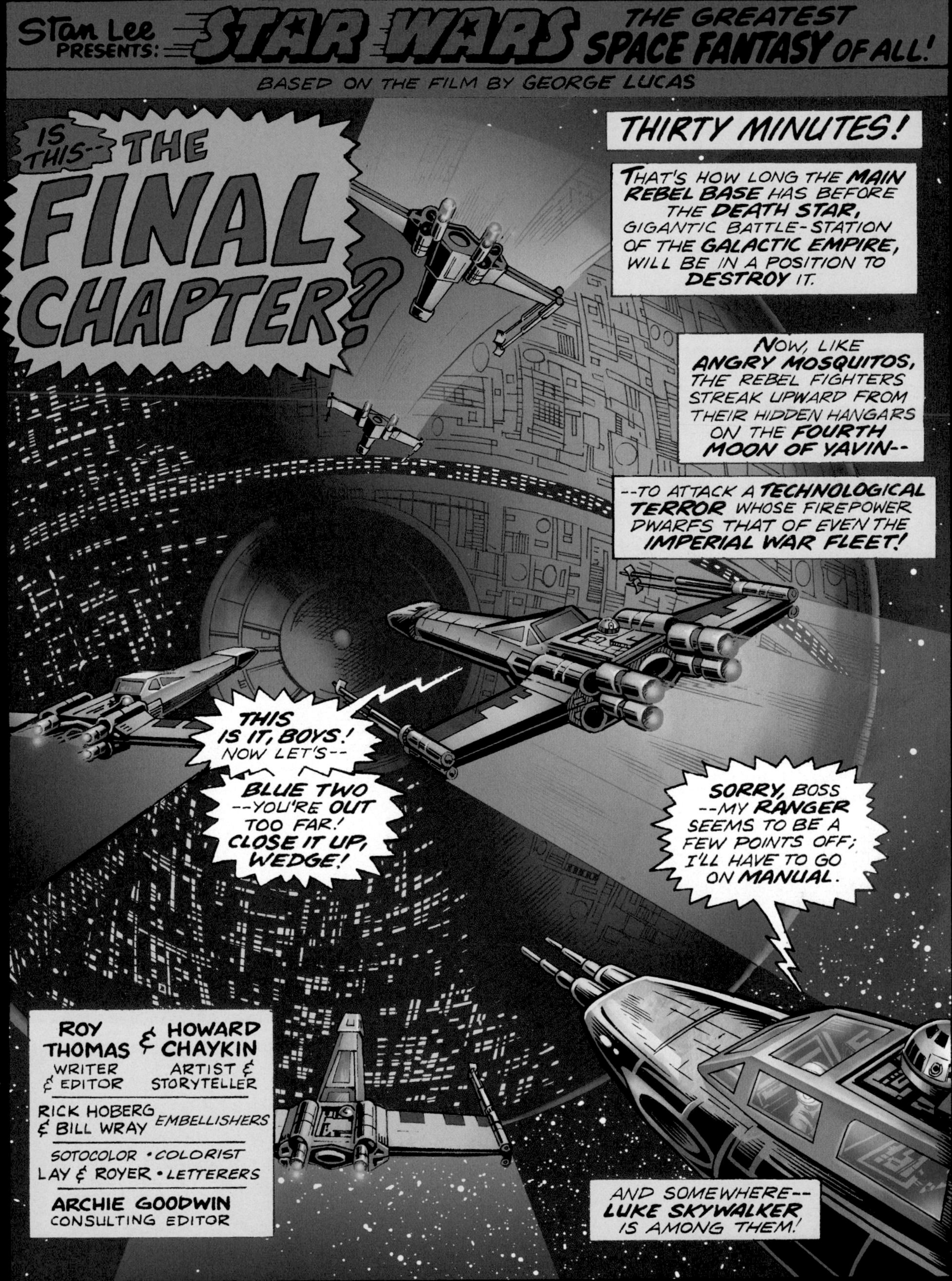
Stan Lee PRESENTS: STAR WARS THE GREATEST SPACE FANTASY OF ALL!
BASED ON THE FILM BY GEORGE LUCAS
IS THIS-- THE FINAL CHAPTER?
THIRTY MINUTES!
THAT'S HOW LONG THE MAIN REBEL BASE HAS BEFORE THE DEATH STAR, GIGANTIC BATTLE-STATION OF THE GALACTIC EMPIRE, WILL BE IN A POSITION TO DESTROY IT.
NOW, LIKE ANGRY MOSQUITOS, THE REBEL FIGHTERS STREAK UPWARD FROM THEIR HIDDEN HANGARS ON THE FOURTH MOON OF YAVIN--
--TO ATTACK A TECHNOLOGICAL TERROR WHOSE FIREPOWER DWARFS THAT OF EVEN THE IMPERIAL WAR FLEET!
THIS IS IT, BOYS! NOW LET'S--
BLUE TWO --YOU'RE OUT TOO FAR! CLOSE IT UP, WEDGE!
SORRY, BOSS --MY RANGER SEEMS TO BE A FEW POINTS OFF; I'LL HAVE TO GO ON MANUAL.
ROY THOMAS WRITER & EDITOR & HOWARD CHAYKIN ARTIST & STORYTELLER
RICK HOBERG & BILL WRAY EMBELLISHERS
SOTOCOLOR • COLORIST
LAY & ROYER • LETTERERS
ARCHIE GOODWIN CONSULTING EDITOR
AND SOMEWHERE-- LUKE SKYWALKER IS AMONG THEM!

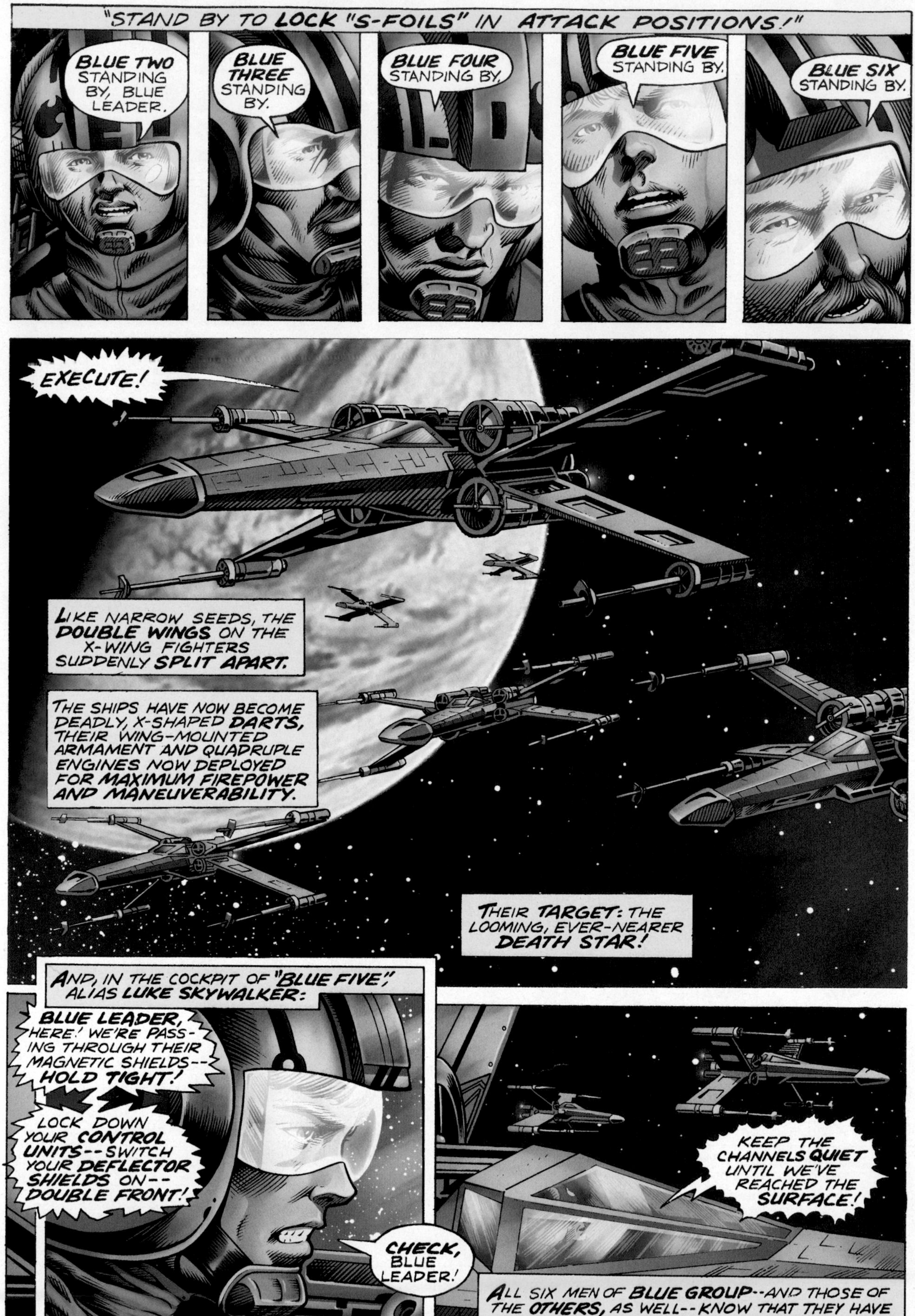
"STAND BY TO LOCK "S-FOILS" IN ATTACK POSITIONS!"
BLUE TWO STANDING BY, BLUE LEADER.
BLUE THREE STANDING BY.
BLUE FOUR STANDING BY.
BLUE FIVE STANDING BY.
BLUE SIX STANDING BY.
EXECUTE!
LIKE NARROW SEEDS, THE DOUBLE WINGS ON THE X-WING FIGHTERS SUDDENLY SPLIT APART.
THE SHIPS HAVE NOW BECOME DEADLY, X-SHAPED DARTS, THEIR WING-MOUNTED ARMAMENT AND QUADRUPLE ENGINES NOW DEPLOYED FOR MAXIMUM FIREPOWER AND MANEUVERABILITY.
THEIR TARGET: THE LOOMING, EVER-NEARER DEATH STAR!
AND, IN THE COCKPIT OF "BLUE FIVE," ALIAS LUKE SKYWALKER:
BLUE LEADER, HERE! WE'RE PASSING THROUGH THEIR MAGNETIC SHIELDS--HOLD TIGHT!
LOCK DOWN YOUR CONTROL UNITS--SWITCH YOUR DEFLECTOR SHIELDS ON--DOUBLE FRONT!
CHECK, BLUE LEADER!
KEEP THE CHANNELS QUIET UNTIL WE'VE REACHED THE SURFACE!
ALL SIX MEN OF BLUE GROUP--AND THOSE OF THE OTHERS, AS WELL--KNOW THAT THEY HAVE NO CHANCE OF DENTING THE IMPREGNABLE DEFENSES...

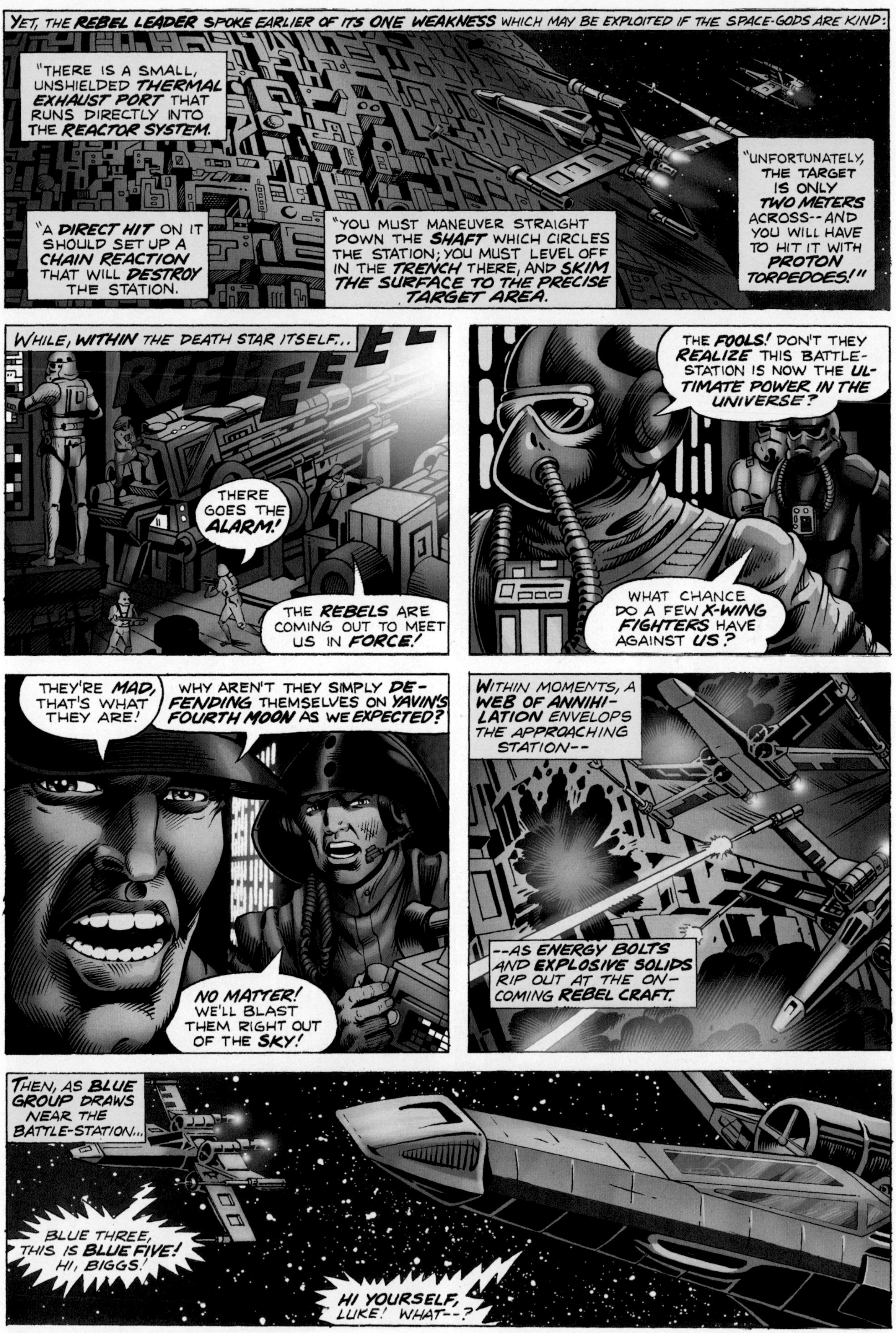

YET, THE REBEL LEADER SPOKE EARLIER OF ITS ONE WEAKNESS WHICH MAY BE EXPLOITED IF THE SPACE-GODS ARE KIND:
"THERE IS A SMALL, UNSHIELDED THERMAL EXHAUST PORT THAT RUNS DIRECTLY INTO THE REACTOR SYSTEM.
"A DIRECT HIT ON IT SHOULD SET UP A CHAIN REACTION THAT WILL DESTROY THE STATION.
"YOU MUST MANEUVER STRAIGHT DOWN THE SHAFT WHICH CIRCLES THE STATION; YOU MUST LEVEL OFF IN THE TRENCH THERE, AND SKIM THE SURFACE TO THE PRECISE TARGET AREA.
"UNFORTUNATELY, THE TARGET IS ONLY TWO METERS ACROSS--AND YOU WILL HAVE TO HIT IT WITH PROTON TORPEDOES!"
WHILE, WITHIN THE DEATH STAR ITSELF...
REEEEEE
THERE GOES THE ALARM!
THE REBELS ARE COMING OUT TO MEET US IN FORCE!
THE FOOLS! DON'T THEY REALIZE THIS BATTLE-STATION IS NOW THE ULTIMATE POWER IN THE UNIVERSE?
WHAT CHANCE DO A FEW X-WING FIGHTERS HAVE AGAINST US?
THEY'RE MAD, THAT'S WHAT THEY ARE!
WHY AREN'T THEY SIMPLY DEFENDING THEMSELVES ON YAVIN'S FOURTH MOON AS WE EXPECTED?
NO MATTER! WE'LL BLAST THEM RIGHT OUT OF THE SKY!
WITHIN MOMENTS, A WEB OF ANNIHILATION ENVELOPS THE APPROACHING STATION--
--AS ENERGY BOLTS AND EXPLOSIVE SOLIDS RIP OUT AT THE ON-COMING REBEL CRAFT.
THEN, AS BLUE GROUP DRAWS NEAR THE BATTLE-STATION...
BLUE THREE, THIS IS BLUE FIVE! HI, BIGGS!
HI YOURSELF, LUKE! WHAT--?

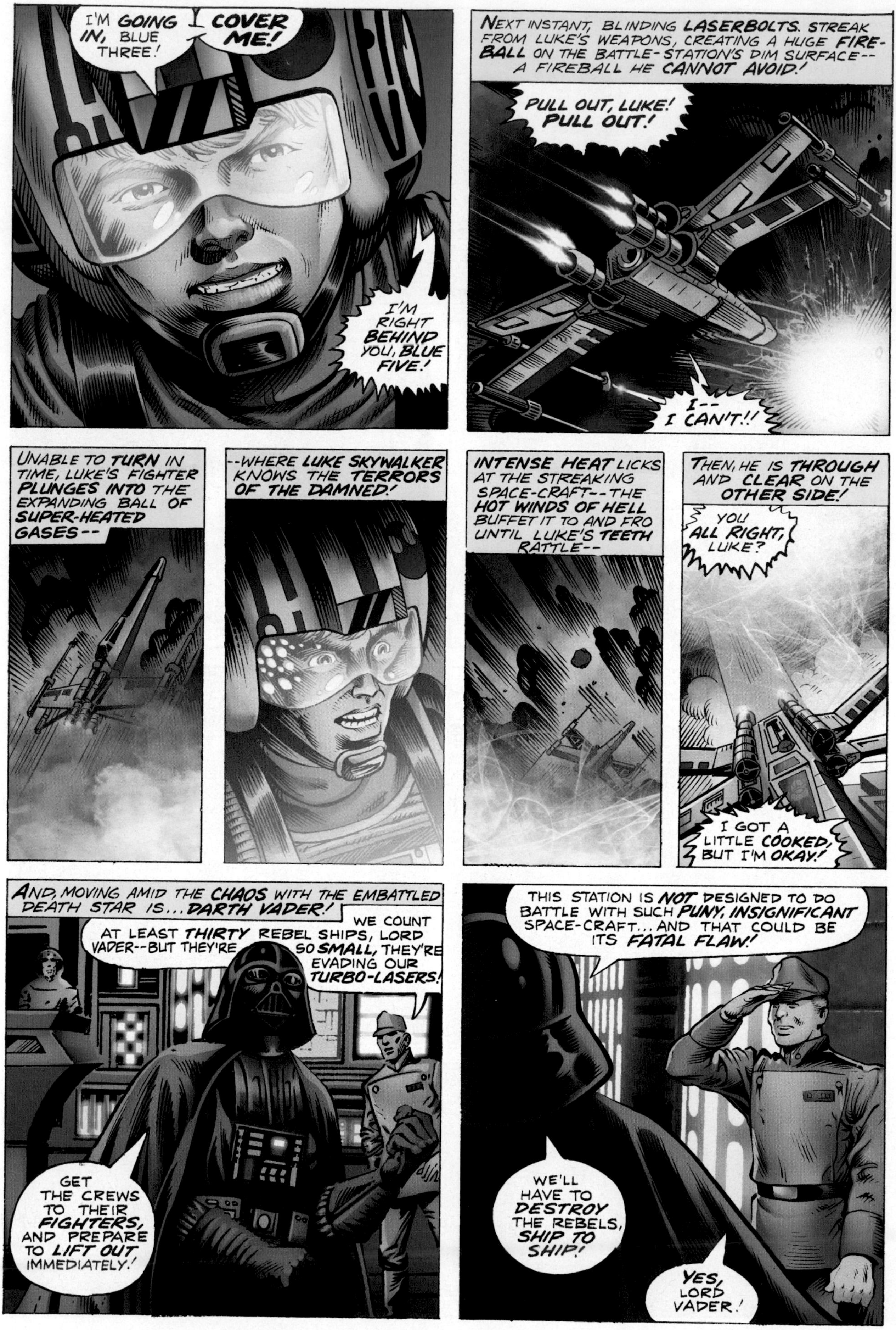
I'M GOING IN, BLUE THREE!
COVER ME!
I'M RIGHT BEHIND YOU, BLUE FIVE!
NEXT INSTANT, BLINDING LASERBOLTS STREAK FROM LUKE'S WEAPONS, CREATING A HUGE FIRE-BALL ON THE BATTLE-STATION'S DIM SURFACE-- A FIREBALL HE CANNOT AVOID!
PULL OUT, LUKE! PULL OUT!
I-- I CAN'T!!
UNABLE TO TURN IN TIME, LUKE'S FIGHTER PLUNGES INTO THE EXPANDING BALL OF SUPER-HEATED GASES--
--WHERE LUKE SKYWALKER KNOWS THE TERRORS OF THE DAMNED!
INTENSE HEAT LICKS AT THE STREAKING SPACE-CRAFT--THE HOT WINDS OF HELL BUFFET IT TO AND FRO UNTIL LUKE'S TEETH RATTLE--
THEN, HE IS THROUGH AND CLEAR ON THE OTHER SIDE!
YOU ALL RIGHT, LUKE?
I GOT A LITTLE COOKED, BUT I'M OKAY!
AND, MOVING AMID THE CHAOS WITH THE EMBATTLED DEATH STAR IS... DARTH VADER!
WE COUNT AT LEAST THIRTY REBEL SHIPS, LORD VADER--BUT THEY'RE SO SMALL, THEY'RE EVADING OUR TURBO-LASERS!
GET THE CREWS TO THEIR FIGHTERS, AND PREPARE TO LIFT OUT IMMEDIATELY!
THIS STATION IS NOT DESIGNED TO DO BATTLE WITH SUCH PUNY, INSIGNIFICANT SPACE-CRAFT... AND THAT COULD BE ITS FATAL FLAW!
WE'LL HAVE TO DESTROY THE REBELS, SHIP TO SHIP!
YES, LORD VADER!

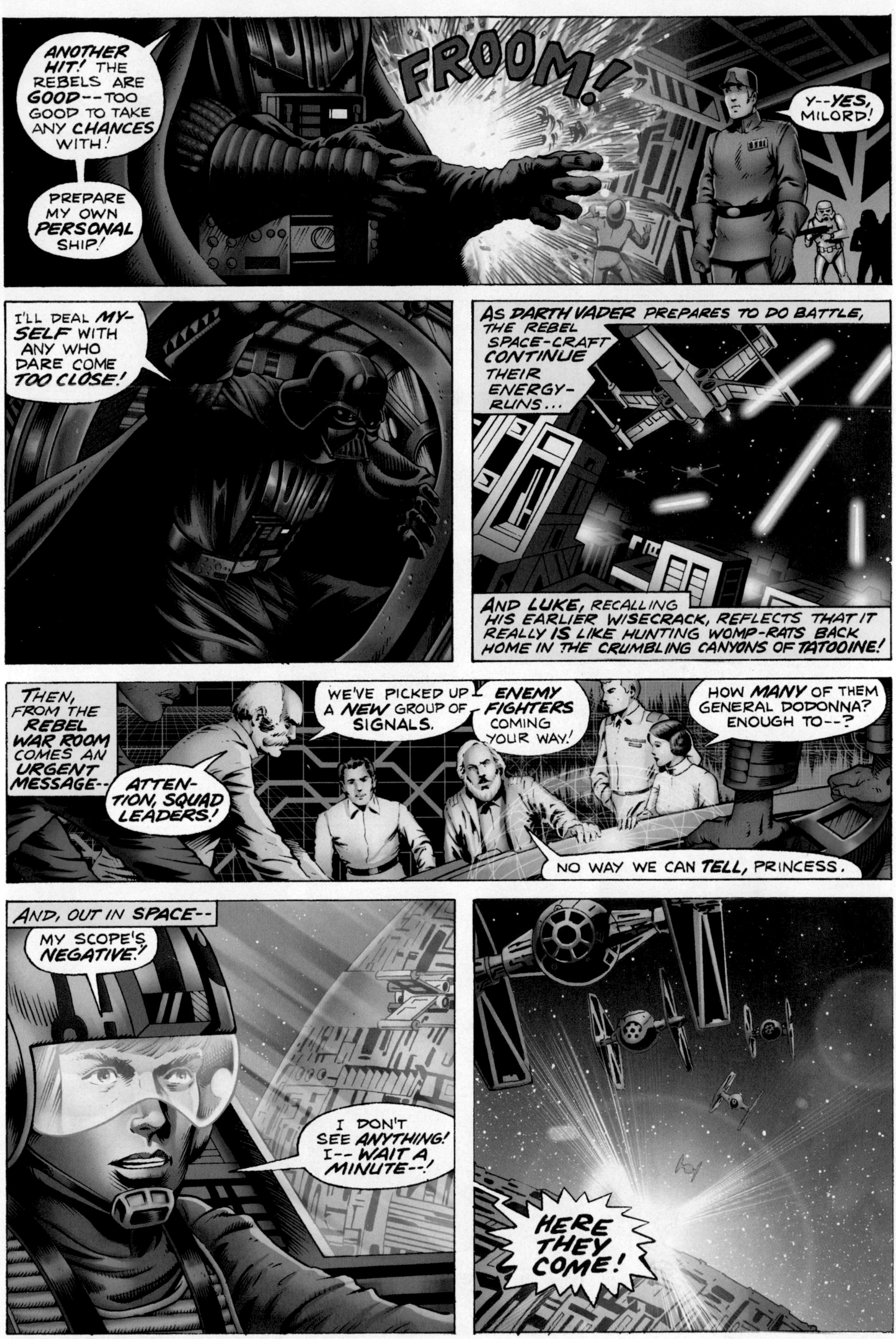
ANOTHER HIT! THE REBELS ARE GOOD--TOO GOOD TO TAKE ANY CHANCES WITH!
PREPARE MY OWN PERSONAL SHIP!
FROOM!
Y--YES, MILORD!
I'LL DEAL MYSELF WITH ANY WHO DARE COME TOO CLOSE!
AS DARTH VADER PREPARES TO DO BATTLE, THE REBEL SPACE-CRAFT CONTINUE THEIR ENERGY-RUNS...
AND LUKE, RECALLING HIS EARLIER WISECRACK, REFLECTS THAT IT REALLY IS LIKE HUNTING WOMP-RATS BACK HOME IN THE CRUMBLING CANYONS OF TATOOINE!
THEN, FROM THE REBEL WAR ROOM COMES AN URGENT MESSAGE--
ATTENTION, SQUAD LEADERS!
WE'VE PICKED UP A NEW GROUP OF SIGNALS.
ENEMY FIGHTERS COMING YOUR WAY!
HOW MANY OF THEM GENERAL DODONNA? ENOUGH TO--?
NO WAY WE CAN TELL, PRINCESS.
AND, OUT IN SPACE--
MY SCOPE'S NEGATIVE!
I DON'T SEE ANYTHING! I--WAIT A MINUTE--!
HERE THEY COME!

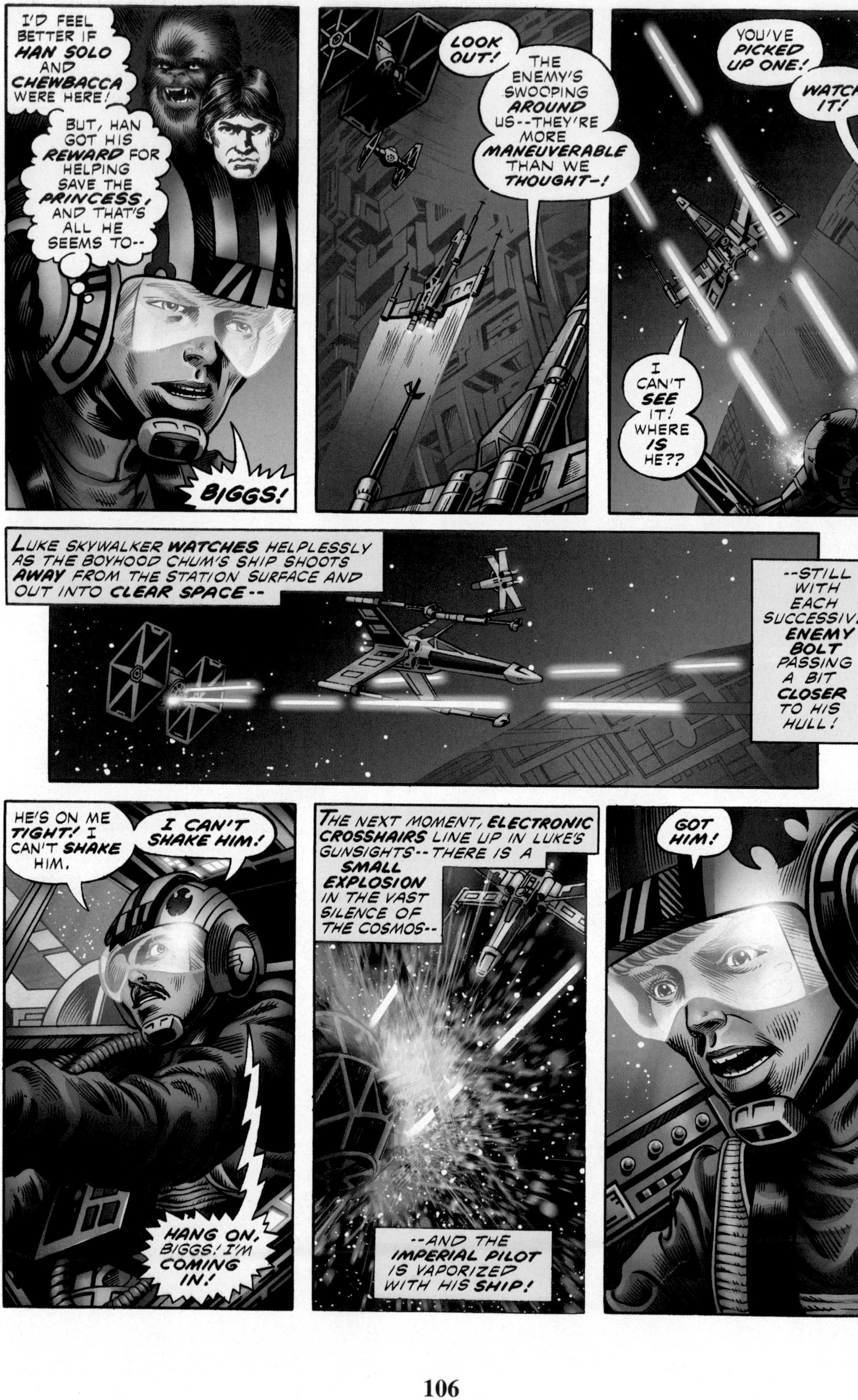
I'D FEEL BETTER IF HAN SOLO AND CHEWBACCA WERE HERE!
BUT, HAN GOT HIS REWARD FOR HELPING SAVE THE PRINCESS, AND THAT'S ALL HE SEEMS TO--
BIGGS!
LOOK OUT!
THE ENEMY'S SWOOPING AROUND US--THEY'RE MORE MANEUVERABLE THAN WE THOUGHT-!
YOU'VE PICKED UP ONE!
WATCH IT!
I CAN'T SEE IT! WHERE IS HE??
LUKE SKYWALKER WATCHES HELPLESSLY AS THE BOYHOOD CHUM'S SHIP SHOOTS AWAY FROM THE STATION SURFACE AND OUT INTO CLEAR SPACE--
--STILL WITH EACH SUCCESSIVE ENEMY BOLT PASSING A BIT CLOSER TO HIS HULL!
HE'S ON ME TIGHT! I CAN'T SHAKE HIM.
I CAN'T SHAKE HIM!
HANG ON, BIGGS! I'M COMING IN!
THE NEXT MOMENT, ELECTRONIC CROSSHAIRS LINE UP IN LUKE'S GUNSIGHTS--THERE IS A SMALL EXPLOSION IN THE VAST SILENCE OF THE COSMOS--
--AND THE IMPERIAL PILOT IS VAPORIZED WITH HIS SHIP!
GOT HIM!

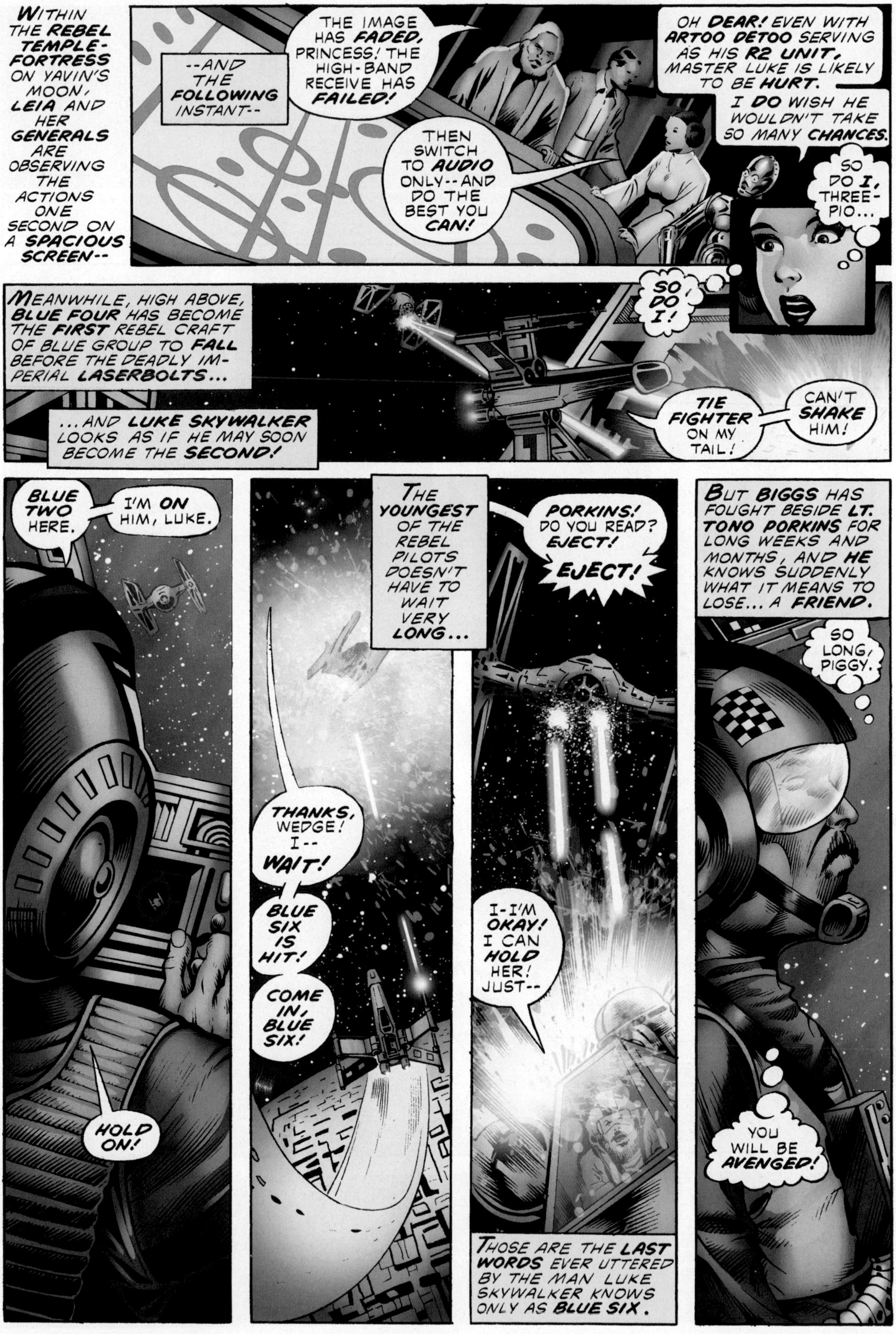
WITHIN THE REBEL TEMPLE-FORTRESS ON YAVIN'S MOON, LEIA AND HER GENERALS ARE OBSERVING THE ACTIONS ONE SECOND ON A SPACIOUS SCREEN--
--AND THE FOLLOWING INSTANT--
THE IMAGE HAS FADED, PRINCESS! THE HIGH-BAND RECEIVE HAS FAILED!
THEN SWITCH TO AUDIO ONLY--AND DO THE BEST YOU CAN!
OH DEAR! EVEN WITH ARTOO DETOO SERVING AS HIS R2 UNIT, MASTER LUKE IS LIKELY TO BE HURT.
I DO WISH HE WOULDN'T TAKE SO MANY CHANCES.
SO DO I, THREEPIO...
SO DO I!
MEANWHILE, HIGH ABOVE, BLUE FOUR HAS BECOME THE FIRST REBEL CRAFT OF BLUE GROUP TO FALL BEFORE THE DEADLY IMPERIAL LASERBOLTS...
...AND LUKE SKYWALKER LOOKS AS IF HE MAY SOON BECOME THE SECOND!
TIE FIGHTER ON MY TAIL!
CAN'T SHAKE HIM!
BLUE TWO HERE.
I'M ON HIM, LUKE.
HOLD ON!
THANKS, WEDGE! I-- WAIT!
BLUE SIX IS HIT!
COME IN, BLUE SIX!
THE YOUNGEST OF THE REBEL PILOTS DOESN'T HAVE TO WAIT VERY LONG...
PORKINS! DO YOU READ? EJECT!
EJECT!
I-I'M OKAY! I CAN HOLD HER! JUST--
THOSE ARE THE LAST WORDS EVER UTTERED BY THE MAN LUKE SKYWALKER KNOWS ONLY AS BLUE SIX.
BUT BIGGS HAS FOUGHT BESIDE LT. TONO PORKINS FOR LONG WEEKS AND MONTHS, AND HE KNOWS SUDDENLY WHAT IT MEANS TO LOSE... A FRIEND.
SO LONG, PIGGY.
YOU WILL BE AVENGED!

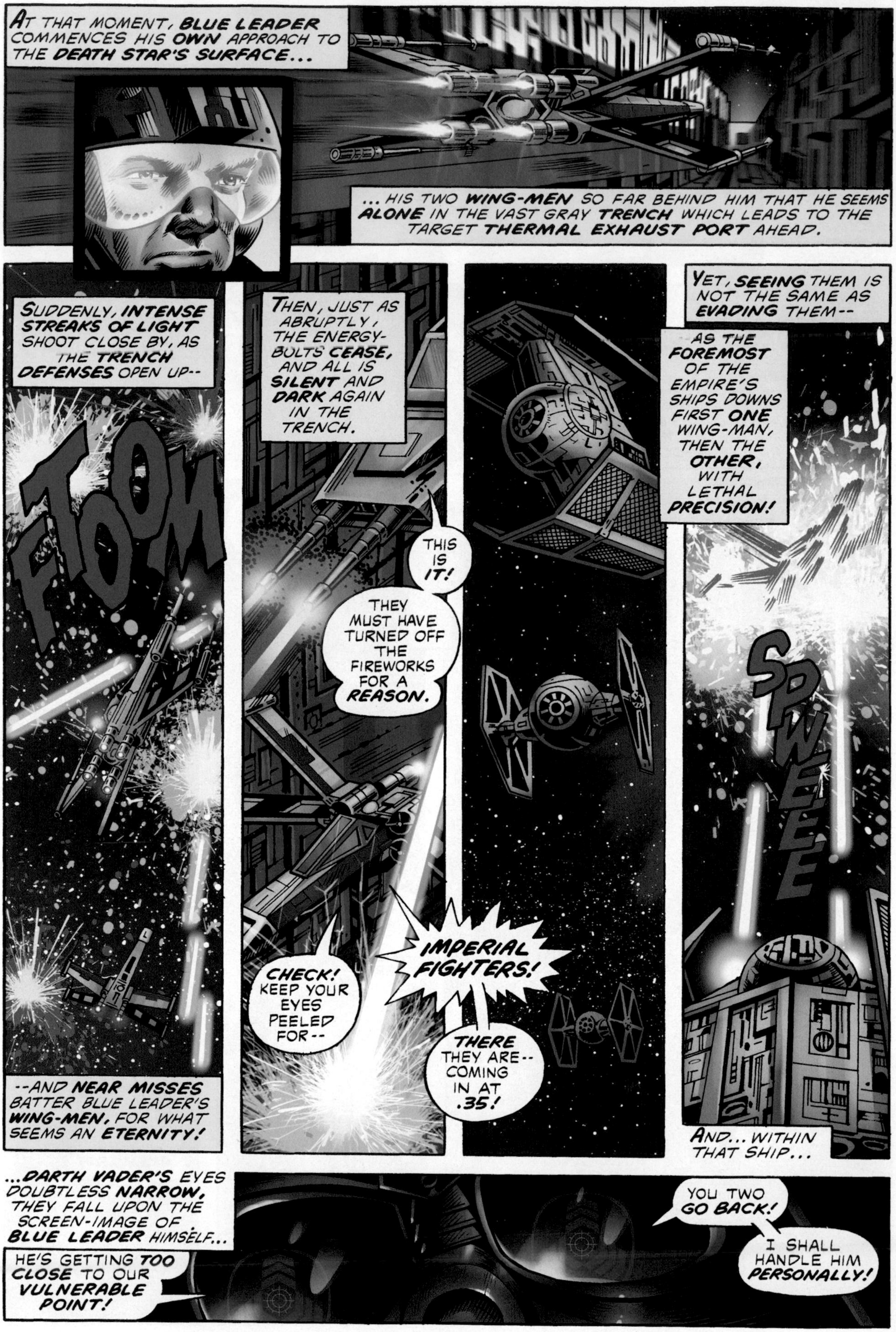

AT THAT MOMENT, BLUE LEADER COMMENCES HIS OWN APPROACH TO THE DEATH STAR'S SURFACE...
...HIS TWO WING-MEN SO FAR BEHIND HIM THAT HE SEEMS ALONE IN THE VAST GRAY TRENCH WHICH LEADS TO THE TARGET THERMAL EXHAUST PORT AHEAD.
SUDDENLY, INTENSE STREAKS OF LIGHT SHOOT CLOSE BY, AS THE TRENCH DEFENSES OPEN UP--
FTOOM
--AND NEAR MISSES BATTER BLUE LEADER'S WING-MEN. FOR WHAT SEEMS AN ETERNITY!
THEN, JUST AS ABRUPTLY, THE ENERGY-BOLTS CEASE, AND ALL IS SILENT AND DARK AGAIN IN THE TRENCH.
THIS IS IT!
THEY MUST HAVE TURNED OFF THE FIREWORKS FOR A REASON.
CHECK! KEEP YOUR EYES PEELED FOR--
IMPERIAL FIGHTERS!
THERE THEY ARE-- COMING IN AT .35!
YET, SEEING THEM IS NOT THE SAME AS EVADING THEM--
--AS THE FOREMOST OF THE EMPIRE'S SHIPS DOWNS FIRST ONE WING-MAN, THEN THE OTHER, WITH LETHAL PRECISION!
SPWEEE
AND... WITHIN THAT SHIP...
...DARTH VADER'S EYES DOUBTLESS NARROW, THEY FALL UPON THE SCREEN-IMAGE OF BLUE LEADER HIMSELF...
HE'S GETTING TOO CLOSE TO OUR VULNERABLE POINT!
YOU TWO GO BACK!
I SHALL HANDLE HIM PERSONALLY!

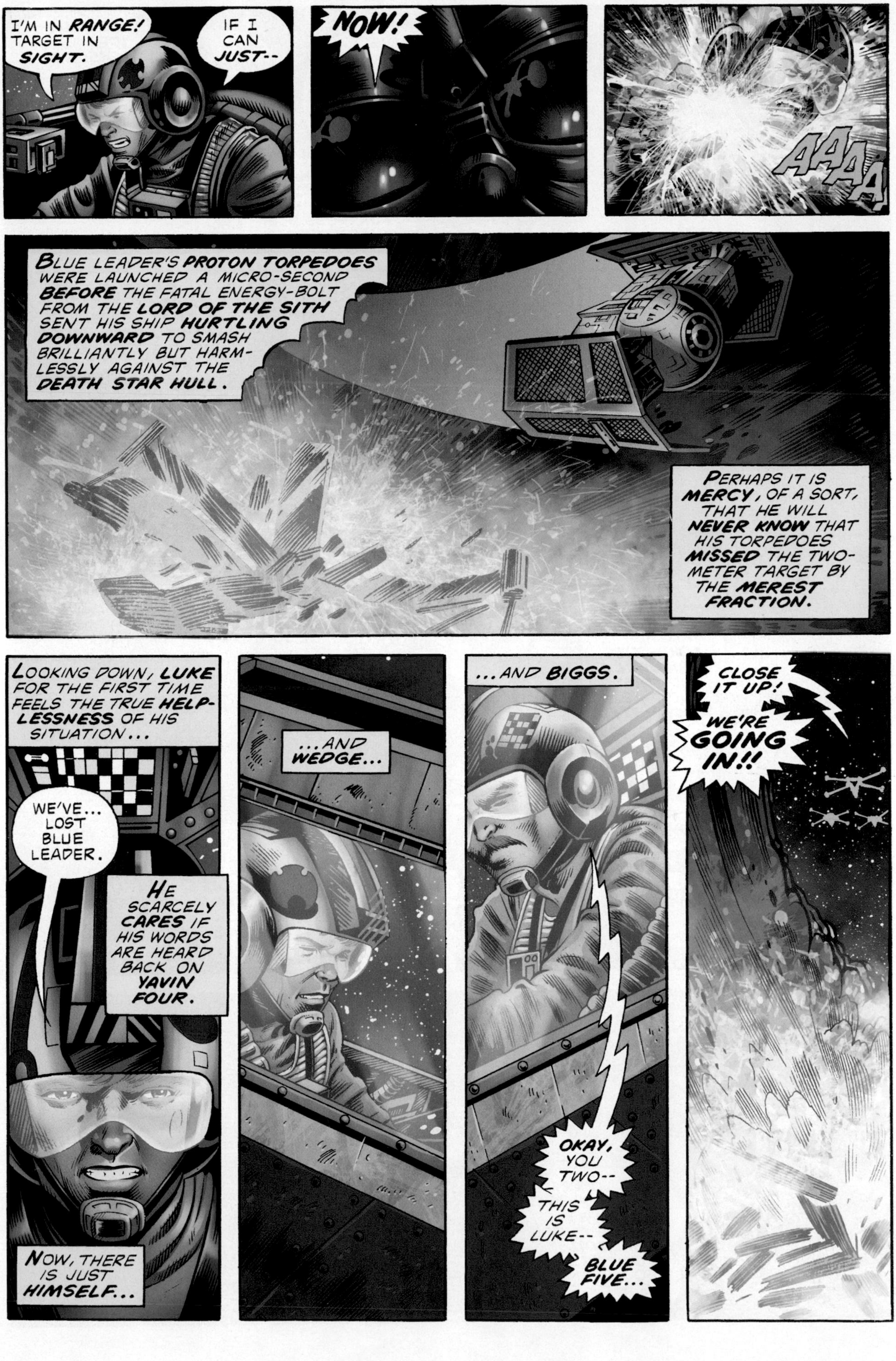
I'M IN RANGE! TARGET IN SIGHT.
IF I CAN JUST--
NOW!
AAAA
BLUE LEADER'S PROTON TORPEDOES WERE LAUNCHED A MICRO-SECOND BEFORE THE FATAL ENERGY-BOLT FROM THE LORD OF THE SITH SENT HIS SHIP HURTLING DOWNWARD TO SMASH BRILLIANTLY BUT HARMLESSLY AGAINST THE DEATH STAR HULL.
PERHAPS IT IS MERCY, OF A SORT, THAT HE WILL NEVER KNOW THAT HIS TORPEDOES MISSED THE TWO-METER TARGET BY THE MEREST FRACTION.
LOOKING DOWN, LUKE FOR THE FIRST TIME FEELS THE TRUE HELPLESSNESS OF HIS SITUATION...
WE'VE... LOST BLUE LEADER.
HE SCARCELY CARES IF HIS WORDS ARE HEARD BACK ON YAVIN FOUR.
NOW, THERE IS JUST HIMSELF...
...AND WEDGE...
...AND BIGGS.
OKAY, YOU TWO--
THIS IS LUKE--
BLUE FIVE...
CLOSE IT UP!
WE'RE GOING IN!!

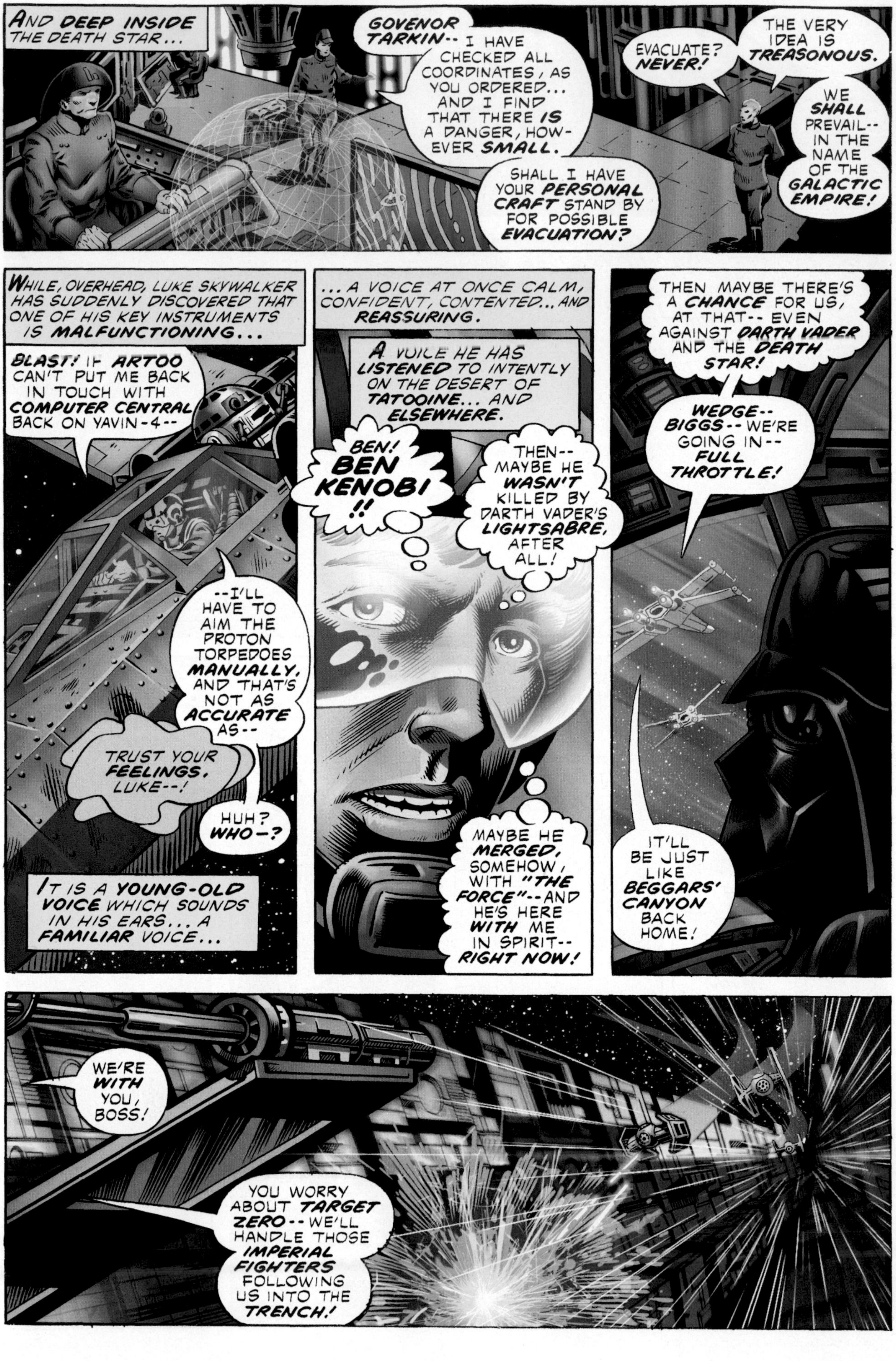
AND DEEP INSIDE THE DEATH STAR...
GOVENOR TARKIN-- I HAVE CHECKED ALL COORDINATES, AS YOU ORDERED... AND I FIND THAT THERE IS A DANGER, HOWEVER SMALL.
SHALL I HAVE YOUR PERSONAL CRAFT STAND BY FOR POSSIBLE EVACUATION?
EVACUATE? NEVER!
THE VERY IDEA IS TREASONOUS.
WE SHALL PREVAIL-- IN THE NAME OF THE GALACTIC EMPIRE!
WHILE, OVERHEAD, LUKE SKYWALKER HAS SUDDENLY DISCOVERED THAT ONE OF HIS KEY INSTRUMENTS IS MALFUNCTIONING...
BLAST! IF ARTOO CAN'T PUT ME BACK IN TOUCH WITH COMPUTER CENTRAL BACK ON YAVIN-4--
--I'LL HAVE TO AIM THE PROTON TORPEDOES MANUALLY, AND THAT'S NOT AS ACCURATE AS--
TRUST YOUR FEELINGS, LUKE--!
HUH? WHO--?
IT IS A YOUNG-OLD VOICE WHICH SOUNDS IN HIS EARS... A FAMILIAR VOICE...
...A VOICE AT ONCE CALM, CONFIDENT, CONTENTED... AND REASSURING.
A VOICE HE HAS LISTENED TO INTENTLY ON THE DESERT OF TATOOINE... AND ELSEWHERE.
BEN! BEN KENOBI!!
THEN-- MAYBE HE WASN'T KILLED BY DARTH VADER'S LIGHTSABRE, AFTER ALL!
MAYBE HE MERGED, SOMEHOW, WITH "THE FORCE"-- AND HE'S HERE WITH ME IN SPIRIT-- RIGHT NOW!
THEN MAYBE THERE'S A CHANCE FOR US, AT THAT-- EVEN AGAINST DARTH VADER AND THE DEATH STAR!
WEDGE-- BIGGS-- WE'RE GOING IN-- FULL THROTTLE!
IT'LL BE JUST LIKE BEGGARS' CANYON BACK HOME!
WE'RE WITH YOU, BOSS!
YOU WORRY ABOUT TARGET ZERO-- WE'LL HANDLE THOSE IMPERIAL FIGHTERS FOLLOWING US INTO THE TRENCH!

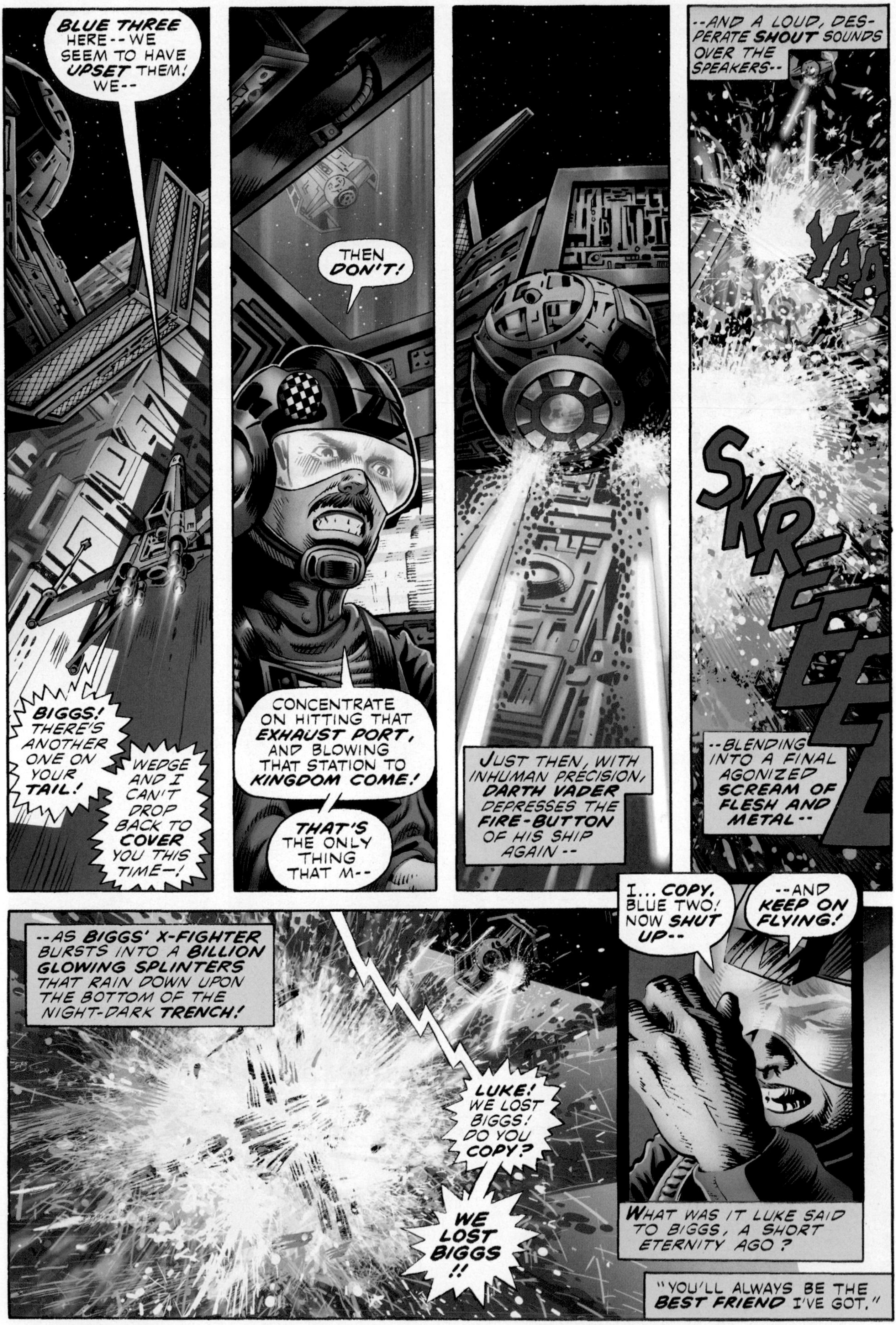
BLUE THREE HERE--WE SEEM TO HAVE UPSET THEM! WE--
BIGGS! THERE'S ANOTHER ONE ON YOUR TAIL!
WEDGE AND I CAN'T DROP BACK TO COVER YOU THIS TIME--!
THEN DON'T!
CONCENTRATE ON HITTING THAT EXHAUST PORT, AND BLOWING THAT STATION TO KINGDOM COME!
THAT'S THE ONLY THING THAT M--
JUST THEN, WITH INHUMAN PRECISION, DARTH VADER DEPRESSES THE FIRE-BUTTON OF HIS SHIP AGAIN--
--AND A LOUD, DESPERATE SHOUT SOUNDS OVER THE SPEAKERS--
SKR-EEEE
--BLENDING INTO A FINAL AGONIZED SCREAM OF FLESH AND METAL--
--AS BIGGS' X-FIGHTER BURSTS INTO A BILLION GLOWING SPLINTERS THAT RAIN DOWN UPON THE BOTTOM OF THE NIGHT-DARK TRENCH!
LUKE! WE LOST BIGGS! DO YOU COPY?
WE LOST BIGGS!!
I... COPY, BLUE TWO! NOW SHUT UP--
--AND KEEP ON FLYING!
WHAT WAS IT LUKE SAID TO BIGGS, A SHORT ETERNITY AGO?
"YOU'LL ALWAYS BE THE BEST FRIEND I'VE GOT."

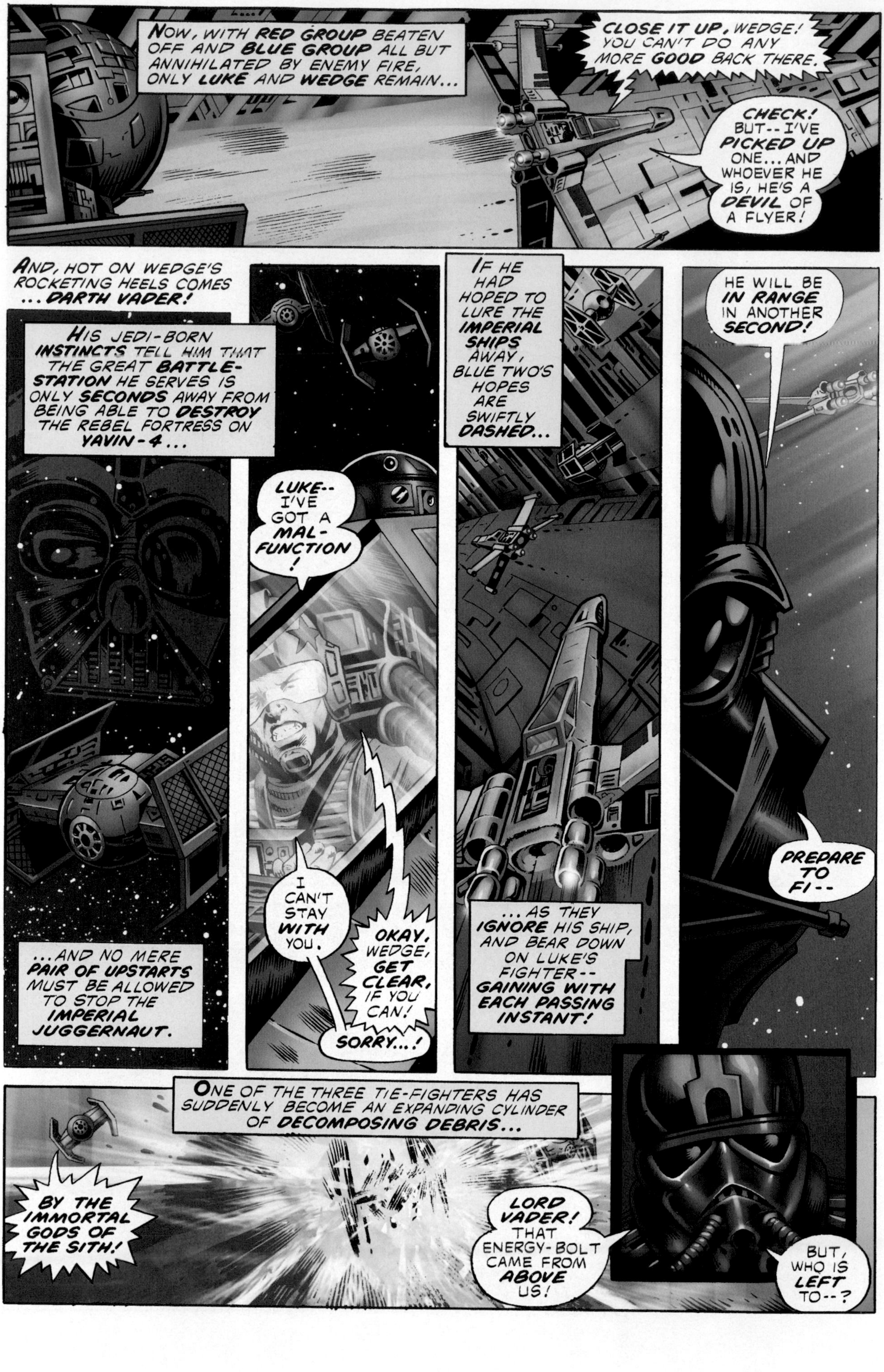
NOW, WITH RED GROUP BEATEN OFF AND BLUE GROUP ALL BUT ANNIHILATED BY ENEMY FIRE, ONLY LUKE AND WEDGE REMAIN...
CLOSE IT UP, WEDGE! YOU CAN'T DO ANY MORE GOOD BACK THERE.
CHECK! BUT--I'VE PICKED UP ONE... AND WHOEVER HE IS, HE'S A DEVIL OF A FLYER!
AND, HOT ON WEDGE'S ROCKETING HEELS COMES ...DARTH VADER!
HIS JEDI-BORN INSTINCTS TELL HIM THAT THE GREAT BATTLE-STATION HE SERVES IS ONLY SECONDS AWAY FROM BEING ABLE TO DESTROY THE REBEL FORTRESS ON YAVIN-4...
...AND NO MERE PAIR OF UPSTARTS MUST BE ALLOWED TO STOP THE IMPERIAL JUGGERNAUT.
LUKE-- I'VE GOT A MAL-FUNCTION!
I CAN'T STAY WITH YOU.
OKAY, WEDGE, GET CLEAR, IF YOU CAN!
SORRY...!
IF HE HAD HOPED TO LURE THE IMPERIAL SHIPS AWAY, BLUE TWO'S HOPES ARE SWIFTLY DASHED...
...AS THEY IGNORE HIS SHIP, AND BEAR DOWN ON LUKE'S FIGHTER-- GAINING WITH EACH PASSING INSTANT!
HE WILL BE IN RANGE IN ANOTHER SECOND!
PREPARE TO FI--
ONE OF THE THREE TIE-FIGHTERS HAS SUDDENLY BECOME AN EXPANDING CYLINDER OF DECOMPOSING DEBRIS...
BY THE IMMORTAL GODS OF THE SITH!
LORD VADER! THAT ENERGY-BOLT CAME FROM ABOVE US!
BUT, WHO IS LEFT TO--?

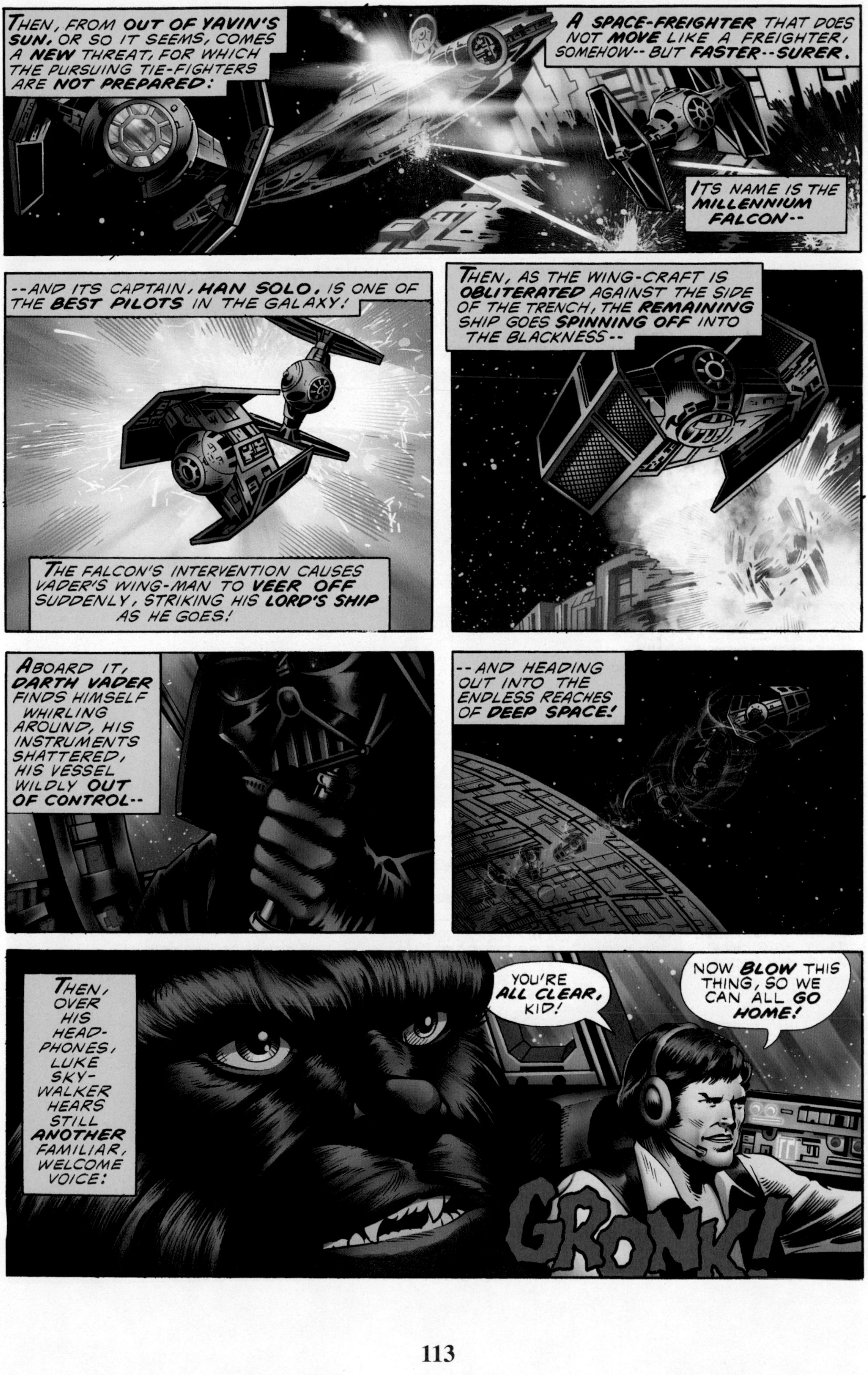
THEN, FROM OUT OF YAVIN'S SUN, OR SO IT SEEMS, COMES A NEW THREAT, FOR WHICH THE PURSUING TIE-FIGHTERS ARE NOT PREPARED:
A SPACE-FREIGHTER THAT DOES NOT MOVE LIKE A FREIGHTER, SOMEHOW-- BUT FASTER--SURER.
ITS NAME IS THE MILLENNIUM FALCON--
--AND ITS CAPTAIN, HAN SOLO, IS ONE OF THE BEST PILOTS IN THE GALAXY!
THE FALCON'S INTERVENTION CAUSES VADER'S WING-MAN TO VEER OFF SUDDENLY, STRIKING HIS LORD'S SHIP AS HE GOES!
THEN, AS THE WING-CRAFT IS OBLITERATED AGAINST THE SIDE OF THE TRENCH, THE REMAINING SHIP GOES SPINNING OFF INTO THE BLACKNESS--
ABOARD IT, DARTH VADER FINDS HIMSELF WHIRLING AROUND, HIS INSTRUMENTS SHATTERED, HIS VESSEL WILDLY OUT OF CONTROL--
--AND HEADING OUT INTO THE ENDLESS REACHES OF DEEP SPACE!
THEN, OVER HIS HEAD-PHONES, LUKE SKY-WALKER HEARS STILL ANOTHER FAMILIAR, WELCOME VOICE:
YOU'RE ALL CLEAR, KID!
NOW BLOW THIS THING, SO WE CAN ALL GO HOME!
GRONK!

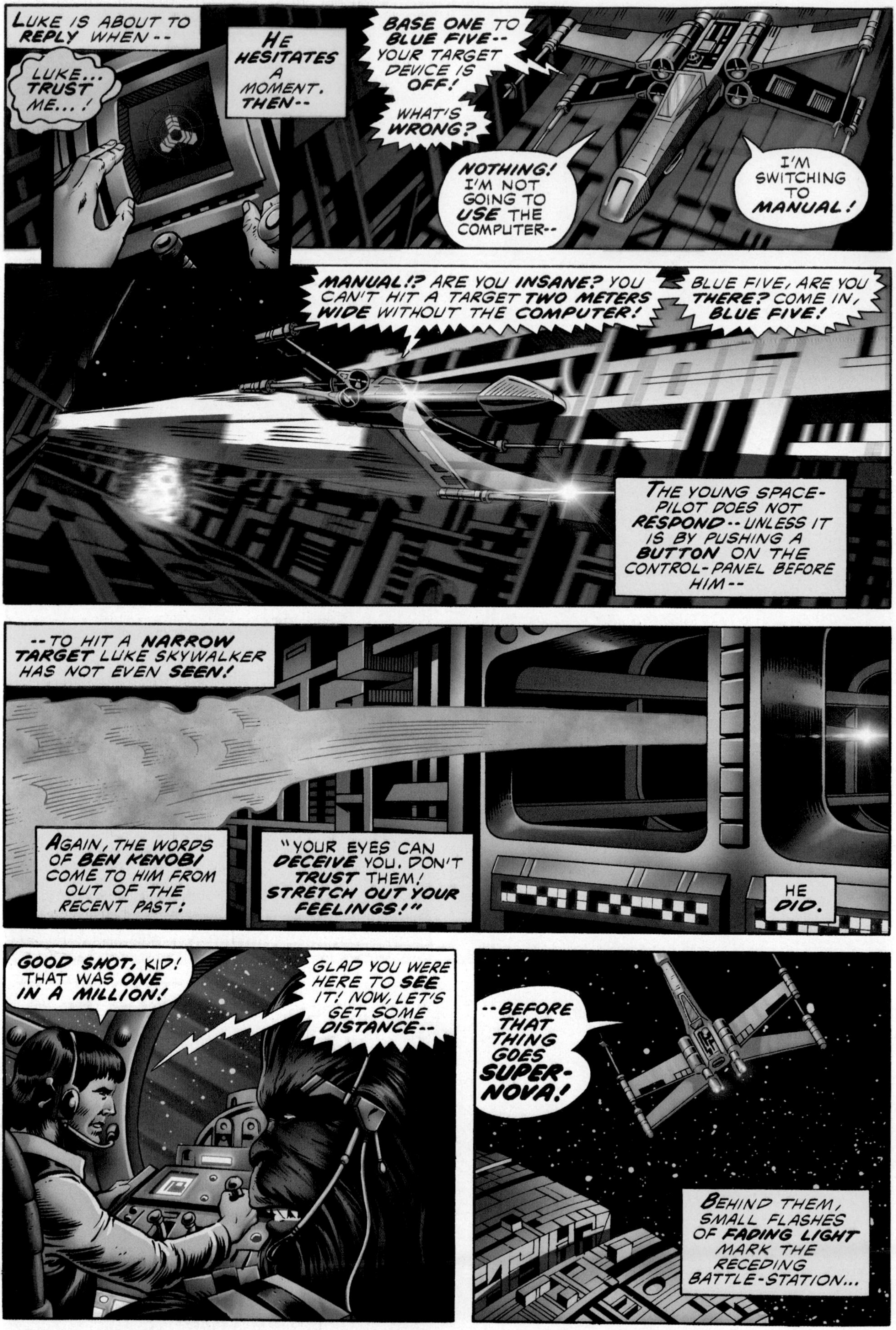
LUKE IS ABOUT TO REPLY WHEN --
LUKE... TRUST ME...!
HE HESITATES A MOMENT. THEN --
BASE ONE TO BLUE FIVE -- YOUR TARGET DEVICE IS OFF!
WHAT'S WRONG?
NOTHING! I'M NOT GOING TO USE THE COMPUTER --
I'M SWITCHING TO MANUAL!
MANUAL!? ARE YOU INSANE? YOU CAN'T HIT A TARGET TWO METERS WIDE WITHOUT THE COMPUTER!
BLUE FIVE, ARE YOU THERE? COME IN, BLUE FIVE!
THE YOUNG SPACE-PILOT DOES NOT RESPOND -- UNLESS IT IS BY PUSHING A BUTTON ON THE CONTROL-PANEL BEFORE HIM --
-- TO HIT A NARROW TARGET LUKE SKYWALKER HAS NOT EVEN SEEN!
AGAIN, THE WORDS OF BEN KENOBI COME TO HIM FROM OUT OF THE RECENT PAST:
"YOUR EYES CAN DECEIVE YOU. DON'T TRUST THEM! STRETCH OUT YOUR FEELINGS!"
HE DID.
GOOD SHOT, KID! THAT WAS ONE IN A MILLION!
GLAD YOU WERE HERE TO SEE IT! NOW, LET'S GET SOME DISTANCE --
-- BEFORE THAT THING GOES SUPER-NOVA!
BEHIND THEM, SMALL FLASHES OF FADING LIGHT MARK THE RECEDING BATTLE-STATION...

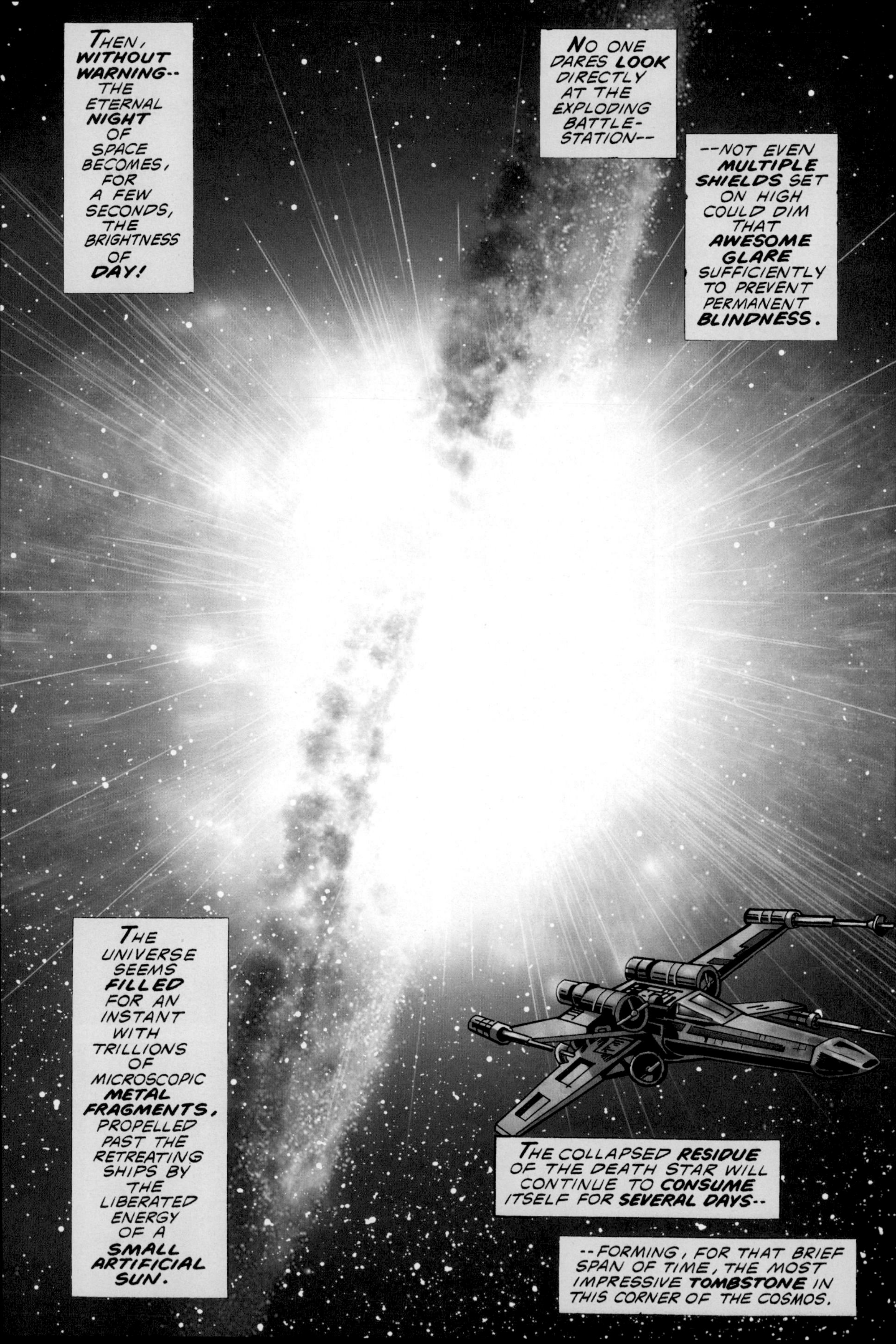
THEN, WITHOUT WARNING-- THE ETERNAL NIGHT OF SPACE BECOMES, FOR A FEW SECONDS, THE BRIGHTNESS OF DAY!
NO ONE DARES LOOK DIRECTLY AT THE EXPLODING BATTLE-STATION--
--NOT EVEN MULTIPLE SHIELDS SET ON HIGH COULD DIM THAT AWESOME GLARE SUFFICIENTLY TO PREVENT PERMANENT BLINDNESS.
THE UNIVERSE SEEMS FILLED FOR AN INSTANT WITH TRILLIONS OF MICROSCOPIC METAL FRAGMENTS, PROPELLED PAST THE RETREATING SHIPS BY THE LIBERATED ENERGY OF A SMALL ARTIFICIAL SUN.
THE COLLAPSED RESIDUE OF THE DEATH STAR WILL CONTINUE TO CONSUME ITSELF FOR SEVERAL DAYS--
--FORMING, FOR THAT BRIEF SPAN OF TIME, THE MOST IMPRESSIVE TOMBSTONE IN THIS CORNER OF THE COSMOS.

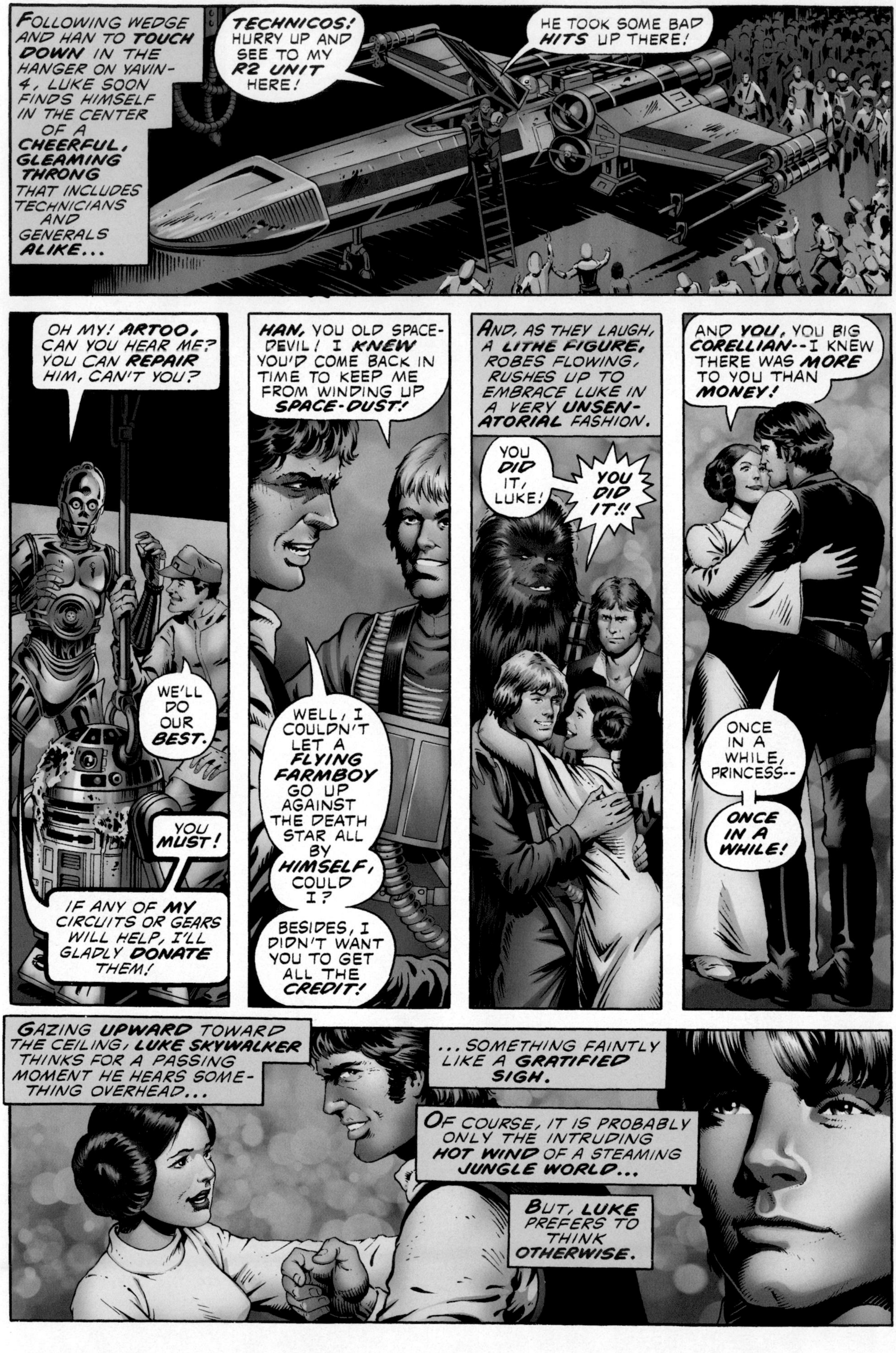

FOLLOWING WEDGE AND HAN TO TOUCH DOWN IN THE HANGER ON YAVIN-4, LUKE SOON FINDS HIMSELF IN THE CENTER OF A CHEERFUL, GLEAMING THRONG THAT INCLUDES TECHNICIANS AND GENERALS ALIKE...
TECHNICOS! HURRY UP AND SEE TO MY R2 UNIT HERE!
HE TOOK SOME BAD HITS UP THERE!
OH MY! ARTOO, CAN YOU HEAR ME? YOU CAN REPAIR HIM, CAN'T YOU?
WE'LL DO OUR BEST.
YOU MUST!
IF ANY OF MY CIRCUITS OR GEARS WILL HELP, I'LL GLADLY DONATE THEM!
HAN, YOU OLD SPACE-DEVIL! I KNEW YOU'D COME BACK IN TIME TO KEEP ME FROM WINDING UP SPACE-DUST!
WELL, I COULDN'T LET A FLYING FARMBOY GO UP AGAINST THE DEATH STAR ALL BY HIMSELF, COULD I?
BESIDES, I DIDN'T WANT YOU TO GET ALL THE CREDIT!
AND, AS THEY LAUGH, A LITHE FIGURE, ROBES FLOWING, RUSHES UP TO EMBRACE LUKE IN A VERY UNSEN-ATORIAL FASHION.
YOU DID IT, LUKE!
YOU DID IT!!
AND YOU, YOU BIG CORELLIAN--I KNEW THERE WAS MORE TO YOU THAN MONEY!
ONCE IN A WHILE, PRINCESS--
ONCE IN A WHILE!
GAZING UPWARD TOWARD THE CEILING, LUKE SKYWALKER THINKS FOR A PASSING MOMENT HE HEARS SOME-THING OVERHEAD...
...SOMETHING FAINTLY LIKE A GRATIFIED SIGH.
OF COURSE, IT IS PROBABLY ONLY THE INTRUDING HOT WIND OF A STEAMING JUNGLE WORLD...
BUT, LUKE PREFERS TO THINK OTHERWISE.

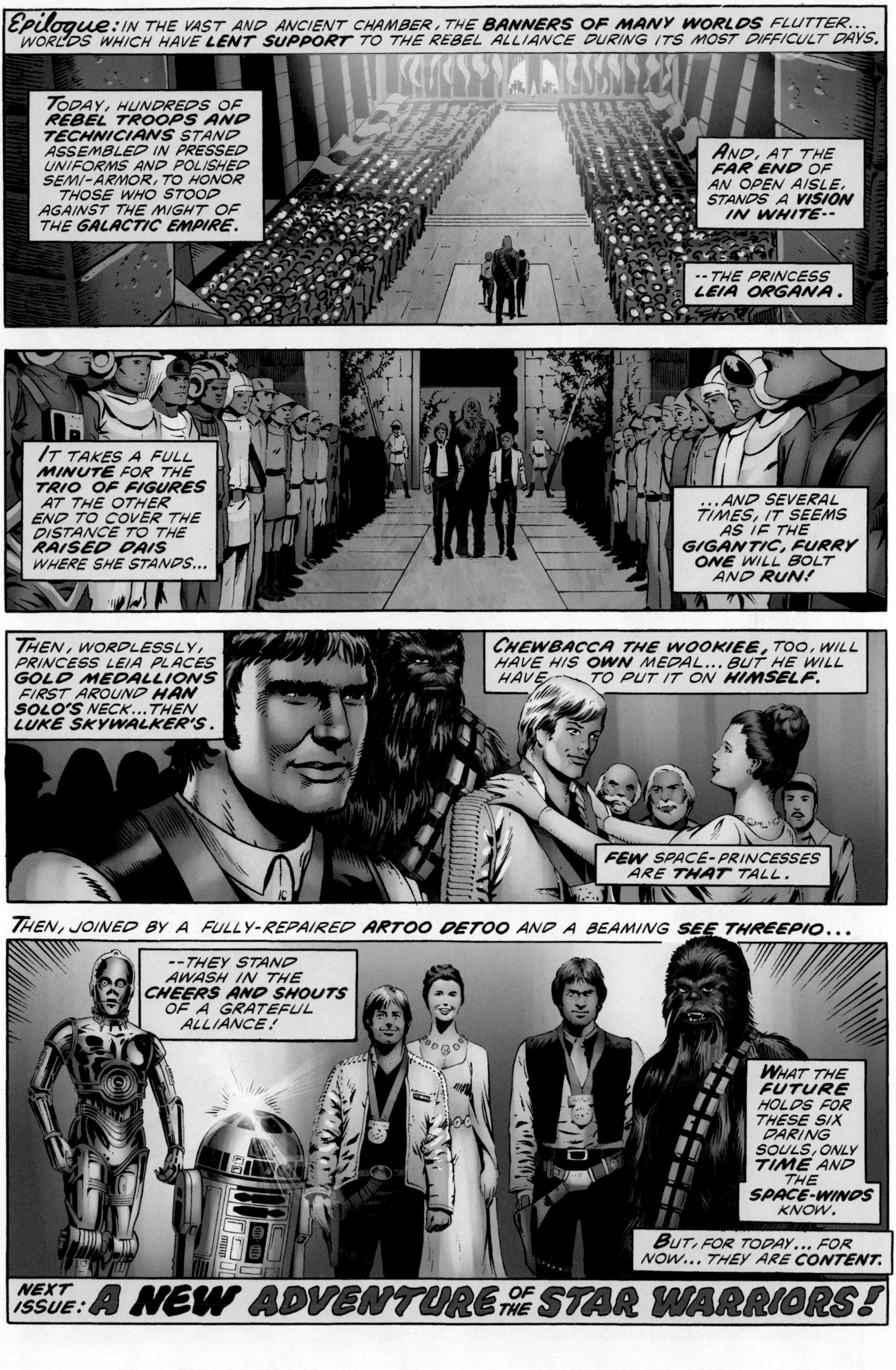

Epilogue: IN THE VAST AND ANCIENT CHAMBER, THE BANNERS OF MANY WORLDS FLUTTER... WORLDS WHICH HAVE LENT SUPPORT TO THE REBEL ALLIANCE DURING ITS MOST DIFFICULT DAYS.
TODAY, HUNDREDS OF REBEL TROOPS AND TECHNICIANS STAND ASSEMBLED IN PRESSED UNIFORMS AND POLISHED SEMI-ARMOR, TO HONOR THOSE WHO STOOD AGAINST THE MIGHT OF THE GALACTIC EMPIRE.
AND, AT THE FAR END OF AN OPEN AISLE, STANDS A VISION IN WHITE--
--THE PRINCESS LEIA ORGANA.
IT TAKES A FULL MINUTE FOR THE TRIO OF FIGURES AT THE OTHER END TO COVER THE DISTANCE TO THE RAISED DAIS WHERE SHE STANDS...
...AND SEVERAL TIMES, IT SEEMS AS IF THE GIGANTIC, FURRY ONE WILL BOLT AND RUN!
THEN, WORDLESSLY, PRINCESS LEIA PLACES GOLD MEDALLIONS FIRST AROUND HAN SOLO'S NECK...THEN LUKE SKYWALKER'S.
CHEWBACCA THE WOOKIEE, TOO, WILL HAVE HIS OWN MEDAL... BUT HE WILL HAVE TO PUT IT ON HIMSELF.
FEW SPACE-PRINCESSES ARE THAT TALL.
THEN, JOINED BY A FULLY-REPAIRED ARTOO DETOO AND A BEAMING SEE THREEPIO...
--THEY STAND AWASH IN THE CHEERS AND SHOUTS OF A GRATEFUL ALLIANCE!
WHAT THE FUTURE HOLDS FOR THESE SIX DARING SOULS, ONLY TIME AND THE SPACE-WINDS KNOW.
BUT, FOR TODAY... FOR NOW... THEY ARE CONTENT.
NEXT ISSUE: A NEW ADVENTURE OF THE STAR WARRIORS!

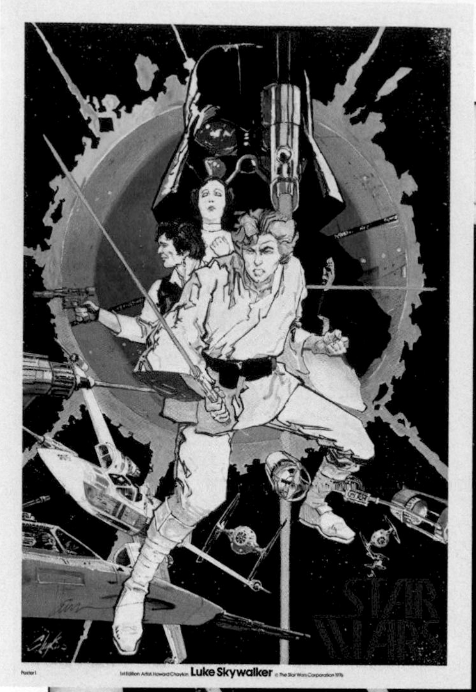
STAR WARS
Luke Skywalker

Star Wars poster by Howard Chaykin released at San Diego Comic-Con 1976 to promote the film and Marvel's adaptation

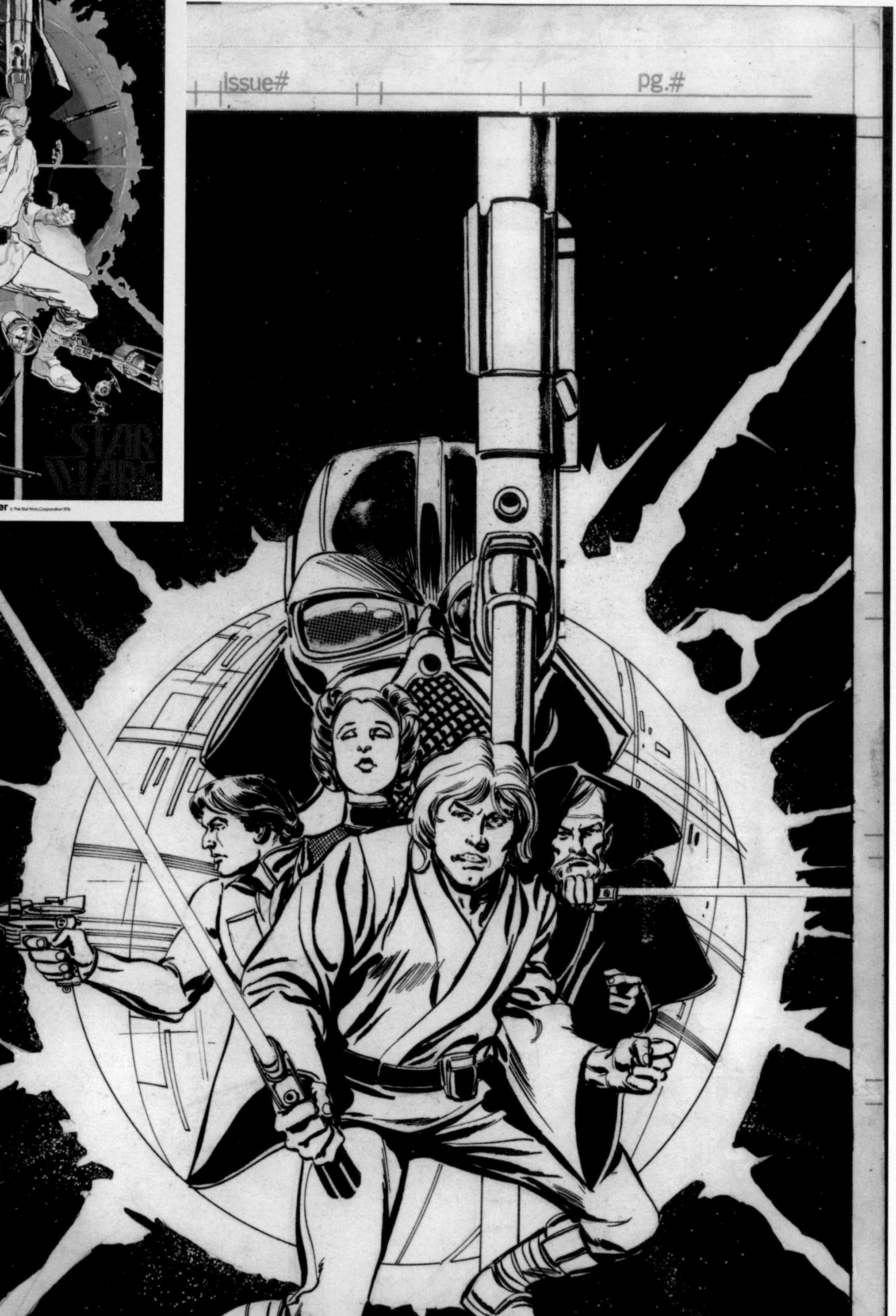
Issue#
pg.#

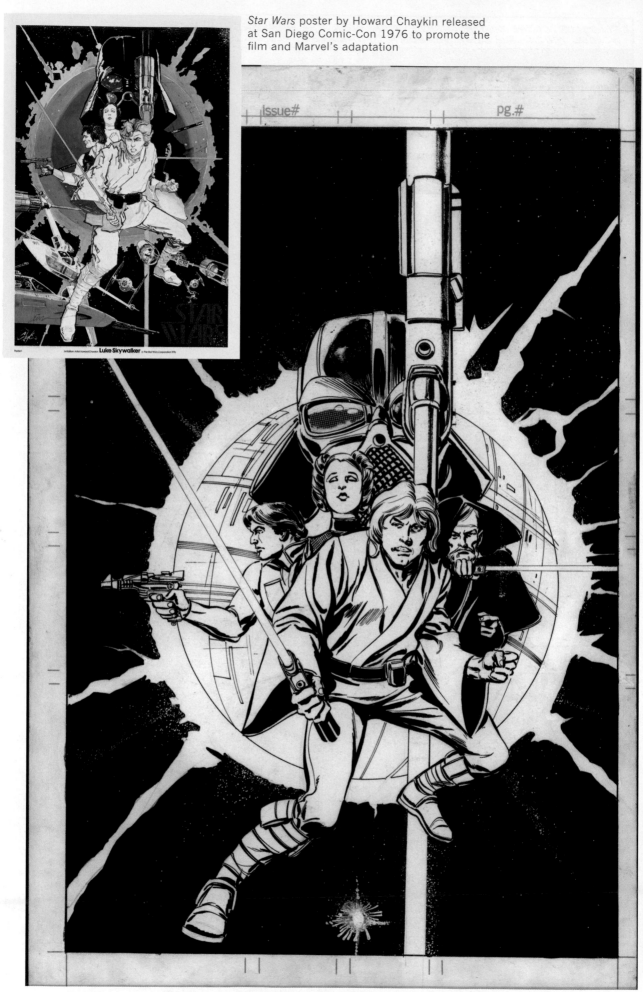

Early version of *Star Wars #1* cover; art by Howard Chaykin

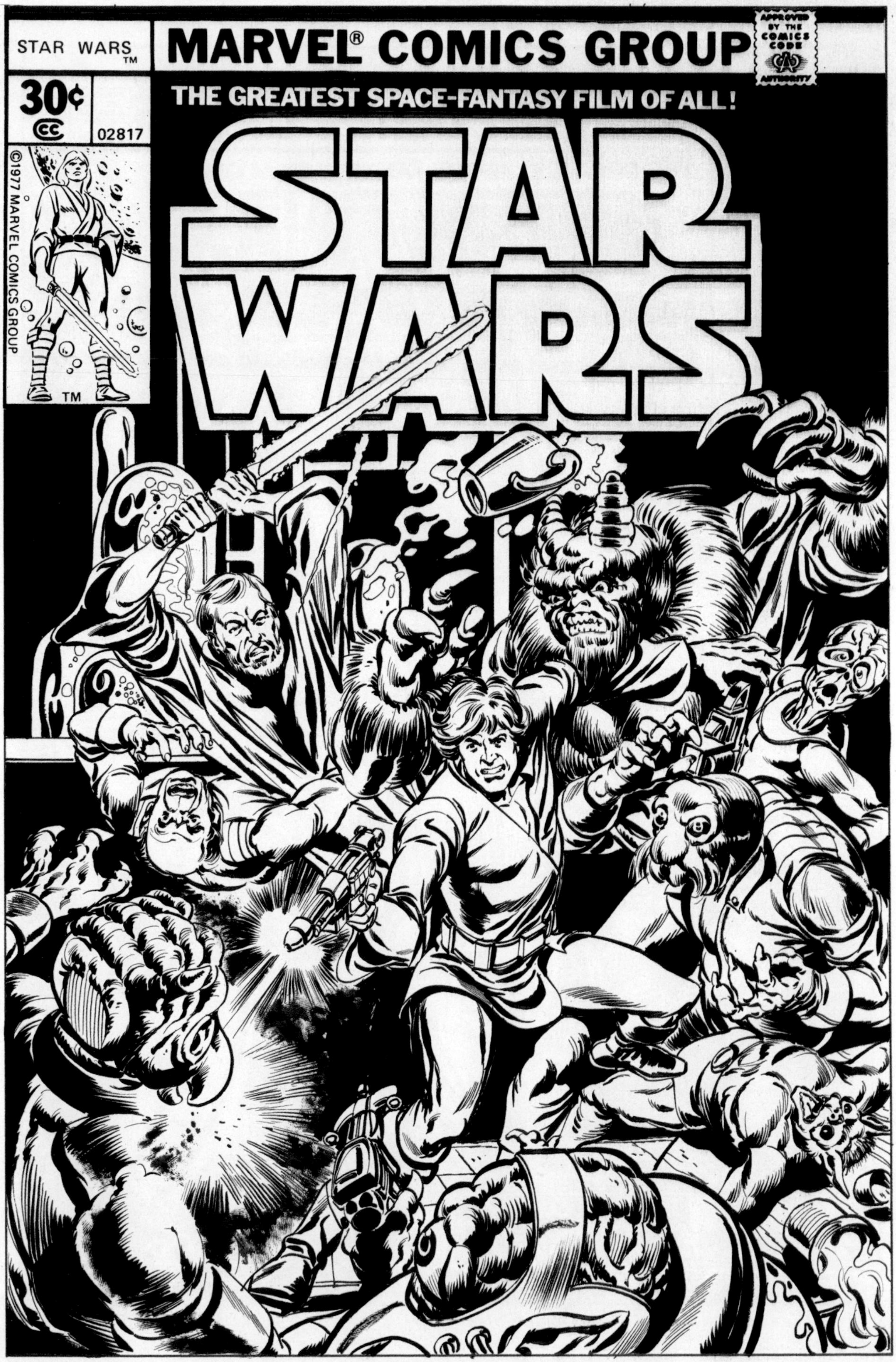
STAR WARS TM
MARVEL® COMICS GROUP
APPROVED BY THE COMICS CODE AUTHORITY
30¢
CC
02817
©1977 MARVEL COMICS GROUP
TM
THE GREATEST SPACE-FANTASY FILM OF ALL!
STAR WARS

Star Wars #2 original cover art by Howard Chaykin & Tom Palmer

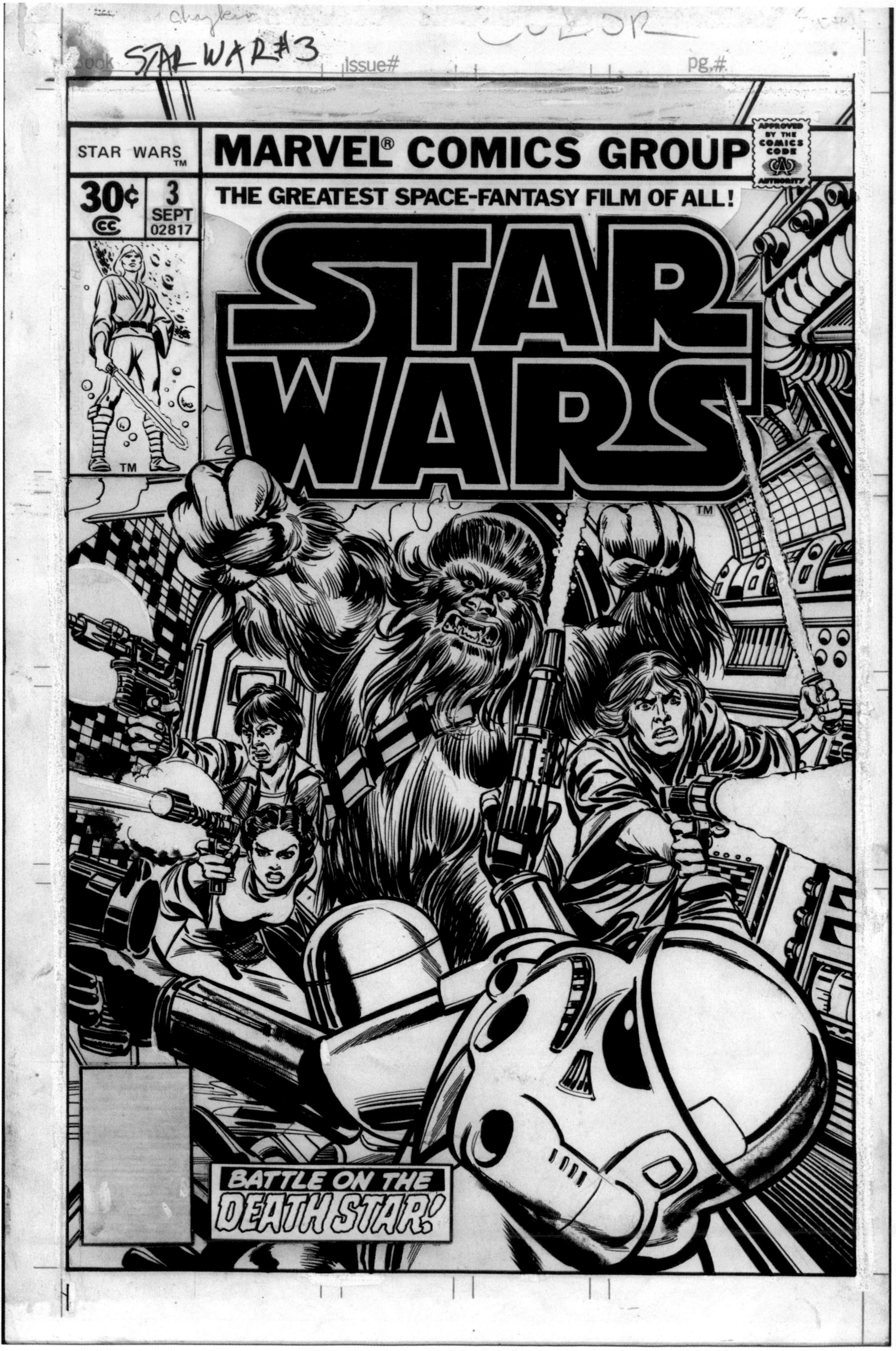
chaykin
STAR WAR#3
COLOR
book
issue#
pg.#
STAR WARS TM
MARVEL® COMICS GROUP
APPROVED BY THE COMICS CODE AUTHORITY
30¢
3
SEPT
02817
THE GREATEST SPACE-FANTASY FILM OF ALL!
STAR WARS
TM
TM
BATTLE ON THE
DEATH STAR!

Star Wars #3 original cover art by Gil Kane & Tom Palmer

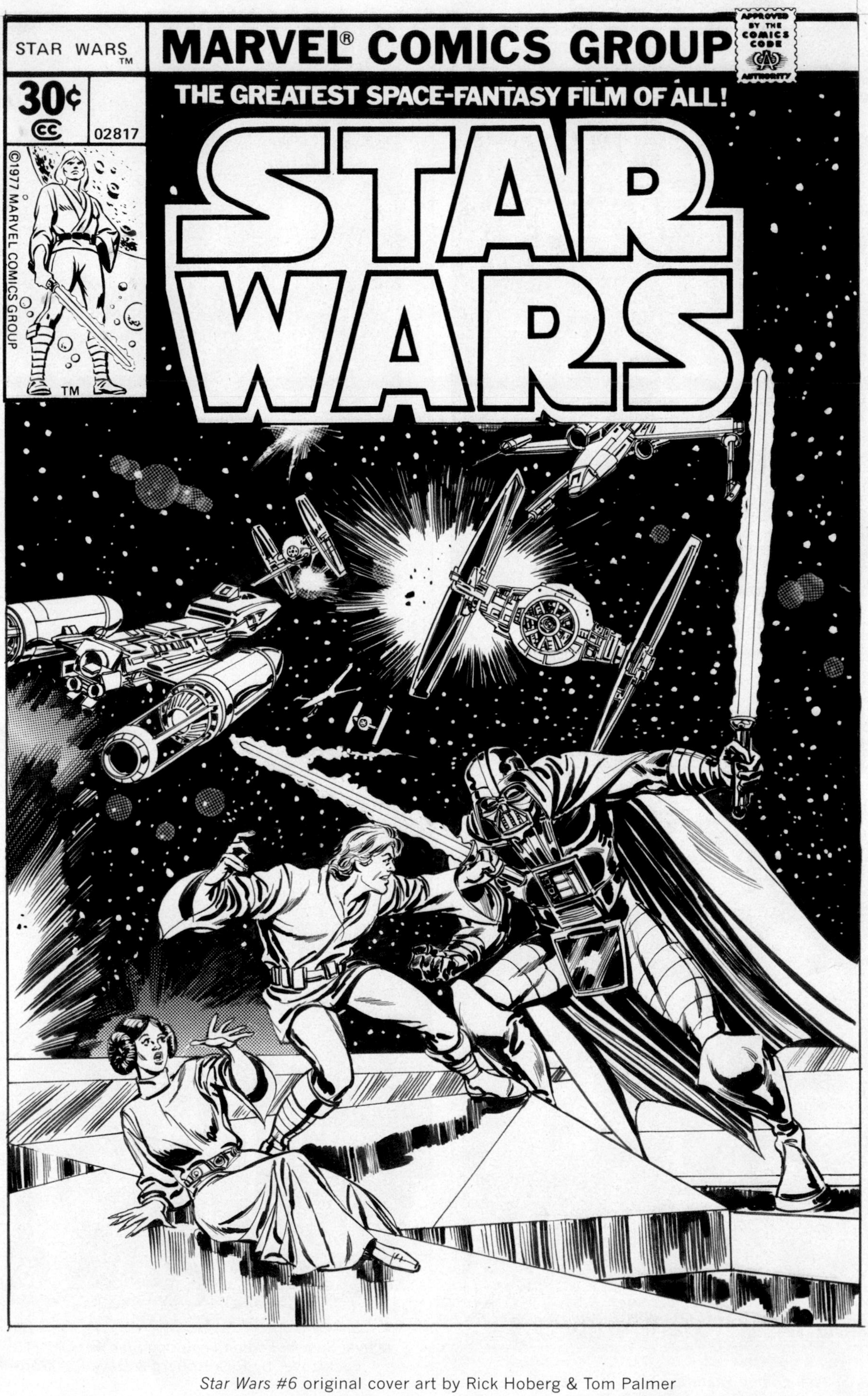
STAR WARS TM
MARVEL® COMICS GROUP
APPROVED BY THE COMICS CODE AUTHORITY
30¢
02817
THE GREATEST SPACE-FANTASY FILM OF ALL!
STAR WARS
©1977 MARVEL COMICS GROUP
TM

Star Wars #6 original cover art by Rick Hoberg & Tom Palmer

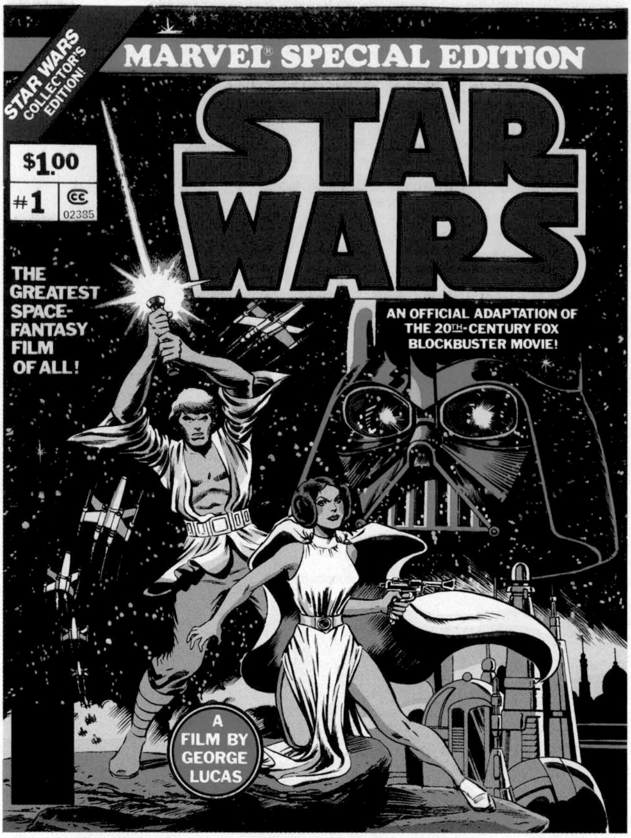
MARVEL SPECIAL EDITION
STAR WARS COLLECTOR'S EDITION!
$1.00
#1
02385
STAR WARS
THE GREATEST SPACE-FANTASY FILM OF ALL!
AN OFFICIAL ADAPTATION OF THE 20TH-CENTURY FOX BLOCKBUSTER MOVIE!
A FILM BY GEORGE LUCAS

Marvel Special Edition Featuring Star Wars #1 (1977) reprinted *Star Wars #1-3* with a new cover by Rick Hoberg & Dave Cockrum.

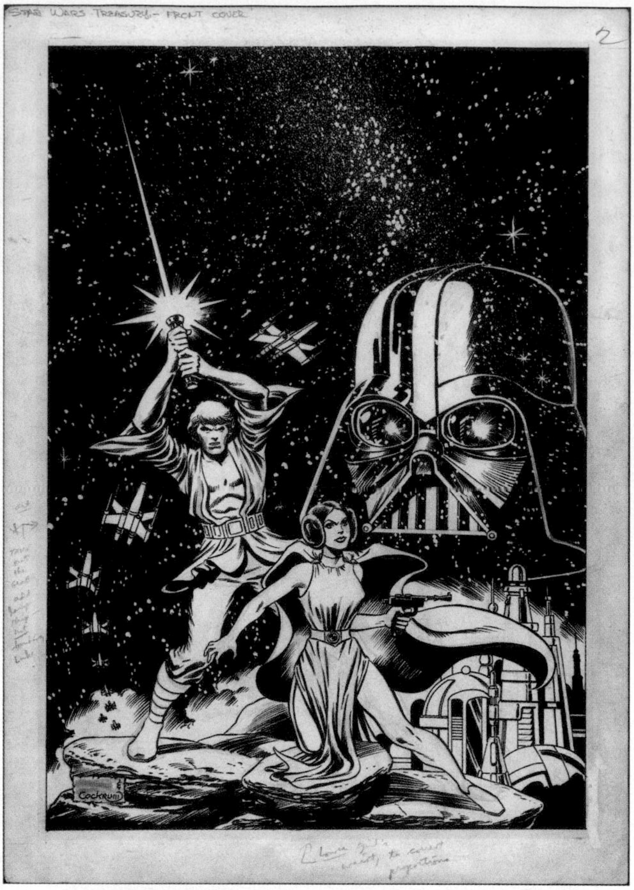
2
Cockrum

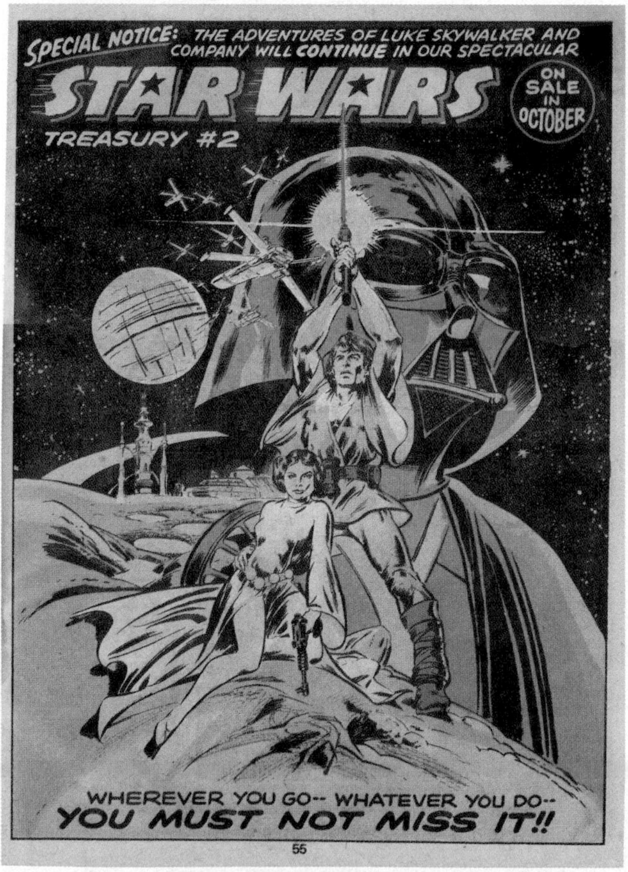
SPECIAL NOTICE: THE ADVENTURES OF LUKE SKYWALKER AND COMPANY WILL CONTINUE IN OUR SPECTACULAR
STAR WARS
TREASURY #2
ON SALE IN OCTOBER
WHEREVER YOU GO-- WHATEVER YOU DO--
YOU MUST NOT MISS IT!!
55

Marvel Special Edition Featuring Star Wars #1 (1977) ad for issue #2 art by Tony DeZuniga

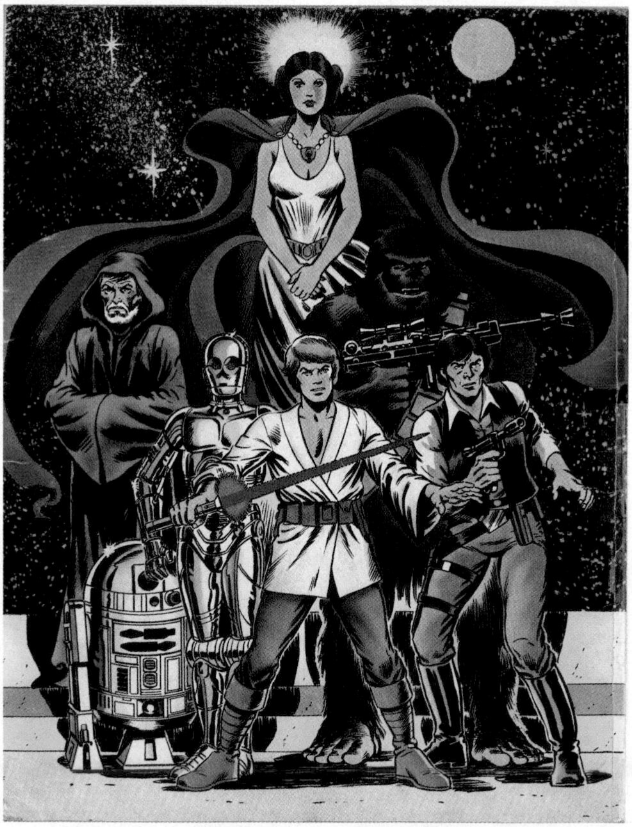

Marvel Special Edition Featuring Star Wars #1 (1977) back cover by Rick Hoberg & Dave Cockrum

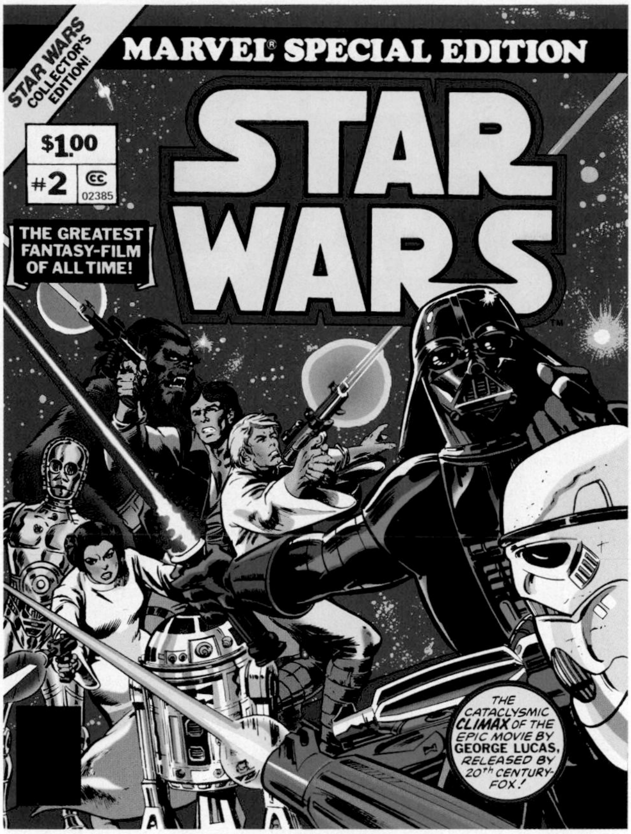
STAR WARS COLLECTOR'S EDITION!
MARVEL® SPECIAL EDITION
$1.00
#2
02385
STAR WARS
THE GREATEST FANTASY-FILM OF ALL TIME!
THE CATACLYSMIC CLIMAX OF THE EPIC MOVIE BY GEORGE LUCAS, RELEASED BY 20TH CENTURY-FOX!

Marvel Special Edition Featuring Star Wars #2 (1977) reprinted *Star Wars #4-6* with a new cover by Howard Chaykin & Tony DeZuniga along with several recap pages.

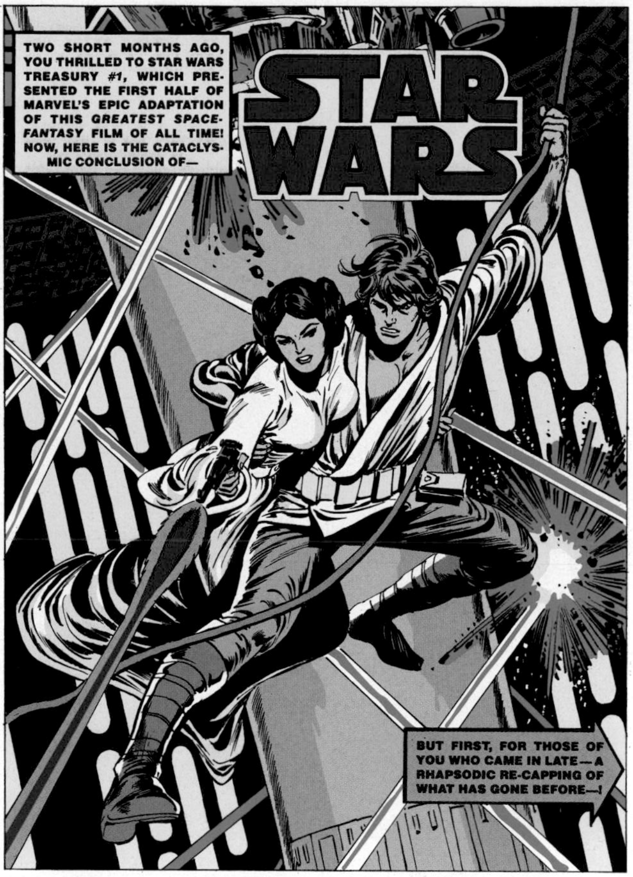
TWO SHORT MONTHS AGO, YOU THRILLED TO STAR WARS TREASURY #1, WHICH PRESENTED THE FIRST HALF OF MARVEL'S EPIC ADAPTATION OF THIS GREATEST SPACE-FANTASY FILM OF ALL TIME! NOW, HERE IS THE CATACLYSMIC CONCLUSION OF—
STAR WARS
BUT FIRST, FOR THOSE OF YOU WHO CAME IN LATE—A RHAPSODIC RE-CAPPING OF WHAT HAS GONE BEFORE—!

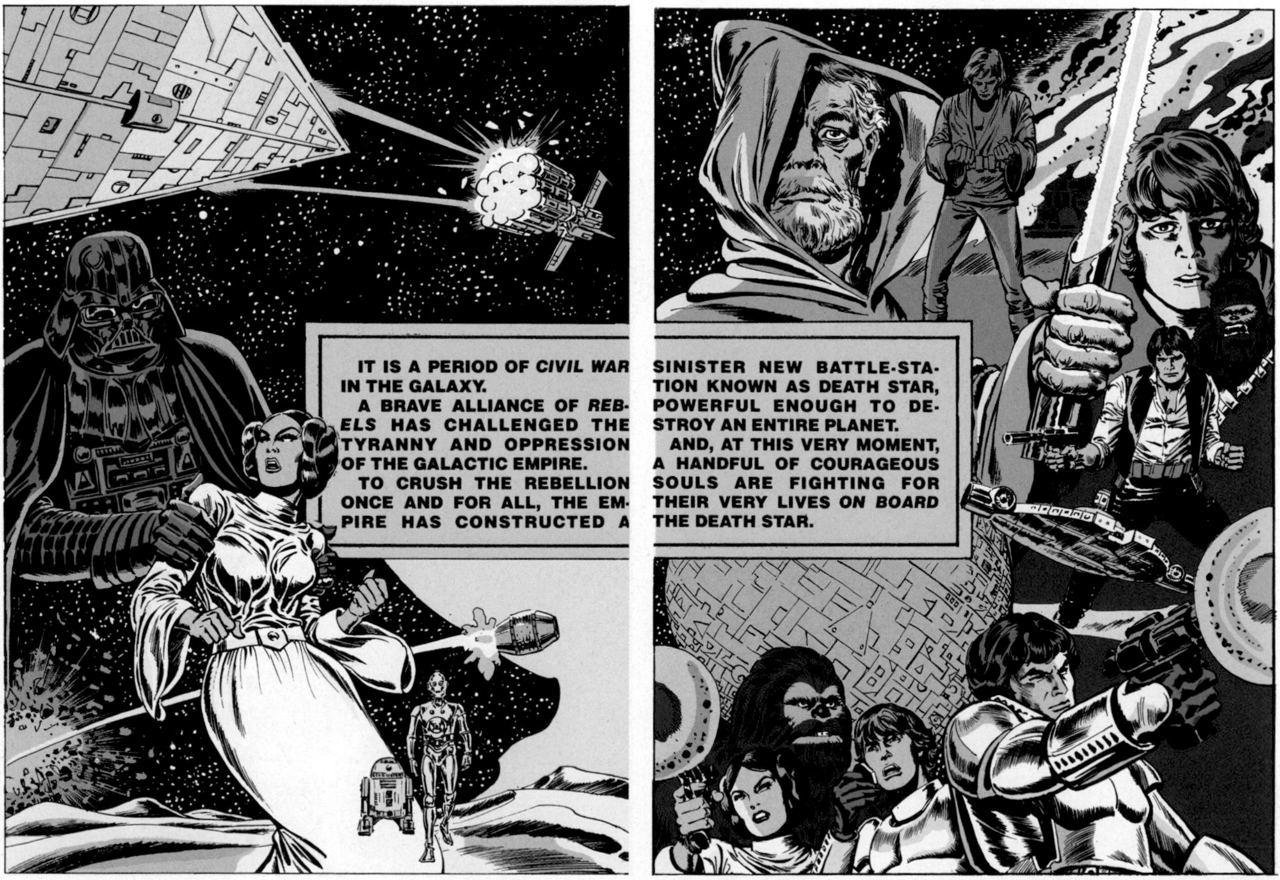
IT IS A PERIOD OF CIVIL WAR IN THE GALAXY.
A BRAVE ALLIANCE OF REBELS HAS CHALLENGED THE TYRANNY AND OPPRESSION OF THE GALACTIC EMPIRE.
TO CRUSH THE REBELLION ONCE AND FOR ALL, THE EMPIRE HAS CONSTRUCTED A SINISTER NEW BATTLE-STATION KNOWN AS DEATH STAR, POWERFUL ENOUGH TO DESTROY AN ENTIRE PLANET.
AND, AT THIS VERY MOMENT, A HANDFUL OF COURAGEOUS SOULS ARE FIGHTING FOR THEIR VERY LIVES ON BOARD THE DEATH STAR.

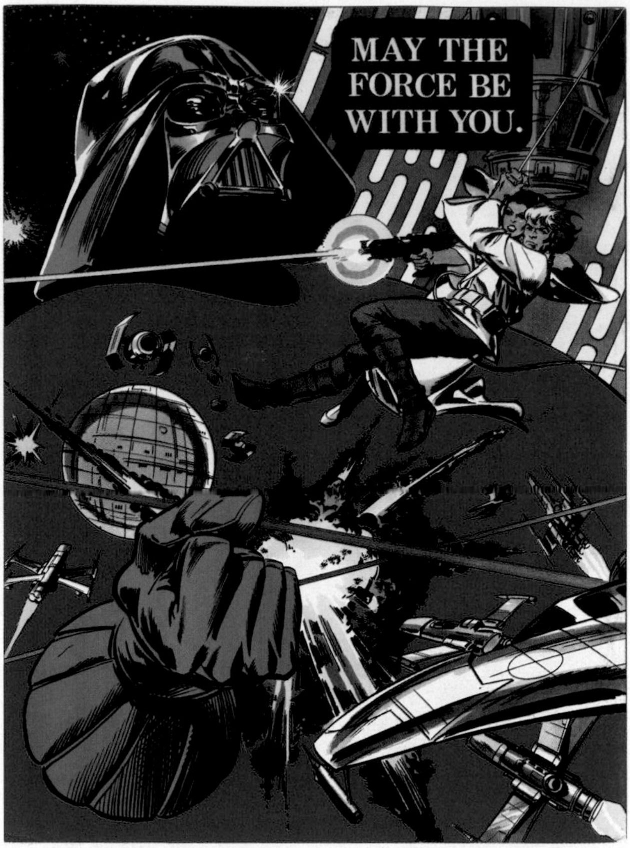
MAY THE
FORCE BE
WITH YOU.
Marvel Special Edition Featuring Star Wars #2 (1977)
back cover by Howard Chaykin & Tony DeZuniga

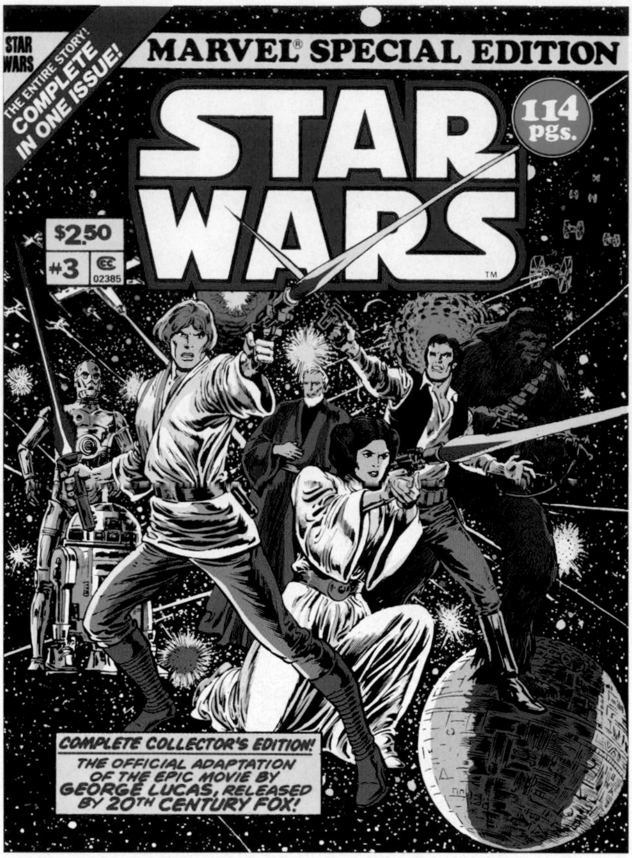
STAR WARS
MARVEL® SPECIAL EDITION
THE ENTIRE STORY! COMPLETE IN ONE ISSUE!
STAR WARS
114 pgs.
$2.50
#3
02385
TM
COMPLETE COLLECTOR'S EDITION!
THE OFFICIAL ADAPTATION OF THE EPIC MOVIE BY GEORGE LUCAS, RELEASED BY 20TH CENTURY FOX!
Marvel Special Edition Featuring Star Wars #3 (1977) reprinted the entire adaptation of *Star Wars #1-6* with new cover art by Ernie Chan.

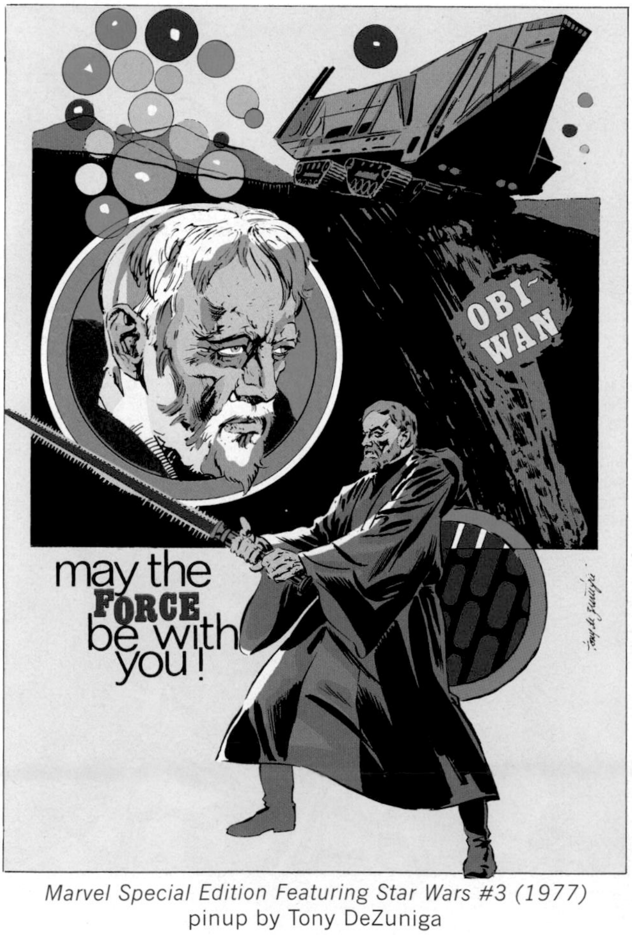
OBI-
WAN
may the
FORCE
be with
you!
Marvel Special Edition Featuring Star Wars #3 (1977)
pinup by Tony DeZuniga

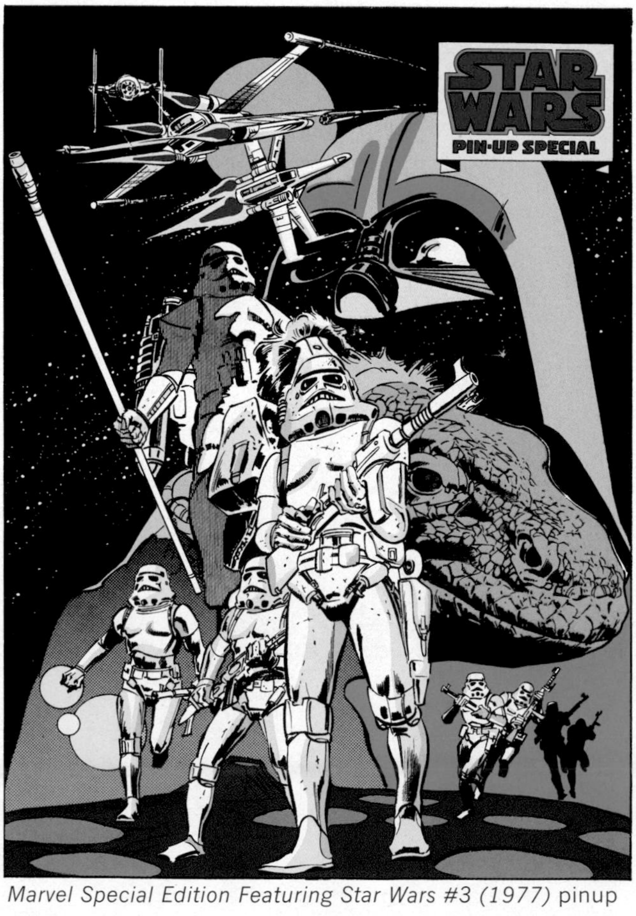
STAR
WARS
PIN-UP SPECIAL
Marvel Special Edition Featuring Star Wars #3 (1977) pinup

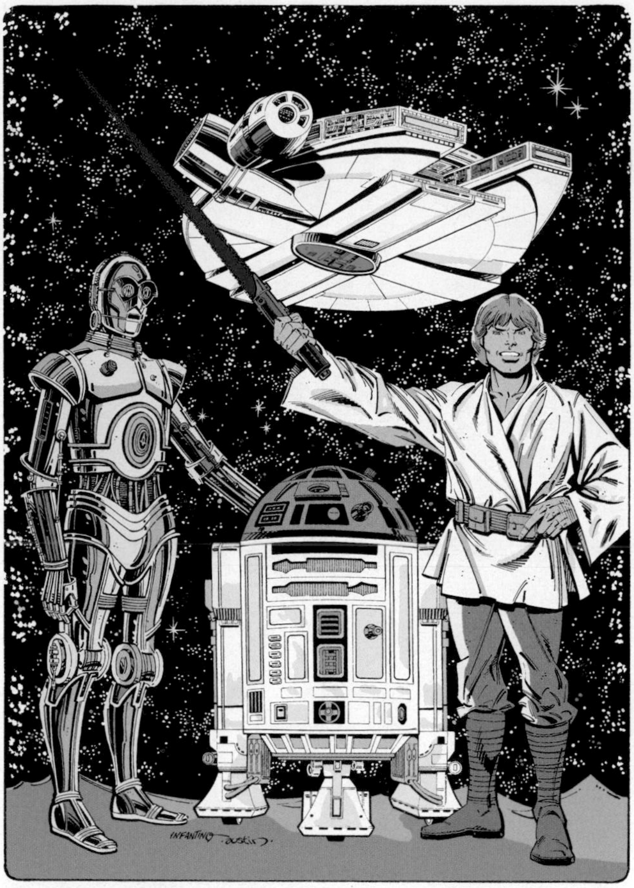
INFANTINO austin

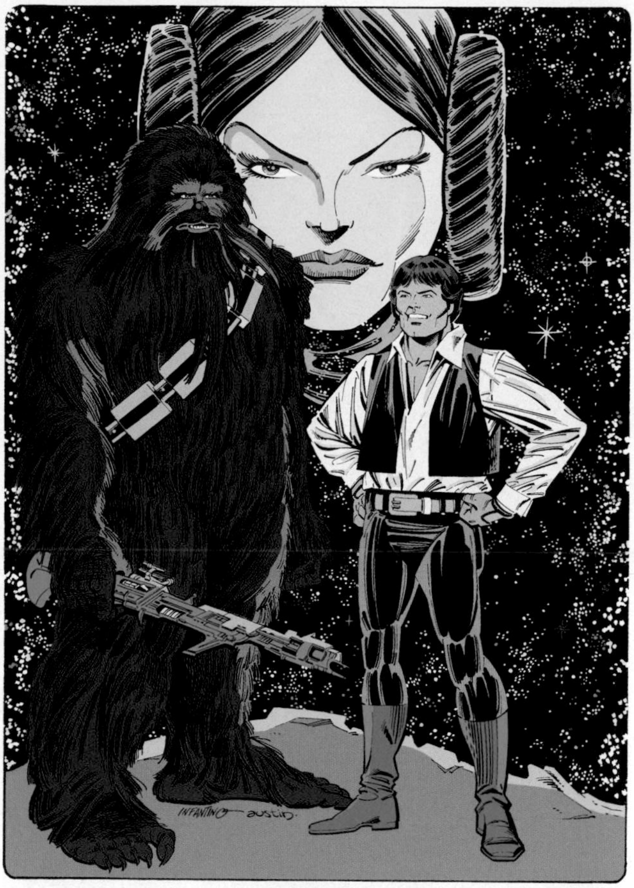
INFANTINO austin

Marvel Special Edition Featuring Star Wars #3 (1977) pinups by Carmine Infantino & Terry Austin

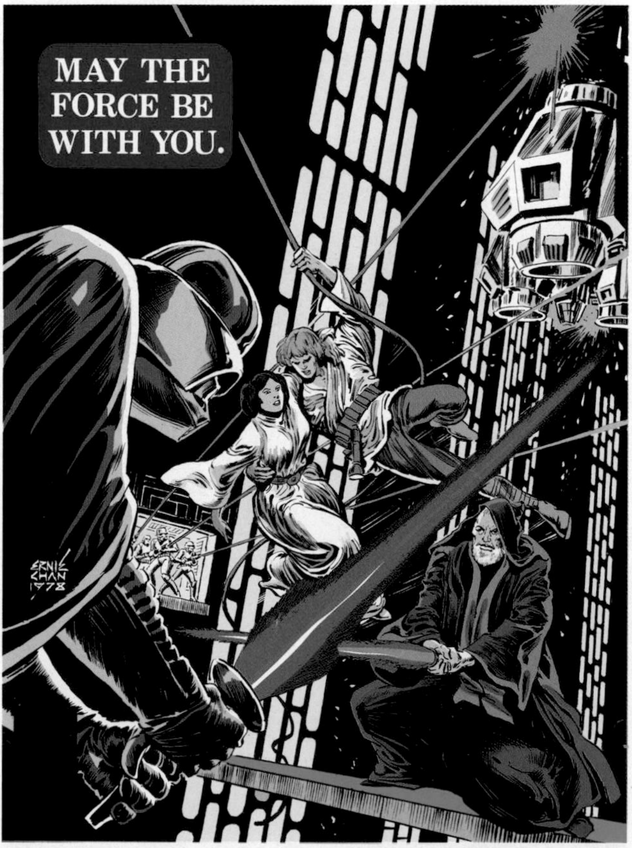
MAY THE FORCE BE WITH YOU.
ERNIE CHAN 1978

Marvel Special Edition Featuring Star Wars #3 (1977) back cover by Ernie Chan

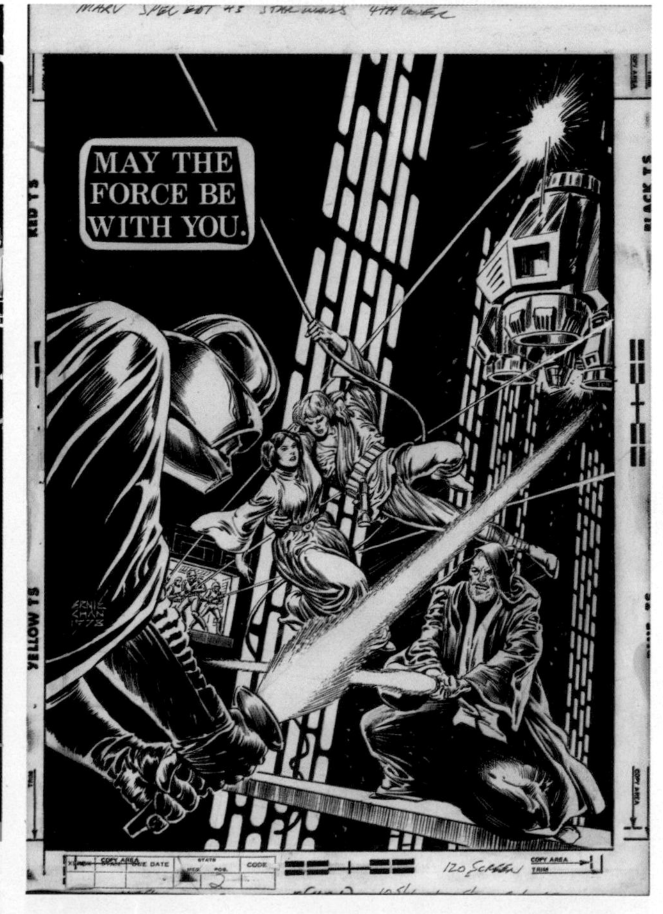
MAY THE FORCE BE WITH YOU.

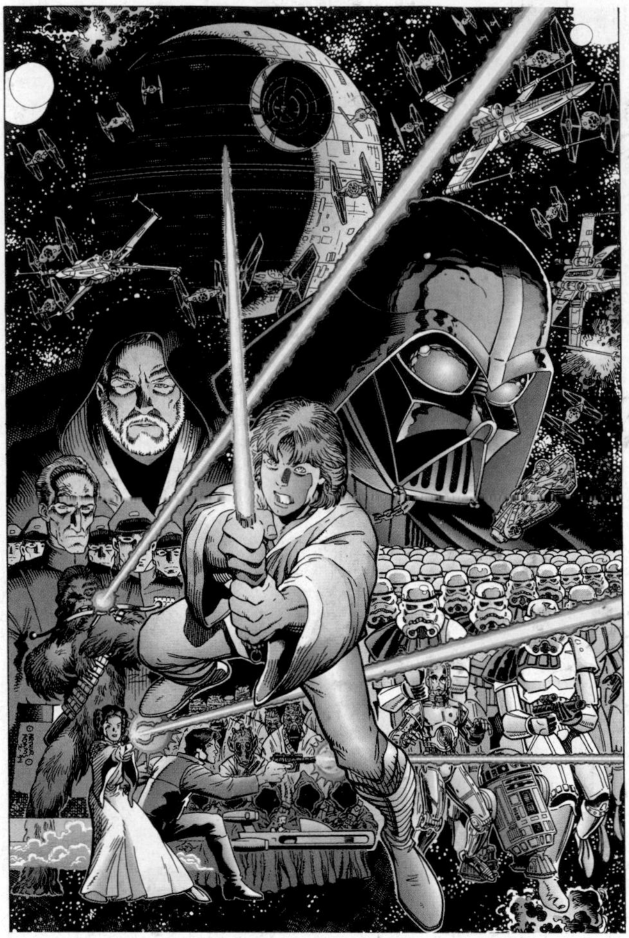

Classic Star Wars: A New Hope #1 (1994)
reprinted *Star Wars #1-3* with new cover art
by Arthur Adams & Matt Hollingsworth.

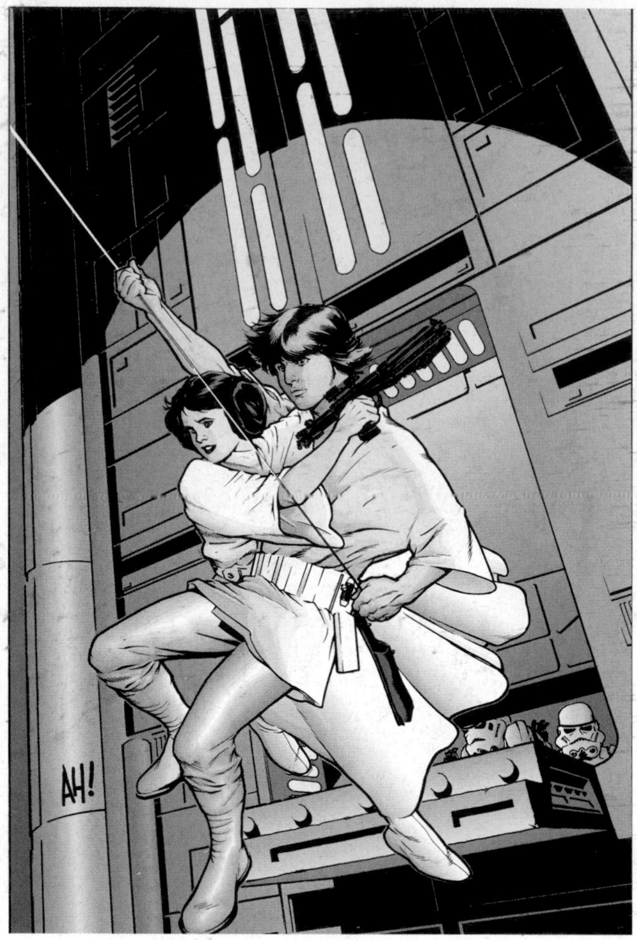

Classic Star Wars: A New Hope #2 (1994)
reprinted *Star Wars #4-6* with new cover art
by Adam Hughes & Matt Hollingsworth.

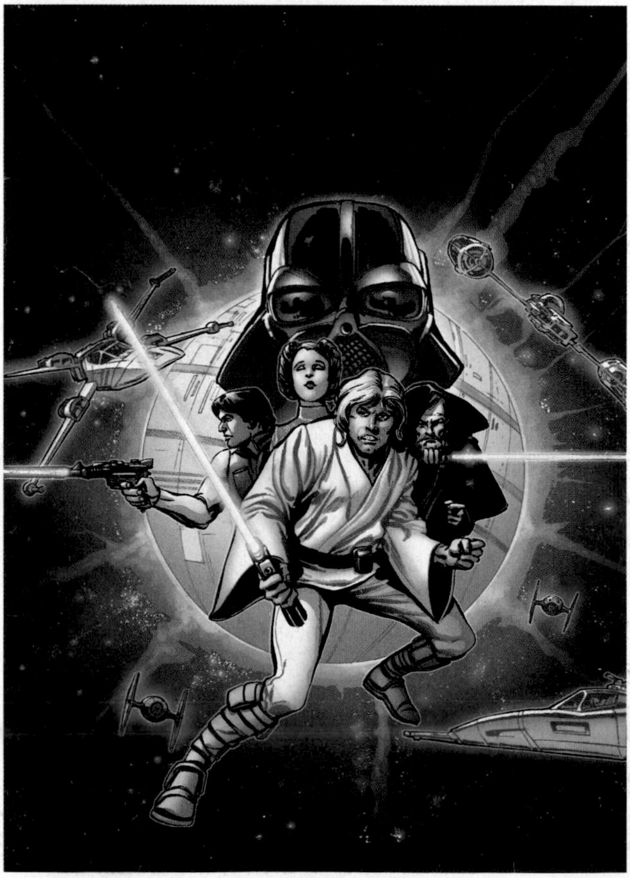

Star Wars: The Original Marvel Years Omnibus Vol. 1
HC cover by Howard Chaykin & Edgar Delgado

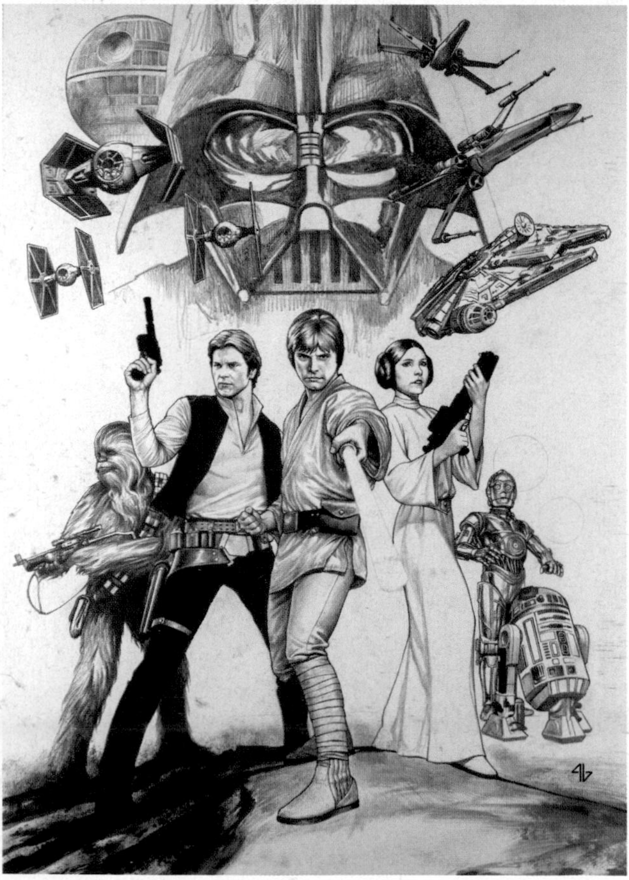

Star Wars Episode IV – *A New Hope HC*
cover pencils by Adi Granov

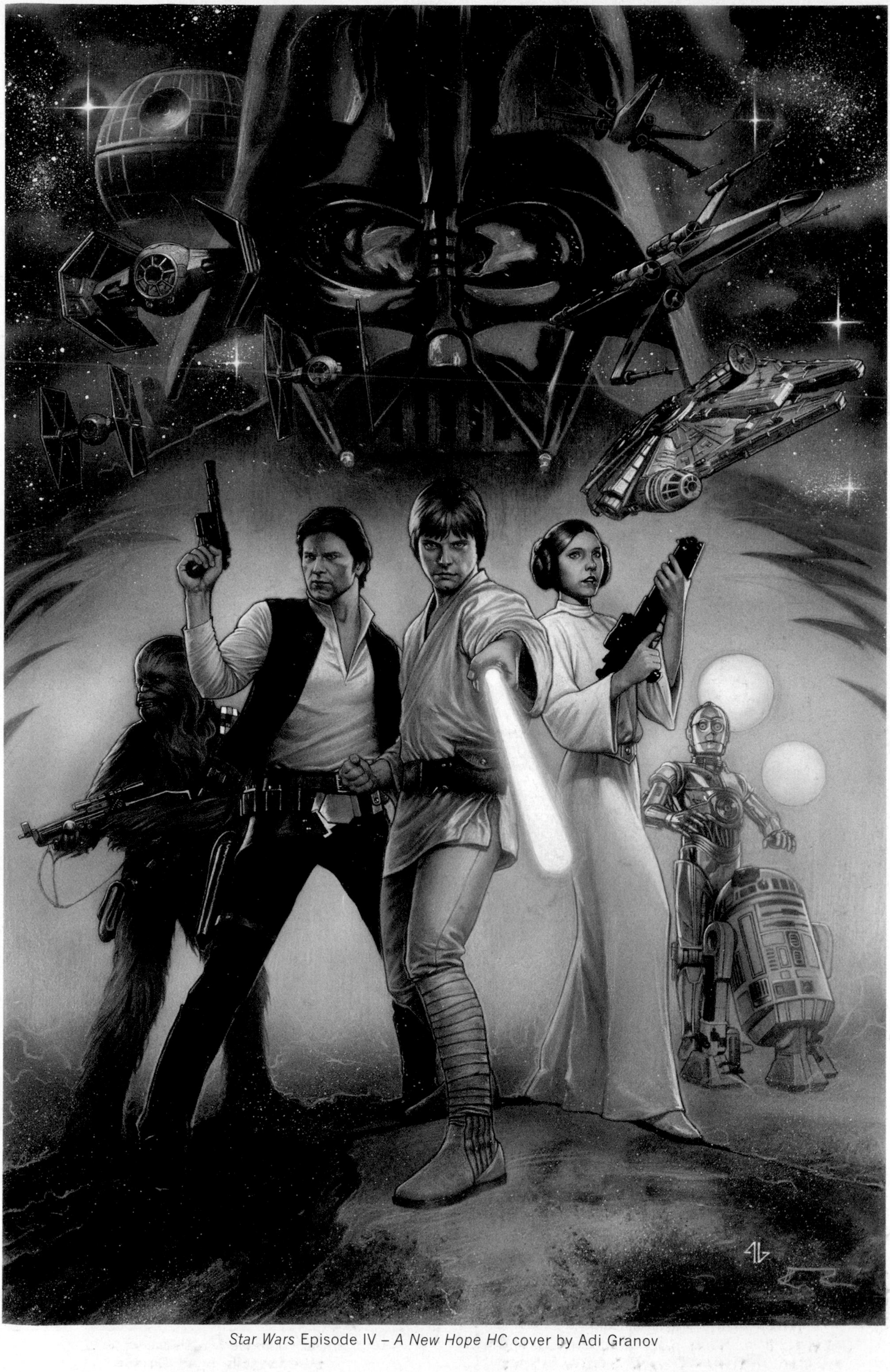

Star Wars Episode IV – *A New Hope HC* cover by Adi Granov

The story continues in....

MARVEL
STAR
THE
EMPIRE
STRIKES BACK
WARS
EPISODE V

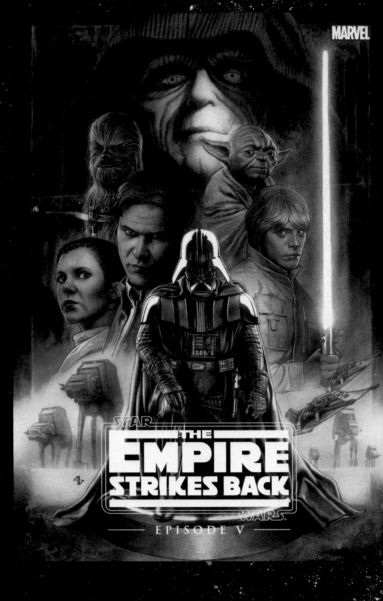